GCSE
PSYCHOLOGY

Cara Flanagan

EDUCATIONAL

Letts Educational
Aldine House
Aldine Place
London W12 8AW

Tel: 0181 740 2266
Fax: 0181 743 8451
E-mail: mail@ lettsed.co.uk

First published 1995
New edition 1997

British Library Cataloguing in Publication Data
A CIP record for this book is available from the British Library.

ISBN 1 85758 590 9

Acknowledgements
I acknowledge the Midland Examination Group, Northern Examinations and Assessment Board and Southern Examinations Group for permission to use their exam material. These boards cannot accept any responsibility for the answers or methods given in this book.

I am most indebted to Phil Banyard, who read through the manuscript at various stages giving me much appreciated advice and support. The officers-in-charge of psychology at the examination boards have been most patient with my persistent queries; my thanks to Elizabeth Dolman, Emma Talbot, Margaret Heritage and Mrs. Wagstaff. My dear parents, Dennis and Geraldine, have offered help both in the form of unpaid research and unflagging appreciation of my efforts. And finally, a tribute to those at home who suffer my absences and moods, to Rob, Philippa, Jack and Rosie, with love.

Cara Flanagan

The author and publishers gratefully acknowledge the following:

Fig. 2.3 reprinted from *A First Course in Psychology*, Nicky Hayes, 1984, by kind permission of Thomas Nelson & Sons, Ltd.; random dot stereogram in margin of p23, and Figs. 2.7, 2.8, 2.11 reprinted by kind permission of Weidenfeld and Nicolson Ltd.; article on p26 reprinted from 'Errors by a Tense U.S. Crew Led to Downing of Iran Jet, Navy Inquiry is Said to Find', by Bernard E. Trainor, August 3, 1988, copyright © 1988 by the New York Times Company, reprinted by permission; rat-man figure in margin on p31 adapted from 'The Role of Frequency in Developing Perceptual Sets', by B.R. Bugelski and D.A. Alampay, 1961, *Canadian Journal of Psychology*, 15, 205-211, copyright © 1961 by the Canadian Psychological Association, reprinted with permission; Fig. 2.9 adapted from 'The Role of Autism in a Visual Figure-Ground Relationship', by R. Schafer and G. Murphy, 1974, *Journal of Experimental Psychology*, 32, 335-343, copyright © 1974 by the American Psychological Association, reprinted with permission; Fig. 2.13 based on data from 'The "Visual Cliff"' by E.J. Gibson and R.D. Walker, April 1960, *Scientific American*, 202, 64-71, reprinted with permission; Fig. 2.14 based on a photograph by David Linton from "The Origin of Form Perception", by R.L. Fantz, May 1961, *Scientific American*, 204, 69; Fig. 4.1 reprinted from 'Two Storage Mechanisms in Free Recall', by M. Glanzer and A.R. Cunitz, 1966, *Journal of Verbal Learning and Verbal Behavior*, 5, 351-360, reprinted by kind permission of Academic Press; Fig. 4.2 reprinted from 'Depth of Processing and the Retention of Words in Episodic Memory', by F.I.M. Craik and E. Tulving, 1975, *Journal of Experimental Psychology*, 104, 268-294, copyright © 1975 by the American Psychological Association, reprinted with permission; Fig. 4.3 reprinted from Cognitive Psychology: *A Student's Handbook*, by M.W. Eysenck and M.T. Keane, 1990, reprinted by permission of Lawrence Erlbaum Associates Ltd., Hove, UK; Fig. 4.4 adapted from *A Study of Thinking*, by J.S. Bruner et al, 1956, John Wiley & Sons, Inc., reprinted by permission of Jerome Bruner; Fig. 4.5 redrawn from 'Intelligence Tests with Tits' by M. Brooks-King and H.G. Hurrell, by permission of the Editors of the monthly journal *British Birds*; Fig. 4.6 reproduced by permission of *Pediatrics*, vol 79, page 343, copyright © 1987; Fig. 5.1 reprinted from the *Journal of Psychology*, 9, 302-310, 1940, reprinted with permission of the Helen Dwight Reid Educational Foundation, published by Heldref Publications, 1319 Eighteenth St NW, Washington, D.C. 20036-1802, copyright © 1940; article on p149 reprinted from "The 'Real Hero of This'", by Phil Gailey, January 14, 1982, copyright © 1982 by the New York Times Company; human sex chromosomes in margin on p194 from Biophoto Associates; Fig. 9.1 reprinted from 'Attitudinal Effects of Mere Exposure', by R.B. Zajonc, 1968, *Journal of Personality and Social Psychology*, 9, 1-29, copyright © 1968 by the American Psychological Association, reprinted with permission; Fig. 10.1 adapted from 'The Relation of Strength Stimulus to Rapidity of Habit Formation', by R.M. Yerkes and J.D. Dodson, *Journal of Comparative Neurology*, copyright © 1908, reprinted by permission of Wiley-Liss, Inc., a subsidiary of John Wiley & Sons, Inc.

Printed in Great Britain by Nuffield Press

Letts Educational is the trading name of BPP (Letts Educational) Ltd

Contents

Introduction

How to use this book

This book is specially written to help you in preparing for GCSE Psychology exams. It contains:

- Hints on **studying, revising, exam techniques** and **coursework** (in Section 1).

- **Syllabus tables** for each examination board (in Section 1). These indicate broad areas of each Board's syllabus plus examination details. It is only a very general guide to the compulsory and optional topics covered by each syllabus, but should help you work your way through the relevant sections of this book. You should consult your teacher or the actual syllabus for precise details about what will be examined. If you are a private student, write to the board. All private students must be registered and accepted by a recognised educational institution in order to sit the final examination.

- **Thirty-six units of text** covering all the the requirements for GCSE. These units are concise, clear and easy to read. Units are grouped together in chapters. Each chapter and each unit begins with a leading article intended to give you a taste of the information which follows. It might be from a newspaper or a classic piece of research.

- A **quick test** at the end of each unit. The questions are similar to those used in GCSE exams, in their form and content. Some of them are taken from the exams themselves.

- A **summary** at the end of each unit representing the key facts in diagrammatic form.

- An **examination section** (Section 3) providing a bank of exam questions from which you can select relevant questions.

- Suggested **answers** (also in Section 3) are given for the quick test and longer examination questions. Your answers need not be identical, but should be similar in terms of content and depth.

Studying GCSE Psychology

Aims

The main aims of GCSE Psychology courses are:

1. To promote an awareness of how psychological theory:
    - Helps to understand the relationship between individuals and between groups.
    - Is influenced and limited by social, cultural, economic, technological, ethical and political factors.
    - Has contributed to the process of change in such areas as conflict and co-operation, and individual and cultural diversity.

② To develop abilities and skills which are relevant beyond the study of psychology:
- To acquire, select and handle information.
- To analyse information critically and to recognise bias.
- To draw inferences and make judgements from a reasoned consideration of information.
- To recognise the usefulness and limitations of the scientific method.

③ To encourage personal and academic development:
- To plan and carry out research.
- To have an awareness of ethical issues.
- To take an informed role and make a positive contribution to society.
- To stimulate curiosity, interest and enjoyment in psychology.

The importance of empirical data is a vital element of all courses. This is shown in the practical work that candidates are required to undertake, in the fact that candidates are examined on research principles and on a critical knowledge of actual studies undertaken by psychologists.

In all syllabuses, 5% of the marks available in both the terminal examinations and the coursework are awarded for accurate spelling, punctuation and grammar.

Analysis of examination syllabuses

MEG

Midland Examining Group
Elsfield Way, Oxford OX2 8EP   Tel. 01865 54421

Foundation tier (Option F)	Paper 1 (core)	1½ hours	40%
	Paper 2 (methodology and options)	1½ hours	40%
	Coursework		20%
	Target grades C–G		
Higher tier (Option H)	Paper 3 (core)	1½ hours	40%
	Paper 4 (methodology and options)	1½ hours	40%
	Coursework		20%
	Target grades A★–D		

Spelling, punctuation and grammar are assessed in all components of the examination.

A knowledge of themes and processes of methodology, ethics, applications and cultural diversity will be required to answer all these papers.

The examination set for the higher tier (Option H) will expect candidates to show greater understanding of wider implications and to have developed the ability to evaluate, interpret and critically analyse their knowledge.

Paper 1 or 3 (Core)
    Section A: Short answer questions covering the six topics in the core.
    Section B: One general question to which the key questions in the syllabus will be
                applied.
    Section C: Questions based on source material.

Paper 2 or 4 (Methodology and options)
    There is a choice of two out of four options. Each option is divided into two
    'sources' followed by a set of questions. Both are compulsory.

The coursework

● One enquiry described in a written report containing no more than 1500 words.

Topics		Unit	✓
THE CORE			
Methodology, ethics, applications and cultural diversity		11.1, 11.2, 11.3, 11.4, 5.3	
The Behaviourist Approach:	Learning theory	1.1, 3.1	
The Cognitive Approach:	Memory	1.1, 4.1	
The Biological Approach:	Stress	1.1, 10.2	
The Social Psychological Approach:	Prejudice	1.1, 5.3, 5.4	
The Developmental Approach:	Moral development	1.1, 3.2, 9.1	
The Humanistic Approach:	Personality	1.1, 8.3	

Topics (cont.)	Unit	✓
OPTION 1: COGNITIVE PSYCHOLOGY		
Perception	2.2, 2.3	
Problem solving and creativity	4.2	
Development of language	4.5	
OPTION 2: DEVELOPMENTAL PSYCHOLOGY		
Attachment	8.1	
Cognitive development	4.4	
Sex and gender	9.2	
OPTION 3: SOCIAL AND ENVIRONMENTAL PSYCHOLOGY		
Social influence	6.1	
Crowds and crowding	6.3, 7.2	
Territorial behaviour and privacy	6.3	
OPTION 4: BIOLOGICAL AND COMPARATIVE APPROACH		
Biological bases of behaviour	10.3	
Ethological approach	1.1, 3.3	
Aggression	7.1	

NEAB

Northern Examinations and Assessment Board
Devas Street, Manchester M15 6EX   Tel. 0161 953 1180

Foundation tier (Option F)	One written paper	2 hours	80%
	Coursework		20%
	Target grades C–G		

Higher tier (Option H)	One written paper	2½ hours	80%
	Coursework		20%
	Target grades A★–D		

Spelling, punctuation and grammar are assessed in all components of the examination.

The examination set for the higher tier (Option H) will expect candidates to show greater understanding of wider implications and to have developed the ability to evaluate, interpret and critically analyse their knowledge.

The written paper will have a set of compulsory, short-answer and structured questions.

The coursework

- At least two investigations are probably required to cover the necessary skills which are listed for assessment.
- Candidates may present a set of shorter investigations.
- No single report should be more than 1000 words.

Topics	Unit	✓
1 INDIVIDUAL PROCESSES		
Perception	2.1, 2.2	
Learning	3.1	
Memory	4.1	
Emotion (including stress)	10.1, 10.2	
2 INTERPERSONAL PROCESSES		
The development of social behaviour (e.g attachment, sexual development)	3.2, 8.1, 8.2, 9.2	
Social Perception (e.g. impression formation, stereotyping, prejudice)	5.1, 5.2, 5.3, 5.4	
Social Influence (e.g. norms, conformity, obedience, social facilitation, bystander behaviour, self-fulfilling prophecy)	6.1, 6.2, 7.2	
3 METHODS OF INVESTIGATION (e.g. techniques and ethics)	11.1, 11.2, 11.3, 11.4	

SEG

Southern Examining Group
Stag Hill House, Guildford, Surrey GU2 5XJ   Tel. 01483 506506

Foundation tier (Option F)	Paper 2	2 hours	80%
	Coursework		20%
	Target grades C–G		

Higher tier (Option H)	Paper 3	2 hours	80%
	Coursework		20%
	Target grades A★–D		

Spelling, punctuation and grammar are assessed in all components of the examination.

The examination set for the higher tier (Option H) will expect candidates to show greater understanding of wider implications and to have developed the ability to evaluate, interpret and critically analyse their knowledge.

The examination paper is divided into:

- Section A: short–answer questions (compulsory).
- Section B: one structured question based on a flawed study (compulsory).
- Sections C/D/E:
  - Each section has a choice from two structured questions.
  - Not more than one question can be answered from any one section.
  - Candidates must answer a total of two questions.

The coursework
- One practical exercise, 1000–1500 words in length.

Topics	Unit	✓
CORE SECTION A: WAYS OF EXPLAINING HUMAN ACTION		
1 The influences of inborn characteristics (nature/nurture debate, maturation, instincts, psychodynamic explanations)	1.1, 2.3, 3.1, 3.3, 4.3, 4.4, 5.3, 7.1, 8.1, 8.3, 8.4, 9.1, 9.2, 11.1	
2 The role of learning in shaping behaviour (learning and social learning explanations of the development of perception, prejudice, aggression, personality, morals and gender)	1.1, 2.3, 3.1, 3.2, 4.3, 5.3, 5.4,7.1, 8.3, 9.1, 9.2	
3 Social and cultural influences (the effects of the environment, the influence of others, affiliation, cross-cultural perspectives)	1.1, 2.3, 4.3, 5.1, 5.2, 5.3, 6.1, 6.2, 6.3, 7.2, 8.1, 8.2, 9.2, 9.3, 11.1	
4 The influences of thinking and perception (processing and representing information, schemas, filters; development of self, gender, pro-social and other concepts)	2.1, 2.2, 2.3, 4.1, 4.2, 4.3, 4.4, 5.1, 5.2, 5.3, 7.2, 8.1, 8.2, 9.1, 9.2, 9.3	
CORE SECTION B: PSYCHOLOGICAL METHODOLOGY		
1 Ways of discovering and testing psychological knowledge	11.1	
2 Carrying out practical research	11.2, 11.3	
3 Ethical concerns in research	11.4	
OPTIONAL SECTION C: SOCIAL AND ANTI-SOCIAL RELATIONSHIPS		
1 Making attachments to others	8.1	
2 Widening social relationships	6.1, 6.2, 9.3	
3 Prejudice	5.2, 5.3, 5.4	
4 Aggression	7.1	
OPTIONAL SECTION D: INDIVIDUALITY AND IDENTITY		
1 The development of personality (including temperament)	8.3, 8.4	
2 Intelligence	4.3	
3 The development of gender	9.2	
4 Towards a concept of self (labelling, effects on behaviour)	8.2	
OPTIONAL SECTION E: COGNITIVE AND SOCIAL COMPETENCE		
1 Cognitive development (Piaget, nature/nurture)	2.3, 4.4	
2 The development of moral behaviour and moral judgements	9.1, 7.2	
3 Prosocial behaviour: empathy, altruism, social norms	6.1, 7.2	
4 Construction of social 'reality' (impression formation)	5.1	

Revision, exams and coursework

Study strategies

Many of the ideas discussed below are drawn directly from theory and research in psychology.

1. **Enjoy it.** You do best at things you enjoy (and vice versa).

2. **Develop skills.** Taking examinations is a skill like any other. You should identify the components (memorising data, answering set questions, working under pressure, working without notes, etc.) and practise them. One element of skill training is feedback and then acting on it. You should be ready to change in line with any positive criticism. Practising a skill under non-stressful conditions helps reduce stress in exams. The questions set in this book should help you to practise some of these skills and improve where necessary.

3. **Organising your material.** It is easier to remember things which have been organised into a structure or hierarchy (see the unit on 'Memory' in Chapter 4). The end-of-unit summaries in this book are presented in a way to help structure your ideas. Throughout the book information is presented in lists as another means of organisation.

4. **Memory techniques.** The main skills are storing information and being able to recall it when required. If information is stored in a structured form, it can be recalled much better.

   There are methods to improve the way you store data, called mnemonics. These are described in the unit on 'Memory' in Chapter 4 (for example: repetition, organisation, cues, the loci system and mental imagery).

   There are methods for reading which improve memory of what you read, variously called the SQ3R or PQRST method:
   - survey or preview a unit,   S   P
   - list questions to actively involve yourself,   Q   Q
   - read the text,   R   R
   - recall or self-recite,   R   S
   - review or test yourself.   R   T

5. **Writing notes.** The purpose of notes is to record highly condensed material from which you can revise later. Some ideas for condensing and organising data:
   - use abbreviations, either your own or standard ones (ψ stands for 'psychology'),
   - highlight keywords,
   - record information in diagrammatic summaries and flowcharts,
   - write numbered lists,
   - flexibility helps for re-organising: use a card index, word processor or database.

6. **Class notes.** Many students start with the intention of copying up their class notes after each lesson, this is probably a waste of time, unrealistic and usually not done. It is a better use of time to read the notes after each lecture, writing in additional comments or side headings and using a highlighter for key words. This helps to consolidate the day's learning and to make the notes more readable later.

7. **Handwriting and expressive skills.** These can be practised like any other. If you know that these are likely to cause problems for you, you should practise them. The skills taught in English lessons apply to all subjects.

8 Set targets and work plans. Success is related to motivation. Find ways to increase yours. It helps to have:
- Realistic targets so that you can have a sense of achievement, otherwise you end up feeling the work is a never-ending task.
- Rewards which are task related ('after finishing the this task I can go out for the evening') or time related ('after each hour I can have a snack').
- Work in short bursts appropriate to *your* optimum length of concentration. It is better to spend a half hour of solid study than one hour of some study and some staring out the window.
- Set aside one pleasant place to study. This means you can associate studying with a sense of relaxation.
- Good equipment, such as: a good file for keeping notes, sharp pencils, pens, highlighters.

Revision techniques

Revision techniques are closely related to study skills:
- In the act of studying you are also learning and revising.
- The notes you make during study will later be useful for revision.
- Both study and revision techniques are related to means of improving memory.

1 Set a **revision timetable**, with realistic goals and, very importantly, small rewards for reaching them. The timetable should record how much you did and a list of things to do.

2 Work for **short spells** with adequate breaks. You may not feel tired but a change of activity will make you more able to concentrate.

3 **Make notes** of your notes every time you revise. You can improve them in line with what you found was successful (skill feedback).

4 Compile a **personal glossary** or **summary cards** to revise from.

5 Revise with **friends** (as long as you can stay on the task) and criticise each other's question answers.

6 Study **past papers**, not for question-spotting but to see how the questions relate to the syllabus. The questions throughout this book come from past papers and should be helpful.

Stress

Psychological theory and research suggests ways of coping with stress (see Unit 10.2). These can be adapted to studying or in the examination itself:

1 Increasing your **sense of control**. This can be achieved using work timetables and positive thinking e.g. 'It's too late to worry now, just get on with it'.

2 Avoiding **ego defence** mechanisms such as denial. Recognise the feeling of stress and devise a coping strategy rather than pretending you are OK.

3 **Relaxation** and **rest periods**. Have short breaks when studying. During the exam, stop for a minute or two and think nice thoughts away from the exam. Use self-hypnosis.

4 **Social support.** Spend time with friends when you're not studying, or for some study sessions. In the exam think about comforting people or things.

5 **Physical exercise** and **emotional discharge**. Go for a run before the exam. In the exam stretch your legs, or find some other means of discharging tension which doesn't distract other candidates.

Final preparation

- Check the time, date and place for the examination.
- Check you have the necessary equipment.
- Take some physical exercise before the exam to relieve tension and clear the mind.
- Arrive in good time.
- Practice relaxation techniques while waiting for the exam to start.
- Look forward to the conclusion of your studies.

Types of examination questions

❶ **Multiple choice questions** are used occasionally as part of the structured questions. An example:

The following are definitions of perception.
(i)   reception of visual information   ☐
(ii) interpretation of visual information   ☐
(iii) interpretation of sensory information   ☐
(iv) recognising shapes and patterns   ☐
(v)   reception of sensory information   ☐
*Tick the box which corresponds to the **best** definition of perception. [1 mark]*

(NEAB, 1988)

Multiple choice questions sound easy because they involve simply choosing one answer from a number of alternatives. But don't be deceived! They are a way of testing difficult ideas and subtle differences. Think carefully before placing your tick. Always indicate your best guess. Don't leave it blank and intend to return later, you can always write a question mark next to it, so that if you have time you can think again.

❷ Some questions require you to **fill in the blank**. For example:

When a child copies the behaviour of someone else, this is known as ....

(NEAB, 1988)

❸ Some exam papers have series of **short answer questions**. These are used to cover a wide range of the syllabus. The answer may be one word, several words or a sentence. The number of marks available is shown, these are usually related to the length of the answer required. For example:

What is meant by the term prejudice? [2 marks]

(MEG, 1993)

Answer: An attitude towards a person or group (*1 mark*) held prior to direct experience of the person or group (*1 mark*).

❹ **The structured question** is the most common on GCSE papers. It consists of some introductory information, the 'stimulus material', which is followed by a series of questions. These questions are structured. They start with a simple question requiring a short answer and progress to more complicated ones worth more marks. The simpler questions may involve multiple choice or short answers. The later questions may involve an essay-type answer. In between are questions which require thinking rather than producing rote answers. Much assistance can be gained from careful reading of the stimulus material.

The marks given for each part of the question, and the space provided for your answer, indicate the general length of answer required. Don't feel you have to fill the space, but if your answer is much too short, think again.

Examples of these questions can be found in Section 3, Questions and answers.

5 **Essay questions** (extended prose writing) require some planning. Answers should be accurate, detailed and critical. The MEG exam provides guidelines (hints) in the exam about how to answer these. For example:

What have psychologists discovered about how we form impressions and make judgements about people and their behaviour? [HINT: You might like to describe three studies by psychologists that show how we make judgements about people and their behaviour. You could then explain what conclusion we can draw from these studies.]

(MEG, 1993)

Mark schemes for essay questions are given in Section 3.

Answering examination questions

1 **Time.** There is plenty of time in the exam for you to consider your answer carefully. It is very easy to panic when you can't talk through the answer with anyone. You must not hurriedly write down the first thing which comes into your head. You should not struggle to present a lengthy answer to a question worth 1 mark.

2 **Stress.** Exam conditions alter everyone's behaviour, but some people suffer more than others. Some ideas for preventing stress during the exam were given on page 8.

3 Writing **essay plans**. This means you can concentrate on detail and structure while you're writing.

4 **Answering the question** rather than writing down what you know. It is very tempting, particularly under conditions of stress, to write down anything in the hope that it is relevant. Sheer volume of material does not get credit.

Don't ignore *features of the question*. For example, some questions say 'describe' rather than 'give', which means a fuller answer is required.

5 Understand the difference between a 'reason' and a 'reason that a psychologist might give'. Avoid common sense answers, as if you were talking to a friend. Psychology aims to be an objective science. In addition you must convince the examiner that your answer is drawn from what you have learned, not from casual knowledge.

6 Use **specific references** where possible. If you know the author's name and date, use them. If you're not sure, say so or leave it out, a mistake looks worse then an honest approach. The names strengthen the answer but arguments are more important. An examiner will be able to identify standard pieces of research without the specific reference.

7 Be able to **evaluate** the evidence you present. This can be done in terms of its methodology and/or ethics. You may also be asked if such findings have any applications.

Coursework

Coursework is stressful in a different way from exams. You have a large amount of time and may feel pressured to go to extraordinary lengths to produce a brilliant piece of work. This is not necessary, your aim should be maximum gains at minimum cost.

1 It's the **report** that gets the marks, therefore make sure you put as much effort into that as into the research itself.

xaminer's tip

The subject area of your coursework should be directly related to your other psychological studies.

② Research methods are a **compulsory** part of the final exam. Conducting your research and writing the report helps enormously when tackling this part of the syllabus.

③ When writing the introduction for your report you inevitably learn about a particular part of the syllabus in depth. This will lead you to a **greater understanding** of that part of the syllabus, so you have killed two birds with one stone.

④ A successful project is by no means one which produces the expected result. All results are significant and, in any case, **a flawed project** can lead to a worthwhile discussion.

⑤ If you **enjoy** something you are more likely to produce good work, therefore choose topics of interest to you. However, you may be tempted to choose some obscure subject which does not lend itself to student investigation, and therefore spend a lot of time with little to show. Be advised by those who know.

⑥ **The best design is a simple one.** One hypothesis, one group of subjects is all that is needed. Many students try to do too much, which leads to poor methodology and confused reporting.

⑦ **Borrow material.** Don't design your own questionnaire. It is difficult and time-consuming. use existing ones. Don't design your own method, replicate a previous study, or adapt some features of the design. Use a book that gives 'recipes' for student projects.

Ethics and public relations

Ethical considerations are paramount to any research, so you should be familiar with ethical guidelines (see Unit 11.4). In particular do not use any drugs or alcohol, do not use any restricted psychological tests, and only use children under close supervision, with parental consent. Animals should be avoided as participants except where naturalistic observation is involved.

You are in a position of responsibility when acting as an experimenter, do not treat your participants trivially even if they are friends or family. Remember, for many people you may be their first and last close call with psychology. Do nothing which will bring psychology into disrepute.

Copying

① **From a textbook:** If a textbook says exactly what you want to say, copy it and use quotation marks and state the source.

② **From another student:** Never risk copying someone else's project. It may mean disqualification for both of you.

Writing the report

Your report should look like a journal article. Different exam boards suggest different length reports. MEG proposes 1500 for your one report, NEAB gives a maximum length of 1000 and SEG recommends between 1000 and 1500 words. The presentation should be neat, clearly labelled and orderly. Typed scripts are easily readable but not compulsory. Folders are nice but more importantly the pages should turn so that they can be read easily.

There is no single correct format but the following is a useful guide:

① **Title:** Not too short and vague but also not too long. Something which gives the reader a good idea what the study is about.

② **Table of contents.**

③ **Summary or abstract.** About 150 words. A brief summary of your study, *not* in note form. This gives the reader a chance to find out the bare essentials without going any further. Include where possible:
- *A one sentence summary*, giving for example: the topic(s) to be studied, the hypothesis, some brief theoretical background, similar research findings.
- *Subjects* and *setting*, who, when, where, how many, what groups.
- The *method*, what design, what experimental treatment, what questionnaires, surveys or tests used.

- The *major findings*, which may include a mention of the statistics or simply one sentence summing up the outcome.
- *What does it all mean?* Mention the implications of your findings and suggestions for further research.

④ **Introduction.** Your hypothesis must come from somewhere. This is the task of the introduction.
- *Introductory paragraphs*. Outline the general theoretical background. Don't turn this introduction into an essay.
- Move on to *specific psychological theory and research* which is directly relevant to your study. One or two studies will be sufficient. Don't spell out the details of the study unless it is one you are replicating. Don't include material more appropriate to the discussion or you won't have anything left.
- The theory or research you have described should lead logically into the aims. Something like, '… therefore I have decided to try to find out …'. It is useful to record these aims for your own sake. Many candidates simply don't know what they're aiming to find out.
- *Hypothesis*. The aims are formally stated by the alternate and null hypothesis. It may help to name the independent and dependent variables as well and to state whether your hypothesis is one or two-tailed.

⑤ **Method.** The precise details of what you did must be described so that, theoretically, your project could be *replicated*. Include:
- *Design*: Type of design (independent, repeated, matched pairs), variables (independent, dependent, participant, confounding variables), data collected, controls.
- *Participants* (subjects): Sample (e.g. age, sex, etc.), sampling method, situation, experimenter(s).
- *Materials* used. Be sure to include copies of any stimulus materials in the appendices, e.g. pictures or psychological measures plus marking keys.
- *Procedure*: Standardised instructions, may be given in appendices.

⑥ **Results and findings:**
- *Raw data* presented in a table in the appendix.
- *Descriptive statistics*: numerical and graphical (see Unit 11.3). Numerical statistics include mean and range. All graphs and tables should have clear titles, axes should be labelled, column headings should be clearly explained, and all graphs should be drawn on graph paper.
- *Inferential statistics* may be used where appropriate. Clear reasons should be given for their use. You can use a computer or calculator program as long as the data and results are included and explained.

⑦ **Interpretation and discussion.** The purpose is to comment critically on the theoretical significance of your findings, with reference to the introduction.
- Explain the outcome in terms of *hypotheses* and/or aims.
- Discuss the outcome in terms of *theory/related research*, relating this to the introduction. If your results agree with previous theory/research the discussion will be brief, if your results are different look for alternative explanations.
- Mention any *additional outcomes*, such as matters raised by participants during debriefing.
- Comment on any *methodological flaws*, and suggest remedies. Even a well-designed study will have flaws but don't nit-pick.
- Discuss *wider implications* and ideas for follow-up research.

⑧ **Conclusions.** Clearly and briefly state your findings and conclusions.

⑨ **References.** Full details of any reference books or research should be given, in a style which would allow someone else to follow it up.
- Journal article: Author (s), date, title, journal name, volume (underlined or italics), pages.
- Book: Author (s), date, title, publisher.

⑩ **Appendices.** Some details are better in an appendix. For example: standardised instructions, debriefing details for participant, raw data, statistical calculations, questionnaires, observation checklists, mark schemes for any test or survey, stimulus materials (pictures).

Chapter 1
Perspectives in psychology

How might a psychologist explain the behaviour of two people in love?

A **biological psychologist** would describe their behaviour in terms the activity of neurons, muscles and hormones. He might explain love in terms of arousal and inherited drives.

A **behaviourist** would think in terms of a stimulus and a response. Love is learned through conditioned associations and positive reinforcement.

A **cognitive psychologist** would focus on the mental activities involved, the fact that each of the participants' perceptions are influenced by their expectations or the images and thoughts which are passing through their minds. Love is a belief about another, a mental label given for arousal.

A **psychoanalytic psychologist** would be most interested in the unconscious forces influencing their behaviour. Our sexual desires are determined by biological drives and early experiences. Love has its origins in mother-love and self-love.

A **humanist** views their behaviour in terms of how each person feels. Love depends on a sense of self-worth and unconditional acceptance.

Each of these different descriptions/explanations is called a **perspective**. These are the five main psychological perspectives.

Psychology is the scientific study of behaviour and experience. (It literally means 'mind-study', from the Greek words *psyche* + *logos*). Psychologists present explanations of why human beings, and animals, *behave* in the ways they do. They are also interested in explaining the subjective *experience* of consciousness.

Explanations vary depending on the perspective you start with. Each perspective has different assumptions, what you see depends on what you assume is there. No one view is correct, they complement each other. Sometimes they are mutually exclusive, but not always. They each contribute to a full understanding of any behaviour. An *eclectic* perspective is one which combines the best features of different perspectives.

The biological perspective

[Physiological psychology, bio-psychology, neuropsychology, neuroscience, psychobiology, psychophysiology]

Biological systems are offered as a means to describe and explain behaviour. Biology refers to all the physiological systems we find in the body: Muscles, blood, hormones (the autonomic nervous system), nerves and the brain (the central nervous system). It also includes genetic factors.

Concepts: Nervous impulses, arousal, maturation, heredity, genes.
Theorists: Hubel and Wiesel, Cannon, Chomsky, Piaget.

Positive points:
● A particular *level* of explanation which is sometimes viewed as the simplest and therefore best, when available.

<u>Criticisms</u>:

- *Reductionist*. It cannot explain complex behaviour adequately. Even if we knew all the biological foundations of memory, learning, emotion, etc. we might still lack an explanation of human behaviour.
- *Narrow*. It does not explain cognitive, emotional and environmental influences, and subjective experience.
- More appropriate for *animal* behaviour. In humans, our conscious minds exert strong influences on behaviour so that most biological processes can be modified.

<u>Major areas in this book</u>: Chapter 2: The Visual System; Chapter 3: Instinct and Learning; Chapter 4: Theories of Cognitive Development (Piaget's maturational perspective); Chapter 6: Crowds, Crowding and Territorial Behaviour (stress); Chapter 7: Aggression; Chapter 8: Attachment and Separation (innate responses), Personality, Temperament; Chapter 9: Gender Development; Chapter 10: Emotion, Stress, Biological Bases of Behaviour.
<u>Other areas</u>: Memory, learning, effect of drugs, consciousness, sleep, motivation.

The behaviourist perspective

[Learning theory, behavioural theory]

Behaviourists focus on objectively observable behaviour, rather than any internal processes. They explain behaviour in terms of how it is learned through interactions with the environment (rather than any innate factors). *Radical* behaviourism refers to the view that *all* behaviour is caused and maintained in this way.

<u>Concepts</u>: Conditioning (classical and operant), reinforcement (positive and negative), punishment, reward, stimulus–response, shaping.
<u>Theorists</u>: Watson, Pavlov, Thorndike, Skinner.

<u>Positive points</u>:

- Classic learning theory has been a *major influence* in all branches of psychology. Few psychologists today would regard themselves as strict behaviourists, but many theories incorporate behaviourist concepts.
- It has given rise to many *practical applications* such as programmed learning, behaviour therapies, advertising and animal training.
- It is an *empirical perspective,* which lends itself to scientific research.
- *Social learning theory* is an adaptation of learning theory, plus psychoanalytic and cognitive approaches.

<u>Criticisms</u>:

- *Mechanistic* perspective which ignores consciousness and subjective experience.
- *Deterministic* perspective. Behaviour is determined by the environment and not by free will.
- *Reductionist*. Simplifies complex behaviour to stimulus–response links.
- It is largely based on work with *animals*.

<u>Major areas in this book</u>: Chapter 3: Conditioning and Cognitive Explanations of Learning, Social Learning; Chapter 4: Intelligence, Language Acquisition; Chapter 7: Antisocial Behaviour: Aggression, Prosocial Behaviour; Chapter 8: Attachment and Separation, Personality (Eysenck, Skinner); Chapter 9: Moral Development, Gender Development, Parenting.
<u>Other areas</u>: Abnormal behaviour and therapy, teaching.

The cognitive perspective

[Information processing]

Explanations are given in terms of internal mental process as well as external factors, and often use concepts borrowed from computer technologies. 'Cognitive' refers specifically to the mental processes. It comes from the Latin 'to know'.

<u>Concepts</u>: Input, storage, retrieval, levels of processing, schema, scripts, information filters.

Theorists: Bruner, Gregory, Newell and Simon, Chomsky, Piaget, Kohlberg.

Positive points:
- Restored the concept of *mind* which behaviourists had dismissed.
- Emphasises *individual* control.
- Has stimulated a large amount of *research*.

Criticisms:
- *Humans are not machines.* Cognitive theory tends to omit emotional influences on behaviour and other external factors such as family conditions. More recently there have been attempts to change this.
- Experimental findings tend to laboratory based and *artificial*.

Major areas in this book: Chapter 3: Conditioning and Cognitive Explanations of Learning (insight learning); Chapter 4: Memory, Thinking and Problem Solving, Theories of Cognitive Development, Language Acquisition; Chapter 5: Impression Formation, Stereotyping and Categorising, Prejudice and Discrimination, Reduction of Prejudice; Chapter 8: Self-concepts and the Role of Expectations; Chapter 9: Moral Development, Gender Development, Attraction and Friendships; Chapter 10: Emotion, Stress.
Other areas: Language production and comprehension, reading, attention, cognitive psychotherapies.

The psychoanalytic perspective

[Psychodynamic, Freudian, post-Freudian, Jungian]

A theory of personality, as well as a form of therapy, which explains human behaviour in terms of unconscious, biological drives and early experience. The approach is dynamic, which means it explains how personality develops rather than just describing what is there.

Concepts: Ego, id, super-ego, ego defence, psychosexual stages (oral, anal, phallic, genital), Freudian slips, neurotic personality, transference, dream analysis.
Theorists: Freud, Bowlby, Erikson, Jung.

Positive points:
- The theory has been enormously *influential* within psychology (for example, psychotherapy and developmental theories) and also beyond in art, literature and other sciences.
- Introduced the concept of the *unconscious*.

Criticisms:
- Lacks rigorous *empirical support*, especially regarding normal development.
- *Reductionist.* Reduces human activity to a basic set of structures, which can't account for all behaviour.
- *Too biological.* It relies too much on the influence of basic instincts and physical drives.

Major areas in this book: Chapter 5: Prejudice and Discrimination (Scapegoat Theory); Chapter 7: Antisocial Behaviour: Aggression; Chapter 8: Attachment and Separation (Bowlby), Personality (Freud); Chapter 9: Moral Development, Gender Development.
Other areas: Abnormal behaviour (psychotherapy), sleep (dreams).

The humanistic perspective

[Phenomenological, existential, Rogerian]

An approach which emphasises subjective experience and individual uniqueness. Humanists reject deterministic and mechanistic approaches, instead taking the view that we control our actions rather being controlled by external forces.

Concepts: Self-esteem, unconditional positive regard, personal constructs.
Theorists: Rogers, Kelly, Maslow.

Positive points:
- Has encouraged psychologists to accept the view that there is *more to behaviour* than objectively discoverable facts. Subjective experience and the importance of the individual are also valuable perspectives.

Criticisms:
- *Vague and unscientific.* It is less concerned with scientific methods and more with enabling individuals to achieve their potential.

Major areas in this book: Chapter 8: Self-concepts and the Role of Expectations, Personality (Rogers, Kelly).
Other areas: Psychotherapy, counselling.

There are some other perspectives which are also important:

The sociocultural perspective

[Social psychology, sociology]

Behaviour can be understood in terms of our social context: family, friends, institutions society, culture and political systems. This perspective focuses on behaviour within and between groups, and on cross-cultural similarities and differences.

Concepts: Norms, ingroup and outgroup, bias, ethnic, ethnocentric.
Theorists: Adorno, Sherif, Asch, Milgram, Zimbardo, Nobles.

Positive points:
- The *cross-cultural* perspective reminds us that much of psychological theory is limited to white middle-class Europeans.
- Social factors are an *important* ingredient in all aspects of behaviour.

Major areas in this book: Chapter 2: Perceptual Processes, Development of Perception; Chapter 5: Impression Formation, Stereotyping and Categorising, Prejudice and Discrimination, Reduction of Prejudice; Chapter 6: Group Norms, Conformity and Obedience, Presence of Others, Crowds, Crowding and Territorial Behaviour; Chapter 7: Antisocial Behaviour: Aggression, Prosocial Behaviour; Chapter 8: Attachment and Separation, Self-concepts and the Role of Expectations, Personality (Bandura, Mischel); Chapter 9: Moral Development, Gender Development, Attraction and Friendships, Parenting; Chapter 10, Emotion, Stress.
Other areas: Attitudes, group behaviour, attribution theory, media influence.

The ethological perspective

[Sociobiology, comparative psychology, animal behaviour]

Behaviour is understood in terms of its adaptive or evolutionary value, the extent to which the behaviour contributes to the survival of the species. Ethology literally means 'the study of behaviour'. Ethologists emphasise the importance of naturalistic observation.

Concepts: Instinct, imprinting, fixed action patterns (FAPs), critical and sensitive periods, kin selection.
Theorists: Lorenz, Tinbergen, Bowlby.

Positive points:
- Has introduced some *important concepts* to many areas of human behaviour.
- Stimulated psychologists to use *naturalistic observation*, a method first used by ethologists.

Criticisms:
- More appropriate to *animal behaviour*. Human behaviour is less influenced by innate factors.

Major areas in this book: Chapter 3, Instinct and Learning; Chapter 6, Crowds, Crowding and Territorial Behaviour; Chapter 7, Antisocial Behaviour: Aggression, Prosocial Behaviour; Chapter 8, Attachment and Separation.
Other areas: animal behaviour.

The developmental perspective

[Lifespan psychology]

An approach which focuses on how humans change over time from infancy to old age, showing how experience and maturation affect social, emotional and cognitive development. Most of the perspectives already mentioned offer developmental accounts of behaviour.

Concepts: Maturation, sensitive periods, nature/nurture, ages of man.
Theorists: Skinner, Piaget, Freud, Kohlberg, Bowlby.

Positive points:
- A *dynamic* view of human behaviour.
- Provides a *useful perspective* on different stages of a person's life such as childhood, adolescence, middle age.

Major areas in this book: Chapter 4: Intelligence and Intelligence Tests, Tests, Theories of Cognitive Development, Language Acquisition; Chapter 7: Antisocial Behaviour: Aggression, Prosocial Behaviour; Chapter 8: Attachment and Separation, Self-concepts and the Role of Expectations, Personality; Chapter 9: Moral Development, Gender Development, Attraction and Friendships, Parenting.
Other areas: Adolescence, adulthood (work, marriage, parenthood), ageing (retirement and death), life events.

The nature/nurture question

[Heredity/environment, nativism/empiricism]

A fundamental issue found throughout psychology. Can behaviour be explained in terms of inherited factors or environmental ones? Which one is more important?

The importance of these questions is both philosophical and practical. If biological factors (nature) are predominant, then any programs of enrichment or attempts to teach people to change their nature are largely irrelevant. If, on the other hand, social and environmental experiences (nurture) do affect behaviour, then we must investigate these and find ways to improve the human condition.

Positive points:
- It is an *inevitable* question about behaviour.

Criticisms:
- Neither nature or nurture *alone* can ever explain behaviour, nor can they be easily separated. The *interactionist* position represents this view.

Major areas in this book: Chapter 2: Development of Perception; Chapter 4: Intelligence, Language Acquisition; Chapter 7: Antisocial Behaviour: Aggression; Chapter 8: Personality, Temperament.

Other areas: Causes of mental illness.

The scientific method

[Experimental, empirical]

An approach to problem solving which aims to produce a body of objective facts.

Science is knowledge gained through critical and systematic testing. Rigid scientific techniques are essentially the same as those that we all use in our everyday observations: we make generalisations from the particular, we form hypotheses (expectations for the future), we note when our hypotheses are wrong, and finally, readjust our expectations accordingly.

It is an approach used by all perspectives and research methods in order to test their theories. The scientific *experiment* is the most precise of all methods because all variables are (potentially) controlled. This control also means that it can be *replicated*, enhancing the validity of the results.

'Experimental psychology' usually refers specifically to research in perception, emotion, learning, and memory.

The steps involved in the scientific method are:
- Stating a problem in relation to existing theory and known facts.
- Formulating a testable hypothesis.
- Designing a controlled procedure to investigate the hypothesis.
- Analysing the data.
- Stating a conclusion.
- Adjusting existing theory to fit any new facts uncovered.

This method relies on the development of theories. Facts are meaningless without a theoretical basis. They can be explained in terms of many different theories. The test of a *good* theory is that it explains the facts and can generate further research questions to test it. Research and theory work together:
- Data is organised into a theory in order to explain the facts.
- Theories generate predictions which can then be tested by research.
- New facts produced from research are used to refine the theory.

Positive points:
- *Facts* can only be established using scientific methods. The alternative methods include introspection and rational argument, which are very subjective.
- In order for Psychology to be considered a *science*, psychologists must use scientific methods to support their views or theories.

Criticisms:
- Objective study of behaviour is *not always possible* because perceptual biases and personal values of experimenters and participants often affect empirical results. This is true in all sciences, but particularly so in psychology.
- Using controlled methods means that the findings lack *real life validity*. The same things which are advantages are also disadvantages.

Major areas in this book: Chapter 11: Methods, Design, Statistical Treatments, Ethical and Practical Considerations.

Quick test

1 What is meant by the nature/nurture debate in psychology?
2 Give a definition of psychology.
3 Give **one** example of a biological system.
4 What does *cognitive* mean?
5 Why is the behaviourist perspective called *behaviourist*?
6 Which approach introduced the idea of *information filters*?
7 What perspective reintroduced the importance of subjective experience?
8 What is *ethology*?
9 What **two** approaches is Freud an example of?
10 What is the difference between the terms *experiment* and the *scientific method*?

Summary

Different kinds of explanation are used in psychology to understand the causes of behaviour and experience:

APPROACH/PERSPECTIVE	KIND OF EXPLANATION
Biological	biological systems
Behaviourist	learning
Cognitive	mental factors
Psychoanalytic	unconscious motives
Humanist	subjective factors and individual uniqueness
Sociocultural	the influence of others and society generally
Ethological	adaptive value
Developmental	change with age
Nature/nurture	what you're born with versus experience
Scientific method	producing objective facts

Chapter 2
Perception

SEEING FOR THE FIRST TIME

Some people are born blind because they have cataracts. This means that the lenses of their eyes are not clear but opaque, not letting any light through. In the 1950s it became possible to replace the lens of the eye. This gave a number of people the chance to see for the first time in their lives. S.B. was a well-known example of this. He was a man of 52 who had longed to see all his life, though he had always been very active. His progress and ultimately sad end, was recorded by Gregory and Wallace (1963).

When the bandages were first removed he saw a confusion of colours in front of him but knew by the voice that this was his surgeon's face. Within a few days he began to make sense of his visual sensations.

One day he looked out of his fourth floor hospital window and was curious about the small objects below. He tried to crawl out of the window to touch them, demonstrating a lack of depth perception. He could not see depth in 3D drawings, nor was he disturbed by visual illusions.

He continued to touch things to help himself 'see', as he had done when blind. Then he could match his internal concept of the object with his new perceptions. For example, when he was first shown a lathe he shut his eyes and explored it with his hands. Then he opened his eyes and said, 'Now that I've felt it I can see it.'

This raises questions about what we 'see'. We assume that our visual images are photographs of the real world. It seems that, in fact, the light patterns recorded by the eye must be organised by the brain before they make sense. This chapter explores the issue of seeing: sensation and perception, and in what way it is innate or learned.

S.B.'s story ends sadly. He never really mastered sight, preferring to use the senses he had become accustomed to and only pretending to 'see'. He died three years after he gained his sight. 'He found disappointment with what he took to be reality' (Gregory and Wallace).

2.1 The visual system

NO VISION WITHOUT MOVEMENT

Pritchard (1961) used a device to stabilise the retinal image. The participant looks at a picture which is projected onto a screen using a tiny projector mounted on the retina. Any movement of the participant's eye is exactly followed by the small slide projector. After a few seconds the participant no longer sees the picture!

Why? The answer lies in the small movements of the eye and the behaviour of the cells of the **retina**.

The eyes are constantly in motion due to small, rapid jerks called saccades and nystagmus. This means that the image which is thrown on the retina is constantly shifting and thus stimulating different retinal cells. If a retinal cell continues to receive *the same* stimulus it ceases to transmit a message to the brain.

Blinking may be related to this. It is a means of renewing the retinal image as well as sometimes moistening the eye. Otherwise why does blinking increase when extra vigilance is needed?

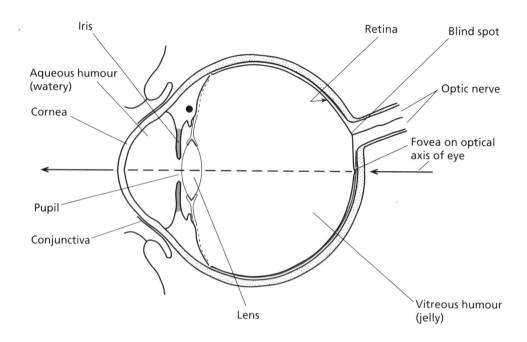

Fig. 2.1 The human eye

DEFINITIONS		
cornea	Contributes to the action of the lens in bending light.
iris	The coloured part around the pupil, containing muscles which control the amount of light let through the pupil.
pupil	A hole, dilates and constricts in response to the amount of available light.
lens	Bends incoming light so that it is focused on the fovea. When focusing on near objects the lens is round. For distant objects the muscles around the lens relax and it becomes flat. This process is called *accommodation*.
retina	A thin sheet of interconnected nerve cells, including the rods and cones, and bipolar and ganglion cells.

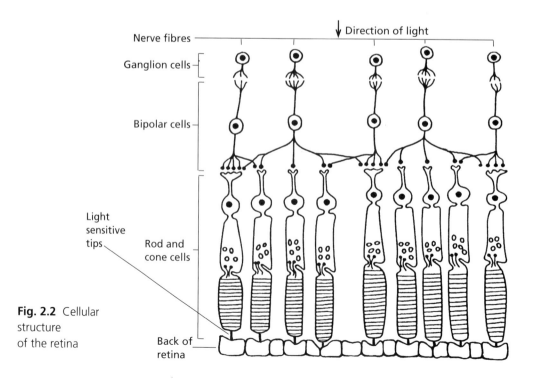

Fig. 2.2 Cellular structure of the retina

photoreceptors or photosensitive cells	Specialised cells (rods and cones) which convert light into a nervous impulse which is transmitted to a specific part of the brain. Photosensitive means 'light' sensitive.
rod	Long and thin (rod-like) photosensitive cell. Rods respond to shades of grey, movement and edges. They function in conditions of low lighting. The outer parts of the retina contain mainly rods. The number of rods in one retina is roughly 120 million.
cone	Cone-shaped photosensitive cell which reports colour by mixing the signals from three different types of cone cell: red-, blue- and green-sensitive (short, medium and long wavelengths respectively). Cones function in daylight conditions. The outer parts of the retina have no colour vision. The number of cone cells in one retina is approximately 6 million.

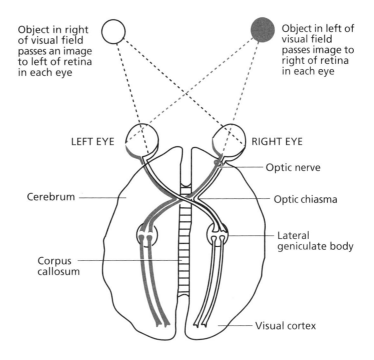

Fig. 2.3 Pathways of the optic nerve

fovea	The central region of the retina, containing densely packed photoreceptors, mainly cones. Specialised for acute, detailed vision.
blind spot	A region of the back of the eye with no photoreceptors. Also called the **optic disc**. This is where the optic fibres collect to pass back to the optic nerve. It generally doesn't disrupt vision because the brain fills in gaps in data. Try this: Draw two small black circles, about 6 inches apart, on a piece of white paper. Cover your left eye and focus on the left circle. Move the paper until it's about 9 inches from your face while staring at one circle. The other circle should disappear because the image is falling on your blind spot.
bipolar cell	Every photoreceptor is connected to more than one bipolar cell, and each bipolar cell receives impulses from more than one photoreceptor. These in turn connect to retinal ganglion cells.

ganglion cell	The third layer of cells, closest to the light source. They receive input from one or more bipolar cells and are bundled into the optic nerve.
optic nerve	Formed from the nerve fibres of the ganglion cells. They leave the eye via the optic disc and pass on to the visual cortex.
optic chiasma	The point of cross-over. Each side of the brain receives information from both eyes. Nerves from the half of each retina closest to the nose cross over to the other side of the brain. Those from the outer side of the retina carry on.
lateral geniculate body	A relay station, where the nerves from the retina meet (synapse with) nerves to the visual cortex.
visual cortex	The part of the cerebral cortex which receives the most direct input from the both retinas. Located in the occipital lobe of the brain (at the back).
striate cortex	The primary visual cortex, striped in appearance.
parastriate cortex	Surrounds the striate cortex.

monocular	Relating to one eye.
binocular	Information combined from both eyes, providing important data for depth perception.
afterimage	Sensed after a stimulus is removed, and created by over-stimulation of the receptors.
bottom–up processing	Visual perception based on the sensory data itself, as opposed to **top–down processing**, where perceptions are influenced by expectations (see Unit 2.2 for theoretical discussion).

Sensory transduction

Transduction is the process by which some 'thing' is transformed. In the case of vision the thing transformed is light, a physical source of energy. It is changed into neural impulses. The image which is received by the retina needs to be processed for two reasons:

❶ It is poor quality.   In some ways the eye is like a camera, an image is focused on a photosensitive surface. However, unlike a camera, the retinal image is neither complete or true. It is blurred due to imperfections in the lens and the cells lying in front of the photo receptors. It is also curved and constantly in motion. A camera is intended to produce a picture, whereas the eye transmits information for the brain for active interpretation.

❷ There is too much data to be processed rapidly or usefully.   The retina collects 126 million points of light, many of which are repetitive. Therefore it is necessary to produce the data in condensed form consisting of the most important data, such as edges and movement. This is achieved by a limited amount of information processing taking place at the retina, one example of which is **lateral inhibition**. When one retinal cell is stimulated, it inhibits activity in surrounding cells. The end result of this is that the borders between light and dark are emphasised. This begins the process of summarising visual information and extracting meaning from it.

The visual cortex

Part of the process of transduction has already taken place in the eye itself. The visual cortex continues this information processing.

Hubel and Wiesel (1962) The visual cortex of the cat

RESEARCH QUESTION: How do the individual cells of the visual cortex respond to the input from the retina?

METHOD: Experiment. An anaesthetised cat is placed facing a screen. **Microelectrodes** are placed in the cat's visual cortex so that a record can be made of the electrical signals produced by individual cells while the cat is viewing a pattern on a screen.

RESULTS: They found that a particular cell in the visual cortex only fired when a line of a particular orientation and from a particular part of the visual field was detected. They called these **simple cells**.

Later they found cells that were equally sensitive to other features, such as a stationary or moving dot, or the direction of movement.

They also found **complex cells**, which respond to several simple cells, and **hypercomplex cells**, which respond to simple patterns or shapes (such as angles) from the information they receive from many complex cells. Additionally, they found that cells are organised into **functional columns** of simple, complex and hypercomplex cells which all respond to a particular feature from one eye.

INTERPRETATION: These findings transformed the physiological study of vision, demonstrating how the visual cortex is related to the retina and the specific mechanisms in the brain for detecting specific features. The functional columns may predispose the brain to be able to make certain comparisons, such as those used in depth perception.

RELATED STUDIES: See Blakemore and Cooper, in Unit 2.3.

Seeing depth

The perception of depth is turning the two-dimensional proximal image into three dimensions. It also enables distance to be recorded.

Using one eye (monocular), we can judge depth using perceptual cues, such as shading on the top surface or shadow behind (see Unit 2.2 for a list of depth cues).

Two eyes (binocular) located at the front, rather than on the side of the head, enable precise judgements of distance, by convergence and disparity.

1. Convergence.   When two eyes converge on a near object the angle is greater than for a distant object. This calculation of an angle serves as a range finder.

2. Disparity.   If you look at an object with your right eye, then cover it and look with your left eye, the object appears to shift sideways in relation to more distant objects. Closer objects shift more than distant ones. This is **stereoscopic vision**.

Julesz (1964) Random dot stereo images

RESEARCH QUESTION: Can disparity alone produce a sensation of depth?

METHOD: Investigation. A pair of random dot patterns (100,000 dots) are generated by a computer. Some of the dots in one picture are shifted horizontally in relation to corresponding dots in the other picture. The only depth cue available is disparity between the two retinal images, does this produce a perception of depth?

RESULTS: When the pictures are viewed individually they appear as dots only, but when they are shown one to each eye (stereoscopically) the pair is vividly seen in depth and an image emerges.

INTERPRETATION: Binocular cells in the visual cortex compare corresponding points from both retinas and compute depth from this disparity. Such cells have been detected by microelectrode recording.

This illustrates how the brain combines the images from both eyes at the level of the physiological processes.

APPLICATIONS:
Disparity explains the fact that, in aerial reconnaissance, objects camouflaged by a complex background are difficult to detect monocularly but jump out when viewed stereoscopically.

Seeing brightness

Brightness or illumination is the simplest of visual sensations, found in the simplest eyes (for example, a limpet). The stronger the light, the faster the rate of firing from the photoreceptor. This straightforward coding is dependent on two other factors:

1 <u>Dark-light adaptation</u>.   When the eye is kept in a low light for some time, it grows more sensitive and a given light will look brighter.

2 <u>Differences in illumination</u>.   Whatever the level of brightness, it is the contrasts between adjacent areas which are most information-rich. Therefore, brightness is a function of :
- intensity of light at a particular point,
- the intensity of light the retina has been exposed to in the recent past,
- the intensities of light falling on other regions of the retina.

Seeing movement

Movement is detected by changes in brightness (on/off). Its detection is complicated by three things:

1 <u>Constancy</u>.   A retinal image moves across the photoreceptors when you move your head. How does the image remain constant rather than being seen as movement? The brain must co-ordinate the eye-head movements with the retinal image to determine movement and constancy. For example, if you are sitting on a train, and another train pulls out of the train station, it is sometimes difficult to know whether it is your train or the other one which is moving.

2 <u>Apparent motion</u> (also called the phi phenomenon).   When a row of lights flash in sequence, they may appear to be a single light moving across the row. This works as long as the distance between the lights and the time between flashes is right. An everyday example is to be found in some advertising displays. It is because the cells of the retina don't notice a time gap of very limited duration. Television also relies on our inability to notice the gaps, the TV screen is refreshed once every 50th of a second.

3 <u>Saccades and nystagmus</u>.   The eye is constantly subject to small tremors. Nystagmus are random tremors, saccades are small jumps that enable the eye to keep tracking an object or words across a page. If the eye did not move in such jumps, vision would be smeared. During a saccade some vision occurs, but small details are not picked up. Additionally, these small movements are necessary to stop the photoreceptors adapting to the stimulus and ceasing to respond (as described in the experiment by Pritchard at the beginning of this unit).

Visual disturbances and visual illusions

Fig. 2.4 Ray figure and white diamonds

The ray figure is disturbing to look at. One explanation is that it upsets the visual system because it over stimulates the edge detectors. Stroboscopes, television flicker and even driving past a row of trees with the sun behind can all be annoying because they overload the visual system, which tries to follow and signal rapidly changing intensities. This illusion is not only uncomfortable, but also produces an illusion of wavy lines in the centre.

Similarly, the white diamonds picture produces an illusion of diamonds at the crossroads. These illusions are due to overload on movement and edge detectors. These visual illusions can be explained in terms of processes in the eye, whereas most illusions are due to other perceptual processes (see Unit 2.2).

Quick test 2.1

1 Are there more rods than cones?
2 What are rods and cones collectively called?
3 Why do we have a blind spot?
4 What is the name given to the point where parts of the optic fibre cross over?
5 What visual input is received by the right visual cortex?
6 Some cells in the visual cortex respond only to line orientation. Give **one** other example of the kind of information another group of cells might respond to.
7 A person with only one eye loses some but not all of the ability to perceive depth. Why?
8 What is *disparity*?
9 What is the *phi phenomenon*?
10 What everyday process uses this phenomenon?

Summary

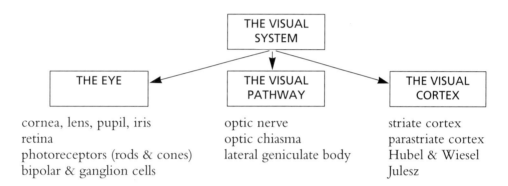

Sensory transduction is the transformation of light into activity in the nervous system. The eye records various features of perception:

DEPTH	BRIGHTNESS	MOVEMENT	ILLUSIONS
convergence	dark–light adaptation	constancy	ray figure
disparity	differences in illumination	apparent motion	white diamonds
		saccades and nystagmus	

APPLICATIONS: Aerial reconnaissance

2.2 Perceptual processes

ERRORS BY A TENSE US CREW LED TO DOWNING OF IRAN JET, NAVY INQUIRY IS SAID TO FIND

A MILITARY INVESTIGATION of the shooting down of an Iranian airliner by an American warship last month has blamed crew error arising from the psychological stress of being in combat for the first time, Defense Department officials familiar with the inquiry said today.

The investigation of the incident in the Persian Gulf on July 3, in which 290 people were killed, found no malfunction in the sophisticated radar technology aboard the Vincennes, the ship that shot down the Iranian Airbus.

The inquiry found that in the stress of battle, radar operators on the Vincennes mistakenly convinced themselves that the aircraft they had spotted taking off from the airport in Bandar, Abbas, Iran, was hostile and intended to attack the Vincennes.

With the perceived threat fast approaching, they wrongly interpreted what they saw on their radar screens in a way that reinforced this preconceived notion.

There is much practical interest in the effect of expectations on what we perceive. This unit is concerned with how we acquire and use such expectations.

Sensation and perception

Sensations are the raw data of the perceptual system, the unaltered record of the physical stimulus. **Perceptions** are based on sensations, but they are altered through interpretation and elaboration so that what is seen has meaning.

Where does sensation end and perception begin? In Unit 2.1 we saw that the process of interpretation starts very early in the visual process. It might be said that photoreceptors *sense* light, but the next cells in the chain (bipolar cells) *perceive* it.

Fig. 2.5 Leeper's Lady. How old is she?

DEFINITIONS		
sensation	Coding. As distinct from perception, sensation is the process by which information about external, physical events is detected by the sense receptors and transmitted to the brain.
perception	A dynamic searching for the best interpretation of the available data. Gregory describes it as the process of forming a hypothesis, which is suggested, and then tested, by sensory data.
distal stimulus	The physical object which gives rise to the proximal stimulus. We may touch the distal stimulus to test our perceptual hypotheses.
proximal stimulus	That which is near, the sensory stimulation.
percept	That which is perceived. It is not the same as either the physical object (distal stimulus) or the energy which impinges on the receptor (proximal stimulus).
2D image	The retinal image which has only two dimensions, as opposed to the 3D percept.

3D image or percept	The image that is constructed by the perceiver, which has a third dimension (depth) added by inference.
ambiguous figure	One sensory input but several possible perceptions.

FACTORS WHICH AFFECT PERCEPTION

perceptual organisation	Part of the perceptual process is to organise sensory data into meaningful patterns.Gestalt psychologists are associated with this view of perception as an active process.
Gestalt psychology	An approach taken by a group of German psychologists in the first part of this century. 'Gestalten' means the 'whole'. Their main contribution was to emphasise the view that 'the whole is greater than the sum of the parts'. The way a set of physical objects are organised leads to a perception which does not exactly correspond to its individual elements.
perceptual constancy	Several sensory inputs (e.g. produced when a book is turned over) which result in one perception (of an object with constant size and shape). This is the reverse of an ambiguous figure. Constancy depends on knowledge of the real object. We persist in seeing it in line with our expectations despite changed retinal images which may distort the image.
perceptual set	'Set' is the tendency to respond in a certain manner, in line with expectations built on past experience. This is a parallel process to visual constancy but results in biased selection.
visual illusions	The unconscious mistakes of perception. In fact they are not really mistakes, but are normal, relatively consistent phenomena which are subject to regular rules of perception. Illusions are distinct from hallucinations or delusions. Illusions are usually associated with an element of surprise. However, many commonplace visual techniques, such as using shadow to infer 3D in pictures, are also illusions.

Perceptual organisation

The experiences of S.B. were described at the beginning of this chapter. An adult recovering his sight finds no meaning in the mass of sensory data. Similarly, James (1890) described the visual world of an infant as one of 'blooming, buzzing confusion'.

The next stage is to learn to how to give a visual scene meaning.

Gestalt principles of perception

The Gestalt psychologists argued that humans tend to organise sensory data in certain typical ways to build up meaningful perceptual units:

1. Figure / ground organisation. When looking at a picture we see figures set against a background. In certain ambiguous drawings, what is figure and what is ground may change. Nevertheless, at any time, only one part is figure. It is not truly possible to see both as 'figure' at the same time.

2. Similarity. When viewing a group of objects we tend to group together those which are similar. For example:
   ooooooooooxxxxxxoooooooooooxxxxxxxxoooooooooo.

3. Proximity. Both in space and time. For example: •• ••• • •• Placing some dots closer together within a line serves to organise the sensory data into groups.

4. Closure. We tend to complete images with sections missing. When participants are presented with a picture like the one on the next page and later asked to draw it, they fill in the missing gaps.

⑤ <u>Continuity</u>.   A series of dots which make a recognisable shape, such as a square, are seen as a square rather than their constituent parts.

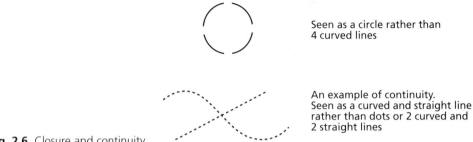

Seen as a circle rather than 4 curved lines

An example of continuity. Seen as a curved and straight line rather than dots or 2 curved and 2 straight lines

Fig. 2.6 Closure and continuity

Navon (1977) Seeing the woods instead of the trees

RESEARCH QUESTION: Given a choice, will the visual system perceive the overall *gestalt* or the constituent parts of a pattern?

PARTICIPANTS: 14 college students, as part of their course requirement. They were paid a monetary bonus for accuracy and speed.

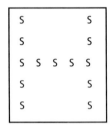

METHOD: Experiment. Participants were briefly (40 milliseconds) shown a stimulus like the one in the diagram. The large letter is termed the 'whole' or global letter, the smaller letters are the constituent or local parts. On some trials the stimuli were consistent (the global and local letters were the same). On other trials they were conflicting.

Participants were directed beforehand to identify either the global or local letter. In all they were shown 288 stimuli.

RESULTS:

1 Global letters were more quickly identified.
2 When local and global letters were in conflict, participants were slowed in their identification of the local letters but not the global ones.

INTERPRETATION: This supports the idea of global precedence, the Gestalt approach to perceptual organisation. Initial perceptions are based on the overall representation rather than the overall picture being built up from its individual elements (top-down rather than bottom-up).

This would be useful in speeding up the perceptual process so that important objects in a visual scene can be identified with minimal delay.

EVALUATION:

1 The results may be due to the fact that, given limited time, a person only partially processes the retinal stimulus.
2 It is not always true. In a later study, Kinchla and Wolfe (1979) found that when the global letter takes up a greater part of the visual field, or if the local features were larger or more prominent, then the local features were easier to respond to. Nevertheless it certainly explains some aspects of early perceptual processing

APPLICATIONS: The instrument panel in an airplane is designed with human factors such as these in mind. Analogue displays (such as the traditional clock face) provide better immediate impressions whereas digital displays are more precise.

Visual constancies

Visual constancies are one example of the way we organise our sensory data. The perceived visual world tends to remain the same despite drastic alterations in the retinal image. Essentially all perceptual qualities display constancy to some extent.

An everyday example of constancy is the ability to draw perspective. A child records the world in two dimensions, a book is always rectangular. The child learns to add depth cues, such as shading and making the near end of the book wider. Is the same true for the visual system? Do we have to *learn* that certain distortions of the retinal image have to be reorganised to make sense? Or is this *innate*? This nature/nurture question is looked at in Unit 2.3.

In what ways does the visual system make adjustments to the proximal image?

❶ <u>Shape constancy</u>.   A book is seen as a rectangle despite the fact that the retinal image is rarely a rectangle.

❷ <u>Brightness constancy</u>.   When the sun goes behind a cloud, our eyes adjust to changes in light so that what was white is still described as white rather than grey.

③ Colour constancy.   Different wavelengths of light reach the eye, yet the same colour is perceived. For example, light outdoors is bluer than indoors, however, colours look the same due to unconscious adaptation.

④ Size constancy.   In the case of the Ponzo illusion, the white bars are the same length yet we perceive them as different. The oblique lines seem to show perspective, and therefore our perceptual processes adjust for size. A distant object of the same retinal size is seen as longer. **Apparent distance** is the key to understanding size constancy. When something appears to be more distant we make adjustments for size.

Fig. 2.7 Ponzo illusion and railway lines

RESEARCH EXAMPLE   **The Ames Room: when size constancy fails**

RESEARCH QUESTION: How can the perceptual system be so completely fooled?

METHOD: Investigation. A room is constructed as shown in the diagram.

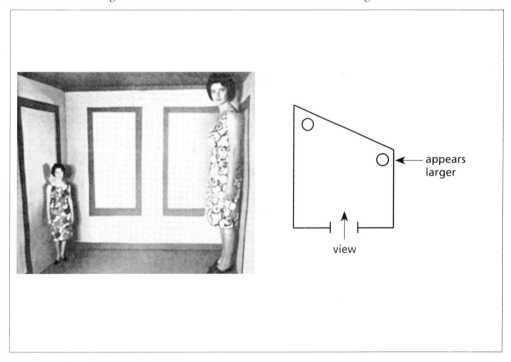

Fig. 2.8 The Ames room

RESULTS: One person looks much larger than the other and the room looks rectangular. Interestingly, if the person on the left is familiar, the illusion disappears. Also, if the participant is given a long stick to poke around the room and discover its true proportions, the illusion disappears slowly.

INTERPRETATION: This illusion shows that apparent distance affects the perception of size. We judge the size of objects according to cues and expectations we have about distance. When a person stands at the end of a room, the retinal image is smaller than when they are immediately in front of you. Nevertheless, you see them as being similar in size.

In the Ames Room the retinal image of the two people is different, but if the room was rectangular they should be the same distance away. Therefore the smaller, more distant retinal image is scaled up. The perceptual system 'prefers' the interpretation that the room is rectangular (as almost all rooms are) rather than that the people are similar in size (we occasionally see some very large or very small adults).

RELATED STUDIES: The study by Turnbull (see Unit 2.3) shows that size constancy may be learned.

---

⑤ <u>Location constancy</u> (movement).   In Unit 2.1 some of the features of movement detection were listed. There are several instances when the visual stimulus may move across the retina, such as when you turn your head or due to saccades or, of course, when the object you are viewing has moved. The perceptual system must use feedback about eye-head/body movement or eyeball flicker to maintain a constancy.

Motion parallax describes a number of cues which are used to perceive *relative* motion. As the observer moves, there are systematic movements in the visual field. For example, objects which are closer move faster in comparison with those in the distance (this contributes to depth perception). Another example is when driving down a road, your sense of speed will be determined by how quickly objects are moving across your eye.

RESEARCH EXAMPLE | **An application of motion parallax: Optical brakes**

RESEARCH QUESTION: Have you ever seen a roundabout with tyre marks going straight across it? A contributory factor in accidents at road junctions, particularly at junctions on high speed roads, is that drivers do not reduce their speed sufficiently to allow them to negotiate the junction safely.

Can drivers be given false feedback to suggest that they are driving faster than they actually are, thus causing them to slow down more?

PARTICIPANTS: Drivers.

METHOD: Field experiment, observation. The road leading up to a junction is marked with a series of parallel lines which progressively become closer together.

RESULTS: The Transport Research Laboratory reports that accidents were reduced by as much as 57% on roads with optical brakes.

INTERPRETATION: The driver receives visual data which suggests that their speed is increasing, because the lines are becoming closer. The driver should be slowing down anyway because of the approaching junction, but this feedback should cause him to slow down even more.

Distance and depth perception

Apparent distance influences the perception of size, and apparent size influences the perception of distance.

There are many cues related to distance perception, though none absolutely determines it. The perceptual system selects the best solution according to experience, accepting the most probable explanation:

① <u>Convergence</u> of eyes and <u>disparity</u> (see Unit 2.1).

② <u>Relative size</u>: More distant objects appear smaller.

③ <u>Linear perspective</u>: Parallel lines converge, as in the Ponzo illusion.

④ <u>Texture gradients</u>: Distant parts of a surface appear denser because the constituent parts are closer together.

⑤ <u>Shade</u>: Shading on an object or shadow behind it.

⑥ <u>Brightness</u>: A brighter object appears closer.

⑦ <u>Relative clarity</u>: Things in the distance are less in focus and also bluer, due to refracted light (aerial haze).

⑧ <u>Interposition</u>: When one object overlaps another, it is assumed to be in front and therefore closer.

⑨ <u>Motion parallax</u>: When the observer is in motion, things which are closer move faster with respect to those farther away.

Perceptual set

Set is a predisposition or bias to perceive a scene one way instead of any of the other alternatives. Such a set influences you in two ways:
- Set as *selector*   It produces an expectation of what to look for.
- Set as *interpreter*   It guides the classification and inferences made from data.

The cues may come from:
- The *situation*   Cues from the surrounding visual scene (e.g. context).
- The *perceiver*   Expectations arising from internal states (e.g. emotion).

Set is a plus and a minus:
- Plus: It speeds up the perceptual process and enables constancies to be kept.
- Minus: We make perceptual mistakes.

Some of the factors which may influence set:

1 Attention.   In order to perceive something it must be focused upon or noticed. In the case of vision, attention is a matter of selecting what to look at.

This may be determined by external factors such as intensity, contrast (as in sudden changes), repetition, or movement. Or it may be an internal decision, such as being told to find someone wearing a pink carnation.

2 Context.   Often visual data is incomplete or ambiguous. Then other information present is used to resolve uncertainties.

RESEARCH EXAMPLE   **Bruner and Minturn (1955) TA13LE or 12 13 14**

RESEARCH QUESTION: How does context affect the perception of an identical sensory input?

PARTICIPANTS: 24 undergraduate students.

METHOD: Experiment, deception. Using a tachistoscope participants were typically shown the following stimulus sequence:

L, M, Y, A, 13	16, 17, 10,12, 13	K, 19, 15, W, 13
series 1	series 2	series 3

Some participants were given series 1 followed by 2. Others were shown series 2 and then 1, to counterbalance any order effects.

Each character was exposed for a very short time and participants were told they were being tested for speed and accuracy. They were asked to draw and read out each character.

RESULTS: Participants tended to close the figure (B rather than 13) when shown letters, though the longer the characters were exposed on the tachistoscope the less this effect occurred.

Exposure level	Expectation	% of subjects identifying the stimulus to conform with expectation
Short	number letter	83% 92%
Long	number letter	88% 58%

INTERPRETATION: Prior context predisposes a person to resolve an ambiguous stimulus in certain predictable ways.

RELATED STUDIES: Carmichael *et al.* (1932), described in Unit 4.1, showed how language can affect the way a picture is perceived.

Siipola (1935) used animal or nautical words to create context, followed by the ambiguous stimulus 'sael' or' dack'. Participants read 'seal', 'sail', 'duck' or 'deck' depending on prior context.

Bugelski and Alampay (1961) showed participants a series of animal pictures, then the ambiguous ratman, followed by a series of human pictures and finally the ratman again (for half of the participants the order was reversed). When participants first saw the ratman, most of them perceived the image in agreement with the first series of pictures. On the second exposure, most of them did not change their perceptions. Therefore set affected their perceptions but subsequent experience didn't significantly alter their initial perceptions.

③ <u>Expectations</u>.   Context influences expectations. Expectations help us to identify a stimulus more quickly, though not always more accurately. In fact expectations may lead to mistaken perceptions as in the 'Iran Jet Tragedy' described at the beginning of this Unit.

For example, Tulving and Gold (1963) found that the more information a participant is given about an incomplete sentence, the faster they were able to recognise the final word. As a person reads a sentence, they build up expectations about what will come next. When these are correct, the perceptual process is enhanced in terms of speed of processing.

However, expectations bias subsequent perceptions. For example, expectations may lead to incomplete processing and errors, consider:

ONCE IN

IN A BLUE

MOON

When expectations are wrong, the perceptual process is slowed down.

④ <u>Previous experience</u>.   Such expectations may be drawn from our vast store of general knowledge.

RESEARCH EXAMPLE **Bruner and Postman (1949) The perception of incongruity**

RESEARCH QUESTION: If you see something incongruous, something unusual, do you perceive what you expected to see or what is actually there?

PARTICIPANTS: 28 undergraduates.

METHOD: Experiment. Participants were shown five different playing cards using a tachistoscope. Some of these were incongruous ('trick') cards. For example, a black three of hearts or a red six of clubs.

Each card was shown for progressively longer exposures until it was correctly described. Participants were shown 1, 2, 3 or 4 trick cards.

RESULTS:
1 It took participants longer to identify the trick cards correctly.
2 Participants dealt with trick cards by:
  • Perceiving it as a normal card.
  • Resolving the conflict by reporting a compromise. For example, the red six of clubs is seen as purple or black clubs illuminated by a reddish light.
  • Experiencing a sense of illusion, 'I don't know what the hell it is now, I'm not even sure whether it's a playing card'.
  • Reporting it correctly.
3 The more trick cards a participant was shown, the more quickly they were able to recognise any trick cards. Their set had changed in the light of new experience.

INTERPRETATION: Perceptions are based on what you know to be likely. Any conflict is resolved, at least initially, by seeing what you expect rather than what is there. Or you may reach some kind of unconscious perceptual compromise. However, it doesn't take long for the system to change expectations in line with new experience.

---

xaminer's tip

When you are asked to describe a study remember to include aims, participants, method, results and the conclusion.

⑤ <u>Motivation and deprivation</u>.   A drive state occurs when a person is deprived of something, for example, food. The person is then motivated to satisfy their need. This appears to increase their sensitivity towards need–related objects, which would speed the process of satisfying their need.

RESEARCH EXAMPLE **Gilchrist and Nesburg (1952) Food looks better when you're hungry**

RESEARCH QUESTION: If a person is experiencing a need, will this distort their perception of objects related to that need?

PARTICIPANTS: 26 undergraduate students who volunteered to go without food for 20 hours.

METHOD: Experiment, deception. A participant was shown a slide for 15 seconds of a meal (a T-bone steak, fried chicken, hamburgers or spaghetti). They were told that this was an exercise in matching pictures. The slide projector was turned off, and then turned on again, this time dimmer. The participant was asked to adjust the lighting knob so that the picture looked the same as before.

The participants were shown the same four pictures at two levels of lighting and at three different sessions, 0, 6 and 20 hours after last eating.

A control group did the same but were not deprived of food.

RESULTS: As participants got hungrier, the pictures of the food were perceived as being brighter. The experimenters also tested hungry participants on thirst and found similar results.

INTERPRETATION: Motivation increases the sensitivity of the observer for the need-related object. Such perceptual sensitivity would be useful in seeking out objects which will reduce the drive state, in this case food. Thus supporting the adage, 'Hunger is the best cook'.

RELATED STUDIES: Sanford (1936) also found that the number of food-responses increased the longer participants were deprived of food.

6 Reward and punishment. Rewards are a means of increasing a person's motivation. Punishment decreases it. For example, Schafer and Murphy (1974) gave participants a reward every time they named a particular face, one facing left or one facing right. They were punished (losing two or four cents) when they did not name the correct face. Later, when the participants were shown an ambiguous image made up from both faces, the participants 'saw' the one they had been rewarded for. Such experiences of reward and punishment underlie other examples of perceptual set described in this unit.

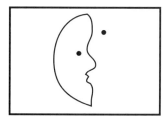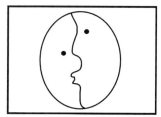

Fig. 2.9 Two stimulus faces and one ambiguous card

7 Emotion. Emotion is a motivating condition. It acts as a selector because it biases the observer. This bias increases the speed of recognition.
   a) *Perceptual defence*: Things which are threatening or unpleasant are ignored or less likely to be attended to (as in Schafer and Murphy's study).
   b) *Sensitisation* or *accentuation*: Things which are relevant or outstanding are perceived as brighter and more attractive (as in Gilchrist and Nesburg's study).

RESEARCH EXAMPLE | **McGinnies (1949) Emotionality and perceptual defence**

RESEARCH QUESTION: Are perceptions affected by emotionally threatening stimuli such that you aren't even aware of them?

PARTICIPANTS: Eight male and eight female undergraduate students.

METHOD: Experiment. Participants are shown a list of words, 11 neutral and 7 critical (emotionally-toned) words using a tachistoscope. Exposure time was gradually increased starting from 0.01 seconds until the word was correctly identified.

Stimulus words (the critical words are shown in italics):

apple	river	*penis*
dance	*whore*	music
raped	sleep	trade
child	*kotex*	*filth*
belly	broom	clear
glass	stove	*bitch*

Participants were asked to report whatever they saw or thought they saw. At the same time a physiological measure of emotionality was taken using the galvanic skin response (GSR), similar to a lie detector. This measures the amount of moisture (sweat) on the skin. Emotional states are associated with arousal and sweating.

RESULTS: On both measures, participants showed that emotion is related to critical words:
1 When shown critical words participants had higher mean GSRs. This happened before the words were recognised.
2 Participants required significantly longer exposure times to report the critical words correctly.

INTERPRETATION: The fact that participants had an emotional response but didn't simultaneously recognise the words, shows that selection of visual data takes place early on and not necessarily with conscious knowledge. In this case, set acts as a defence.

EVALUATION: The results might be explained in different ways:
1 When participants only partly perceive a word, because of the short exposure times, they prefer to report seeing a non-taboo word because they don't expect such words in an experiment.
2 Alternatively, they might avoid saying such words through embarrassment. Bitterman and Kniffen (1953) found that there is no effect if participants can write down their responses rather than report out loud.
3 Some participants may be less familiar with the taboo words or not even know them.

RELATED STUDIES: Solley and Haigh (1958) asked children to draw pictures of Santa Claus at intervals in the month leading up to Christmas, and again two weeks after Christmas. The first pictures showed Santa as bigger, nearer and with a more elaborate costume and a larger bag of toys. This shows how positive emotions *increase* sensitivity and affect perceptual organisation.

8 <u>Cultural factors</u>.   Culture can influence perception in a number of ways (see Unit 2.3). It can also affect perceptual set profoundly. Our culture has a major impact on the way we view the world. For example, Pettigrew *et al.* (1958) presented pairs of photographs of members of five ethnic groups stereoscopically (two pictures, one to each eye) for 2 seconds. When the photographs are conflicting this creates binocular rivalry, which the brain resolves by fusing the images into one perception. Many participants 'saw' the stimulus as either black or white, particularly participants who were Afrikaners. This has vital relevance to studies of eyewitness testimony, as we can only remember what we perceived in the first place (see Unit 4.1)

Visual illusions: Surprises of active processing

Visual illusions appear throughout this chapter as a means of demonstrating how the perceptual system works. This is because illusions illustrate normal functioning in abnormal conditions. The visual system continues to apply rules of constancy, but in the case of illusions your perceptions misinform you.

Some illusions are due to physiological mechanisms of the visual system (see Unit 2.1), others are psychological.

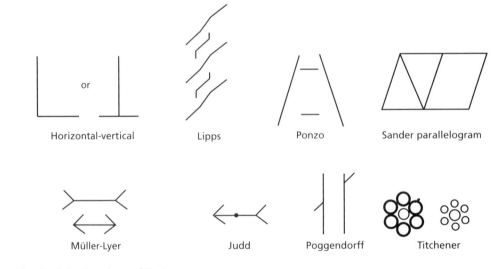

Fig. 2.10 Explanations of illusions:
Horizontal-vertical: Both horizontal lines, and both vertical lines are of the same length
Lipps: The oblique lines in the middle are parallel
Ponzo: The two horizontal lines are the same length
Sander parallelogram: Both lines inside the parallelogram are the same length
Müller-Lyer: The horizontal lines are the same length
Judd: The dot is the midpoint of the horizontal line
Poggendorff: The two oblique lines form a straight line
Titchener: The two inner circles have the same diameter
Kanizsa triangle: A white triangle is seen although not being present
Delboeuf: The outer circle on the left and the inner circle on the right are the same size
Zöllner: The oblique lines are parallel

❶ <u>Gregory's explanation of size constancy</u>. Gregory (1966) suggested that illusions are due to size constancy mechanisms. Consider the Ponzo illusion. The slanted lines suggest perspective and therefore the top line appears to be farther away. In which case the retinal image, which is the same size for both lines, must actually represent a longer line for the more distant one. Therefore we perceive the top line as being longer. Many of the examples above can be similarly explained in terms of normal distance cues being misleading.

How can you explain the Müller-Lyer illusion?

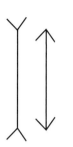

The line with the ingoing fins looks like the corner of a building, and this makes the vertical line seem closer. The outgoing fins are like the corner of a room and therefore the vertical line appears to be receding and as a result is perceived as longer. Both lines produce the same retinal size which is *interpreted* as longer (for a more distant object) or shorter (for something nearer).

Fig. 2.11 The Müller-Lyer illusion

RESEARCH EXAMPLE **Segall *et al.* (1963) Cultural differences in perceiving illusions**

RESEARCH QUESTION: Are illusions an example of learned perception, or do they exist in everyone's perceptual system (i.e. innate)? If illusions *are* a product of size constancy, they should be learned rather than innate.

PARTICIPANTS: 1878 adults and children from Africa (experimental group) and the US (control group).

METHOD: Experiment. Participants were shown four illusions, each illustrated by more than one item: Müller-Lyer, Sander parallelogram, and two versions of the horizontal-vertical illusion. They were asked to indicate the longer line length by selecting a line of the same length.

RESULTS: More American participants perceived the difference in line length than African participants.

INTERPRETATION: Supports the view that perception is a function of learned habits. People in the western world live in *carpentered* environments where they experience sharp corners (rectangularity). Africans may have less experience of this and therefore have not learned the cues for distance which are exploited by illusions.

EVALUATION:
1 Cross-cultural studies must be regarded with some scepticism. For example, we cannot always be sure that the participants understood the instructions as intended.
2 The reason the Africans did not 'see' the illusions may be because they were unused to interpreting paper-and-pencil drawings (see Hudson, in Unit 2.3)

RELATED STUDIES: Annis and Frost (1973) studied Canadian Cree Indians, some who led a nomadic life while others lived in houses and towns (a carpentered environment). When shown pairs of parallel and non-parallel lines the 'traditional' Crees were good at judging all lines, not just horizontal and vertical ones, whereas this was not true of the 'urban' Crees.

---

❷ <u>Counter-arguments</u>. If the perspective cues are removed the illusion remains.

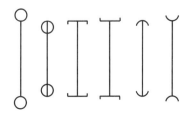

Fig. 2.12 Altered Müller-Lyer illusions. The vertical lines are all the same length

③ A conclusion.   There is no doubt that size constancy can explain some illusions, such as the Ponzo illusion. However, other illusions are explained by other features of the perceptual system. For example:

● The moon appears to move when clouds move across it. This can be explained by movement constancy, the smaller object (the moon) appears to move.
● Interference patterns are disturbances of the retinal system (see Unit 2.1).
● Vertical–horizontal line illusion is caused by experience. Far-off objects are projected higher on the retina than nearer ones. Therefore a line which is the same length, but lower appears shorter.
● Kanizsa triangle shows our tendency to organise data on the basis of sufficient cues.

Major explanations of visual perception

We obtain perceptual information from:

1 BOTTOM-UP   Sensory data arising directly from the physical stimulus.
2 TOP-DOWN   Our expectations based on previous experience.

In order to build up a 3D image which has meaning, do we mainly use sensory data or our expectations?

❶ Bottom-up processing: Gibson's direct perception theory
Also known as: data-driven processing or ecological psychology (based on the real world).
The argument: Gibson (1979) argued that sensory information contains enough information to explain the process of perception. He said that the amount of data contained in the retinal image is often underestimated. The child learns to identify the crucial features of any stimulus in order to build up an accurate perception. Gibson claimed that theorists need look no further than the visual stimulus to explain 3D perception.
Support:
● Aspects of depth and movement perception are coded physically, leading directly to a 3D image. For example, many monocular depth cues (aerial haze, texture gradients) exist in sensory data.
● Explains functioning of animal perception.
● Explains much of human perception.

Counter-arguments: This position does not explain:
● The effects of set.
● The functioning of constancies.
● Illusions.
● The experience of cataract patients (see Unit 2.3).

Application: Gibson's theory arose in connection with training pilots. He produced an unambiguous training stimulus based on his principles of data-driven perception.

❷ Top-down: Gregory's theory of cues and hypotheses
Also known as: Concept-driven processing or a constructionist approach.
The argument: Gregory (1966) suggested that a perceived object is a hypothesis, suggested and tested by sensory data. The stimulus provided to our senses is often incomplete or ambiguous, perception is therefore 'driven' by cognitive expectations. In this way, it is an active process.
Support:
● The fact that perception is sometimes inaccurate, as with visual illusions, supports the position that an incomplete visual stimulus is only perceived by hypotheses.

Counter-arguments: If this is always the case, it doesn't explain:
● Why vision is generally so accurate even in novel situations.
● Why the system is sometimes slow to adjust (as in inverted images) and sometimes faster (as in seeing ambiguous images).

Application: Situations where quick judgements need to be made of ambiguous stimuli, as with the Iran Jet tragedy described at the beginning of this unit.

❸ Bottom–up and top–down: Neisser's analysis-by-synthesis model
The argument: The most obvious, and in fact the best, solution lies in joining the

two approaches. Neisser (1976) suggests how the two systems might interact. Perception starts with sampling the available environment (bottom-up). For example, a stimulus of four legs might generate the hypothesis 'dog'. The next step is to employ a top-down approach looking for other expected features, in our case, a wet nose and a hairy body. If these are not found, disconfirming the original hypothesis, a new model has to be tested.

Support: The two processes, bottom-up and top-down, need not be seen as rivals but rather complementary. It may be that the former represents innate sensory mechanisms whereas the latter depends on learned experience. Or that their relative importance varies with particular circumstances. For example, during the reading process one deals with familiar (top-down) and unfamiliar (bottom-up) contexts, or in situations of variable viewing conditions top-down processes become more important when conditions deteriorate.

Counter-arguments:
- Gibson would argue that one should not complicate matters more than necessary.
- Such a perceptual cycle would be slower than most perceptual functioning.

Quick test 2.2

1. How are perceptions different from sensations?
2. Name **two** examples of the Gestalt laws of perception.
3. What are *visual constancies*?
4. Name **four** visual constancies.
5. What term describes the process of selecting and interpreting sensory data?
6. When standing at one end of a long beach, it may be difficult to estimate the distance to the other end. Why might this be? (adapted from *MEG, 1992*)
7. What is an *ambiguous figure*?
8. What do ambiguous figures tell us about the process of perception?
9. How does emotion affect perception?
10. What is *bottom-up processing*?

Summary

Perception is not the same as sensation.

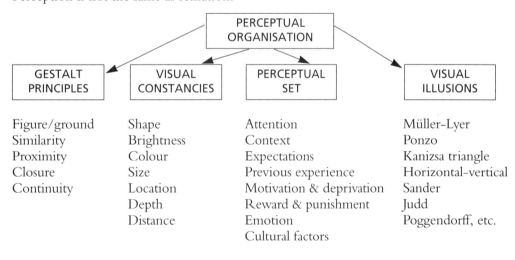

GESTALT PRINCIPLES	VISUAL CONSTANCIES	PERCEPTUAL SET	VISUAL ILLUSIONS
Figure/ground	Shape	Attention	Müller-Lyer
Similarity	Brightness	Context	Ponzo
Proximity	Colour	Expectations	Kanizsa triangle
Closure	Size	Previous experience	Horizontal-vertical
Continuity	Location	Motivation & deprivation	Sander
	Depth	Reward & punishment	Judd
	Distance	Emotion	Poggendorff, etc.
		Cultural factors	

THEORIES OF PERCEPTION	
	1 Bottom-up: Gibson's direct perception theory
	2 Top-down: Gregory's theory of cues and hypotheses
	3 Bottom-up and top-down: Neisser's analysis-by-synthesis model

APPLICATIONS: optical brakes, instrument panels, eyewitness testimony

2.3 Development of perception

THE VISUAL CLIFF

Gibson and Walk (1960) asked the question 'Do infants fall from high places because they have yet to develop their muscular co-ordination, or is it because they have to *learn* to perceive depth?'

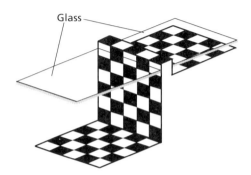

Fig. 2.13 The visual cliff

They constructed a table covered in a checked pattern (see Fig. 2.13). On one side there was a big drop (the cliff) which was covered with glass so that a participant could safely move across it. Under the glass was a sloping surface so that one side appeared to be a greater drop than the other.

The participants were 36 infants aged between 6 and 14 months.

Depth could be perceived using the monocular cue of more distant squares having smaller retinal images than nearer ones. Or by the binocular cues of disparity and motion parallax.

When an infant is encouraged to crawl over the cliff by its mother standing on the other side, most of them do it on the shallow side, but 92% refused to crawl over the deep side. This was true even if they had a patch across one eye, which showed that they were using monocular cues only.

They also experimented with 4-week-old kittens and day-old goats. The age was determined by when they could first move. Both kittens and goats showed depth perception.

They compared 3-month-old rats who had been reared in the dark, to eliminate any learning, with normal rats. There again appeared to be no differences, suggesting that depth perception was innate. They also looked at whether binocular or monocular cues were innate in rats, by placing the patterned material directly beneath the glass on both sides, but using smaller squares on one side to signal depth. The dark-reared rats showed no preference for the deep or shallow side under these conditions. This supported the view that binocular cues were innate while monocular ones were not.

Gibson and Walk suggest that depth discrimination is a vital capacity which must develop by the time independent locomotion is possible. Therefore we would expect it to have an innate basis in animals who are mobile from birth. The human infants were relatively old by the time they were tested so it's not possible to be certain whether their depth perception was learned or innate. In any case, they appear to have developed depth perception by the critical age of mobility.

DEFINITIONS		
	nature	Those characteristics which are inherited. This is the position taken by *nativists*.
	nurture	The collective impact of all environmental factors which affect growth and behaviour. This is the position taken by *empiricists*, those who believe that all knowledge is gained through experience.
	maturation	A process of development determined by biological or inherited forces. The organism may not be able to do certain things at birth, such as walk, but later physical or mental, innately programmed maturity enables such development.
	neonate	A newborn animal.

Nature: The hereditarian view

The Gestalt psychologists (see Unit 2.2) believed that certain principles of perception were innate, studies of young humans and animals appear to support this view.

1 <u>Human neonate studies</u>. Physically, the neonate's eye is reasonably well developed. It is sensitive to colour, brightness and movement. Their visual acuity is limited by a focal length of about 20 centimetres, a useful distance for studying their mother's face while they are being fed.

Techniques:
- *Discrimination*, as shown by interest (see Fantz) or how often the infant turns its head towards an object (see Bower).
- *Avoidance response*, as shown by covering their face (see Bower *et al.*) or refusing to cross the cliff (see Gibson and Walk).

Difficulties:
- Testing a somewhat immobile and unresponsive participant is difficult and prone to *subjective* interpretation and *experimenter bias*.
- Testing an infant who has had no visual experience is impossible. Even in the womb infants are able to see and move, and therefore start the learning process. In fact all the neonates tested were more than one week old, and usually more than six months old. Therefore they had had plenty of learning opportunities. Consequently such experiments cannot claim to show innate performance, though they might show evidence of maturation.
- Separating *maturation* from learning is difficult. An ability may still be innate even if an infant has not developed it yet. Some abilities, the results of maturation, are inherited but they don't show until a child has reached a certain age.

RESEARCH EXAMPLE | **Fantz (1961) The origin of form perception**

RESEARCH QUESTION: Can infants respond to shape, pattern, size and solidity? Taken together these add up to perception of form.

PARTICIPANTS: Human neonates, aged from 1 week to 6 months.

METHOD: Experiment. Ability to perceive form can be tested by observing the visual interest of an infant. The point of fixation was determined by noting the reflections in the participant's eyes.

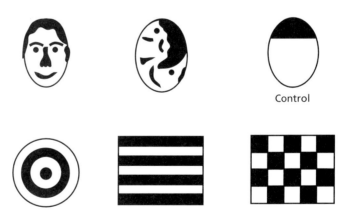

Control

Fig. 2.14 Fantz's test stimuli

RESULTS:
1 The more complex patterns received more interest.
2 The youngest participants (1 to 6 weeks) preferred some patterns to others (e.g. stripes to bull's eye).
3 The real face was looked at most by infants of all ages, the scrambled face received somewhat less attention, and the control pattern was largely ignored.

INTERPRETATION:
1 Strongly suggests that, at least some aspects of form perception, are innate.
2 Some aspects of form perception are a function of age, though this could be explained by learning *or* maturation.
3 The preference for a face cannot be explained in terms of pattern complexity, since the same pattern jumbled receives less interest.

THEORETICAL SIGNIFICANCE: The results support the nativist position. Recognition of the human face can be explained in terms of important survival functions. Fantz concluded that the 'infant sees a patterned and organised world' not one which is a 'big, booming confusion'.

APPLICATIONS: A knowledge of what is 'normal' for infants at particular ages provides a useful baseline for evaluating those who may have delays in development.

EVALUATION:

1 His results regarding the preference for the face may be because infants prefer a symmetrical pattern.
2 Like all neonate studies, it is impossible to claim completely that performance is due to innate factors alone.

RELATED STUDIES:

Ahrens (1954) found that infants not only preferred faces but smiled at them, and smiling is the beginning of socialisation.

Bower (1966) taught infants aged 6 to 8 weeks to respond to a certain sized or shaped cube, by rewarding the infant with a game of 'peek-a-boo' every time the correct response is made. The infant is then shown the same cube placed at a different distance or angle. Therefore the retinal image changes, but an infant with shape or depth constancy should perceive it as the same stimulus. The infants did this even with a patch over one eye, which means that the infants were using motion parallax to determine depth, moving one or both eyes to determine relative distance. Bower proposed the theory from this, and other studies, that infants can *register* most of the information that adults can, but can *handle* less information. Learning appears to be a process of developing the necessary information-handling capacity.

Bower *et al.* (1970) tested depth perception in infants aged 6 to 20 days old, by observing their response to an approaching object. The infants signalled awareness by opening their eyes, moving their head back and putting their hands in front of their face. If the infant had no depth perception their response to a large disc stopping further away should be the same as their response to a smaller, closer one because they both create the same *retinal* image. In fact the infants were so upset by the smaller, closer one that Bower *et al.* abandoned the experiment and concluded that the infants could perceive depth.

---

② Animal neonates.   Many of the studies reported already in this unit, were also tried with animal participants. For example:
  - Fantz did earlier work with chicks, testing their pecking response and discrimination with different patterns.
  - Gibson and Walk found evidence with rats, goats and kittens.
  - Hess (below) found that chickens could not adapt to new environmental situations.

The evidence suggests that these animals have innate perceptual systems which do not benefit from experience in the same way as humans.

Advantage of animal studies: Animals can be raised in conditions which prevent learning, in other words, in the dark.

Disadvantage of animal studies: Most animals are more mature at birth than humans, so such evidence may have little bearing on the *human* nature/nurture debate.

Nurture: The empiricist view

Argument: If a perceptual skill is inherited then all people should develop it whatever their visual experiences (deprivation or restriction) or wherever they were brought up (cross–cultural studies). If we find a difference, then it suggests that this perceptual skill is due to experience or learning. If the perceptual system is innate, it should not be able to adapt to changed circumstance (studies of distorted vision). If it can adapt, this shows that perception can be learned.

① Readjustment studies: Adults who have regained their sight.   At the beginning of this chapter, there was a description of S.B., an adult who regained his sight after being born blind. There have been many similar cases which have been studied, usually as a result of cataracts being removed. von Senden (1932) gave a summary of 66 such cases:
  1 Initially participants were confused by an array of disordered visual stimuli.
  2 From the start they were able to distinguish figures against a background.
  3 Furthermore they could fixate on the figures and follow them.
  4 Participants were able to discriminate between objects but not identify the nature of the differences nor name the objects.

5 Judgements of depth were particularly poor.

Advantage of such studies: Since adults are involved, unlike neonates, they can provide verbal reports of their experiences.

Difficulties in interpretation:

- The evidence from studies of restricted or deprived environments in animals (see below), suggests that parts of the *visual cortex* may actually degenerate if not used. Any problems such adults have may be due to degeneration.
- Such patients may have undergone physical and psychological *trauma* when their eyesight was restored.
- Such patients may have learned to rely on *other senses* and may in fact still be using these to aid what appears to be 'seeing'. For example, using touch.
- Often the data has been collected in *unsystematic* ways. For example, merely talking to the participants rather than using standard visual tests.

② Distortion studies.   What happens if you wear goggles which turn the world upside down? Can the perceptual system 'learn' or is perception a fixed (innate) ability?

- Stratton (1896) wore a lens on one eye that turned the world upside down and kept his other eye covered. Within a few days he was bumping into things less and less and by the seventh day he no longer noticed that things were upside down.
- Snyder and Pronko (1952) found that participants learned to cope easily with inverted images.
- Hess (1956) placed prism lenses on chickens so things appeared ten degrees to one side of where they actually were. The chickens never learned to adjust their sight and this prevented them from pecking in the right place.

Explanation: It may be that participants are developing appropriate motor behaviour rather than learning how to 'see'. Nevertheless a *totally* innate system would not allow such a development to take place.

RESEARCH EXAMPLE   **Kohler (1966) Experiments with goggles**

RESEARCH QUESTION: How does the visual system unconsciously respond to images which are systematically distorted?

METHOD: Investigation. The participant wears a pair of prism goggles which produce distortions as if the world were made of rubber. Participants can record their degree of adaptation using a device that presents horizontal and vertical lines which the participant can adjust in orientation and curvature until they look 'right'. Alternatively they can look through other prisms, identifying the one which cancels out the after-effects of wearing the goggles.

RESULTS: Participants begin to see the world normally in less than a week.

INTERPRETATION: The experience of the goggle-wearing mimics the development of the normal visual system, indicating that the perceptual system can change with experience.

APPLICATIONS: Very strong glasses (used for example to correct a squint) produce refraction on the edges, creating colour which might disturb the wearer. Some eye operations involve 'folding' the retina, resulting in some loss of vision. Investigations of distorted vision suggest that all these changes will be fairly easily adapted to in time and perception will be undisturbed.

RELATED STUDIES: Peterson and Peterson (1938) trained participants to adapt to inverted images. They re-tested the participants eight months later and found they readapted quickly. This suggests that the original learning was an addition to original perception rather than a reorganisation of the entire system.

---

③ Deprived environments.   These studies inevitably use animal participants, since it would be unethical to deprive human infants. The same disadvantages as mentioned in relation to animal neonates (above) should be considered.

- Riesen (1950) raised chimpanzees in total darkness until the age of 16 months. They couldn't distinguish simple patterns and were developmentally deprived in other respects, such as not responding to conditioning with an electric shock.

- Wiesel (1982) sewed one eye of a kitten shut. If this is done early enough and long enough the eye becomes blind. These studies suggest that experience is necessary to maintain the innate system.

Explanations:
- Such total sensory deprivation has major emotional effects (see Unit 8.1), which could explain the retardation.
- It is also possible that the cells in their visual cortex had simply wasted away when they were not used, though this doesn't seem to be true in the case of the cataract patients above.
- Post-mortem examinations show degeneration of the retina as well as the visual cortex.

Consider:
- The results of animal experiments may not apply to humans.
- Such experiments raise ethical questions, is such deprivation defensible?

4 Restricted environments.   A preferable approach is to restrict elements in the environment, though this is still only acceptable in animal experiments.

- Riesen (1956) this time fixed goggles on the chimpanzees so that they could see light but not patterns. This still led to impaired perceptual performance.
- Held and Hein (1963) worked with a pair of kittens. One kitten could walk around, and in doing so, turned a carousel so that the other kitten was moved as well. The active kitten developed normal vision whereas the passive one didn't seem to be able to see at all even though it had had the same visual experiences. This suggests that physical experience is just as important as visual experience for normal development of visual perception.

Consider:
- The same criticisms as mentioned above apply here, to a lesser degree.
- The finding that experience alters visual development might be used to explain the experience of blind adults who recovered their sight and also the variation in terms of perception between different cultures.

RESEARCH EXAMPLE **Blakemore and Cooper (1970) A vertical world**

RESEARCH QUESTION: Does visual experience affect the *type* of perception that is developed?

PARTICIPANTS: Kittens from birth housed in a dark room. At the age of two weeks, before their eyes opened, they were placed in special environment for five hours a day.

METHOD: Experiment. The kittens were placed in a drum which had only vertical or only horizontal lines. They had no other visual experience until the age of five months, an age well beyond the critical period for visual development.

RESULTS:
1 They had difficulty with depth perception.
2 They were virtually blind for the contours perpendicular to those they had experienced. For example, the vertically experienced kittens only responded to things like table legs (vertical) but tripped over ropes stretched in front of them (horizontal).
3 By anaesthetising the kittens they could test the activity of cells in visual cortex while exposing the eye to horizontal and vertical lines. (See the work of Hubel and Wiesel, in Unit 2.1, who found specific cells in the visual cortex which respond to specific line orientations). Blakemore and Cooper found no cells in the deprived kittens' brains which responded to the orientation *not* experienced by the cat.

INTERPRETATION: This suggests that the ability to perceive other line orientations had been lost due to adjustments made in the visual cortex during the critical period. Blakemore and Cooper propose that the visual system adapts to match experience.

---

5 Cross–cultural studies.

RESEARCH EXAMPLE **Turnbull (1961) The forest people**

RESEARCH AIM: Turnbull's aim, as an anthropologist, was to observe the behaviour and practices of another culture.

PARTICIPANTS: The BaMbuti Pygmies who lived in the dense Ituri Forest in the Congo (now Zaire).

METHOD: Naturalistic observation. On a journey Turnbull was accompanied by a Pygmy guide, Kenge. They happened to emerge into a clearing where there was a distant view of the mountains. Noting Kenge's surprise, Turnbull offered to take him to visit the mountains.

RESULTS: Since mountains were outside Pygmy experience, Kenge had no words to describe what he saw and was literally speechless. Looking out across the plain Kenge saw a herd of buffalo grazing in the distance and asked what kind of insect they were. He laughed when Turnbull told them they were buffalo, and when Turnbull drove him closer Kenge thought it was some form of trickery which had made them larger.

Similarly, when they visited a lake where men were fishing in boats farther out, Kenge claimed it was just a bit of wood.

INTERPRETATION: Kenge clearly did not have a knowledge of depth cues and size constancy. Presumably this was because, in the environment in which Pygmies lived, there was no opportunity to experience these.

The Pygmies may have other more highly developed perceptual abilities, such as figure-ground since it would be necessary in the forest to be able to distinguish dangerous animals from the undergrowth hiding them.

This supports the view that size constancy, at least, is not innate.

EVALUATION: All cross-cultural studies should be treated with caution (see Unit 11.1).

RELATED STUDIES:

Segall *et al.* (1963) compared the ability to perceive certain visual illusions in some Africans and Americans, finding that Africans were less likely to be fooled by certain illusions (see Unit 2.2).

Hudson (1960) showed pictures containing depth cues to over 500 children and adults from southern Africa, both White and Black. He found that the 'school-going' participants interpreted the depth cues correctly whereas the 'non-school-going' participants did not. This suggests that the ability to decode depth cues is learned. Such findings are relevant to multicultural education where not all students will have the same understanding of pictorial representations.

Quick test 2.3

1 Outline **two** problems which arise when psychologists use human babies to study perception.
2 What does the word *innate* mean?
3 In what way are adults better subjects than children or animals?
4 If kittens are raised in a vertical environment, what happens?
5 Name **one** drawback of cross-cultural research.

Summary

NATURE (what you're born with)	Human neonate studies (Gibson & Walk, Fantz, Bower) Animal neonates (Gibson & Walk, Fantz, Hess)

NURTURE (the experience you have)	Readjustment studies (Gregory & Wallace, von Senden) Distortion studies (Stratton, Snyder & Pronko, Hess, Kohler) Deprived environment (Riesen, Wiesel) Restricted environment (Riesen, Held & Hein, Blakemore & Cooper) Cross-cultural studies (Turnbull, Hudson, Segall *et al.*)

APPLICATIONS:
1 Distortions caused by heavy glasses needed for impaired vision.
2 Multicultural education.

Chapter 3
Learning

LEARNING INSIDE THE WOMB

Infants inside their mother's womb can hear various noises. They are soothed by the sound of their mother's heartbeat and learn to recognise the voices of their mother and other family members. This *learning* is important for the bonding which takes place between mother and infant immediately after birth.

It is possible that infants may learn more than sounds. DeCasper and Spence (1986) arranged for mothers to read selected passages from books repeatedly, including the *Cat in the Hat*. After birth the infants showed recognition of the known passages, when compared with a control group. This shows that experiences before birth can have profound and lasting effects.

Can this be learning? The infant is acquiring a set of behaviours through experience. Is it conditioning, observation or imprinting? This chapter looks at these and other psychological explanations of learning.

3.1 Conditioning and cognitive explanations of learning

PAVLOV'S DOGS

Pavlov is one of the most familiar names in psychology. His work had two important effects:
1 It demonstrated classical conditioning, one of the key explanations of human behaviour.
2 It launched psychology as a science.
He was a physiologist not a psychologist. One of his areas of study was the process of digestion and salivation in dogs. He placed various substances in the dog's mouth and recorded the rate and amount of saliva. To do this he redirected the dog's salivary duct through its cheek and into a tube to collect the saliva.

One of the things that he observed was that production of saliva is a **reflex**. This means that you cannot produce saliva at will, but a plate of food will make you salivate whether you want to or not.

He also noticed that the dogs began to salivate *before* they were given the food. The sight of the person bringing the food was a sufficient stimulus. This led him to formulate the principles of classical conditioning.

To test his theory he needed a **neutral stimulus**, unrelated to food. He used the sound of a metronome. He placed the dogs in a soundproof room to exclude all but the stimulus noise. Just before feeding the dog, he exposed it to the ticking metronome. The dog salivated when it received food. After several 'conditioning' trials, the dog would salivate when it heard the metronome ticking. The metronome had become a **conditioned stimulus**.

He tried out various other things, such as a bell, the odour of vanilla, apomorphine (a drug which causes vomiting) and a rotating object. They could all become conditioned stimuli (Pavlov, 1927).

If the stimulus was presented *after* the food, it did not result in conditioning.

DEFINITIONS

learning	A relatively permanent change in behaviour, caused by reorganising existing habits and skills. It is not change as a result of growth, neither is it a result of reversible changes, such as fatigue or hunger.
classical conditioning	Learning that results from the association of two stimuli. Sometimes also referred to as **Pavlovian conditioning** or respondent behaviour.
operant conditioning	Learning that occurs when an organism learns to associate its behaviour with the consequences or results of that behaviour. Also called **instrumental conditioning**.
law of effect	A response that is followed by positive reinforcement is more likely to happen again. Thorndike used the phrase 'a satisfying state of affairs' rather than reinforcement.
reflex	An involuntary, unlearned predictable response which is important for the protection and/or survival of the organism. Examples include: salivation, fear, blinking. In babies there is a wide range of reflex behaviours: Moro, Babinski, grasping, rooting, stepping and sucking.
stimulus (S)	Anything that has some effect on the organism so that its behaviour is changed in some detectable way.
response (R)	Any action from the organism, including movements, thoughts or glandular secretions.
unconditioned stimulus (UCS)	The stimulus that elicits an unlearned response.
unconditioned response (UCR)	An unlearned response to a stimulus.
neutral stimulus (NS)	In classical conditioning, a neutral stimulus is one which does not naturally produce the UCR. In operant conditioning, it is any stimulus which has no effect upon behaviour.
conditioned stimulus (CS)	The neutral stimulus after conditioning has taken place.
conditioned response (CR)	The UCR after conditioning has taken place.
extinction	The gradual disappearance of a learned response when the reinforcer or UCS is removed.
spontaneous recovery	A learned response reappears after apparent extinction.
generalisation	Once a conditioned response has been established, similar stimuli will also lead to the CR.
discrimination	The ability to perceive differences between two or more stimuli.
shaping	Learning through progressive reinforcement. First, the organism is reinforced for behaviours vaguely like the desired behaviour. Gradually reinforcement becomes more specific, only behaviours which are increasingly similar to the desired behaviour are reinforced, until the desired behaviour finally occurs.

reinforcement	A stimulus which strengthens learning. Both positive *and* negative reinforcement increase the probability of a response occurring.
negative reinforcement	Removal of an aversive stimulus, escape.
reinforcer	Any event or behaviour which acts as reinforcement.
punishment	A procedure used to decrease the probability of a response using an aversive stimulus. Punishment may be given when a response occurs, or for the absence of a response.
reward	A procedure or stimulus used to increase the probability of a response. A concept used in operant conditioning, but essentially the same as positive reinforcement.
behaviourism	An approach to psychology based on conditioning. The view that the only appropriate matter for scientific study is observable behaviour rather than any suggestion of internal mental activity.
latent learning	A form of learning which is not immediately shown as observable behaviour. It occurs without obvious reinforcement.
cognitive map	A mental representation of the environment.
trial and error learning	Learning that is achieved by gradually eliminating all ineffectual responses and strengthening those responses which are satisfactory. In other words, operant conditioning.
one trial learning	Learning which takes place after only one exposure to the reinforcer. This would be of especial value in situations where danger is involved (see Unit 4.2).
insight learning	The process by which problems are resolved in an instant. No trial-and-error learning is involved, but internal schema must change (see Unit 4.2).
transfer of learning	Earlier learning influences later learning, either positively or negatively.

Classical conditioning

- The basic unit of conditioning is stimulus–response (S–R).
- Unlearned **reflexes** consist of an innate or **unconditioned** response (UCR) to a naturally occurring or **unconditioned stimulus** (UCS). For example, food (UCS) produces salivation (UCR) or a blast of air (UCS) causes you to blink your eye (UCR). The reflex is the stimulus and the response together.
- A **neutral stimulus** (NS) is paired with the UCS so that an individual comes to expect them together (association or conditioning).
- In time, the NS produces the UCR on its own. We now called the NS a **conditioned stimulus** (CS) and the response is a **conditioned response** (CR).

1 BEFORE   NS (bell) $\longrightarrow$ no response
                                                    UCS (food) $\longrightarrow$ UCR (salivation)

2 DURING CONDITIONING   NS and UCS are paired by occurring together (the NS is presented slightly *before* the UCS)

3 AFTER   CS (bell) $\longrightarrow$ CR (salivation)

- If the stimuli stop being paired, the CR is **extinguished**.
- If there is a rest interval after extinction, the CR will reappear. This is **spontaneous recovery**. This shows that extinction is not unlearning but temporary suppression of the CR.

- The conditioned response can be **generalised**. For example, if the UCS is a circle, then other shapes (ellipse, square, triangle) also will elicit the CR.
- A **generalisation gradient** expresses the relationship between the new object (e.g. ellipse) to the original one. The more similar they are the stronger the response.
- If the circle continues to be paired with the food and the ellipse is shown without food, the participant learns to **discriminate**, but only if the two shapes are significantly different.
- It is possible to acquire a conditioned response after **one trial**. Usually the NS and UCR have to be paired more than once for learning to take place.

RESEARCH EXAMPLE **Watson and Rayner (1920) Little Albert**

RESEARCH QUESTION: Can emotions be conditioned in the same way as reflexes?

PARTICIPANT: An infant boy, Albert, aged 11 months.

METHOD: Experiment, case study. A white rat was put in front of the baby and as he reached out to touch it, the researcher made a loud noise with a steel bar. Albert showed a reflex fear response. This classical conditioning procedure was repeated six times.

RESULTS:

1 The next time Albert was shown the rat, he began to cry. This is a **conditioned emotional response** (CER).

	reflex response		learned response	
rat (NS)	noise (UCS)	fear (UCR)	rat (CS)	fear (CER)

2 Later this was shown to **generalise** to other objects such as a fur coat, a rabbit and white cotton wool. A year later the CER was still evident.

3 Unfortunately the experimenters never had the opportunity to extinguish the CER because Albert's mother withdrew her consent.

INTERPRETATION: Watson suggested, very controversially, that the same process may underlie the learning of emotions (such as love) and abnormal behaviours (such as phobias).

APPLICATIONS: In the same way, phobic patients can be conditioned to associate their feared object with pleasure rather than anxiety (see Systematic Sensitisation, in this unit).

EVALUATION: This study contravenes ethical standards. Deliberate psychological and physical harm was done to a vulnerable individual. In this case parental consent is not sufficient.

RELATED STUDY: Remember, conditioning works on **reflexes**. Menzies (1937) asked subjects to put their hands in ice-cold water whenever a buzzer sounded. The cold temperature caused vasoconstriction (the blood vessels get narrower). After a number of conditioning trials, the vasoconstriction occurred just in response to the sound of the buzzer.

Operant conditioning

Thorndike (1913) observed that learning may take place without any association between two stimuli. Instead, he suggested that learning is dependent on the consequences of a behaviour. Positive effects (rewards) lead to **stamping in** behaviour. Negative effects (punishments) do not produce unlearning (**stamping out**), they merely stop the behaviour being displayed. This is the **Law of Effect**. It is also called **instrumental learning**, because certain behaviours are useful or instrumental in obtaining a reward (or punishment).

Skinner (1938 onwards) introduced the terms **operant** behaviour and **respondent** behaviour (classical conditioning). In operant behaviour the learner **operates** on their environment, which brings about certain consequences. These consequences strengthen or weaken S–R links.

$$\text{Situation (\underline{A}ntecedents)} \rightarrow \underline{B}\text{ehaviour} \rightarrow \underline{C}\text{onsequence [a useful mnemonic: ABC]}$$

→ Reinforcement (reward) strengthens

→ Punishment weakens

RESEARCH EXAMPLE   **Skinner (1938) The Skinner box**

RESEARCH AIM: To demonstrate that being given reinforcement *after* a response is made leads to conditioning as well as learning through association.

PARTICIPANTS: Pigeons.

METHOD: Animal experiment. A pigeon is placed in a special box called a Skinner box. If it presses a lever or pecks at a disc within the box, a door opens and a pellet of food will be delivered. The lever is a UCS and the food is a reinforcer or reward.

RESULTS: The pigeon first pecks randomly around the box as part of its natural exploratory behaviour. Accidentally it presses the lever on a number of occasions. Each time food appears. The more that the reward and the lever are paired, the greater the likelihood of the behaviour being repeated.

Reinforcement is both positive and negative. When the lever is pressed, it is positive. Receiving no food when pecking elsewhere is negative reinforcement.

INTERPRETATION: The lever becomes the CS and pressing the lever is a CR. Behaviour has been bought under **stimulus control**.

VARIATIONS: A lighted button is placed next to the food door. Only when it is lit will pecking result in the door opening. The pigeon must learn to **discriminate** the state of the button, called a **discriminative stimulus**.

1 Shaping.   It might take the organism a long time to perform the right behaviour and receive a reward. But learning is not such a lengthy process. Therefore Skinner proposed the notion of shaping. Operant behaviours are gradually built up by reinforcing behaviours which progressively become closer to the final goal.

2 Avoidance learning.   It is a type of operant conditioning where a response is learned as a means of avoiding an unpleasant (aversive) stimulus. However the organism never has the chance to discover if the painful stimulus is still there, so it can't be extinguished.

Reinforcement, rewards and punishment

Likelihood of a response re-occurring:		Effect	An example
Increased	Decreased		
positive reinforcement		agreeable	Receiving a smile when you say 'please'.
negative reinforcement		agreeable (absence of a negative stimulus or escape from a negative stimulus)	*Not* being punished for being naughty because you apologised or running away from punishment.
reward		agreeable	Receiving a gold star for good work.
	punishment	disagreeable (noxious)	Receiving a detention for bad behaviour

E xaminer's tip

Make sure you understand the difference between negative reinforcement and punishment.

Another way of looking at the same information:

	Stimulus present	Stimulus absent
Stimulus pleasant	Positive reinforcement or reward	Omission
Stimulus noxious	Punishment	Negative reinforcement

1 Is punishment effective? (see Hoffman (1970) Unit 9.1)
  ● It may produce *hostility* and a desire to rebel.

- A person may *get used* to punishment, which means it has to be increased continually to be effective. In the end some other means may be necessary.
- The *attention* associated with punishment may be positively reinforcing. Some children are naughty because it is an easy way of gaining attention.
- It may be as effective to *ignore* bad behaviour, which will then disappear through lack of reinforcement, and just use positive reinforcement and rewards.
- The *threat* of punishment may be sufficient. This is contrary to Behaviourist theory because it suggests a cognitive component.
- Useful in situations where an *immediate effect* is needed, such as a child putting its hand near the fire.

2 What helps increase the effectiveness of punishment?
- If you also show the person the right way to behave.
- If punishment is consistent.
- If it is not too severe.
- If it is immediate.

3 Reinforcement schedules. **Partial reinforcement schedules** are more effective and more resistant to extinction. This may be because, under continuous reinforcement, the organism 'notices' the absence of the reinforcer more quickly.

SCHEDULE OF REINFORCEMENT	DESCRIPTION
Continuous reinforcement	Reinforcement is given *every time* the correct behaviour is performed.
Partial reinforcement	Reinforcement is not consistent or continuous.
Fixed ratio	Reinforcement is given after a *regular* number of correct behaviours. For example, every fifth time.
Variable ratio	Reinforcement is given after a *variable* number of correct behaviours. Sometimes a correct behaviour is reinforced but sometimes it isn't. It might be on average every fifth time.
Fixed interval	Reinforcement is given only after a *fixed time* since the previous reinforcement. For example, every 30 seconds.
Variable interval	Reinforcement is given after a *variable* time since the previous reinforcement.

4 Secondary or conditioned reinforcement. Things which act as **primary reinforcers** are innate, such as food, approval or fear. **Secondary reinforcers** work because at sometime they have been paired with a primary one. The classic example is money. An example of a negative secondary reinforcer is a hot cooker.

Classical versus operant conditioning

CLASSICAL	OPERANT
Learning through *association*.	Learning through *reinforcement*.
Concerned with *reflex* or automatic response.	Concerned with *voluntary* behaviour, any behaviour which is *naturally produced*.
Reinforcement is presented *before* the CR.	Reinforcement occurs *after* the CR.
The reinforcement is not related to anything the organism might do.	The organism is *instrumental* in obtaining reinforcement.

However, the *theoretical* distinction may not always be so clear in practice. For example, when bell plus food are paired, is the food a UCS or a reward? If the bell comes immediately *after* the food it can still result in an association being formed, though such backward conditioning is rare.

Cognitive explanations of learning

Behaviourist explanations of learning are concerned only with observable behaviour. Cognitive explanations suppose that other, unseen activity may take place so that stimulus, response and reinforcement are not the only explanations for learning.

❶ <u>Latent learning</u>.   Learning without reinforcement and in behavioural 'silence'. The organism does not appear to be learning but later behaviour reveals hidden learning.

RESEARCH EXAMPLE   **Blodgett (1929) The effect of reward on maze learning in rats**

RESEARCH QUESTION: What happens if behaviour is not reinforced?

PARTICIPANTS: About 100 rats.

METHOD: Animal experiment. Rats were placed in a six-alley maze unit. Each animal had one trial per day.

  Group 1   The control group: always found food in the goal box.
  Group 2   The experimental group: did not find food for the first six days. They showed no signs of learning, they choose the wrong alley as often as the right one. On each day they were fed one hour after being removed from the maze.
  Group 3   Another experimental group: did not find food for the first two days.

RESULTS: As soon as the experimental group received food in the maze, their error rate dropped. Within two days of being rewarded they had caught up with the control group.

INTERPRETATION: The rats in the experimental group did not appear to be learning anything. But in fact they had done something which enabled them to subsequently learn much faster. They had stored a mental representation of the maze. Tolman called this a **cognitive map** of the maze. This **latent learning** was hidden until it became worthwhile to show it.

---

❷ <u>Insight learning</u>.   The main stages of insight learning are:
  1 An initial helplessness.
  2 A pause in activity.
  3 A sudden, smooth performance of the solution.

RESEARCH EXAMPLE   **Köhler (1925) The mentality of apes**

RESEARCH QUESTION: Köhler was a Gestalt psychologist. He disagreed with the idea that all behaviour could be explained in terms of stimulus–response. Some learning was possible by having a flash of insight (the 'aha! experience'). Can this be demonstrated?

PARTICIPANTS: Köhler set chimpanzees various problems to solve.

METHOD: Animal experiment. In one study he placed a chimpanzee called Sultan in a cage. A banana was outside of the cage, just out of reach. Inside the cage was a stick and some boxes.

RESULTS: Sultan first tried to reach the fruit with his hand. He sat down and gazed around. Suddenly he grabbed the stick and got the fruit.

INTERPRETATION: Köhler claimed that the problem was solved through insight, in the absence of any trial-and-error learning or reinforcement. Sultan had worked out the solution in his mind and planned his actions before starting.

EVALUATION: Insight learning may be similar to the process of generalisation. Solutions to previous problems are applied in a new situation.

---

❸ <u>Observation or social learning</u>.   This is described in Unit 3.2.

❹ <u>The transfer of learning</u>.   Earlier learning influences later learning. This is an important aspect of the learning process.
  • **Positive transfer** occurs when learning task A has a positive effect on learning task B. For example, learning to swim backstroke after breaststroke.
  • **Negative transfer** occurs when learning task A interferes with learning task B.

This usually happens when there is some conflict between tasks A and B. For example, learning to play badminton after becoming proficient at tennis, because badminton involves a flick of the wrist rather than the whole arm. Learning badminton skills requires unlearning tennis first.

- There is usually both positive and negative transfer. For example, when learning badminton there is also positive transfer such as previously learning ball sense.

Applications

CLASSICAL CONDITIONING

1 Systematic desensitisation.   First used by Wolpe (1958) to treat phobias. The patient learns how to relax, and then relaxes while imagining increasingly threatening situations involving the feared stimulus. This new pairing of the feared stimulus and relaxation acts to *inhibit* and *weaken* the old bond between the stimulus and anxiety. You cannot experience relaxation and fear at the same time.

2 Aversion therapy.   Used, for example, with alcoholics or drug addicts. A drug which produces vomiting (UCS) is given at the same time as the patient has a drink (NS). The vomiting, a reflex response (UCR) becomes associated with drinking (now CS) so that the patient vomits when given a drink.

3 Advertising.   The aim is to produce a desirable CR every time the punter is exposed to your product. To this end, you see the product (NS) paired with an attractive girl (UCS). Ultimately you associate the product (CS) with feelings of pleasure (CR).

RESEARCH EXAMPLE | **Gustafson *et al.* (1974) Coyote predation**

RESEARCH QUESTION: Can classical conditioning techniques be applied to the problem of coyotes and wolves killing sheep?

PARTICIPANTS: Wild coyotes and wolves.

METHOD: Field, animal experiment. The participants were given hamburger, lamb and rabbit meat containing small amounts of lithium chloride. This makes the animal feel dizzy, with severe nausea and vomiting. The poison is the UCS, the sickness is the UCR.

RESULTS:
1 If the animals were again offered the same meat they refused to eat it, though they accepted other food. This shows that the aversion was to specific conditioned foods.
2 A second test was to place the coyotes in a pen with a rabbit or sheep. Some of the animals continued to attack their prey but they resisted in eating the meat. On subsequent occasions they did not attack.
3 If the animals experienced no further poison they eventually returned to their original habits, though initially they tested the dead prey cautiously. The CR was extinguished.

INTERPRETATION: The poisoned meat (UCS) is associated with the smell of sheep (NS). The vomiting, a reflex response (UCR) becomes paired with the smell (now CS). The predator learns to avoid the CS. The result is a form of aversion therapy resulting in changed food preferences.

OPERANT CONDITIONING

1 Token economy.   Patients are given tokens as **secondary** reinforcers when they engage in correct or socially desirable behaviours. These tokens can be exchanged for **primary** reinforcers, such as food or privileges. The drawback of this therapy is that it often fails to transfer to life outside the institution.

2 Behaviour modification.   The process of changing an undesirable behaviour. The steps involved are: specify the behaviour to change (the goal), study the behaviour and try to determine what is maintaining it (a hyperactive child may be gaining attention through his unruly behaviour), plan treatment so that everyone involved behaves in the same manner, monitor progress and change treatment if necessary.

3 Shaping verbal behaviour.   Autistic children are taught to speak through a process of progressive reinforcement. Initially the child is reinforced for any sound.

Gradually, the rewards are given for vocalisations which become successively closer to actual words.

④ Biofeedback.   A technique to learn voluntary control of involuntary muscles or voluntary muscles not normally controlled. For example, some patients with spinal cord injuries lose consciousness when they sit up because their blood pressure drops. Training such people to control their blood pressure (involuntary muscles) enables them to lead fuller lives. Children suffering from asthma can be taught to better control their breathing (voluntary muscles).

Learning occurs through feedback. The patient is connected to various monitoring devices. A light comes on or a tone sounds each time the required response is made. The technique relies on giving patients instructions about what they might do to produce the response.

Biofeedback certainly works with **voluntary** responses. Apparent changes in **involuntary** control may be due to relaxation and control of unused voluntary muscles.

⑤ Programmed learning.   Skinner advocated the benefits of learning based on small but rigorous steps, each of which is rewarding. A programmed learning system consists of breaking down the topic into **frames** or very small steps. A correct response acts as a reward and leads on to the next question. The success of the approach is due to the fact that learning happens a small step at a time, giving students plenty of opportunity to make correct responses. A programme may be linear (a list of frames) or branching. A branching programme can 'respond' to mistakes by presenting the student with special help on a topic.

Quick test 3.1

1 Give **one** example of a reflex found in newborn human babies.
2 What is meant by 'one-trial learning' and give **one** example. (*NEAB, 1993*)
3 When learning is not immediately shown, what is it called?
4 How have psychologists measured learning in animals?

Summary

CLASSICAL CONDITIONING	NS paired with UCS [bell + food] *leads to a* CS producing a CR [bell causes salivation]	
	EXAMPLES: Pavlov, Watson and Rayner (Little Albert), Menzies. KEY CONCEPTS: reflex responses	

OPERANT CONDITIONING	ABC Consequences strengthen or weaken S–R links.
	EXAMPLES: Thorndike (Law of Effect), Skinner (pigeons). KEY CONCEPTS: positive and negative reinforcement, shaping, discrimination, generalisation.

3.2 Social learning

LEARNING BY IMITATION – THE BOBO DOLL STUDY

Bandura, Ross and Ross (1961) used Bobo-the-Clown, an adult-sized inflatable doll. Children were placed in a room:

1 With a model who behaved aggressively (punching the doll, shouting at it and hitting it with a hammer).
2 With a model who behaved non-aggressively.
3 With no model (control group).

The participants were 36 boys and 36 girls, aged from 3 to 6 years. They made sure that all groups contained equally aggressive children by using teachers' ratings.

After 10 minutes with the toys and/or model, the children were moved to another room. In order to create a sense of frustration, the children had to walk some distance to the second room. The new room contained both aggressive and non aggressive-type toys, including Bobo. The children were observed through a one-way mirror for 20 minutes, and rated for their aggression.

The findings were:

1 Children in the aggressive group imitated the exact violent behaviours they observed, whereas neither of the other groups showed these behaviours.
2 Children watching non-aggressive models were neither more nor less aggressive.
3 Boys were more generally aggressive than girls.
4 This was especially so when they observed a same-sex model.

A number of other related studies, some by Bandura, found that:

- A live model was more effective than ones on film. However, a filmed or cartoon model still produces more violent behaviour than a non-aggressive one or no model. This is evidence for the effect of media violence on children's behaviour.
- If children saw violence rewarded, this increased their aggressive acts. If the aggressive model was punished, this decreased the imitation.
- Models who are high in prestige or status are more likely to be imitated.
- People who are low in self-esteem are more likely to imitate.

There are three important criticisms of this work:

1 It is oversimplified. In reality models are not clearly rewarded or punished.
2 The unfamiliar social situation of the experiment produces demand characteristics. The children look for cues of what to do with Bobo.
3 There are ethical objections to exposing children to violent models.

Examiner's tip

Candidates often have only a very superficial understanding of this key study.

DEFINITIONS

imitation	Copying someone else's behaviour.
modelling	A person observes a model perform some behaviour and then tries to copy it themselves.
Social Learning Theory	The process of acquiring new forms of behaviour through other people. Such learning involves direct and indirect reinforcement. It is also called **vicarious** or **observational learning**.
vicarious reinforcement	Experiencing reinforcement by watching the reward or punishment of another.

Social learning theory

In the 1940s and 1950s Social Learning (SL) Theory was developed as a major alternative to conditioning. It was an attempt to reinterpret psychoanalytic theory. Bandura blended traditional learning theory with Freud's concept of identification (see Unit 9.3) and the concept of internal mental representation from cognitive psychology. The key points of the theory are:

1 <u>Conditioning.</u>   Many aspects of learning can be understood in terms of classical and operant conditioning. However, these are not sufficient to explain all of human behaviour, in particular, novel forms of behaviour.

2 <u>Observational learning.</u>   Other learning occurs through observation. This greatly increases the opportunities for learning.

3 <u>Imitation and modelling.</u>   Observed behaviour may be imitated. This is called modelling. It is a form of identification.
- Imitation may result in exact copying of a behaviour, as with Bobo.
- It may result in a more general imitation of that kind of behaviour. For example just being more aggressive.
- Imitation itself is probably learned through reinforcement. For example, imitating gender–appropriate behaviour is rewarded.

RESEARCH EXAMPLE   **Liebert and Baron (1972) The effect of television violence on children's behaviour**

RESEARCH QUESTION: Would children behave the same towards another person as they did to Bobo? Attacking a plastic doll is not the same as being violent towards another living being.

PARTICIPANTS: 136 children, aged 5–9. The researchers noted that informed written consent was obtained from parents.

METHOD: Experiment, deception. Children were shown $3\frac{1}{2}$ minutes of a television programme. They were randomly assigned to one of two conditions:
1 Experimental group were shown an aggressive sequence, a segment of *The Untouchables* which contained a chase scene, two fist-fights, two shootings and one knifing.
2 Control group saw a highly active sports sequence.
The participant was then asked to play a game with another child. The second child was visible through a window seated in another room. This other child had a game with a handle. The participant could either press a button labelled 'help' and thus make the handle easier to turn. Or press the button labelled 'hurt' which supposedly made the handle feel very hot.

RESULTS:
1 Those who were exposed to the aggressive film behaved more aggressively, pushing the hurt button for longer.
2 Both groups were far more 'helpful' than they were aggressive.
3 The aggressive group were more helpful than the non aggressive group, though the difference was not significant.

INTERPRETATION: Children imitate general aggression levels. The effect may only be temporary.

The fact that the aggression effect was stronger than the helping effect suggests that behaviour was not due to generally increased arousal, but instead to a **disinhibition** of aggressive behaviour: Normally a child is inhibited about behaving aggressively. Watching aggressive behaviour lifts this normal restraint.

APPLICATIONS: This supports the view that violence on TV may have a detrimental influence on those who watch.

---

4 <u>Models.</u>   Who is likely to be imitated?
- Parents, teachers and other *important* adults, especially television, film and pop stars.
- Someone who the person *identifies* with, in terms of gender, age, occupation, similarity or relevance.
- Someone who is seen as having *advantages*, such as status, power, attractiveness.

The model does not deliberately influence the observer.

5 <u>Reinforcement.</u>
- *Learning* is independent of reinforcement. A person may learn a new behaviour without any reinforcement, having merely observed it is enough.
- *Performance* however *is* related to reinforcement. If either the model or the observer receives reward or punishment, this will increase/decrease the likelihood of performance.
- *Vicarious* reinforcement occurs when the model is reinforced.
- This means that even if aggressive behaviour is seen to be punished, the observer still *learns* the response.

Quick test 3.2

1 What is the difference between learning theory and social learning theory?
2 In social learning, how does a person experience reinforcement?
3 What factors make it more likely that a model will be imitated?
4 What does social learning theory have in common with psychoanalytic theory?
5 The original research on social learning was conducted in a laboratory. Give **one** criticism of this method.

Summary

SL theory is more appropriate for explaining human rather than animal learning since it incorporates cognitive factors such as beliefs, observation and identification.

3.3 Instinct and learning

INNATE FEARS – BAIT SHYNESS

Why do so many people have a fear of spiders? Is this fear learned through experience? Is it gained through observation? Or is it innate?

It has been suggested that rats may have evolved a 'bait shyness'. This is an innate set of behaviours which makes them avoid unfamiliar foods or sample them cautiously. Anything which makes them sick is never touched again (one trial learning).

Any rat with this repertoire of behaviours has a better chance of survival than a rat which hasn't. Man has laid poison for centuries, allowing ample opportunity for the process of natural selection: 'bait shy' rats survive to reproduce, rats who are not bait shy die, often with no offspring. Therefore the trait of bait shyness is selected by natural processes.

This unit seeks to explain changes in behaviour in terms of innate factors and the process of natural selection. Unless a behaviour serves some survival function it will cease to be part of the animal's behavioural repertoire.

DEFINITIONS

ethology	Ethology is the study behaviour in terms of its **adaptive** significance. Behaviours are explained in terms of their **survival** value and function. An important feature of ethology is that it relies on **naturalistic observation** as a method of research rather than experiment.
maturation	A change due to age rather than experience. It is an innate and biological process.
innate	Inherited.
instinct	Predisposes an animal to certain forms of learning. It is an inherited behaviour pattern common to all members of a species. It is an unfashionable concept.
imprinting	A maturational process influenced by experience. It is a kind of restricted learning which takes place rapidly and has a lasting effect.
fixed action patterns (FAP)	Units of species-specific behaviour, mainly innate but can have some learnt elements, for example bird song.
releaser	Releasers are certain features in the environment which trigger or release certain patterns of response (FAPs). All releasers are sign stimuli, but not all sign stimuli are releasers.
sign stimuli	An environmental feature which leads an animal to produce an FAP. It acts as a releaser in appropriate circumstances.
super releaser	Sign stimuli which are exaggerated. Sometimes the most effective sign stimulus is not the natural one but a caricature of it.
critical period	A biologically-determined period of time during which the organism is exclusively receptive to certain behavioural or physiological changes. Outside this window of time the changes will not take place.
sensitive period	A looser interpretation of the notion of a critical period. A time during an organism's development when a particular influence is *most likely* to have an effect.

Instinct

An instinctive behaviour has certain key features:

1 It tends to be stereotyped, i.e. it always appears in the same form when displayed.
2 It can be found in individuals reared in isolation.
3 It is fully developed in individuals who have been prevented from practising it.

EXAMPLE | **Cricket song and bird song**

If a male cricket is reared in isolation, it can still sing. Therefore, in crickets, this particular behaviour pattern is instinctive. The same is true for a cock and its crow. In most birds the situation is more complex.

Marler and Mundinger (1971) found that sparrows kept in isolation between the age of 8 to 90 days fail to develop adult bird song, though they are able to produce a basic version. If an isolated chaffinch fledgling is played a tape of another species they can learn the song if the species is closely related. Adult bullfinches can learn the songs of many other birds. Mynah birds extend this ability to being able to imitate the human voice.

Therefore the instinct to produce a song seems to be present in all birds. The basic pattern is also innate, but the full version is something which is imitated. Some species have a greater capacity for learning than others.

---

1 Adaptive value.   Only instincts which have proven value survive, as in the example of bait shyness in rats.

2 Fixed action patterns (FAPs).   They are:
  - Exhibited in a *repertoire* and thus more complex that reflexes.
  - *Independent of learning*, but can be affected by experience.
  - *Inevitable*, triggered by a specific stimulus (sign stimulus).
  - *Ballistic* and *inflexible*, once launched the rest is inevitable.
  - *Distinct*, each serves one function and occurs in one circumstance.

All of these features can be related to the survival value of such behaviours.

EXAMPLE | **The egg retrieval behaviour greylag goose**

The mere sight of an egg triggers a sequence of inevitable behaviours (**repertoire**) in the goose. It stands in the nest, faces the egg, extends its neck outwards until it is over the egg, puts the underside of the beak on the far side of the egg and starts to roll it back, moving its bill from side to side to prevent it slipping away. If the egg does slip away (or is removed) the goose nonetheless continues back to the nest (**ballistic and inflexible**). Then, if it sees the egg again the sequence recommences until it is finally successful. Any goose that doesn't do this probably will lose a lot of eggs and is likely to have little reproductive success (**adaptive value**).

---

3 Sign stimuli.   Examples include the goose's egg, the red underbelly of the male stickleback (see below) and the red spot on the adult herring gull's bill. The importance of these stimuli is that they produce an instinctive response in the target animal.

4 Releasers.
  (a) All releasers are sign stimuli. For example:
    - The egg acts as a releaser for the greylag goose's behaviour.
    - The spot on an adult herring-gull acts as a releaser for the chick's pecking behaviour. In turn, this pecking behaviour 'releases' a regurgitation response in the parent.
  (b) Not all sign stimuli are releasers. They maybe moderated by environmental cues or hormones so that the response is prevented. For example:
    - Changes in daylight trigger the release of certain hormones in birds. Only then will a male bird respond to the sign stimulus of a female and engage in courtship displays.
    - The greylag goose will not retrieve an egg which has rolled into a dangerous place.

Tinbergen (1951) Instinct in male sticklebacks

RESEARCH QUESTION: Tinbergen was studying the territorial behaviour of male sticklebacks in aquariums which were placed against a window. He noticed that whenever a red post office van passed, the males immediately tried to attack it as if it were a rival male. What features in the environment provoke the male stickleback to display aggression? In other words, what sign stimuli combine to trigger the **innate releasing mechanism** (IRM)?

PARTICIPANTS: Male sticklebacks, a freshwater fish about 2–4 inches long.

METHOD: Animal experiment. In spring the male stickleback develops a red underbelly. They each start to defend their territory from other sticklebacks. If another male swims into his territory the owner will swim hard at the intruder and drive him off.

RESULTS:
Experiment 1: Male sticklebacks were shown various models. The one that looked like a stickleback but had no red underbelly elicited no aggressive response. Whereas a model of any shape but with a red underbelly caused aggressive behaviour.
Experiment 2: Does the sight of a red underbelly always result in attack? Two male sticklebacks (A and B) set up their territories in an aquarium. They are then each placed in a test tube. If both are placed in B's territory B will try to attack A and A tries to flee. The opposite happens if they are placed in A's territory.

INTERPRETATION: The red underbelly of the male stickleback acts as a sign stimulus to release aggressive behaviour in another male. However this depends on a second sign stimulus of territory. The aggressive response only occurs if the male is on home ground, otherwise it will flee.

Therefore, a sign stimulus does not always act as a releaser. This depends on other cues.

⑤ Super-releasers. If you like chocolate cupcakes, then it might be reasonable to think that you would really like a large chocolate cake with chocolate chips and fudge icing. In a similar way, the female oyster catcher prefers a gull's egg to her own, which is similar but half the size. Even more, she prefers an absurdly outsized one.

The cuckoo

The cuckoo leaves the business of rearing its young to other birds. Each cuckoo specialises in a particular species of host. It lays its egg in the nest of a host. The cuckoo egg mimics the shade and colour of the host's eggs. The cuckoo chick generally hatches first and ejects the other eggs. To be successful, the cuckoo chick must release feeding responses in its adoptive parent. The parent thrush feeds its young when it sees its gaping mouth which is brightly coloured. The cuckoo has a *huge* gape which acts as a super-releaser.

⑥ Evaluation. The concept of instinct has been used in many different contexts. Freud used it to denote a biological drive. Behaviourists refer to reflexes rather than instincts. Tinbergen introduced the term to ethology.

The concept has become unfashionable because it involves making a distinction between innate and learned behaviours. In fact no such clear distinction exists because all behaviour is influenced by both factors.

Imprinting

The concept of imprinting comes from embryology. During the development of the embryo there are short periods when the individual is especially vulnerable. For example, if testosterone (a male hormone) is given to a mother to prevent miscarriage during the third and fourth months of pregnancy, a female embryo will develop male genitals (see Unit 9.2). The embryo is only vulnerable during **critical** periods. At other times these external factors do not have the same effect.

In the same way, ethologists suggested that the acquisition of certain forms of behaviour have a critical period. The argument is that some behaviours are vital for survival, such as attachment. In order to ensure that the young organism acquires these behaviours they should be predisposed to learn them at specific times. This sort of learning is called imprinting.

RESEARCH EXAMPLE | **Lorenz (1953) King Solomon's Ring**

RESEARCH QUESTION: What is the main factor in determining the figure that a young animal imprints on? Is it some feature or features of its parent, or just the fact that it's the first moving object the young animal sees?

PARTICIPANTS: Greylag goslings and other young birds.

METHOD and RESULTS: Animal experiment, naturalistic observation. Lorenz divided a clutch of greylag goose eggs into two groups. One group was hatched by the goose, the other was put in an incubator. The goslings hatched by their mother followed her around. For the others, the first living thing they saw was Lorenz and they followed him around.

Lorenz marked the two groups to distinguish them and placed them together. When they were shown both their mother and Lorenz, they went to their respective mother-figures. The goslings persisted in following Lorenz as if he were their mother, becoming distressed if they lost sight of him.

Lorenz tried out different objects with different batches of eggs. It has also been found that goslings will imprint on a cardboard box, a flashing light or a rubber ball. Lorenz tried the same experiment with mallard ducks and found that they ran away unless he quacked his best 'Mallardese'. It seems that mallards have an inborn reaction to a call note rather than a visual stimulus.

INTERPRETATION: Neonates seem to have an innate drive to become attached to a thing which possesses certain key features, such as movement or a particular sound. These attachments seem to be fairly irreversible.

EVALUATION: Imprinting is similar to the kind of bonding seen in other animals. At birth new-borns attach themselves to a caretaker, and equally, the caretaker bonds to the newborn (see Unit 8.1). This process is important for survival in terms of protection, food and imitation of adult behaviour.

APPLICATION: Imprinting techniques are used by nature film makers. They rear a bird such as an owl or swan from the time it hatches. The bird will then always fly to their mother-figure enabling unusual close-ups of the bird in flight.

Is imprinting different from learning? To make this claim the following must be true:
- It only occurs during a *critical period*.
- The process is one of *rapid* behavioural change.
- It is *irreversible*, once set the behaviour doesn't change.
- It is *supra-individual*, imprinting is not to a specific individual but to a class of objects.
- It is *lasting* and has repercussions on later behaviours.

① <u>Critical period.</u>   Certain learning takes place at a particular time, or not at all. To test this deprivation studies are used.

RESEARCH EXAMPLE | **Hess (1958) Imprinting ducklings on models**

RESEARCH QUESTION: What is the critical age at which imprinting occurs? How long must young birds be exposed to the imprinting object before they can discriminate between it and similar objects?

PARTICIPANTS: Ducklings just hatched.

METHOD: Animal experiment. The ducklings were kept in a cardboard box until exposed to the imprinting object. They were exposed for 10 minutes, during which time the model moved at various speeds.

RESULTS:
1 Some imprinting takes place immediately on hatching. The strongest response occurs between 13 and 16 hours after hatching.
2 Ducklings exposed to the imprinting model after 32 hours showed almost no imprinting response.
3 Ducklings who had to follow a model at a great distance, therefore exerting more effort, seemed to form stronger attachments.

INTERPRETATION: This is strong evidence for a critical period.

EVALUATION: The current view is that the concept of a critical period is probably too strong. Instead the period should be seen as 'sensitive'. It is a time when the organism is optimally receptive to acquiring certain behaviours. However, it is possible to learn them at other times, though the learning may be more difficult and less effective.

RELATED STUDIES:
Held and Hein (1963) showed how restricted early visual and motor experiences cause problems for the normal development of visual perception (see Unit 2.3).

DeCasper and Spence (1986) gave evidence of aural imprinting in humans, as described at the beginning of this chapter.

2 Rapid change.   Unlike some other forms of learning, imprinting should take place with little effort and relatively quickly. This is supported by Hess' study, where ducklings were exposed for 10 minutes only.

3 Irreversible.   Lack of sensory stimulation appears to cause physical changes (see Unit 2.3), the same may be true for other stimuli. If this is true, it would explain the relative irreversibility.

4 Supra-individual.   Lorenz's experiment showed that the process of imprinting is not tied to the individual species, but rather a class of objects.

5 Lasting effects.   The immediate effects of imprinting are connected to safety and food. There also appear to be long-term effects related to reproduction. For example, Immelmann(1972) studied male zebra finches who were cross-fostered, that is Zebra (Z) finches were reared by Bengalese (B) parents and vice versa. He found that, when offered a free choice of Z or B females, they chose the species of their fostering. This happened even when they were offered females of their own species. Such **sexual imprinting** has a very important function in ensuring that mating is restricted to the same species and thus is successful. The imprinting model gives them a template for recognising their own species.

6 A conclusion.   In what way is imprinting different from learning generally?
- Things which are imprinted can be learned at other times, though perhaps less easily.
- Both learning and imprinting result in neurological changes which may be long lasting.
- Imprinting is an innate *readiness* to learn certain things during sensitive periods. The actual change in behaviour is *learning*.

Quick test 3.3

1 What is meant by the term *imprinting*?
2 Give an example of an instinct, apart from imprinting.
3 How does imprinting help a young animal survive?
4 What is meant by the term *ethology*?
5 What is **one** advantage of innate behaviour?
6 What is the difference between a sign stimulus and a fixed action pattern?
7 Give an example of a sign stimulus.
8 Why is it sometimes helpful for ethologists to study animal behaviour in a laboratory?
9 Why do ethologists prefer to study animals in their natural environment?
10 (a) What is a *critical period*?
   (b) Give an example of a behaviour which has a critical period.

Summary

INSTINCT	1 Has adaptive value. 2 Occurs in units of FAP (fixed action patterns). 3 Triggered by sign stimuli/releasers. 4 Set in motion the IRM (innate releasing mechanism). It is now an unfashionable concept.
IMPRINTING	1 A critical period in development (e.g. Hess). 2 Rapid change (e.g. Hess). 3 Irreversible (e.g. Blakemore and Cooper). 4 Supra-individual (e.g. Lorenz). 5 Lasting effects (e.g. Immelmann). Not distinctly different from ordinary conditioning.

Chapter 4
Cognitive psychology

THE COMPUTER AGE

The computer 'inspired' cognitive psychologists to explain human behaviour using information processing concepts: the brain is a processor which selects, processes, organises, stores and uses data.

Cognitive psychology is characterised by its concern with internal mental processes, unlike the Behaviourist approach. The cognitive approach is criticised for being mechanistic, reductionist and often omitting emotional influences, criticisms that are also levelled at Behaviourism.

In this chapter you will find memory, thinking, intelligence, cognitive development and language. There are other chapters in this book which are examples of cognitive psychology. For example, perception and social cognition.

4.1 Memory

THE MIND OF A MNEMONIST

A mnemonist is a person who excels at remembering. The Russian psychologist, Luria (1969), recorded the case history of a man called 'S'. This is one example of his memory: he was asked to recall a 'mathematical' formula that had been made up:

$$N \cdot \sqrt{d^2 \times \frac{85}{vx}} \cdot \sqrt[3]{\frac{276^2 \cdot 86x}{n^2v \cdot \pi 264}} \; n^2b = sv \frac{1624}{32^2} \cdot r^2s$$

To do this he made up a story:
"Neiman (N) came out and jabbed the ground with his stick (•). He looked up at a tall tree which looked like a square root sign ($\sqrt{}$), and thought to himself: 'No wonder the tree has withered and begun to expose its roots. After all, it was here when I built two houses' (d^2). Once again he poked with his cane (•). Then he said: 'The houses are too old, I'll have to get rid of them (×) (i.e. 'cross them off'), the sale will bring in far more money. He had originally invested 85,000 in them (85). Then I see the roof detached (——), while down below on the street I see a man playing the Termenvox (vx). He's standing near a mailbox, and on the corner there's a large stone (•).'" And so on.

Fifteen years later, S was able to recall this tale, and the formula, in precise detail.

Such extraordinary feats may seem beyond most of us. Yet they are based on straightforward techniques. In this case it is called the method of loci, described later in this unit.

DEFINITIONS	**memory**	<ul><li>The mental function of retaining data, i.e. learning.</li><li>The storage system which holds the data.</li><li>The data that is retained.</li></ul>

STRUCTURE OF MEMORY

sensory memory (SM)	The sensory form of a stimulus remains unaltered in the mind for a brief time. This could be an auditory or visual trace. It is rapidly lost through decay.
short-term memory (STM)	Information receives minimal processing. It has a relatively limited capacity (about 7 items) and rapidly decays unless maintained through rehearsal. Also called primary or working memory.
long-term memory (LTM)	Relatively permanent storage which has unlimited capacity. Information is held in enactive, iconic or symbolic forms (see Unit 4.4). One of the features of LTM is that information is structured in some way. Also called secondary or permanent memory.

TYPES OF LONG-TERM MEMORY

procedural memory	Knowing how. Our knowledge of how to do things, skills such as riding a bicycle.
declarative memory	Knowing that. Memory for specific information or facts. This is either semantic or episodic.
semantic memory	Memory of language, other cognitive concepts and general knowledge. It is well organised, usually isn't forgotten and doesn't disappear in cases of amnesia. Theories of loss of availability cannot account for the behaviour of semantic memory.
episodic memory	Memory for personal events and people, the episodes of your life. It is this kind of memory which is tested in experimental work. It tends to be unstructured and rapidly lost, particularly as new information arrives and interferes.

FEATURES OF MEMORY AND FORGETTING

reconstruction	Information is not reproduced but organised into its supposed original form using expectations.
amnesia	Loss of memory due to trauma. A person maybe incapable of forming new memories, though older memories remain intact (**anterograde**). Or a failure to retrieve memories immediately prior to the trauma (**retrograde**).
trace decay	The physical form of memory disappears in time due to neural decay.
interference	One set of information competes with another, causing it to be 'overwritten' or physically lost.
Proactive inhibition (PI)	Learning one set of data first interferes with later learning.
Retroactive inhibition (RI)	The reverse, learning a second list interferes with memory of the first list.
schema (schemata)	Mental frameworks which organise information. They help understanding and generate expectations. Similar to stereotypes.

TECHNIQUES OF MEMORY RESEARCH

nonsense syllables	Information devoid of meaning, such as trigrams (BDT) or CVCs (consonant-vowel-consonant, HIG)
free recall	Information is directly retrieved from memory at will. Participants are allowed to recall items in any order they please.
recognition	Identifying familiar information. A list of possible stimuli is presented after learning. It is a better test of memory than recall because more data can be gathered rather than just the items currently accessible.

Stages of memory

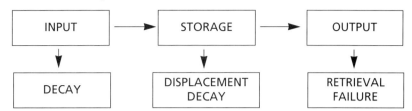

Each stage is a necessary but not sufficient condition for memory to have taken place. Memory can fail (forgetting) at any of these stages.

1 Input: registering √ encoding information.   The physical stimulus is encoded into a form that memory accepts. The input may be visual, acoustic (sounds), motor or verbal. These all need to be translated or coded into a memory trace.

2 Process: storage.   In order for a memory to last it must be stored. The final resting place is called long-term memory. There is intermediate storage, short-term memory, which is limited in capacity and duration.

3 Output: retrieval.   Memories may be stored but are useless unless we can retrieve them. Retrieval may be through recognition, recall or reconstruction.

Short-term and long-term memory

William James (1890) first suggested a distinction between, as he termed them, primary and secondary memories. The evidence still strongly supports two distinct stores (STM and LTM, sometimes referred to as STS, short-term store, and LTS) plus a sensory input store (SIS or SM).

1 Coding differences.   STM is primarily acoustic, whereas LTM is semantic.

RESEARCH EXAMPLE **Baddeley (1966) The influence of acoustic and semantic similarity**

RESEARCH QUESTION: Do STM and LTM differ in the way they code information?

PARTICIPANTS: 147 servicemen and women.

METHOD: Experiment. Each participant was shown one of 4 lists of 10 words. The words were shown for 3 seconds at a time. After each list there was an interpolated task for 20 minutes to prevent rehearsal. Participants were then asked to recall the words.
- List A: acoustically similar (e.g. man, cab, can, cap, mad, max).
- List B: a control list of acoustically dissimilar words. The words were matched for length and frequency of usage.
- List C: semantically similar (e.g. great, large, big, huge, tall)
- List D: a control list of semantically dissimilar words.
Experiment I: tested STM.
Experiment II: tested LTM. Participants were given 1 minute to write out all the words (i.e. rehearse) before doing the interpolated task.

RESULTS:
Experiment I: Participants' performance was affected by acoustic similarity.
Experiment II: Performance was affected by semantic similarity.

INTERPRETATION: This supports the idea of two different kinds of memory, each based on different coding systems: acoustic and semantic.

RELATED STUDIES: Conrad (1964) showed that even when letters are presented visually they are acoustically coded in STM. Participants' verbal recall shows mistakes based on sounds (B is confused with P rather than F).

---

2 Differences in duration.   A distinction is made between memories which disappear quickly (STM) and those which may last a lifetime (LTM).

3 Differences in capacity.   LTM has unlimited capacity, but the same is not true for STM.

4 The serial position effect.   In free recall experiments it is found that both items at the beginning of the stimulus list (**primacy effect**) and items at the end of the list (**recency effect**) are better recalled than those in the middle.

Glanzer and Cunitz (1966) Two storage mechanisms in free recall

RESEARCH QUESTION: When people are asked to recall information, they remember the first and last items best. Is this due to the effects of different memory mechanisms?

PARTICIPANTS: 46 Army enlisted men.

METHOD: Experiment. Each participant was shown 15 lists each containing 15 words. After each list the subject had either to immediately recall the list, or to start counting out loud until the experimenter said 'write' after 10 or 30 seconds.

RESULTS:
1 The no delay condition showed a primacy and a recency effect, indicating both LTM and STM retrieval.
2 The delay recall condition showed a primacy effect but no recency effect, indicating only LTM retrieval.

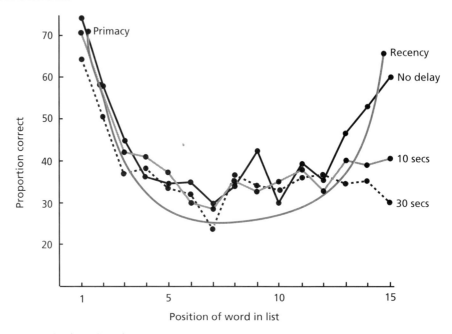

Fig. 4.1 Graph of recall performances

INTERPRETATION: Primacy is due to the fact that the first items are more likely to have entered LTM. Recency occurs because the last items in the list are still in STM. This supports the idea of two distinct memory stores.

⑤ <u>Effects of brain damage</u>.   There are different kinds of amnesia. The differences between them can be related to STM and LTM.
  • STM: **Retrograde amnesia** may be caused by an accident or ECT. It occurs when the events immediately prior to the trauma are permanently forgotten. Presumably this is because information is lost from STM at the time of trauma.
  • LTM: **Anterograde amnesia** leaves permanent memories intact but sufferers immediately forget any new information. It would seem that there is a failure for material to be transferred from STM to LTM because sufferers continue to have normal STM spans and to have LTM for events which preceded their illness. **Korsakoff's syndrome** is an example of this, resulting from severe alcohol poisoning.

H.M.: A severe epileptic

PARTICIPANT and METHOD: Case study. In 1953, H.M. had epilepsy of such severity that it couldn't be controlled by drugs and he was forced to quit his job. As a final measure, surgeons removed the hippocampus from both sides of his brain.

RESULTS: His epileptic seizures were much reduced. His personality and intellect remained intact but his memory was affected. He suffered extensive **anterograde amnesia**.

His memory for events prior to the operation was reasonable, though not as good as usual. He still could talk and recall all the skills he previously knew (**semantic memory**). For many years he reported that his age was 27 and the year was 1953. After a while he realised this was absurd and tried guessing the answer. In other words, he tried to *reconstruct* memories.

He was unable to store any new information. He watched the news every night yet had no recall for major events. He happily reread magazines with no loss of interest. He couldn't memorise lists of words or recall faces of people he met.

INTERPRETATION: The hippocampus may be a specific location for STM. Without STM he couldn't transfer data to LTM but he could still use his LTM.

6 <u>A separate sensory store</u>. The sensory store has very limited duration. If it wasn't cleared almost immediately, the incoming images would become a blur.

RESEARCH EXAMPLE **Sperling (1960) The information available in brief visual presentations**

RESEARCH QUESTION: People 'see' more than they remember. What causes this?

PARTICIPANTS: 5 students trained to do the task.

METHOD: Experiment. Participants were shown a display like the one below for 50 milliseconds. There was a fixation cross in the centre. The stimulus material was chosen to prevent any possibility of the participants interpreting the arrays as words.

7	I	V	F	high tone
X	L	5	3	medium tone
B	4	W	7	low tone

1 *Whole report* condition: Participants filled in a response grid, reporting what they saw or thought they saw for all positions.

2 *Partial report* condition: Participants were instructed that they would hear a tone immediately after seeing the stimulus. They should write down the letters/numbers from the appropriate row only.

RESULTS:

1 Whole report participants typically remember 4–5 items. This represents less than 42% recall.

2 Partial report participants could recall 3 out of 4 items in the row, suggesting that 75% of the information is available immediately after presentation.

INTERPRETATION: Information is initially held in a **sensory store**. The capacity is greater than that for STM but the information decays rapidly.

A similar memory exists for the auditory mode. We can usually still 'hear' information 3 or 4 seconds after it was first heard. This explains why sometimes when you say 'Pardon?' you simultaneously are aware of what was said.

Models of memory

The aim of a model is to provide a framework for the known evidence about memory.

1 <u>Multistore model</u> (also called the <u>two-process theory</u>) e.g. Atkinson and Shriffrin (1968). The evidence reported above suggests that the functioning of memory can be explained in terms of different kinds of storage. Information enters SM, it is initially stored in STM. If it is not rehearsed, it is lost. Rehearsal or practice leads to its eventual storage in LTM.

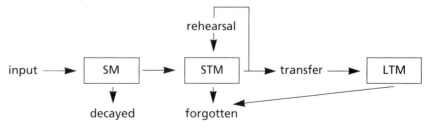

Evaluation:

● Some of the evidence related to coding, duration, capacity, brain damage, position effects and forgetting supports three qualitatively different kinds of memory store. However not everyone shares this view.

● Rehearsal doesn't adequately explain LTM.

● It is a useful concept but is over-simplified. In practice there are no clear distinctions between stages of memory. For example, what kind of memory are you using when learning lists for an experiment?

② Modifications of the multistore model:
- Subdivisions of STM: Baddeley (1986) replaced the term STM with **working memory,** which is subdivided into a central executive controlling both an articulatory loop and a visuo-spatial scratchpad. This would account for the fact that people can perform two tasks involving STM simultaneously. It also presents a more active role for STM.
- Subdivisions of LTM: Amnesiacs do not lose their memory for everything, they retain memories of how to do things and of general knowledge. This suggests a more complex picture of LTM. Cohen and Squire (1980) divided LTM into a knowledge about knowing how to do things (**procedural system**) and a knowledge about facts (**declarative system**). Tulving (1972) further divided the procedural system into memory for personal events and people (**episodic memory**) and memory of language and other general knowledge and concepts (**semantic memory**).

Evaluation:
- Subdivisions make more sense of the experimental data.
- Laboratory studies of memory concentrate on episodic memory, these models suggest why such studies lack everyday validity.

③ Levels of processing model.   Craik and Lockhart (1972). LTM should be defined in terms of how 'deeply' information has been processed rather than the length of storage. 'Depth' is a matter of meaning, when information is given more meaning it is processed more. Retention is not a matter of rehearsal alone. It's a question of what is done with the material during rehearsal, memory is a by-product of processing.

RESEARCH EXAMPLE   **Craik and Tulving (1975) Depth of processing in episodic memory**

RESEARCH QUESTION: Is it reasonable to see memory as an automatic by-product of cognitive operations? The more meaning information has, the more it should be memorable.

METHOD: Ten experiments. Participants were asked a question about a word which was subsequently exposed. The questions were meant to encourage different levels or processing and were to be answered with 'yes' or 'no'. Questions belonged to one of three levels of analysis:
1 *Shallow* or structural, for example 'Is the word in capital letters?'
2 *Phonemic*, for example, 'Does the word rhyme with *able*?'
3 *Semantic* or sentence, for example, 'Would the word fit in the sentence "They met a —— in the street"?'

In one experiment participants were given an unexpected recognition test. In another experiment they were told beforehand that they would be asked to recall the words.

RESULTS:
1 Those participants who had been given semantic-type questions remembered most words. The phonemic coding was next best.
2 Where participants were warned about recall, their performance was not always better. Semantic recall was still better.

INTERPRETATION: Semantic processing creates an automatic memory. It is equivalent or even superior to conscious storage (when a person is told to remember something).

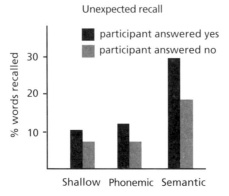
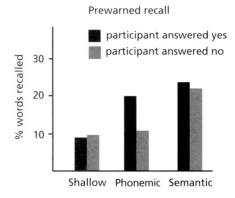

Fig. 4.2 Bar charts showing recall performance

APPLICATIONS: Giving meaning to material is one means of improving your memory.

EVALUATION: It is possible that the better recall of semantic coding is due to the way the participants' memories were tested. Morris *et al.* (1977) found that if participants were given a rhyming recognition test they remembered the words which had received shallow processing better than the more deeply processed ones.

RELATED STUDIES: Craik and Lockhart (1972) gave participants lists of words, followed by a surprise recall. Those who had been asked questions about, for example, the type of letter, recalled an average of 15%. Those who were asked about rhymes recalled 35%. Those who were asked what the words meant recalled 70%.

Evaluation:
- This is also an over-simplified account of how memory functions. Depth is not the only factor which affects memorability. Relevance, for example, can be important.
- The depths of processing model in some ways describes rather than explains what is happening.
- The concept of depth is hard to define and it is circular: deeply processed material is remembered better, the definition of depth is that it leads to greater processing and memory.

Comparison:
- The levels of processing model suggests that the kind of coding (semantic) *causes* LTM.
- The multistore model supports the view that there is an *association* between LTM and semantic coding.

4. Reconstructive model. e.g. Bartlett
   Recalling information is not simply a matter of accessing a piece of information. Memories are often very incomplete and recall requires some reconstruction. This is done with the help of **schemata**. Schemata (or schema) are also discussed in Units 2.2, 4.4 and 5.2.

RESEARCH EXAMPLE **Bartlett (1932) The War of the Ghosts**

RESEARCH QUESTION: How is a person's memory for stories affected by their own attitudes, beliefs, motivation and general cognitive style? Bartlett called this the 'social psychology of remembering' because transformations of memorised material are influenced by social conventions and beliefs which are current in an individual's social group.

PARTICIPANTS: 20 adults.

METHOD: Experiment. Participants were shown one of eight different stories or drawings. They were asked to recall these repeatedly, at intervals of increasing length (days, weeks or even years later).

One of the best known stories was a legend about a tribe of North American Indians. The tale belongs to a culture very different from ours, with unexpected concepts. This makes it ideal for persistent transformation.

The story told of a young man who accompanied a canoe full of warriors to a battle up the river. During the battle he realises that the warriors are ghosts. He returns home, having been shot but not feeling it. He tells his friends about the ghosts. In the morning something black came out of his mouth and he died.

RESULTS: Participants distorted the story rather than remembering it exactly. The transformations were consistent with the participants' Western assumptions and expectations. For example, they used the word 'boat' rather than 'canoe', they often left out the supernatural aspects of the story, and they translated 'something black came out of his mouth' into something more familiar such as 'he foamed at the mouth'.

The commonest omissions or transformations were:
- The title.
- Proper names, which disappeared or were changed.
- Definite numbers.
- The precise significance of the ghosts.
- The canoes.

INTERPRETATION: These distortions are necessary rationalisations because the tale did not fit pre-existing schemas. The process of remembering is not passive recording, but rather active processing, reducing material to a form which can be readily dealt with. This is done by making connections with existing schemas.

Much human memory is influenced by factors that are social in origin and which may be obscured by laboratory methods because of the artificial nature of the material.
APPLICATIONS: Eyewitness testimony.

Evaluation:
- Schema theory is a more *general* approach to cognitive processes than just memory.
- It accounts for the fact that memory is an *active* process.
- It does not explain some important features of memory, such as why some material *cannot be retrieved*.

Forgetting

The other side of remembering is forgetting. 'Forgetting' assumes that something was once stored in STM or LTM, and now either it has disappeared (a failure of availability), or that it is there, somewhere, but you can't 'bring it to mind' (a failure of accessibility).

FAILURE OF AVAILABILITY

1 Encoding failure. You may think you've forgotten something, whereas the truth of the matter was that it never even got as far as STM let alone LTM. This is usually the reason why you can't remember a person's name after having just been introduced to them. People who are good at remembering names usually rehearse the name as soon as they've heard it so that it is stored in LTM.

2 Trace decay:
- In *STM*: trace decay explains the limited duration of STM and the effect of rehearsal. Rehearsal continually renews the physical trace which otherwise would vanish.
- In *LTM*: Are there permanent memories? It is said that the elderly never lose their childhood memories and many skills, such as riding a bicycle, are never forgotten. It is hard to prove or disprove whether memory is permanent. Evidence includes: the success of recall under hypnosis (not always accurate), electrical stimulation of the brain (recovery of some long-lost memories), the reconstructive nature of memory (gives the illusion of long-term memories), re-learning studies (the second time you learn something it's easier suggesting that some trace may be left) and accessibility (given the right cue the memory is there).
- *Brain damage* or *degeneration* is an example of physical alteration of the memory trace. It may occur through ageing, illness or injury.

3 Interference. Proactive (PI) and retroactive (RI). Interference is typically tested by giving participants two lists of word pairs (A–B and A–C), the same nonsense syllable being paired with a different word.

A	B	A	C
BEM	*lawn*	BEM	*aisle*
TAQ	*barge*	TAQ	*cave*
MUZ	*host*	MUZ	*bass*
PEZ	*tube*	PEZ	*vine*
LUF	*weed*	LUF	*dame*
ROH	*mate*	ROH	*file*
VID	*ache*	VID	*gown*
JOP	*cart*	JOP	*whip*
KUG	*quart*	KUG	*budge*
GAV	*zinc*	GAV	*dough*

RI   learn A–B   learn A–C   recall A–B   poorer performance on A–B
PI   learn A–C   learn A–B   recall A–B   poorer performance on A–B
Such memory loss can only be due to interference.
- The greater the similarity between the two sets, the greater the interference. McGeoch and McDonald (1931) gave participants a list of words to learn, then an interference task and then asked them to recall the original list. If the interference task was a list of synonyms to the original list, recall was poor (12%), nonsense syllables interfered less (26% recall), numbers (37% recall) and finally jokes had the least effect (43% recall). Only interference can explain such findings.
- RI is stronger than PI.

④ <u>Gestalt theory of forgetting</u>.   Gestalt psychologists emphasised the form of memory and suggested that memories changes over time to maintain consistency.

RESEARCH EXAMPLE | **Ceraso (1967) Recognition and recall**

RESEARCH QUESTION: Does interference affect recognition and recall differently?

METHOD: Experiment. He gave participants two word lists, such as A and B above.
1 To test recognition he gave participants a list of the nonsense syllables to be matched with a jumbled list of the other words.
2 To test recall, he asked participants to list any of the words and scored this without regard to order.

RESULTS:
1 Recall and recognition showed significant losses of memory.
2 If memory was tested again after 24 hours, recognition (accessibility) showed considerable spontaneous recovery, whereas recall (availability) remained the same.

INTERPRETATION: This suggests that:
1 Some interference effects are temporary.
2 Recognition, as opposed to recall, is almost immune to interference.
3 Interference is more due to lack of *accessibility* than lack of availability.

FAILURE OF ACCESSIBILITY

❶ <u>Cue-dependent forgetting</u>.   There is more in memory than is accessible at any particular time, if only you had the right cue.

RESEARCH EXAMPLE | **Tulving and Psotka (1971) Retroactive inhibition in free recall**

RESEARCH QUESTION: How do cues affect forgetting or memory?

METHOD: Experiment. Participants were given lists of 24 words. The words belonged to 1 of 6 categories, such as buildings or earth formations. Participants were given 1, 2, 3, 4, or 5 lists to learn.
1 *Noncued* recall: after seeing each list three times, they were asked to recall the words.
2 *Cued* recall: they were given an interpolated task for 10 minutes, and then given the category names and asked to recall the words again.

RESULTS:
1 In *noncued* recall, the more lists the participants were given the fewer words they recalled.
2 In *cued* recall, performance remained the same no matter how many words the participant learned.

INTERPRETATION: Retroactive interference does not affect *cued* recall. Forgetting is due to a lack of good enough cues at the time of recall. If the task is recognition, no cue is necessary.

RELATED STUDIES:
Tulving (1968) presented participants with a list of words followed by three successive recall trials. The *specific* words recalled each time were different though participants always got about 50% right. The information was clearly available but not accessible. On each recall trial the participants were using different retrieval cues.

---

❷ <u>Repressed memories</u> (motivated forgetting).   Freud suggested that painful or disturbing memories are put beyond conscious recall. Hypnosis is one means of retrieving such inaccessible memories, though it may rely on reconstructions and therefore inaccurate recall.

Repressed memories can be more commonplace. Most people 'forget' or 'don't bring to mind' things they don't want to do such as go to the dentist or clean their room. However, some of these are failures of availability not accessibility.

KEY POINTS ABOUT FORGETTING
● Decay explains lack of availability which may occur in STM.
● *If* LTM is not permanent, the cause must be decay.
● Interference, as an explanation of forgetting, has limited application. It is relevant to occasions when two sets of data are very similar. This is rare in everyday life.
● Cue-dependent forgetting explains how memories are available but not accessible.

- Some memory experiments suffer from accessibility being confused with availability. Just because you can't bring an item of information to mind, doesn't mean you haven't got it in your memory. For this reason recognition is a better test than recall.
- When discussing forgetting, some of the difficulties arise from confusions between *types* of long-term memory. Semantic memories do not suffer from forgetting in the same way that episodic memories do.

Factors which influence memory

❶ <u>Organisation</u>.   Memory benefits when information is organised. Memory, like perception (see Unit 2.2), is a matter of active organisation rather than passive storage.

RESEARCH EXAMPLE   **Mandler (1967) Sorting cards**

RESEARCH QUESTION: Is organisation alone sufficient to cause long-term storage?

METHOD: Experiment. Participants were given a pack of 52 cards each with a word printed on it. They were asked to sort the pack into categories according to any system they wished. They continued this until they achieved two identical sorts. Participants who had not achieved consistency within $1\frac{1}{4}$ hours were excluded!

After the last sort participants were asked to write all the words they could recall. In one group the participants had been warned about this. In another group there was no prior warning.

RESULTS:
1 The instructions made little difference to the number of words recalled.
2 The more categories a participant used, the more words were recalled.

INTERPRETATION: The fact that participants recalled *anything* when they had no prior warning shows that the act of organising alone created a memory. The act of organising appears to be equivalent to memorising. (Remember that the act of giving meaning also appears to be equivalent to memory, see Craik and Tulving, earlier in this unit).

RELATED STUDIES:
Bower *et al.* (1969) gave participants a list of 112 words arranged into conceptual hierarchies. When participants were given the same words arranged randomly, recall was found to be half as good.

Collins and Quillan's (1969) hierarchical network model of thought (see Unit 4.2) also applies to memory. A hierarchy enables efficient searches of stored data. This shows how organisation helps both storage and retrieval processes.

❷ <u>Language</u>.   Language creates expectations which cause distortions.

RESEARCH EXAMPLE   **Carmichael *et al.* (1932) The effect of language on the reproduction of visually perceived forms**

RESEARCH QUESTION: How do labels affect subsequent recall?

METHOD: Experiment. Participants are shown a set of ambiguous drawings. The drawings are accompanied by 1 of 2 word lists labelling each drawing. For example:

Word List – 1	Stimulus figures	Word List – 2
Curtains in a window		Diamond in a rectangle
Bottle		Stirrup
Crescent moon		Letter "C"

RESULTS: Later reproduction of the drawings was seen to be influenced by the words which had accompanied the drawings. For example, the picture was reproduced as or depending which list the participant had seen.

INTERPRETATION: Language creates expectations which alter our perceptions. You can only remember what you perceived in the first place.

RELATED STUDIES:
See Loftus *et al.* (1978), later in this unit, on leading questions.
See Bartlett (1932), earlier in this unit, on reconstructive memory and the effects of schemata.

③ <u>Context effects</u>. The place where learning takes place may influence subsequent recall. This context acts like a cue (see 'cue-dependent forgetting', earlier in this unit).

For example Abernethy (1940) found that students performed better on a test if the room and teacher were the same as they had had during their initial learning. Godden and Baddeley (1975) gave divers lists of words to learn on land or underwater. Recall was better when the context was constant.

State dependent recall also occurs. For example, Goodwin *et al.* (1969) report clinical evidence of drinkers who hide money when drunk and can't remember where when sober. However they can recall the location when drunk again.

Applications

① <u>Police reconstructions of crimes</u> are based on context-dependence. They restage the events of a crime using actors at a similar time and place to the original events to jog observers' memories. This 'jogging' is essentially providing cues to access 'lost' memories.

② <u>Eye witness testimony</u>. People think they can accurately identify a stranger's face or recall events related to a crime. However psychological evidence suggests that our memories are not so reliable. We unconsciously replace partial recall with reconstructions of such memories, based on expectations.

RESEARCH EXAMPLE | **Loftus (1979) Expert witness**

José Garcia was accused of robbing a liquor store in California. He shot one of two clerks in the store. The surviving clerk, Joseph Melville, identified Garcia but this was the only evidence against him. At the trial Loftus was called as an expert witness to help the jury decide how much weight to give to Melville's testimony. There were three issues for Loftus to consider:
1 Identification was made two weeks after the crime. How does retention interval affect memory?
2 Melville was in a state of extreme distress after seeing his colleague shot. How are stress and memory related?
3 Garcia was a Mexican-American, Melville was white. How does race affect identification?
Loftus gave the following replies:
1 Memory decays rapidly at first and then more gradually.
2 Under very high stress, memory is less good than under moderate levels of stress (see 'Yerkes-Dodson Law' in Unit 10.2).
3 People are less good at identifying members of a different race.

It might be asked, given that the memory may not be accurate, what was Melville recalling? Most likely he was unconsciously filling in the gaps in his memory on the basis of expectations and prejudices.

INTERPRETATION: In the case of this trial, the jury could not agree on a verdict and Garcia was acquitted.

EVALUATION: The evidence presented by Loftus is based on laboratory experiments and may not be valid in real-life.

RELATED STUDIES:
Loftus *et al.* (1978) showed how the use of leading questions may influence a witness's testimony. The use of 'a' or 'the' in a question changes the way people answer a question. 'Did you see the broken headlight?' assumes that there was a broken headlight whereas 'Did you see a broken headlight?' is more open-ended.

Wells *et al.* (1979) left a participant in cubicle with a calculator, a confederate appears and pops it in her purse. When the experimenter asked the participant (witness) to identify the 'thief' from six pictures, 58% were correct. Moreover, in a follow-up mock trial, 80% of the witnesses were believed. Such unreliability and influence needs careful monitoring.

③ <u>Exam revision</u>.

EXAMPLE | **A guide to better revising: Mnemonics**

A mnemonic is a technique for improving one's memory.
1 <u>Repetition</u>. Rehearsal and relearning enhance long-term memories.

2 <u>Organisation</u>.   Revision notes should be made in a structured manner. The act of categorising is equivalent to memorising. Visual imagery (see below) is one means of organising data.

3 <u>Elaboration</u>.   Expanding and discussing material increases its meaning.

4 <u>Chunking</u>.   Break material down into chunks with keyword headings. For example, using numbered lists.

5 <u>Cues</u>.   Organising notes is also means of establishing cues. For example, creating category headings, numbered lists or maintaining a personal glossary of keywords.

6 <u>Visual imagery</u>.   Images help connect or organise pieces of information. This improves recall by reducing the chunks of information, forming links and imposing structure.

7 <u>Loci system</u>.   The method of locations. Objects to be remembered are 'placed' by forming strong visual images. This is similar to the technique used by S, described at the beginning of this Unit. Its success can be related to context cues, organisation of material and imagery.

8 <u>Keyword system</u>.   A useful method for learning a foreign language. A **keyword** is identified which sounds very similar to the foreign word. An image is formed which links this word to the meaning of the foreign word. For example:

Spanish word	keyword (sounds like Spanish word)	English translation	visual image
sopa	soap	soup	imagine a picture of a bar of soap in a soup tin.
perro	pear	dog	imagine picture of dog holding a pear.

9 <u>Peg word system</u>.   A previously learned system of words are used as **pegs** on which to hang data. For example, you could use the list: one–bun, two–shoe, three–tree, etc. A long list of new words could be memorised by associating each with words in the known list.

10 <u>Abbreviations</u>.   Giving meaning to an otherwise meaningless groups of letters or words. Meaning implies deeper levels of processing.
   - **Acronyms**, such as ROY G. BIV for the colours of the spectrum,
   - **Acrostics**, using the first letter of each word, such as 'Some old hippies can always have tankards of ale' for the trigonometry formula sine = opp/hyp, cos = adj/hyp, tan = opp/adj.
   - **Rhymes**, such as 'thirty days hath September ...'.

4 <u>Everyday memory</u>.   The application of memory research to everyday situations is relatively recent.

RESEARCH EXAMPLE **Ley (1978) Memory for medical information**

RESEARCH QUESTION: How can doctors help patients' remember what they tell them?

PARTICIPANTS : Four doctors and their patients.

METHOD: Natural experiment. Patients often fail to remember what their doctor told them. Ley prepared a booklet for doctors with suggestions about how to improve this:
1 Give instructions and advice *before* other information.
2 *Stress* the importance of the instructions and advice you give.
3 Use *short* words and *short* sentences.
4 Use *explicit terms* where possible.
5 *Repeat* information.
6 Give *specific* detailed advice rather than general rules.
All these suggestions are based on the findings of psychological studies.

RESULTS: Before the arrival of the booklet, patients recalled 55% of what their doctors said. Afterwards this increased to 70%.

INTERPRETATION: Everyday situations can benefit from psychological research.

Quick test 4.1

1 What is the difference between:
   (a) *primacy* and *recency*?
   (b) *short-term* and *long-term* memory (give at least **three** differences)?
2 What is a *mnemonic*?
3 Name **three** techniques which might help you improve your memory.
4 When revising, put a few drops of a favourite fragrance on your wrist and use it again during the actual exam. What is this an example of? (*NEAB, 1992*)

5 Why does visual imagery improve our memory recall? (*MEG, 1993*)

6 (a) Give an example of a nonsense syllable.

(b) What is **one** advantage and **one** disadvantage of using nonsense syllables to study memory?

7 People often forget their dental appointments. What explanation might a psychologist give for this?

8 Using your psychological knowledge, give **two** factors which could affect the accuracy of eyewitness testimony. (*MEG, 1994*)

9 List **three** ways that past experience can affect memory.

10 Describe **two** methods used to measure memory.

Summary

FEATURES OF MEMORY	SENSORY MEMORY (SM or SIS)	SHORT-TERM MEMORY STM or STS)	LONG-TERM MEMORY (LTM or LTS)
CODING	Modality based (visual SM is iconic, acoustic SM is acoustic).	Mainly acoustic.	Mainly semantic, but others too e.g. imagery.
DURATION	Generally very brief (less than 1 second) though some may remain up to 18 seconds.	Brief (less than 30 seconds if there is no rehearsal).	Supposedly unlimited.
CAPACITY	Large capacity.	2.5–7 chunks.	Supposedly unlimited.
SERIAL POSITION EFFECT		Recency effect.	Primacy effect.
BRAIN INJURY		Retrograde amnesia.	Anterograde amnesia.
FORGETTING	Trace decay, displacement.	Trace decay, displacement, interference.	Lack of accessibility: encoding failure, cue-dependence, repression. Lack of availability: trace decay, brain injury.
FACTORS WHICH INFLUENCE MEMORY	Attention.	Rehearsal, perception (e.g. context, expectations).	Organisation, language.

MODELS OF MEMORY	FORGETTING		FACTORS WHICH INFLUENCE MEMORY
	AVAILABILITY	ACCESSIBILITY	

MODELS OF MEMORY	AVAILABILITY	ACCESSIBILITY	FACTORS WHICH INFLUENCE MEMORY
1 Multistore model (e.g. Atkinson and Shriffrin) 2 Levels of processing (Craik and Lockhart) 3 Reconstructive models (e.g. Bartlett)	1 Encoding failure 2 Trace decay 3 Interference (PI and RI) 4 Gestalt theory	1 Cue-dependent 2 Repressed memory	1 Organisation 2 Language 3 Context effects

APPLICATIONS:

1 Reconstructions of crimes.

2 Eyewitness testimony.

3 Exam revision (repetition, organisation, elaboration, chunking, cues, visual imagery, loci system, keyword system, peg wordsystem, abbreviations.

4 Everyday memory.

4.2 Thinking and problem solving

DOES THIS MAKE SENSE?

The procedure is actually quite simple. First you arrange items into different groups. Of course one pile may be sufficient depending on how much there is to do. If you have to go somewhere else due to lack of facilities, that is the next step; otherwise you are pretty well set ... After the procedure is completed one arranges the materials into their appropriate places. Eventually they will be used once more and the whole cycle will then have to be repeated. However, that is part of life.

It might have helped you to be told the title of this passage is 'Washing clothes'. Bransford and Johnson (1972) gave some participants the title before reading the passage. They were significantly better at a comprehension and a recall test than those who received the title afterwards.

The title enables you to interpret all the ambiguous details in terms of expectations. It provides a necessary schema or a frame of reference.

DEFINITIONS

thinking	The mental processing of information stored in the form of concepts (schema), images or action memories. This includes: concept formation, problem-solving, creativity, reasoning, decision-making and imagination. Intelligence is a measure of the quality of your thinking.
concept	The mental representation of a group of things which share some attribute(s).
concept formation	Selecting features common to a class of objects and discovering rules which relate these features.
schema	A structured cluster of concepts based on experience and used to generate future expectations.
scripts	Schemata about events, plans for action. The knowledge of appropriate behaviour: who does what, when, to whom and why. There are different kinds of scripts: ● situational (social situations, like a restaurant), ● personal (expectations and behaviours), ● instrumental (goal directed behaviour, such as getting to school).
prototype	The most typical example of a class of things. A set of characteristic attributes.
modes of thinking	Enactive, iconic and symbolic (see Unit 4.4).
convergent thinking	Producing one correct solution to a problem by bringing information together, like deductive reasoning.
divergent thinking	Creating one or more novel and unusual solutions to a problem which are appropriate in context and valued by others ('crazy' behaviour would not be regarded as creative). 'Correctness' depends on some subjective evaluation. Also called **creativity** or **lateral thought**.
creativity	Problem-solving which results in a novel solution to a problem.
cognitive style	The difference between individuals in terms of the cognitive approaches they tend to use. For example, convergent and divergent thinking, use of imagery, field dependence or independence, reflectivity and impulsivity.

| rigidity of thought | Our tendency to view objects as serving only the function for which they are commonly used. Also called **Einstellung** by the Gestalt psychologists, or **functional fixedness**. |
| mental set | A readiness to respond in a particular manner. |

The organisation of concepts

① <u>Defining attributes</u>.   A concept has a set of attributes (features) which are all necessary and distinct. For example, the concept 'cup' *must* have the following features: a handle, contains liquid and a characteristic shape. It is *distinct* from the concept 'mug'.

Hierarchical semantic network: Collins and Quillan's (1969) model organises concepts into hierarchies on the basis of defining attributes.

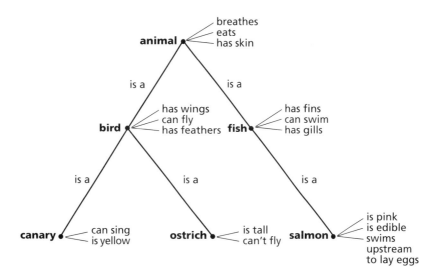

Fig. 4.3 Example of a hierarchical semantic network

② <u>Characteristic attributes: prototypes</u>.   The real world does not divide so neatly into distinct categories. Some concepts, such as 'bachelor', are clearly defined. Others, such as 'bird', have ill-defined or *fuzzy* boundaries. For example, a bird may or may not include the attribute 'can fly'.

Prototype model: Rosch (1975) argued that concepts are prototypes. We hold ideas about typical features, but these features do not all need to be present to recognise an instance of a concept.

③ <u>Schemata and scripts</u>.   Schema theory considers how concepts are related to each other in a more complex manner than a hierarchy. We use schemas to understand incoming information and to generate expectations.

Script theory: Schank and Abelson (1977) developed a model to show how schema could be used in everyday comprehension of the world around us. For example, they used a test like this: 'Ruth and Mark had lunch in a restaurant today. They really enjoyed the meal but worried about the eventual cost of it. However, after the ice cream, when the bill arrived, they were pleasantly surprised to find that it was very reasonable.'

When reading this passage, we unconsciously make many inferences based on our knowledge of eating in a restaurant. For instance, we assume that the meal involved ice cream and the bill was brought by a waiter. We fill in those bits that are missing using our pre-existing knowledge or scripts.

The term schema was used by Bartlett to explain how people's memories are shaped by expectations (see Unit 4.1), and by Piaget to describe cognitive development (see Unit 4.4).

Concept formation

Some concepts are probably inborn, such as time and space. Others have to be learned or formed. The strategies for concept formation are innate and may reflect cognitive style.

1 <u>Assimilation and accommodation.</u>   Piaget suggested that schemata are adapted to fit in with experience through these twin processes (see Unit 4.4).

2 <u>Integrating concepts.</u>   Each new concept is placed within existing hierarchies.

3 <u>Prototype formation.</u>   This is a process of identifying the key features of a concept to use as a template for recognising all instances.

4 <u>Hypothesis testing.</u>   People form a hypothesis about a new instance of a concept and then test to see if this is valid.

RESEARCH EXAMPLE   **Bruner et al. (1956) A study of thinking**

RESEARCH QUESTION: What strategies do people use when forming concepts?

PARTICIPANTS: Various groups of undergraduates

METHOD: Experiment. They gave a participant 81 cards, representing every combination of the available features (colour, number of symbols, type of symbol and border). The participant had to work out the concept (i.e. card) the experimenter was thinking of by selecting cards which tested their hypothesis and seeing how many attributes were correct. (Like the game of Mastermind).

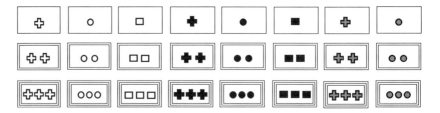

Fig. 4.4 Examples of cards used by Bruner, each of them given with borders of one, two or three lines

RESULTS: Participants used **scanning** or **focusing** strategies.

1 Focusing involves choosing a feature from a correct card and selecting another card which differs in only one attribute. For example, if one circle in green is correct but one square in green isn't, the circle must be correct. A person might be using a conservative-focusing or focus–gambling strategy.

2 Scanning involves choosing a card and remembering all the remaining cards which this logically eliminates. This is done for many different cards, so that all outcomes have to be remembered and combined. One attribute at a time may be excluded. It tends to be less effective than focusing. There is simultaneous-scanning and successive-scanning.

INTERPRETATION: These might represent differences in cognitive style. However, subjects rarely hold to a single strategy.

Problem solving

1 <u>Convergent and divergent thinking.</u>   These are two approaches to problem-solving. Neither is 'better' but each is more appropriate for different problems.

2 <u>Testing divergent or creative thinking.</u>   Psychologists are expected to suggest methods for measuring all aspects of behaviour. Creativity is assessed in terms of the number and variety of answers to certain problems. For example:

- Unusual uses for objects, such as a brick or paper clip.
- Elaboration, for example, draw as many pictures as possible using a circle or write as many meanings for duck as you can.
- Think of common problems, for example when making a cup of tea.
- Think of consequences, for example, what would happen if national laws were abolished?
- Suggest improvements for common articles such as toys or toasters.
- Make remote associations, for example, find a fourth word to go with 'rat, blue, cottage'.

❸ <u>Cognitive style</u>.   People show characteristic differences in their approach to problem-solving. Training may encourage the use of a less favoured method. For example, deBono (1970) wrote a popular book on how to develop lateral thinking.

RESEARCH EXAMPLE | **Hudson (1962, 1963) Personality and scientific aptitude**

RESEARCH QUESTION: How do convergers differ from divergers?

PARTICIPANTS: 95 English sixth form pupils, aged 15–17.

METHOD: Psychometric, correlation. The boys were tested on IQ, creativity measures and personality differences.

RESULTS: The most marked difference was between 'arts' and 'science' students.

The 'converger'	The 'diverger'
More likely to study sciences.	More likely to study arts.
Does well on the kind of reasoning task set in intelligence tests.	Is weak on logical argument.
Poor on open-ended tasks, and answers lack humour.	Fluent on open-ended tasks.
Unlikely to express attitudes which are out of the ordinary or non-authoritarian. They are conformers.	Attitudes avoid stereotypes.

INTERPRETATION: Science students differ from arts students in terms of their personality.

EVALUATION: Attempts to replicate Hudson's findings haven't been successful suggesting that there isn't such a neat divide between arts and science students.

---

❹ <u>Rigidity of thought</u>.   Cognitive style may hinder problem-solving, particularly divergent thinking.

RESEARCH EXAMPLE | **Luchins (1942) The water jar problem**

RESEARCH QUESTION: To what extent is problem solving affected by **Einstellung**, 'the set which immediately predisposes an organism to one kind of motor or conscious act'?

PARTICIPANTS: More than 2,500 students of various kinds (222 college students, 913 adults attending education classes, 1, 259 state school pupils, 275 university students).

METHOD: Experiment. Participants are given a series of water jar problems, written on paper.

	Jar A	Jar B	Jar C	required amount of water
1	92	9	0	20
2	21	127	3	100
3	14	163	25	99
4	18	43	10	5
5	9	42	6	21
6	20	59	4	31
7	23	49	5	16
8	10	36	3	7
9	28	76	3	25

(Amount of water measured by each jar)

- Problems 2, 3, 4, 5 and 6 are the *Einstellung* problems which can be solved using: B − A − 2C. This may generate an *Einstellung* effect for subsequent 'critical' problems, 7 and 8, which can be solved by an easier method, A − C.
- Problem 9 can only be solved using the easier method (A − C), and therefore should be affected by the *Einstellung* effect.
- Control groups are given problems 7, 8 and 9 only.
- There was also a 'don't be blind condition' (DBB) where participants were told, after question 6, to write 'Don't be blind' on their answer paper! To warn participants not to be fooled by their 'set'.

RESULTS:

1 Participants soon realise the solution and continue to rigidly apply the same method even to problems 7 and 8.
2 The control groups solved problems 7 and 8 using the simpler method, because they had no prior set.
3 On question 9, only 4% of the control group failed, but the majority (66%) of the others failed. The DBB condition did slightly better with 47% failure.

INTERPRETATION: Participants demonstrated set. Past experience may lead to **positive transfer effects**, as in the case of the early problems which were solved. Or **negative transfer**, as in the later ones.

APPLICATIONS: deBono's suggestion is that you must make yourself aware of your pre-existing assumptions. These can then be avoided.

Techniques of problem solving

1 Stages of problem-solving:
- Familiarisation Identify the problem.
- Incubation   Acquiring necessary skills or simply 'sitting on it'.
- Activity   Develop a solution. This is a convergent stage.
- Illumination   Solution emerges. This is a divergent stage.
- Verification   Testing the solution.

2 Trial-and-error learning.   Operant conditioning (see Unit 3.1) is a form of learning through successive trials where errors act as negative reinforcement and success is positively reinforcing. Eventually a solution will be found. This technique works for convergent problems. Thorndike (1898) demonstrated how cats learn to escape from a 'puzzle box' to reach the food placed outside. The solution was to pull a string dangling from the ceiling. The cats eventually discover this by trying various solutions, being unsuccessful and eventually hitting on the correct behaviour.

3 Insight learning.   A different approach is necessary for divergent problems. Köhler (see Unit 3.1) set chimpanzees various open-ended problems to solve. The animals soon gave up and sat down, seemingly inactive. Later, they would solve it in a flash, presumably having worked out the solution in their minds and planning their actions before starting.

4 Brainstorming.   This is generally a group process. In the initial phase, ideas are generated uncritically, then evaluated and finally elaborated, again uncritically. This may not be efficient in terms of man hours but produces a greater range of ideas.

5 Means-end analysis.   People working with computers have to design systems which will solve problems.

RESEARCH EXAMPLE | **Newell and Simon (1963) The General Problem Solver (GPS)**

RESEARCH QUESTION: How can a computer be programmed to solve problems? What does this tell us about human problem-solving?

METHOD: Investigation. The method involves breaking a problem down into smaller stages or **sub-goals**, which will reduce the **problem space**. The problem space is the distance between your current state and the goal state.
- Note the problem space.
- Create a sub-goal to reduce this difference
- Select an operator which will solve the sub-goal.
- Recalculate the problem space and set a new sub-goal.

INTERPRETATION: This is a **heuristic** approach. A heuristic is a trial-and-error method for problem solving using rules. An alternative method is the use an **algorithm**, a set of instructions like a knitting pattern, which guarantees a solution.

APPLICATIONS: Computer programs which play chess use a similar process of 'chunking' (setting sub-goals). They also use number crunching methods which examine all the available possibilities (a **scanning** strategy).

EVALUATION: Means-end analysis works with well-defined goals but in everyday life people have to solve problems with unclear goals and many ambiguities.

RELATED STUDIES:
Simon and Reed (1976) applied this technique to a variation on the missionaries and cannibals problem. Participants had to move five missionaries and five cannibals to the other side of a river, at no time can there be more missionaries than cannibals. Participants who were told to move three cannibals to the target side were able to solve the problem faster. This sub-goal seems to be moving away from the solution and so would be avoided in a means-end approach. The fact that people weren't doing this, shows that they were using a means-end approach.

Quick test 4.2

1 Match the methods of problem solving (left column) to types of problem (right column).

Method of problem solving	Problem
1 Convergent thinking	A A group of people trying to come up with an original name for a new product.
2 Means-end analysis	B An unusual problem like finding your car has frozen locks.
3 Brainstorming	C A science problem with only one right answer.
4 Lateral thinking	D A complicated problem with a lot of stages to go through before it is completed.
5 Divergent thinking	E Developing a scientific invention.

(adapted from *MEG, 1993*)

2 What is the difference between:
   (a) an *algorithm* and a *heuristic*?
   (b) a *schema* and a *script*?
3 Describe **one** strategy which may be used in concept formation.
4 What is *functional fixedness*?
5 Why might convergent thinkers be better at science subjects?
6 Give an example from everyday life when *divergent* thinking is useful. (*MEG, 1994*)
7 Psychologists often have difficulties in investigating thinking and problem-solving. Describe **one** difficulty that they may have when they want to study how people think or solve problems. (*MEG, 1993*)
8 Give **one** disadvantage to using computers to investigate problem solving in humans.
9 How could a psychologist decide if a creativity test was valid? (*MEG, 1992*)
10 What is *The General Problem Solver*?

Summary

THE ORGANISATION OF CONCEPTS

1 Defining attributes
2 Characteristic attributes
3 Schemata and scripts

THE FORMATION OF CONCEPTS

1 Assimilation and accommodation
2 Integrating concepts
3 Prototype formation
4 Hypothesis testing

PROBLEM-SOLVING

1 Convergent/divergent thought
2 Cognitive style
3 Rigidity of thought

TECHNIQUES OF PROBLEM-SOLVING

1 Stages of problem-solving
2 Trial-and-error learning
3 Insight learning
4 Brainstorming
5 Means-end analysis

4.3 Intelligence

BIRDBRAIN OF BRITAIN

Is it possible to test the intelligence of birds? Brooks-King and Hurrell (1958) observed how various species of birds coped with puzzle boxes.

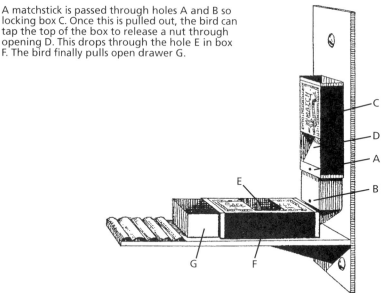

A matchstick is passed through holes A and B so locking box C. Once this is pulled out, the bird can tap the top of the box to release a nut through opening D. This drops through the hole E in box F. The bird finally pulls open drawer G.

Fig. 4.5 The matchbox intelligence test

The matchbox apparatus in Fig. 4.5 was one version they tried. One female blue tit was successful almost immediately, while her mate took three months to work it out. Once a bird had learned the task, they always remembered the solution even if they didn't see the puzzle for many weeks.

A later set of trials involved a more complicated perspex puzzle. Over a period of a month they noted that blue tits and coal tits succeeded whereas great tits and marsh tits did not. They noted individual differences: some solved the problem at once, others persisted until they succeeded, others were permanently defeated.

What ability were the researchers testing by setting these problem–solving tasks? They called them intelligence tests. The tasks involved many cognitive processes: learning, memory, attention, task persistence, reasoning, creativity and so on. Intelligence is a general *ability* which underlies all cognitive *processes*.

DEFINITIONS		
	intelligence	The ability to profit from experience. To learn, apply what has been learned to new situations, to reason, to solve problems, to think abstractly and to use all of these abilities in an effective way.
	monozygotic twins (MZ)	Twins with the same genes. One fertilised egg (a zygote) divides and produces two individuals. Also called identical twins. Used for studying the effects of heredity.
	dizygotic twins (DZ)	Twins which are no more alike than any brothers and sisters. Two eggs were fertilised at the same time. Also called fraternal twins.
	heredity	The biological transmission of genetic information from parent to offspring. Other words which are used include: nature, innate, inherited, biological, inborn, genetic or native (nativism).

environment	Everything around you. This includes your diet while in your mother's womb, or exposure to x-rays which could cause genetic mutation.
IQ	Intelligence quotient. Mental age (MA) is calculated using an intelligence test. As children get older they naturally improve their mental ability and the test score is adjusted for chronological age (CA). Therefore IQ = MA / CA × 100. The mean IQ is set at 100. IQs below 70 or above 130 are extremely rare (educationally subnormal or genius level).

The hereditarian view of intelligence

1 <u>Twin studies</u>. Twins can provide evidence favouring heredity in two ways:
- If MZ twins are reared apart they should nevertheless have very similar IQs. They are identical genetically but have had different environments.
- MZ twins should have more similar IQs than DZ twins. They are more similar genetically.

RESEARCH EXAMPLE

Examiner's tip

Make sure you can explain how twin studies contribute to the nature/nurture debate.

Shields (1962) Twins reared apart

RESEARCH QUESTION: Are early environmental factors an important cause of variation in personality and intelligence?

PARTICIPANTS: In 1953 the BBC broadcast a programme about twins and appealed for any MZ twins who had been reared apart to fill in a questionnaire. Altogether 5,000 twins, MZ, DZ and those reared together and apart answered their questionnaire. From this the researchers selected 44 pairs of MZ twins brought up apart and a matched control group of MZ twins who had been brought up together. There were also 32 pairs of DZ twins of whom 11 were reared apart. The age ranged from 8 to 59 years.

METHOD: Natural experiment, psychometric. The twins were given intelligence tests, questionnaires, interviews and medical examinations.

RESULTS: The correlations between sets of twins on measures of intelligence were:
1 Separated MZ twins   0.77
2 Non-separated MZ twins   0.76
3 Non-separated DZ twins   0.51

INTERPRETATION:
1 The intelligence of MZ twins seems little affected by environment, supporting a hereditarian view.
2 DZ twins have less similar IQs, as we would expect since they are less similar genetically. This again supports a hereditarian view.

EVALUATION: Kamin (1974) has been one of the most influential critics.
1 The sample was relatively small.
2 In reality the twins had often spent a substantial amount of time together. Fourteen sets of MZ twins were only separated after the age of one year. In only 11 sets were one or both twins adopted. The rest were raised by relatives, often visiting each other. Therefore the assumption of different environmental influences was not justified.
3 Theoretically, if intelligence was entirely inherited, the IQ scores of MZ twins reared apart should have a correlation of +1.00. Since correlations are lower than this, this shows that environment must play a role.
4 A correlation is not evidence that one factor *caused* another. A third factor may be important. For example, identical twins may have a similar effect on people around them which creates expectations leading to self-fulfilling performance (see Unit 8.2).

2 <u>Familial studies</u>. By examining the IQs of family members it can be shown that the closer the genetic relationship, the closer the IQ. Familial studies can include adopted children who have no genetic relationship with their parents but share the same environment.

Bouchard and McGue (1981) Comparing IQ in families

RESEARCH QUESTION: What general conclusions can be drawn from world-wide studies of IQ within families?

METHOD: Correlation. Review of 111 studies which calculated the correlation in IQ between family members.

RESULTS:

	median correlation	total number of subjects
MZ twins reared together	0.85	4,672
MZ twins reared apart	0.67	65
DZ twins reared together	0.58	5,546
Parent-offspring reared together	0.38	8,433
Parent-offspring reared apart	0.22	814
Adopted parent-offspring	0.18	1,319
Siblings reared together	0.45	26,473
Adopted siblings (not biological)	0.31	369

INTERPRETATION: The evidence supports the inheritance argument:
1 MZ twins reared apart are more similar in IQ than DZ twins reared together. This suggests that genetic factors are stronger than environmental ones.
2 The closer the genetic link, the greater the correlation between IQ.
3 Biological pairs are closer than non-biological pairs who share the same environment.

EVALUATION:
1 MZ twins reared *together* are more similar than those reared apart. This shows that environment has at least some effect.
2 A review places many studies together, each using different tests and methods. It may not provide a valid result.

RELATED STUDIES: Bouchard *et al.* (1990) reported on the Minnesota Study of Twins Reared Apart. Over 100 participants, MZ and DZ twins and triplets, came from America, Britain and other European countries. The evidence continues to supports the view that IQ is at least partly inherited, finding that about 70% is due to genetic variation.

③ Adoption studies.   These can provide evidence favouring heredity in two ways:
- Comparison of, on the one hand, a child and its adopted parents (environment link) with, on the other hand, a child reared apart from its natural parents (genetic link).
- Comparison of an adopted parent and their own child (genetic link) with the same parent and an adopted child (environment link).

Skodak and Skeels (1949) The effects of adoption

RESEARCH QUESTION: What is the role of heredity in determining intelligence?

PARTICIPANTS: 100 adopted children and their natural mothers. All had been in care from the age of six months, and were White. They were usually adopted within two years of arrival in care.

METHOD: Longitudinal, natural experiment. The IQs of subjects were recorded. Information about IQ and background was available for both the children and parents when the child was placed in care. The children were re-tested at the age of approximately 2, 4, 7 and 13 years using a version of the Stanford-Binet test. In this time the sample dwindled from an original 180 to the final 100.

RESULTS:

Age of child	2	4	7	13
Correlation with natural mother	0	0.28	0.35	0.44

All correlations were significant except at age 2. It appears that the effects of environment become *less* with age, as IQ becomes progressively more similar to the natural parent.

INTERPRETATION: Supports the view that intelligence is inherited. The decline of environmental influence may be due to early enrichment and extra attention levelling out, and genetic factors showing through.

RELATED STUDIES: Genetic view:
Horn (1983) reported on the Texas Adoption Study which looked at about 300 families with adopted children. The biological mothers had all given the children up within one week of

birth. The children at age 8 had a correlation of 0.25 with their biological mother (genetic link) and 0.15 with their adopted mother (environmental link).

Plomin (1988) reported on the same children at age 10. They had a correlation of 0.02 with their adoptive siblings. This suggests that ultimately the environment has very little influence.

RELATED STUDIES: Environmental view:

Schiff *et al.* (1978) found that children born to low SES parents and were subsequently adopted by high SES families, showed significant IQ gains when compared with siblings who had remained at home. Their improved environment did affect their IQ.

Skeels and Dye (1939) followed children in an orphanage where they were deprived of stimulation, unlike most adopted children. Those children who remained in the orphanage showed large decreases in IQ compared to those moved to another orphanage where older children cared for them. Here the children had more attention and showed IQ gains.

CONCLUSIONS:

1 The evidence supports both sides. Genetic factors are more important but environment *can* have a significant contribution.
2 Adoptions are often made to similar environments. Any differences tend to be in a positive direction. Adoptive families are generally smaller, wealthier and better educated than natural families. Both these factors would cause environmental factors to appear stronger.
3 Early adopted children do better, favouring the idea that environment is important under suitable circumstances.

The environmentalist view of intelligence

1 Social class. There are many factors which are positively associated with social class and negatively associated with intelligence. They are all environmental:
- Poor nutrition.
- Lack of mental stimulation.
- Large family size.
- Poor parental education.
- Lack of frequent and sensitive parent-child interactions.

RESEARCH EXAMPLE | **Sameroff *et al.* (1987 and 1993) Rochester longitudinal study**

RESEARCH QUESTION: Is intellectual delay in young children due more to environmental factors than biological ones?

PARTICIPANTS: 215 children were followed from when their mother was pregnant. They were tested aged 4 and 13 years. Their families had a range of socio-economic backgrounds, maternal age groups and number of other siblings. At age 13, 152 families remained in the study.

METHOD: Longitudinal. Ten family risk factors were identified, such as: mental health, education, occupation, family support, stressful life events, family size.

RESULTS:

1 There was a clear negative association between number of risk factors and IQ. At age 4 this correlation was −0.58. At age 13 it was −0.61.
2 At the age of 4, high risk children were 24 times as likely to have IQs below 85 than low risk children. It was calculated that, on average, each risk factor reduced the child's IQ score by 4 points.
3 There was a high correlation between IQ at age 4 and 13 (0.72)

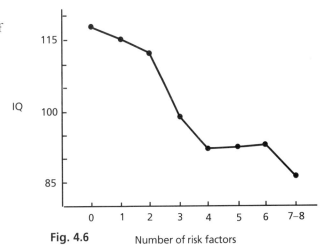

Fig. 4.6   Number of risk factors

INTERPRETATION: This shows that environmental factors can be of great importance. Where a child is not exposed to risk factors, genetic factors will be important in determining intelligence. When there are risk factors, these will be of more importance than the inherited ones.

EVALUATION:

1 There are so many interrelated factors, it is not clear whether social class or specific parental behaviours are more important.

2 It is possible that low socio-economic parents are biologically less intelligent, those with more intelligence become better educated and are able to have higher living standards.

2 Family influence.   Parent–child interactions profoundly affect the development of IQ.
- Parental expectations influence a child's performance (see Unit 8.2).
- Stimulation: studies of deprivation indicate how a *lack* of stimulation leads to IQ deficits (see Unit 8.1).
- Birth order is related to parental attention. Zajonc and Markus (1975) used data from a Dutch longitudinal study of 40,000 males born in 1944 whose IQs were tested at age 19. They found that IQ declines with family size and birth order. They suggest this is because, in larger families, each child has a smaller share of parental attention, less money and more physical deprivation.

3 Special intervention (enrichment) programmes.   Some children may benefit in terms of IQ from educational programmes which supply the stimulation they are lacking in their home environments. If they do, it shows the value of environmental factors.

RESEARCH EXAMPLE | **Operation head start**

BACKGROUND: Pre-school compensatory intervention programmes first appeared in the US in the 1960s. It was reasoned that disadvantaged children failed at school because they lacked the initial social and intellectual advantages that middle-class youngsters were presumably getting in their homes. Once this downward spiral has begun, it is self-fulfilling (see Unit 8.2)

AIM: To compensate for early disadvantages so that all children started school on an equal footing. Enrichment should be in terms of physical, social, emotional and cognitive development.

THE PROJECT: The first Head Start programmes ran during the summer of 1965 for 500,000 children at 4,700 centres. The cost came to nearly one billion dollars. The children were given help with pre-school skills and provided with medical checkups. They were taught games and values appropriate for American schools.

INITIAL ASSESSMENT:

1 Initially participants made significant gains in IQ, vocabulary and school readiness, compared with non-participants.

2 These gains were inconsistent and short-lived. Within two years of starting school any differences had disappeared.

LATER ASSESSMENT: Lazar and Darlington (1982) suggested that there was a 'sleeper' effect:
- Intervention programs may not produce long-term gains in IQ but they foster positive attitudes towards achievement and education. In fact, the initial aims of the project were not simply to boost IQ.
- In adolescence, participants were less likely than non-participants to become pregnant, require welfare assistance or to become delinquents. They were more likely to complete high school, to be employed after high school or to enrol in post high school education.
- It is difficult to assess costs and benefits. One estimate suggests that for every $1 spent, $4–$7 are saved in terms of special education placements, welfare, health and policing.

EXPLANATIONS for the failure to increase IQ:
- Jensen (1969) suggested that failure was due to inherited racial differences which were impossible to compensate for. His claims that Black children had inferior IQs were ferociously attacked. One possibility is that disadvantaged children inevitably score less well on White, middle-class tests of intelligence (see 'culture-fairness', at the end of this Unit).
- The Headstart programme may have failed because it was too directed at middle-class values and therefore missed the problem entirely.
- The effects may be too subtle to be detected on a measure such as IQ, or within one generation. Subsequent generations may benefit from the fact that their parents took part.

OTHER ENRICHMENT PROGRAMS
- Home-based interventions have concentrated on parental involvement.
- Project Follow Through continued to help disadvantaged children through their early years at primary school.

- Nursery education: disadvantaged children who are given day care opportunities score higher on IQ tests at the age of five than similar children cared for at home by their mothers.
- Television intervention, such as *Sesame Street* to help pre-reading skills.

A conclusion

1 Is it nature *or* nurture?

Separating nature and nurture

1 If you plant a seed in good soil and provide it with plenty of warmth, sunshine and water, it will thrive. If you plant an identical seed in poor soil and give little attention, it will grow less well.
2 Babies whose mothers smoke or eat a poor diet during pregnancy may not seem to suffer any physical or psychological ill effects. However, a female baby is born with all her eggs already formed and, amazingly enough, *these* may have been affected. Therefore the *grandchildren* of the mother who smoked may be smaller or less intelligent. This is called a **transgenerational link**. What might appear to be a genetic influence could be an environmental one which has skipped a generation.
3 Very rarely an infant is born with **phenylketonuria**, a genetic disorder which means that certain proteins are not metabolised leaving poisonous substances in the blood which will cause brain damage. The solution is simple. The protein, phenylalanine, must be eliminated from the diet and no harm is done. For this reason all newborns are tested for phenylketonuria to enable immediate action and prevent any irreversible brain damage. If the infant's intellect was impaired, has this been caused by nature or nurture?

Nature and nurture are separate in *ideology* but not in practice.

2 How much is intelligence the result of nature or nurture?   If we can't say it's one *or* the other, can we estimate which contributes more?
- Hebb (1949) said it's like asking 'How much of the area of a rectangle is due to width and how much to length?'. Your genes provide your **potential range** but environment determines the extent to which this is realised. For example, we are born with a potential height range. Experiences such as diet affect the extent to which that range is fulfilled. The same is true for intelligence.
- Width × length = area, potential × environment = intelligence.
- **Polygenetic inheritance:** some characteristics, such as eye colour, are determined by one set of genes. Intelligence is the result of many genes interacting (**polygenetic**). This kind of complex interaction would make it impossible to make clear predictions from the actual genes to observable behaviour even if intelligence was *entirely* due to heredity.

3 Does it matter?   All of this means that the nature/nurture debate over intelligence cannot be resolved. People continue to try for political and practical reasons:
- *Enrichment program*s can only be successful if environment makes a significant contribution to intelligence.
- *Educational placement*: if intelligence is largely fixed at birth, then it would be appropriate to test children and educate them according to their ability.
- *Intelligence tests* only make sense if they are testing a fixed ability. If the ability can change, what does the score mean? This has practical consequences.
- *Eugenics* or selective breeding: through human history there have been humane and inhumane attempts to create a super race. This makes sense only if certain desirable characteristics are inherited.

Intelligence tests

YOUR IQ: WHAT IT MEANS

1 Sampling.   IQ is not the same as 'your intelligence'. It is the result of a test which samples some of your intelligent behaviours. The behaviours it actually samples are selected by the test designer and may be biased by their views of what intelligence is.

2 Validation.   All tests are verified or validated by choosing some measure which should be evidence of intelligence. For example, success at school. The test is considered good or valid if people who do well on the test are those who do well at school.

③ <u>Distribution</u>.   Intelligence, like height and shoe size, is normally distributed. In a **normal distribution** most people have scores around the mean and very few people are found at either the top or bottom extreme. In fact we can be even more precise. A test which has an mean of 100 (the traditional mean IQ) and a standard deviation of 15, should have the following distribution:

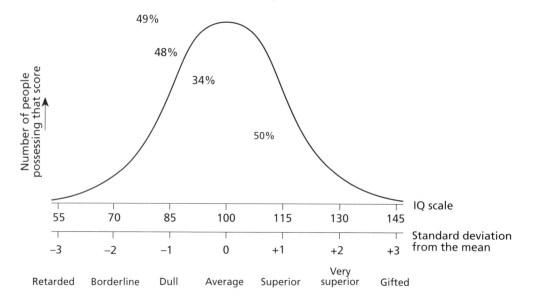

Fig. 4.7 Standard normal distribution for IQ, showing that approximately 68% of the population should have an IQ in the range 85 to 115, and only 16% should have an IQ higher than this. The mean is 100, and standard deviation is 15

HOW IQ TESTS ARE USED

① <u>Educational placement</u>.   To select children for grammar schools, special education or for banding pupils within a school.

② <u>Diagnostics</u>.   Determining whether a person needs special help in certain areas. Such tests are usually not of general intelligence but tests of particular abilities such as reading or mathematics.

③ <u>Job selection</u>.   Employing the right person for the job is an important cost-benefit exercise for any business. Intelligence is a good general predictor of subsequent performance.

LIMITATIONS OF IQ TESTING

① <u>Reliability</u>.   A reliable measuring instrument should give the same result every time it is used. This is true for a ruler, but IQ test performance is affected by many factors. For example, how you are feeling on the day of the test, the temperature of the room you are in or the examiner's behaviour towards you.

② <u>Validity</u>.   To what extent is the score you achieve representative of your actual abilities? Is it true or valid? The result may reflect the fact that you are good at taking IQ tests (practice effect) or that you are fast, but it may not be measuring intelligence.

③ <u>Different kinds of intelligence</u>.   Tests are reasonably good at assessing a person's ability to learn or reason abstractly, but they almost entirely ignore other aspects of intelligence such as divergent thinking.

④ <u>Culture fairness</u>.   A common criticism is that tests are designed by White, middle-class Westerners. This may explain why some races do not score as well as others on IQ tests (see Jensen, earlier in this unit). It is difficult to produce intelligence test items which are culture-fair, in other words items which do not rely on experience. Even nonverbal tests make assumptions about the definition of intelligence which other cultures would disagree with. For example, an Australian Bushman might not agree with the assumptions behind British IQ tests. **Gender bias** is a similar problem.

⑤ <u>The effects of IQ test</u>.   Being given an estimate of your intelligence (your IQ) may act as a self-fulfilling prophecy (see Unit 8.2)

Quick test 4.3

1 What is the difference between *monozygotic* and *dizygotic* twins?
2 Describe **one** problem with using twin studies to measure intelligence. (*MEG, 1994*)
3 Twin studies are **one** way in which psychologists have studied the nature-nurture debate in intelligence. Name a different technique and a study which used this. (*MEG, 1994*)
4 Name **two** factors which are known to affect IQ.
5 Special intervention programmes are developed to help disadvantaged children. Name **one** such programme and describe the results.
6 What does IQ mean and what is the formula used to calculate IQ? (*SEG, 1992*)
7 What is meant by the *validity* of an IQ test?
8 Give **two** reasons why a person's score on an IQ test might not be true. (*SEG, sample Foundation*)
9 Why is it difficult to measure the intelligence of children?
10 If we conclude that intelligence is inherited, then the effect on social policy would be to introduce immigration controls based on IQ scores, and to encourage people with a low IQ not to have children. If, on the other hand, we conclude that intelligence is developed through experience, what effect do you think this would have on social policy? (*MEG, 1992*)

Summary

HEREDITARIAN VIEW	ENVIRONMENTALIST VIEW	A CONCLUSION
1 Twin studies 2 Familial studies 3 Adoption studies	1 Social class 2 Family influence 3 Social intervention programmes (e.g. Headstart)	1 Either/or: nature or nurture? 2 How much of each? 3 Does it matter?

INTELLIGENCE TESTS

WHAT IS IQ?	HOW IQ TESTS ARE USED	LIMITATIONS OF IQ TESTING
1 Sampling 2 Validation 3 Definitions of intelligence 4 Distribution	1 Educational placement 2 Diagnostics 3 Job selection	1 Reliability 2 Validity 3 Different kinds of intelligence 4 Culture fairness

4.4 Theories of cognitive development

CONSERVATION ~ MORE OR LESS?

Piaget worked with Alfred Binet in constructing some of the earliest intelligence tests. He noticed that children of a similar age tended to make the same kind of mistakes. This led him to think that some mental abilities must be dependent on maturation. One of the classic examples of this is conservation (keeping things the same).

To test this Piaget showed a child two equal displays of counters or beakers of water. He asked 'Are they both the same?'. The child answers 'Yes'. Then he transformed one of the displays and asked 'Are they both the same?'. A child over 7 usually recognises that the quantity has not changed and says 'Yes'.

This and other experiments are used as evidence that children's cognitive development proceeds through set, biologically determined stages. A child naturally reaches a particular stage at a particular age.

Some people think that Piaget underestimated what children can do. For example, it might be that younger children are confused by being asked the same question a second time. A second question might mean a second answer. Rose and Blank (1974) asked the question only once, after the transformation, and found that younger children coped better. Younger children also did better if the task made more sense. For example, using a naughty teddy who transformed the displays (McGarrigle and Donaldson, 1974).

However, in all the later experiments there were still age differences, younger children didn't do as well as older children. Piaget's (1926, 1970) main point stands and has had an enormous impact on education and child-rearing.

DEFINITIONS		
	cognitive development	The description and explanation of how mental abilities develop. Theories concentrate on thought, but cognitive development includes language acquisition.
	maturation	A change which is due to age rather than experience. It is an innate and biological process.
	object permanence	Knowing that an object continues to exist even when it out of sight, hearing or touch.
	egocentric	A child's thinking is dominated by its own ideas. It cannot take other people's views into account nor other aspects of the situation.
	conservation	An individual's understanding that quantity is not changed when a display is rearranged or transformed.
	animism	The belief that all living and non-living objects are alive.
	centration	Focusing on the central part of a problem. It is the inability to **decentre**.
	operational thought	A particular kind of logical thinking. Pre-operational thought is also logical, but uses a different and more idiosyncratic set of rules. **Concrete operations** are those where logic can only operate on real concepts. **Formal operational thought** involves abstract logical thinking.
	cognitive structures	Piaget presents a **structuralist** model of the mind. A structure is a framework or organisation of parts. **Variant** structures are those which change. **Invariant** structures are innate.
	schemata (schema)	A plan or an image, like a scheme. A data structure which contains knowledge. Related to the notion of scripts (see Units 4.2 and 5.2).

assimilation	To make something your own. Applying your schemata to data.
accommodation	Change or adjustment. Altering schema to fit new data.
equilibrium	A state of balance.

Piagetian stages of intellectual development

	STAGES	AGE in YEARS (approx)	MODE OF THINKING	CHARACTERISTIC BEHAVIOURS
1	SENSORIMOTOR	0–2	Beginnings of language and symbolic thought, but mainly focused on sensory and motor experiences.	● Reflex activities, e.g. sucking. ● Circular (repetitive) reactions, e.g. kicking. ● Object permanence develops around 9 months.
2	PRE-OPERATIONAL pre-conceptual intuitive	 2–4 4–7	The ability to form and use symbols, as seen in the use of language and numbers. Thought processes are rule based but not using adult logic.	● Animism. ● Egocentric thought. ● Centration. ● Inability to conserve. ● Moral realism (see Unit 9.1).
3	CONCRETE OPERATIONS	7–11	More adult-like but still not abstract or always using adult logic.	● Can now cope with conservation, decentration, class inclusion, understanding numbers reversibility, seriation. ● Problem solving still tends to be random. ● Moral relativity and empathy (see Unit 9.1).
4	FORMAL OPERATIONS	11 onwards	Formal logic and abstract thought.	● Systematic and organised deduction/induction ● Strong idealism. ● Own values, beliefs and philosophies.

Empirical evidence

Piaget's methods involved naturalistic observation and interviews. He used small samples which were often his own children.

1 <u>Object permanence</u>.   Showed an infant a bright, attractive object, then hid it. At 4–5 months they will immediately forget it, by 10–12 months they will look for a completely hidden object. Bower and Wishart (1972) found that younger children had object permanence (see 'Criticisms of Piaget' later in this Unit).

2 <u>Unsystematic nature of thought</u>.   Young children often reason something like: if A has four legs and B has four legs, A must be B. For example, they call all dogs Spot.

3 <u>Egocentrism</u>.   A young child finds it hard to see the perspective of another. In the Three Mountains experiment children between 4 and 12 years were shown a doll placed in various positions around a model of three mountains. In each position, the child is asked what the doll's view would be. The younger children could only work from their own perspective. They selected a picture which showed their own view rather than the doll's. By age 9 they were sure of the doll's perspective. Hughes (1975) found children coped better if the task made sense to them. For example, using a toy policeman and a doll (see 'Criticisms of Piaget' later in this Unit).

4 Centration.   A pre-operational child cannot focus on the whole and the parts at once. If they are given 18 brown beads and 2 white beads (all of which are wooden), and asked 'Are there more brown beads than wooden beads?', the reply is typically that there are more brown beads. McGarrigle *et al.* (1978) found that a more realistic version using cows was easier (see 'Criticisms of Piaget' later in this unit).

5 Conservation tasks.   These are examples of the more general skill of centration. The typical tasks have been described at the beginning of this unit. Many researchers have shown that changes to the method can improve the children's performance on these tasks (see 'Criticisms of Piaget' later in this Unit).

6 Formal operational thinking.   For example, 'Edith is fairer than Susan. Edith is darker than Lily. Who is the darkest?' (from the Stanford-Binet Test). Children find this impossible during the concrete operations stage, unless it is presented in a concrete form, such as using dolls.

   The pendulum task requires deductive reasoning. A person is given some string and a set of weights, and asked to discover what determines the swing of the pendulum. Is it the length, weight, height of release or force of push? Not all 15-year-olds given this task can succeed. It is possible that some people never reach this stage.

The structure of the intellect

Piaget's view of intelligence was that it is **adaptive**. We constantly adapt existing schemas to new situations to advance our understanding and mastery of the world.

1 Variant Cognitive Structures.   Those structures that change as a child gets older:
   - *Schemata*: The child is born with innate schemata which are equivalent to reflex responses, e.g. grasping or sucking schemata. During development, new ones are constantly formed. The content changes but the *structure* remains the same.
   - *Operations*: A higher order mental structure which appears in middle childhood. They involve physical or symbolic manipulations.

2 Invariant Cognitive Structures.   The fundamental processes involved in **adaptation.** The cognitive structures (schemata and operations) are adapted to meet the demands of the environment through the processes of assimilation, accommodation and equilibrium. These processes are present throughout life.
   - *Assimilation*: Taking in new information. A new object or idea is understood in terms of existing schemata which the person already has. The new experience may extend the range of the schemata but not change them. (For example, it has four legs, therefore it is a cow).
   - *Accommodation*: The complementary process. Schemata are changed in order to fit new information. (For example, it has four legs but goes 'baa' instead of 'moo', what shall I call this thing? A sheep.)
   - *Equilibrium*: The driving force. In a new situation the person uses existing schemata (assimilation). If these are inadequate a state of disequilibrium occurs *driving* the person to accommodate the schemata instead, thus ensuring cognitive development.

Criticisms of Piaget

The counter-evidence suggests that children can do more and earlier than Piaget suggested.

1 Age:
   - Object permanence may occur earlier: Bower (1981) showed that infants 5-6 months old showed surprise when an object that had been hidden behind a screen

was no longer there when the screen was lifted. He also demonstrated that babies of 8 weeks tracked an object as it moved behind a screen.

- Formal operations may occur later or not at all: Shayer and Wylam (1978) found that only 30% of 15- and 16-year-olds had achieved formal operations.

2 Appropriateness of the task:
- Some of Piaget's tasks did not make sense. Hughes (1975) found that 3-year-olds could cope with an egocentric task (such as the Three Mountains experiment) if they were asked to hide a doll from a toy policeman. In this case the task was more appropriate.
- Bower and Wishart (1972) suggested that babies don't track an object because of the way it was made to disappear. If a baby is watched after the lights have been turned out (using infra-red cameras) they found that babies continued looking for the objects.
- Frank (1966) tested 4-6-year-olds on the volume conservation task with a screen in front of the beakers so the level was not visible. Almost all the older children coped and half of the 4-year-olds did. When tested without the screen, performance was improved over a pre-test experiment. The children presumably were 'freed' from making judgements based on what they could see.

3 Form of questioning.   Children use contextual cues in deciding how to respond. Like any experimental subject they aim to please and so they respond to demand characteristics and/or experimenter bias. The younger the child, the more suggestive they are.

RESEARCH EXAMPLE **McGarrigle and Donaldson (1974) Conservation accidents: Naughty teddy**

RESEARCH QUESTION: Why can children conserve in some situations and not others? Is it the context?
PARTICIPANTS: Eighty children aged between 4 and 6 years.

METHOD: Experiment. Children were tested on number (using counters) and length (using lengths of string) conservation problems. Before and after each transformation, they were asked 'Are there more here, or more here, or are they both the same number/length?'

Each child was exposed to some trials of each experimental condition, counterbalanced for order effects:
1 Intentional transformation (IT)   The experimenter performs the transformations.
2 Accidental transformation (AT)   Before the transformation the experimenter took a teddy out of a box and said, 'It's a naughty teddy! Oh! Look out, he's going to spoil the game. The teddy then messed up the counters or string'.

RESULTS:
1 In the AT condition 72% of the children conserved, whereas in the IT condition only 34% did.
2 The difference was most marked for children who did the AT condition first.

INTERPRETATION: Traditional methods of assessing egocentrism seriously underestimate a child's ability.

RELATED STUDIES:
Rose and Blank (1974) and Samuel and Bryant (1984)found that asking the question only once, after the transformation, had a significant effect, though there were still age differences.

McGarrigle *et al.* (1978) showed that the class-inclusion (centration) questions do not make sense. Instead of asking the more usual 'Are there more black cows or more cows?', they asked children 'Are there more black cows or more sleeping cows?'. The percentage who answered correctly moved from 25% to 48%.

---

4 Practice.   Children may lack skills simply because they haven't had sufficient experience rather than being immature. For example, Borke (1975) tested preschool children in a situation similar to the Three Mountains. However, she used a familiar character from *Sesame Street* and played with the child first. The children were much more able to cope, suggesting that it is not cognitive immaturity which is limiting their performance.

5 Effects of language.   A key feature of Piaget's view is that thinking develops first and this leads to the ability to use appropriate language. Language is dependent on thought. For example, Furth (1966) has studied deaf children and compiled evidence that many thought processes occur without the benefit of language.

Summary of Piaget's theory

1 <u>Key features of the theory</u>:
  - It is a *biological* approach. Cognitive development is mainly a consequence of *maturation*.
  - It is a *structural* approach. Intelligence consists of innate structures for acquiring and storing knowledge.
  - It is a *cognitive* approach. The emphasis is on cognition, ignoring emotional and social influences.
  - A child's thinking is not merely a less informed version of an adult's but has *qualitative* differences.
  - *Thought shapes language* far more than language shapes thought.

2 <u>Criticisms</u>:
  - *Underestimation* of children's early logical abilities.
  - *Overestimation* of later stages.
  - The influence of *language* and *culture* largely overlooked.
  - Piaget's evidence often lacked *scientific rigour*. The samples were small and open to experimenter bias (using his own children).

3 <u>Support</u>:
  - The most detailed and comprehensive account of cognitive growth that is available.
  - Changed the traditional view of the child as passive and intellectually simpler.
  - Large impact on education, particularly primary schools.
  - Stimulated research, much of it critical.
  - Critics tend to take the model too rigidly. Supporters suggest it should be seen a useful structure for understanding behaviour and generating research.

Application of Piaget's ideas

1 <u>Education</u>:
  - Progression should rely on a child's *readiness*. There is no point teaching cognitive processes unless a child is sufficiently mature.
  - Education should be *child-centred* and *individualised*, directed by a child's readiness.
  - The teacher's role is to ask *questions* rather than to impart knowledge. This helps the process of adaptation. This type of teaching is called **discovery learning.**

2 <u>Parenting</u>.   Good child-rearing practices follow the same advice as for education.

3 <u>Toys</u>.   Toys should be appropriate for the child's level of cognitive development and stage of play.

4 <u>Playgroup practices</u>.   Play is important for social and cognitive development. Stages of play are related cognitive maturity.

TYPE OF PLAY	AGE	ACTIVITIES
Mastery play (sensorimotor)	0–2	Practice and repetition are important for mastering motor and sensory skills. Exploration.
Symbolic play (pre-operational)	2–7	Fantasy and make-believe play allows the child to test schemata and reduce interpersonal conflicts.
Play with rules (concrete operations)	7 onwards	Play becomes more logical, using rules which are progressively less egocentric and more symbolic.

Alternative explanations of cognitive development

BRUNER

1 <u>The main differences</u> between Bruner and Piaget are:
  - *Language*. Bruner suggests that language has a key role in shaping the intellect whereas Piaget felt that the development of the intellect happens anyway, language is a product.

E xaminer's tip

Candidates often overlook applications as a means of evaluating a theory. They are a key route to assessing the validity of any model of development.

- *Social influences*. Cognitive growth occurs not just because of maturation (Piaget's view), but because skills are transmitted from other members of your culture (Bruner's). Language plays an important role.
- *A cognitive description of intelligence*. Bruner is foremost a cognitive rather than developmental psychologist. His is an *information processing approach*, concentrating on how *strategies* for organising information change with age rather than structures.
- *Similar ages and stages*. They both identify key changes around the ages of 2 and 7. For Piaget the change is from sensorimotor to pre-operational to abstract (concrete) thinking. This mirrors Bruner's enactive to iconic to symbolic sequence.

2 The structure of the intellect and developmental stages:
- *Modes of thinking* are 'recurrent themes' which develop sequentially and remain throughout adult life as the three forms of mental representation:

Mode	Age in years (approximate)	Description and function
Enactive	0–1	Thinking is based entirely on physical actions. We learn by doing rather than through internal representation. This mode continues later in many physical activities.
Iconic	1–7	The use of mental images (icons) which may be based on sight, hearing, smell or touch.
Symbolic	7 onwards	Representation of the world through language, and other symbolic systems such as number and music.

- *Thinking* consists of:
- *Categories* (= concepts): Our interactions with the world involve forming categories in order to reduce its complexity and recognise things.
- *Hierarchies*: categories are interrelated and organised into a framework (coding system). This notion of hierarchies enables us to explain how people remember and assimilate knowledge (learn).
- *Knowledge*: is a complex arrangement of categories and coding systems.

3 Evidence.   Support comes from the view that language can affect thinking (see Furth, 1966, above), and the use of categories and hierarchies in thinking (see Units 4.1 and 4.2, for example, Mandler, 1967, and Bruner *et al.*, 1956).

VYGOTSKY

Vygotsky, a Russian, died at the age of 38 from TB. He was born at same time as Piaget but they never met. Piaget only learned of Vygotsky's work when it was translated into English in the 1960s.

1 Essence of his theory.   A complex and far-reaching theory, with three themes :
- *The influence of culture* (i.e. social settings) leads to the development of higher mental functions from the basic, unlearned ones. Social processes shape language, and language makes thought possible.
- *Language* is critical to thought and also regulates behaviour.
- *Zone of Proximal Growth or Development* (ZPD) is the distance between actual and potential capabilities. Development depends on the guidance of more expert peers or adults (expert intervention).

2 Developmental stages:

SPEECH STAGE	AGE	FUNCTION
Social	0–3	Speech controls the behaviour of others, expresses simple thoughts and emotions.
Egocentric	3–7	Speech controls own behaviour but is spoken out loud, a bridge between social and inner speech.
Inner	7 on	Self-talk which directs behaviour and thinking. It is involved in all higher mental functioning, like 'stream of consciousness'.

③ <u>Evidence</u>. Vygotsky (1987) demonstrated the value of instruction in increasing the understanding of 7 and 9 year olds for scientific and everyday concepts. He assumed that the former would be more developed because they would be shaped through direct instruction. The procedure was to give the children sentences ending in 'because …' or 'although' and see if they could finish them appropriately. They did this better for scientific concepts.

Quick test 4.4

1 For each Piagetian stage listed below, give **two** typical behaviours:
   (a) sensorimotor
   (b) concrete operational
   (c) formal operational
2 At what age (approximately) do children develop *object permanence*?
3 What is meant by *egocentricism*?
4 Describe **one** method that Piaget used to test for conservation.
5 According to Piaget, how can adults help a child develop their cognitive skills?
6 Why did Piaget believe that discovery learning was the best way for children to learn? (*SEG, 1991*)
7 What is the difference between:
   (a) *variant* and *invariant* cognitive structures?
   (b) *assimilation* and *accommodation*?
   (c) *concrete* and *formal* thinking?
8 Why did 'naughty teddy' make it more likely that children were able to show conservation?
9 Sue talks to her dolls as though they were alive. She has an imaginary friend. Even at playgroup she talks to her imaginary friend rather than with the other children.
   (a) According to Piaget's theory of intellectual development, what stage of development has Sue reached?
   (b) Name **one** characteristic she is showing which is common at this stage.
   (c) Name and describe **one** other characteristic you would expect her to show. (*SEG, 1994*)
10 Bruner suggested three stages or modes of thinking which continued throughout life. What were they?

Summary

PIAGET

STAGES OF INTELLECTUAL DEVELOPMENT

THE STRUCTURE OF THE INTELLECT

KEY FACTORS

VARIANT COGNITIVE STRCTURES	INVARIANT COGNITIVE STRCTURES

1 Sensorimotor (0–2)
2 Pre-operational (2–7)
3 Concrete operations (7–11)
4 Formal operations (11+)

1 Schema
2 Operations

1 Assimilation
2 Accommodation
3 Equilibrium

1 Biological approach
2 Structural
3 Qualitative differences between adult and child
4 Thought shapes language

Applications: education, parenting, toys, playgroup practices.
Alternative explanations of cognitive development

BRUNER

VYGOTSKY

1 Language
2 Social influences
3 Cognitive
4 Modes of thinking (enactive, iconic, symbolic)
5 Categories and hierarchies

1 Influence of culture
2 Language
3 Zone of proximal growth
4 Speech stages (social, egocentric, inner)

4.5 Language acquisition

WASHOE

Early attempts to teach animals language involved trying to get them to say words. The Gardners reasoned that chimpanzees may not have suitable apparatus for speaking but they do have nimble fingers, so it might be more successful to teach them sign language. They used American Sign Language (ASL or Ameslan). This language is largely iconic (the hand gestures resemble what they represent) but some of it is arbitrary. This *arbitrariness* is a key distinction between language and natural animal communication.

They trained a female chimp, Washoe, from the age of 1 using operant techniques. She was treated like a child and all conversation was held in ASL. By the age of 4 she had 160 signs. She *overgeneralised* and spontaneously combined signs into strings of up to 5 words. She used her language to communicate with the researchers.

Later she went to live with other chimps, where she continues to live. Their accommodation consists of four rooms with five tunnels in a University psychology department. They are given playthings and dressing up clothes. At meal times they feed themselves and can ask for more food. The chimps have been known to sign amongst themselves when no one is present.

The reason behind this research is to see whether language is uniquely human. But many people find it even more fascinating to have the opportunity to communicate with animals. An extraordinary though sad example occurred when one of the researchers had to tell Washoe that her baby, who had been taken away for medical treatment, had died. Washoe thought he was returning with her baby and signed 'baby' enthusiastically. He signed back 'He's dead, he's finished'. And Washoe dropped her head, moved to a corner and stopped signing.

DEFINITIONS		
language	A set of arbitrary conventional symbols through which we convey meaning.
learning theory	A model for explaining how behaviour is changed using the concepts of conditioning and reinforcement (see Unit 3.1).
nativist theory	A model which presupposes that much of behaviour is inherited or biologically determined.
language acquisition device (LAD)	An innate hypothetical brain mechanism which is pre-programmed with the rules of a universal grammar. A set of innate rules. In a sense a 'language organ' though it may not exist as literally as that. Also referred to as **LAS**: language acquisition system.
linguistic universals	Those elements which are common to all languages, such as phonology (vowels, syllables) and syntax (nouns, verbs).
grammar	The rules of language. They enable an infinite number of meanings to be generated from a finite set of sounds (phonemes). This is not the same 'grammar' as children learn at school.

Theories of language acquisition

1. Learning theory: Skinner (1957).   Language is learned through the same processes as all other behaviour. Operant conditioning works through selective reinforcement, shaping and imitation (see Unit 3.1). The key elements are:
   - Echoic responses: a child imitates the sounds made by others and is positively reinforced.

- *Motherese* is a special form of language that adults use when talking to children which helps imitation.
- Children make random sounds (**mands**), such as 'dada'. Adults give the sounds meaning. Initially their expressions may not sound like the actual words, but through *shaping* the sounds become closer and closer to the real thing.
- Children are **positively reinforced** by getting what they want. For example, saying 'cup water'.

Counter-evidence:
- deVilliers and deVilliers (1979) found that mands are not used meaningfully.
- Brown *et al.* (1969) found little evidence that mothers shaped their children's grammar.

Evaluation:
- This account explains how *vocabulary* and *accent* are learned.
- It does not explain *overgeneralisations*.
- It does not explain the *remarkable rate* nor the universal sequence of acquisition.

② Nativist theory: Chomsky (1959).   A child acquires language by hearing words and constructing the necessary rules of syntax (grammar). A child can do this because they have an innate ability to generate grammatical rules and apply these to their native vocabulary. Key elements:
- **Language acquisition device** (LAD or **system**, LAS). A biological system which produces universal linguistic rules.
- **Linguistic universals** are those features of grammar which exist in all languages, such as nouns. These similarities suggest that there are innate rules, a universal grammar.
- **Generativity** of language. Grammatical rules mean that an infinite number of expressions can be generated from a finite set of sounds. This gives language its power.
- Language must be acquired during a **critical period**. This is an ethological concept (see Unit 3.3) applied by Lenneberg (see below) to language. He claimed that a first language must be acquired by puberty or it would be too late.
- **Nature versus nurture**. The vocabulary is learned, the rules of combination are an innate capacity. This capacity is similar to our capacity to walk.

Counter-evidence:
- If animals can use language then the nativist position needs revision (see the next section on animal language). Either animals also have a LAD or grammatical rules can be learned.
- Sachs *et al.* (1981) studied 'Jim', whose deaf and dumb parents wanted him to be able to speak. They exposed him to TV and radio but by three and a half he still could not speak. Later, after three months of speech therapy, he was able to catch up linguistically. This demonstrates that mere exposure to language is insufficient for linguistic development. Social stimulus is vital as well.

Evaluation:
- Chomsky's views, when they were first published, were *revolutionary*. Until then the study of language had been merely a matter of studying vocabulary.
- This account explains *linguistic universals*.
- It explains why virtually all children acquire language at about the same age, in the same sequence and with *relative ease*.
- Children reared in *social isolation* don't develop language on their own, therefore exposure and innate potential are vital but not sufficient factors.
- Any account of language acquisition must involve *learning* the vocabulary and grammar, plus the **pragmatics** of language: the rules of how to conduct conversations.

Sensitive periods in language acquisition

Lenneberg (1967) proposed that there is a specific biological (and innate) mechanism for language acquisition. Such innate mechanisms appear to degenerate if not used by a particular age (see Unit 2.3). Language can't be acquired before the infant has sufficient motor control of its speech organs. The notion of a critical or sensitive period comes from embryology and ethology (see Unit 3.3).

RESEARCH EXAMPLE | **Curtiss (1977) Genie: A psycholinguistic study of a modern-day 'wild child'**

RESEARCH QUESTION: If a child of 13 has had little experience of language, are they still able to acquire language or are they past the **critical age**?

PARTICIPANT: In 1970, a girl of 13 appeared in a Los Angeles welfare office accompanied by her nearly blind mother. Genie had been kept locked in a room. She looked like a child of 6, was incontinent, could not chew solid food or focus beyond 12 feet (3.6m). She spat indiscriminately. She had a ring of hard callous on her buttocks. She had little language, could comprehend about 20 words and said 'stop it', 'no more' and some shorter negatives. Her father had kept her locked in a room. By day she sat on a potty seat, tied in with a harness. By night, if he remembered, she was moved to a cot covered with wire mesh and tied into a sleeping bag.

Neither parent was prosecuted for child abuse. Her father shot himself within a week of Genie's discovery. Her mother claimed she herself had been abused by the father.

METHOD: Case history. Genie presented the ideal opportunity to test the critical period hypothesis. Curtiss followed her over the next 7 years, recording a vast amount of data about her developing speech. At first her linguistic development was promising. She behaved like a young child, pointing to objects to find out their names. She was taught sign language to help her overcome her speech difficulties.

RESULTS: She developed a reasonable vocabulary and could communicate what she wanted or what she was thinking. However her sentences lacked grammar. For example, 'apple sauce by store' meant 'we need to buy more apple sauce at the store'. She should have said 'buy apple sauce store'.

INTERPRETATION: Genie's linguistic progress is evidence both for and against the critical period hypothesis:
1 She did acquire language. She could produce novel sentences and was able to learn without direct instruction.
2 Her language never developed to the point where it could be called 'normal'. It lacked grammar.

EVALUATION: Features of Genie's life history mean that any findings are hard to interpret:
1 She suffered more than linguistic deprivation. The permanent damage due to emotional deprivation may have prevented her ever recovering entirely.
2 Her father was convinced that she was retarded. He kept her locked up to protect her from being exploited by others. If she was retarded this would explain her lack of progress.
3 Her mother later claimed that she *had* been exposed to language.
4 Retrospective data, such as mentioned in (2) and (3), are unreliable and can never be validated.
5 The ethics of this case study should be considered (see beginning of Chapter 11).

RELATED STUDIES:
1 Other children who suffered deprivation for no more than their first six years appear to recover almost completely. This includes and P.M. and J.M. (Koluchova, 1972), Isabelle (Mason, 1942) and a brother and sister (Fujinaga *et al.*, 1990).
2 Singleton and Newport (1993) studied a deaf boy, 'Simon' and his deaf parents. The parents had both learned sign language after the critical age of 15, and they were never able to use grammar. Simon learned sign language from infancy entirely from his parents' defective version. Simon learned to use sign language *grammatically*. Presumably his innate grammatical rules were able to act on the flawed linguistic input to produce grammatical language.
3 Newport (1990) studied Korean and Chinese-born students who had emigrated to America. Those who had arrived before the age of 7 performed identically to American-born students in terms of their grammatical ability. Those who arrived between the ages of 8 and 15 performed increasingly poorly.

CONCLUSION: The *grammatical* aspects of language are biologically-determined. The areas of the brain responsible for rule-driven language will degenerate if not used by puberty. However, the ability to learn words is present throughout life and is also an ability found in animals (see 'Animal Language' below). Therefore there *is* a sensitive period for language acquisition. *Language* is both innate and learned whereas *grammar* is innate and unique to humans.

POSTSCRIPT: Genie's story had a sorry ending. She was fostered in a number of homes over the years. In one home she was abused which resulted in trauma and the end of any speech.

Examiner's tip

When you are asked to describe a study, remember that marks are awarded for accuracy and detail.

Speech landmarks in language acquisition

There seems to be a universal sequence of language acquisition, regardless of culture, cognitive ability or training. Both maturation and experience have a role to play.

PHASE	BEHAVIOUR
Pre-linguistic. 0–12 months	Until around 6 months the nervous system and oral cavity are not sufficiently developed to form or distinguish different sounds. • *Cooing* and *crying*, verbal behaviours which are not linguistic. • *Turn-taking* (2 months): nonverbal conversation. • *Babbling* (6–9 months): producing phonemes (ma, pa). These are the same in all languages and even in deaf children. By 9 months phonemes are restricted to those of the native tongue and deaf children have stopped babbling. • *Echolalia* (11–12 months): the baby echoes itself, phoneme expansion (mamamama). • *Gestures*, a kind of pre-language which uses a grammar.
One word utterances. 12–18 months	The word infant comes from the Latin *infas* meaning 'without speech'. The onset of speech is the end of infancy. • *First words* are often invented. A word is when a sound is consistently matched with meaning. • *Holophrases* are words which convey complex messages. For example, 'milk' may mean 'I want more milk' or 'I spilled my milk'. Adults often amplify the meaning for the child. • *Understanding* is always more advanced than production. • *Vocabulary* is typically 10 words by 15 months, 4 months later it is 50 words and 200 words by the age of 2.
First sentences. Around 2 years	Stage 1 grammar • *Two word utterances* and *telegraphic speech*: only key words are used but they are combined with rules (grammar) to convey meaning. • *Pivot grammar*: key or pivot words appear repeatedly and in the same position. For example, 'see' is always first and 'it' last. Stage 2 grammar • *Overgeneralising*: applying a grammatical rule wrongly. For example 'sheeps' rather than 'sheep'. • *Overextension*: using 'daddy' as a word for all men. • *Pragmatics*: by the age of 2 children use many nonverbal signals, such as raising the head to signal the start of conversation.
Later speech.	• *Overmarking and redundancy*: for example, 'the girl pushed the dog and then the boy he repushed the boy once more'. • *Metalanguage*: listening to and creating rhymes and songs, enjoying jokes based on language. For example, 'Why did the man tiptoe past the medicine cabinet? Because he didn't want to wake the sleeping pills'.

Animal language

Language is different from communication. Hockett (1958) suggested some 'design features' of language, including:
• It is a precise and specialised system.
• The units may be arbitrary. They do not directly represent the thing they stand for.
• The vocabulary is learned not inherited.
• Meaning is communicated by order (a grammar).
• The system allows users to produce their own novel utterances.
There have been many attempts to teach language to animals, for example:
1 Kellogg and Kellogg (1933) raised a chimpanzee called *Gua* who learned to recognise about 95 words and phrases, but was unable to speak.
2 Gardner and Gardner (1969) see beginning of this unit.
3 Patterson and Linden (1981) taught *Koko*, a gorilla, ASL. After 7 years he knew almost all 700 signs and could understand many spoken equivalents. He used grammar and produced some novel sentences (his own form of swearing was: 'you big dirty toilet').
4 Terrace (1979) worked with a chimp called *Nim Chimpsky* (after Noam Chomsky,

mentioned earlier in this unit). Nim never reached Washoe's level but this may because he was deprived of important social stimulation.

5 Premack (1971) taught *Sarah* a language based on small plastic arbitrary symbols placed on a magnetic board. These were called **lexigrams**. The system places less strain on memory.

6 Fouts (1973) continued work with Washoe to see if she would teach ASL to an adopted son, *Loulis*. Loulis did learn a limited vocabulary despite no human intervention.

7 Savage-Rumbaugh (1991) has perhaps made the greatest progress with two chimpanzees, *Kanzi* and *Panbanisha*. She used lexigrams and conversed with the chimps constantly, in the same way that children are taught. The results were a rich use of language: 90% accuracy in being able to identify pictures, novel combinations of words and introduction of new rules.

8 Pepperberg (1983) has taught her parrot *Alex* to name 40 objects. He can answer questions such as 'What shape?' suggesting an understanding of abstract categories.

9 Herman *et al.* (1990) have worked with dolphins. Schusterman and Gisiner (1988) taught sea lions a series of commands, testing their comprehension.

ETHICS

- Any research involving animals must be closely considered. What right have we to interfere in their lives in this way? Do the ends justify the means?
- Any animal used in such research is the researchers' responsibility for life. In the case of language research, these animals have been introduced to a new way of life.

CONCLUSION

- It is clear that animals can be taught to communicate. Are they using language?
- Animals never get beyond a limited form.
- They never achieve a consistent grammar, the thing which humans appear to have innately.
- They never do it without extensive training, unlike the speed and ease with which humans acquire language.

Quick test 4.5

1 Suggest **one** reason why continually correcting children's language mistakes does not always improve the child's use of language. (*MEG, sample Higher*)

2 How might human parents affect the ways in which their children learn language? (*SEG, 1990*)

3 Which theorist suggested that humans have an innate ability to acquire language?

4 Give an example of a *linguistic universal*.

5 What is: (a) *grammar* (according to psychologists)? (b) *telegraphic speech*? (c) a *critical period*?

6 Is there a critical period for learning language?

7 Outline the main stages of language development.

8 How do *overgeneralisations* show that a child is using grammar?

9 Why are psychologists interested in whether animals can learn language?

10 Give **one** criticism which has been made about studies that try to teach language to chimpanzees. Explain why you agree or disagree with the criticism you give. (*SEG, 1990*)

Summary

LEARNING THEORY (SKINNER)	NATIVIST THEORY (CHOMSKY)	SPEECH LANDMARKS	ANIMAL LANGUAGE
1 Echoic responses	1 LAD	1 Pre-linguistic (0–1)	1 Do trained animals do more than communicate?
2 Motherese	2 Linguistic universals	2 One word utterances (1–1½)	2 Animals learn a limited form.
3 Mands reinforced	3 Critical period	3 First sentences (about 2), grammar	3 Extensive training is necessary.
4 Positive reinforcement	4 Explains ease of acquisition and overgeneralisations	4 Later speech	4 They never achieve consistent grammar.
5 Shaping			
6 Explains vocabulary but not grammar			

Chapter 5
Social cognition

EVERY PHOTOGRAPH TELLS A STORY

What would you do if you found a stamped self-addressed envelope in a phone box? Inside the envelope is a college application form, filled in, and a photograph of the applicant. According to psychological research the photograph will probably significantly influence what you do. Benson *et al.* (1976) placed such forms in public phone booths at a busy city airport. The applicant's photograph was varied in terms of race, gender and physical attractiveness; 604 White adults used the phone.

The results were:

Variable	Attractiveness		Race		Gender	
	Attractive	Unattractive	Whites	Blacks	Males	Females
% who received help★	47%	35%	45%	37%	42%	40%
Significance	Significant		Significant		Not significant	

★ Measured in terms of the number of forms which were returned.

Physical attractiveness and, to a lesser extent, race, significantly affected the participants' helping behaviour. Why? Personal characteristics are related to stereotypes. We believe that people who are attractive are also good, kind, happy, genuine, friendly and so on. In other words, that they are more likely to possess socially desirable characteristics. We are more likely to help such people. The opposite is true for unattractive persons. This is called the **halo effect**.

The key points about these stereotypes are:
1 They are based on a small piece of information (the photograph).
2 They are often inaccurate (an attractive or White person is not necessarily 'better' or more deserving of help).
3 They lead to prejudice and discriminatory behaviour (in this case helping or not).
4 It may be possible to change them.

Each of these points is related to a unit in this chapter: (1) impression formation, (2) stereotypes, (3) prejudice, (4) the reduction of prejudice.

5.1 Impression formation

WHAT SORT OF PERSON IS JIM?

Jim left the house to get some stationery. He walked out into the sun-filled street with two of his friends, basking in the sun as he walked. Jim entered the stationery store which was full of people. Jim talked with an acquaintance while he waited for a clerk to catch his eye. On his way out, he stopped to chat with a school friend who was just coming into the store. Leaving the store, he walked toward school. On his way he met the girl to whom he had been introduced the night before. They talked for a short while, and then Jim left for school.

Luchins (1957) asked participants to answer some questions about Jim. For example:

1 'Do you like him?'
2 'Jim was waiting for his turn in the barber shop. The barber overlooked him to call on another customer who had just come in. What did Jim do?'
3 'Is he shy?'

Participants described Jim as an extrovert type: sociable, popular, likeable, happy, athletic and he would protest if the barber overlooked him.

Other participants were given a different paragraph about Jim, which contained more negative words and pictured him more as a loner. This time participants pictured him as an introvert: shy, quiet, unfriendly, unpopular, thin, weak and someone who would not protest to the barber.

This is an example of **impression formation**. Participants form an impression of Jim's personality on the basis of what information they have. This is not as unreasonable as it may sound. When you first meet someone, you only have a glimpse of their characteristics but you need to build an image of this person for future reference: 'Do I trust him?', 'Would I like to see her again?', 'Will I avoid him next time?'. Impressions are a precondition of social life. When you get to know the person better, you might revise this impression, though a bad first impression may prevent that happening.

Some participants were presented with both versions of the 'Jim' account merged together but in different orders. There was a strong primacy effect, first impressions count. If, however, a time interval is allowed between reading both versions, a recency effect was shown ('you're only as good as your last book').

DEFINITIONS		
social perception		Any aspect of perception with a social element. A similar process to physical perception, influenced by expectations. In the case of physical perception there is a physical reality to test against.
person perception		The study of how we perceive other people.
impression formation		A necessary social process where a limited amount of information leads to the perception of a whole, rounded personality. This impression allows us to make inferences about unknown aspects of the personality.
infer		To make a logical judgement based on a sample of evidence. This implies going *beyond* the facts.
halo effect		The tendency for the impression you form to be influenced by one outstanding trait so that it is assumed that all other traits possessed by the individual are equally positive or negative.
primacy effect		The tendency for first received information to dominate subsequent impressions.
recency effect		The dominance of last received information.
central traits		Traits which are seen as more fundamental and which have greater influence over impression formation than peripheral traits. For example, intelligence or warmth.
nonverbal signals		Non-linguistic behaviour. It can be vocal, such a cry. Nonverbal communication (NVC) tends to deal with emotional information.
implicit personality theory		Psychologists develop *explicit* personality theories. Implicit theories are those intuitive notions that each of us has about what personality characteristics tend to go together.
schema		A structured cluster of concepts (see Units 4.2 and 4.4).
scripts		Plans for actions. Who does what, when, to whom and why. People have different scripts for every common occasion.
filters		Anything which screens out particular stimuli. Social filters filter out particular social information.

Studies of impression formation

Evidence has come from three types of study:
1 Lists of adjectives, for example, Asch, Haire and Grunes.
2 Fuller descriptions, for example, Luchins (see the beginning of this unit).
3 Field experiments, for example, Kelley, Jones *et al.*, Argyle *et al.*

RESEARCH EXAMPLE   **Asch (1946) Forming impressions of personality**

RESEARCH QUESTION: Each person displays a range of different characteristics. These are combined in some manner to form a single impression of that individual's personality. Are there lawful principles which govern the way that impressions are formed? Are the characteristics simply added up or are some given more weight than others?

PARTICIPANTS: Over 1,000 university students.

METHOD: Experiment. Participants are read a list of characteristics that belong to a particular person. For example:

energetic – assured – talkative – cold – ironical – inquisitive – persuasive

They are asked to form an impression of the kind of person the characteristics describe. Later they are asked:
1 To write a brief characterisation of the person in a few sentences.
2 They are shown a list of 18 pairs of opposites. They are asked to select one adjective from each pair which they believe best fits the person.
In all there were 10 separate experiments, a few are reported here.

❶ Making inferences

RESEARCH QUESTION: Do people go beyond the bare facts they are given to infer other characteristics?

METHOD: As above.

RESULTS: A typical response was 'He is the type of person you meet all too often: sure of himself, talks too much, always trying to bring you round to his way of thinking, and with not much feeling for the other fellow. He would tend to be an opportunist. Likely to succeed in the things he intends to do. He has perhaps married a woman who would help him in this purpose.'

INTERPRETATION: Participants go beyond the initial bare terms and integrate them into a rounded, meaningful whole. They automatically make inferences about traits which are not included in the original information.

❷ Central traits

RESEARCH QUESTION: Do certain *central* traits carry more weight in impression formation than *peripheral* traits?

METHOD: Experiment. The list of characteristics given to the two experimental groups: (The words 'warm' and 'cold' were not given in italics)
Group A: intelligent – skilful – industrious – *warm* – determined – practical – cautious
Group B: intelligent – skilful – industrious – *cold* – determined – practical – cautious

RESULTS:
1 Group A judged the person to be also generous, wise, happy, good-natured, humorous, sociable, popular, humane, altruistic and imaginative.
2 Group B selected the opposite traits, in other words, the socially-undesirable traits.
3 If *polite* and *blunt* were used instead of warm/cold, there were no significant differences between group A and B.

INTERPRETATION:
1 A change of a single word can alter the entire impression formed. These are central traits.
2 Central traits create a halo effect.
3 Not all words have this power.

❸ Primacy and recency

RESEARCH QUESTION: Do two identical sets of characteristics produce the same impression, despite changes in the order of presentation?

METHOD: Experiment. The list of characteristics given to the two experimental groups:
Group A: intelligent – industrious – impulsive – critical – stubborn – envious
Group B: envious – stubborn – critical – impulsive – industrious – intelligent (reversed)

RESULTS:
1 Group A perceived their target as an able person who possesses certain shortcomings.
2 Group B judged their person as a 'problem' whose abilities are hampered by serious difficulties.

INTERPRETATION: Order affects person perception. Initial traits have greater weight than subsequent ones (primacy rather than recency).

④ **Consistency**

RESEARCH QUESTION: How do the mutual relationships among traits affect the impression formed?

METHOD: Experiment. The list of characteristics given to the two experimental groups:
Group A: kind – wise – honest – *calm* – *strong*
Group B: cruel – shrewd – unscrupulous – *calm* – *strong*

RESULTS:
1 Group A: participants selected traits such as soothing, peaceful, gentle.
2 Group B: participants chose traits such as deliberate, silent, impassive. In other words a 'grimmer' side of 'calm'.

INTERPRETATION:
1 People try to maintain consistency within an impression.
2 Prior expectancies affect the way the same characteristics might be interpreted.

EVALUATION: This effect only occurs when subsequent words in the list can be interpreted in various ways. In other words, the words are ambiguous.

OVERALL EVALUATION:
1 These experiments lacked realism. Ordinarily information does not come in such neat chunks. Observations of real people might involve other processes.
2 The stimulus list consists of two kinds of characteristics: intellectual traits (intelligent, skilful, industrious, etc.) and social traits (warm or cold). Participants then selected traits from an adjective checklist, containing mainly social traits. It is not surprising that such traits are affected by warm/cold.

RELATED STUDIES:
Kelley (1950) demonstrated the importance of *warm* versus *cold* in a field study involving an introductory psychology class and a new instructor. Each student was given a written description of their new teacher, the only difference being the words *warm* or *cold*. After the lecture they were asked to evaluate the teacher. Those participants given the word *warm* rated the instructor as more considerate, informal, sociable, popular, humorous, humane and better natured. Participants given the word *cold* gave the opposite ratings.

Haire and Grunes (1950) gave participants a description of a typical worker: 'He works in a factory, reads a newspaper, goes to movies, average height, cracks jokes, intelligent, strong, active'. Some participants did not have the inconsistent word *intelligent* included in their list. When the participants were asked to describe the worker those without the inconsistent data presented very uniform descriptions of a 'typical American Joe'. The other participants had to make some adjustment in order to integrate the word *intelligent* into their overall picture of a factory worker. They did this by either denying the information or changing it in some way. This shows that people try to maintain their stereotypes and a sense of consistency.

Argyle *et al.* (1972) tested a different kind of inconsistency effect. How do people treat a message that is delivered with contradictory verbal and nonverbal signals? For example, an experimenter who greets a participant by saying 'I enjoy meeting participants who take part in these experiments and find I usually get on well with them' spoken in a harsh voice, with a frown and tense posture. They found that nonverbal signals carry greater weight. This is probably because we are less able to control our nonverbal behaviour (see 'Nonverbal Leakage', Unit 10.1).

Jones *et al.* (1968) tested the primacy effect in another field experiment. Students completed and marked a test alongside a confederate who either had ascending success (15 correct answers, mostly towards the end of the test) or descending success (15 correct answers, mostly towards the beginning of the test). Participants rated the descending group best and the ascending group worst, in terms of performance and intelligence.

Pennington (1982) conducted a mock trial, giving participants a summary of a rape trial. If the prosecution evidence was given before the defence the participants were more likely to give a guilty verdict than the other way around. This is evidence supporting the primacy effect.

APPLICATIONS: In real-life trials the defence always goes last, both in giving evidence and summing up. Psychological research suggests this is not in the best interests of the defendant.

Evaluation of studies of impression formation

To what extent do these studies illustrate real-life processes?

① <u>Demand characteristics.</u>   The way the experiments were set up, participants had little choice but to respond in the way they did. The participants' behaviour may be more a reflection of the experiment than reality. However, they could have said, 'How am I to know?' The fact that they didn't may be because people are used to making such snap judgements or it may be because people do what they are asked to do, particularly by a figure of authority (the experimenter).

② Limited information.   The experiments rely on the use of very limited, superficial information. In a job interview this may well be the case, impressions are formed on the basis of appearance, dress, race, accent and so on. In this sense, the experiments reflect reality.

③ Acting on such behaviour.   People may form impressions, but how much do they rely on them? The experiment on helping behaviour (see Unit 7.2) suggests that these impressions do form the basis of interpersonal *behaviour*. So these experiments illustrate the beginning of the process of prejudiced behaviour.

Sources of bias in impression formation

The research by Asch and others supports the idea that personality traits are not simply added up, but that some are given more 'weight' than others. What factors lead to such bias?

① Centrality: central and peripheral traits.   Characteristics such as warm, cold, murderous or intelligent have greater weight than others such as polite and blunt. Central traits lead to a halo effect. See Asch, Kelley.

② Order effects: primacy and recency.   The primacy effect seems to be stronger than recency effect. This may be because:
  ● It sets up expectations which influence the perception of subsequent data.
  ● Subsequent inconsistent data may be ignored.
  See Luchins, Asch, Jones *et al.*

③ Type of communication: nonverbal and verbal cues.   Nonverbal cues are given greater weight than verbal ones. See Argyle *et al.*

④ Consistency.   Inconsistent data may be ignored. This is because people want the impression they form to make sense. They may find 'excuses' to explain such inconsistent data and give it less weight in the overall impression. See Asch, Haire and Grunes.

⑤ Individual differences:
  ● Women tend to use different cues from men. See Abbey (below).
  ● The traits you possess influence the way you perceive or weight the same or different characteristics in others.

Models of impression formation

IMPLICIT PERSONALITY THEORY
A personality theory (explicit or implicit) is a model based on consistency. We expect that people possess a cluster of associated traits. Once we perceive some information about a person, the model will generate expectations about other traits which are likely to co-occur. Ideally, the model should be modified when we find these expectations are wrong, but we know that many factors prevent us changing our impression once it is formed. Concepts which are related to implicit personality theory:
● A stereotype also provides an overall picture from limited data.
● The halo effect is the process of generating beliefs based on one trait or general evaluation.

SCHEMA AND FILTERS
Schema and filters explain how we understand and select information using existing concepts or expectations (see Units 4.2 and 4.4). This is an cognitive-informational or information processing model of impression formation.
● Schema are built up from past experiences of others' personalities (e.g. stereotypes).
● Schema provide a framework for organising information (e.g. implicit personality theories).
● Schema generate future expectations about personality. These expectations focus our attention on certain traits, thus filtering out other information and simplifying our social perceptions.
● Schema and filters bias the information we perceive. This is both a help and a

hindrance. It makes some aspects of social cognition more efficient but it means that people fail to see some unique qualities of individuals (see Cohen, below).

❶ Personal filters are individual stereotypes or characteristics which determine what information is selected for processing:
- Personal traits: the fact that you possess a particular trait will influence your attention to such traits in others.
- Expectations (schema or scripts): subsequent data is affected by prior expectations, we perceive information in a way that fits existing expectations.
- Attention: those things which attract our attention are not filtered out.
- Learned stereotypes.

RESEARCH EXAMPLE | **Cohen (1981) Social perception**

RESEARCH QUESTION: How do stereotypes affect what information we perceive and remember? Do we seek to confirm existing expectations (confirmatory bias)?

PARTICIPANTS: 56 undergraduates.

METHOD: Experiment. Participants were shown a 15-minute videotape of a woman and her husband having dinner and having a birthday celebration. Half were told that the woman worked as a waitress and the other half were told that she worked as a librarian. Half were told this information before, and half after watching the videotape.

Certain behaviours were included in the video which were consistent with a waitress stereotype and inconsistent with a librarian stereotype, and vice versa.

Afterwards all participants were asked to recall features about the woman's appearance and behaviour, using a personality trait questionnaire and a set of forced-choice questions about specific events in the videotape.

RESULTS: Participants remembered consistent information more than inconsistent data.
Memory accuracy:

Prototype features	Timing of occupational information (per cent of accuracy)	
	Before videotape	After the videotape
Consistent	74%	68%
Inconsistent	66%	57%

INTERPRETATION: This shows that schema bias the information we perceive, filtering the information we store for later use and confirming existing beliefs. Schema also improve memory, as shown by the fact that participants remembered consistent data. Therefore filters have both positive and negative effects.

RELATED STUDIES: Abbey (1982) arranged for a man and woman to talk for five minutes, observed by a hidden man and woman. The men, whether watching or conversing, rated the woman as more seductive than the women did the men. The men also were more sexually attracted to the opposite-sex actor than the females were. These results were interpreted as evidence that men are more likely to perceive the world in sexual terms. In other words, their schema organise and filter information along sexually oriented lines.

---

❷ External filters. External sources of information act as **gatekeepers**, controlling the flow of information and selecting what should be transmitted. For example:
- *Teachers* select and control the information presented to their classes.
- The *media* (books, films, TV) influence stereotypes which then act as filters. For relevant research, see Units 3.2 (observational learning), 7.1 (TV and aggression), and 9.2 (gender stereotypes and the media).
- **Deviance amplification hypothesis** suggests that the media over-report violent crimes thereby altering our perceptions of the frequency of such crimes. They filter information affecting our picture of social reality (see Gerbner and Gross, Unit 7.1).

Applications: making a good impression

The interview. An interview could be for a job, or it could be a consultation with a doctor or a cross-examination by your headmaster relating to some vandalism in school. In all cases the interviewer (I) has or forms an impression of the candidate (C).

- The impression is based on a limited exposure to the personal characteristics of the C.
- This impression will influence subsequent perceptions of the C and subsequent behaviour towards the C.
- Some factors which influence this impression are not be directly relevant to the interview itself. For example, accent, race, dress, appearance, and manners. On the other hand, if you are being interviewed for a job as a receptionist, some of these factors might be directly relevant.
- Some may be outside the C's control (e.g. race). C could deal with this directly.
- First impressions are important (primacy versus recency effects).
- Nonverbal behaviour may be particularly important. For example, a higher level of smiling, direct eye gaze, decisive gestures, and clear speech.
- There is a code of behaviour for every social situation (a script). Cs who fail to recognise this will be judged accordingly.

RESEARCH EXAMPLE   **Leathers (1986) Advice to President Carter on how to make a good impression**

Television debates have become an important feature of American presidential election campaigns. In 1976, then President Ford was running against Jimmy Carter. Most people thought Ford had a serious credibility problem until he 'won' the first television debate. Winning is in terms of the ratings that people gave after the broadcast. Immediately Carter's advisors sought a social psychologist to advise them on what went wrong. Leathers studied tapes of the broadcast and concluded that Ford had used skilful visual cues to convey dominance. He stood at the lectern with his feet apart, used karate-type gestures and fixed his opponent with an unremitting stare. Carter, on the other hand, had his eyes downcast, used few gestures and held a rigid pose. It was clear that Carter had to learn to use more forceful nonverbal signals.

Leather's advice changed Carter's style from submissive and beaten to being Ford's equal in dominance. Carter won the second debate and, ultimately, the election.

Quick test 5.1

1 What is meant by the *halo effect*?
2 List **three** factors which might affect the impression you form of another person.
3 What is the term used to describe the fact that impressions tend to be prejudiced?
4 What is a *nonverbal signal*? Give an example.
5 What is the difference between *implicit* and *explicit* theories of personality?
6 What are *schema*?
7 How does a *gatekeeper* affect your stereotypes and schema?
8 What is *deviance amplification*?
9 Chris has been invited to attend a job interview. She knows that you have studied a psychology course. She has asked you for advice on how to create a good impression. Give **two** suggestions supported by psychological evidence and/or theory. (*NEAB, 1994*)

Summary

STUDIES OF IMPRESSION FORMATION	PROBLEMS WITH SUCH STUDIES	SOURCES OF BIAS IN IMPRESSION FORMATION	EXPLANATIONS OF IMPRESSION FORMATION
1 Asch	1 Demand characteristics	1 Centrality	1 Implicit personality theory
2 Kelley	2 Limited information	2 Order effects	2 Schema and scripts
3 Haire and Grunes	3 Relationship between impressions and actual behaviour	3 Type of message	3 Filters
4 Argyle *et al.*		4 Consistency	
5 Jones *et al.*		5 Individual differences	
6 Pennington			

APPLICATIONS TO REAL LIFE SITUATIONS
1 The interview
2 Making a good impression (Leathers)
3 Judgements of others, such as a lecturer or trial defendant (e.g. Kelley, Jones *et al.*, Pennington)

5.2 Stereotyping and categorising

THEY ALL LOOK THE SAME TO ME

We classify people according to the groups they belong to. This could be in terms of gender, attractiveness, race, age or which football team they follow. For each group we have an impression or stereotype of what its members are like. We tend to perceive members of our own group (the ingroup) as more diverse than members of other groups (outgroups). This can be called the *illusion of outgroup homogeneity*, in other words the false impression that members of an outgroup are all the same.

Linville *et al.* (1989) conducted a number of studies to demonstrate that this occurs. In one study they asked college students and elderly citizens to rate both their own age group and the other group on several traits. For example, the trait of friendliness. They asked each participant to imagine a group of 100 elderly and 100 college students. How many would be very unfriendly, unfriendly, somewhat unfriendly, neutral, somewhat friendly, friendly, and very friendly?

College students evaluate the elderly within a narrow band, whereas they used the entire range to rate students. The elderly perceived college students with less variability and their ingroup as more differentiated.

This process is the result of holding outgroup stereotypes which are less detailed than the ingroup picture. No doubt it occurs because we are more familiar with our ingroup and learn to make finer distinctions. If you rarely encounter a member of the outgroup, your stereotype remains fixed.

The illusion of outgroup homogeneity is therefore an effect of stereotypes. It also contributes to their persistence. People perceive what they expect to perceive. As far as possible, you fit your experiences into pre-existing schemas or stereotypes rather than the other way round. Therefore stereotypes are slow to change.

This aspect of stereotypes is relevant to eyewitness identification. People make more accurate identifications of ingroup members than outgroup members (see Unit 4.1).

DEFINITIONS		
	stereotype	Literally means a solid (*stereo-*) impression (*-type*). For example, a cast metallic plate for printing. As a psychological concept, it is a **cognitive schema** which summarises large amounts of information. It is a social perception of an individual in terms of their group membership or physical characteristics rather than their actual personal attributes. A stereotype tends to be at least partly inaccurate and resistant to change. It can be either positive or negative.
	stereotyping	Using a stereotype to classify people according to a set of pre-established criteria. 'Off-the-peg' impressions.
	categorising	To place in a group where all members of the group can be distinguished in terms of certain attributes from members of another group.
	self-fulfilling prophecy	One person's prediction about another's behaviour comes to be realised *because* of their expectation (see Unit 8.2).

An understanding of stereotypes

xaminer's tip

You must avoid commonsense material and use psychologically informed arguments, when answering questions on this area of the syllabus.

① <u>Why do we have stereotypes?</u>   A cognitive explanation:
  - They are an inevitable part of the process of cognition.
  - We categorise and organise all stimuli to make the social and physical world more manageable. Stereotyping is simply natural category formation.
  - Categorising involves making rules or generalisations. Inevitably rules are applied in some situations where there are exceptions (*overgeneralising*, see Unit 4.5).

2 <u>How do stereotypes develop?</u>   A social learning explanation:
- Indirectly from **gatekeepers**: the media, parents and other adults. For example, gender stereotypes develop partly through seeing men and women portrayed in traditional roles on television (see Unit 9.2).
- Directly through association and reinforcement.

3 <u>Why are stereotypes resistant to change?</u>
- *Confirmatory bias*: We seek out information which supports rather than challenges our beliefs (see Unit 5.1).
- *The self-fulfilling prophecy*: Initial judgements are self-perpetuating. They generate expectations which affect our subsequent perception and the behaviour of others.
- The *illusion of outgroup homogeneity* tends to confirm our existing stereotypes.
- They may contain an *element of truth*.

4 <u>What is the relationship between stereotypes and prejudices?</u>
- Stereotypes are cognitive schema. A prejudice is an *attitude* towards a stereotype. In other words it has an *emotional* component.
- Prejudices draw on stereotypes, but stereotypes do not necessarily lead to prejudice.

RESEARCH EXAMPLE   **Locksley *et al.* (1980) Social categorisation and discriminatory behaviour**

RESEARCH QUESTION: Do people invariably use stereotypes or does the presence of 'individuating' information influence their judgements?

PARTICIPANTS: 130 psychology college students.

METHOD: Experiment.
1 Participants' gender stereotypes were assessed.
2 Participants were given two paragraphs and asked to assess assertiveness, among other things. The paragraphs were:
  A: *Yesterday Tom (or Nancy) went to get his (or her) hair cut. He (or she) had an early morning appointment because he (or she) had classes that day. Since the place where he (or she) gets his (or her) hair cut is near the campus, he (or she) had no trouble getting to class on time.*
  B: *The other day Nancy (or Tom) was in a class in which she (or he) wanted to make several points about the readings being discussed. But another student was dominating the class discussion so thoroughly that she (or he) had to abruptly interrupt this student in order to break into the discussion and express her (or his) own views.*

RESULTS:
1 Gender stereotypes conformed to usual views on male/female assertiveness.
2 When given paragraph A, participants' assessments reflected gender stereotypes. When given paragraph B, which contains individual information, the assessments were the same no matter what sex was given.

INTERPRETATION: The presence of individual information can override stereotyping.

RELATED STUDIES: Bodenhausen (1988) asked participants to assess the guilt of various hypothetical defendants at various stages during a trial. The participants rated defendants with an ethnic last name as more guilty than one with a non-ethnic name. But this only occurred before receiving further information about the case. Participants did not use their stereotypes once they had other information to work with.

---

5 <u>Changing stereotypes.</u>   See Unit 8.2.

6 <u>Advantages of stereotypes:</u>
- They are a necessary part of making sense of the world.

7 <u>Disadvantages of stereotypes:</u>
- They are often inaccurate because they are not based on reality.
- They are often based on superficial characteristics, such as skin colour.
- They do not allow for exceptions. In other words, there is a tendency to overgeneralise.
- They are irrational. Logical argument will not change them.
- They are resistant to change.
- They lead to prejudiced attitudes and discrimination.

8 <u>Stereotypes are not such a problem as long as:</u>
- They don't continue to influence impressions even when other, more relevant information is available.

● They don't become trapped in a cycle: expectations affect behaviour, behaviour confirms expectations.

Factors which arouse stereotypes

Physical attractiveness, race and gender are the three strongest sources of stereotype and prejudice. This is probably because physical features stand out most in initial or superficial encounters.

❶ Physical attractiveness.

RESEARCH EXAMPLE | **Dion *et al.* (1972) What is beautiful is good**

PARTICIPANTS: 60 male and female psychology students. Participants received extra points on their final exam grade.

METHOD: Experiment, deception. The participants were told that the study was about accuracy in person perception. They were shown three photographs: one physically attractive, one average and one relatively unattractive. They were asked to assess the photographs on 32 personality traits and to assess their future happiness in marriage, parenthood, social and professional life. Finally they rated success for 30 different occupations.

RESULTS: On every measure except parenthood, the attractive photograph was rated more highly.

INTERPRETATION: Attractiveness is associated with other socially desirable traits as well as personal and occupational success. This demonstrates a strong positive stereotype for physical attractiveness and is an example of the halo effect in action.

EVALUATION: This stereotype for physically attractive persons may occur because:
1 A calm, relaxed, successful person may develop fewer lines and therefore look more attractive to some people.
2 The self-fulfilling prophecy: if others assume that an attractive person is more sincere, kind, etc., the person may come to believe that and act according to expectation.

RELATED STUDIES:
Stewart (1980) found that attractive defendants received lighter sentences.

Landy and Sigall (1974) gave male college students a set of essays, each with a photograph attached, to be rated in terms of quality. Essays thought to have been written by attractive women were rated more highly overall.

However, attractiveness may sometimes call up a less desirable stereotype. Dermer and Thiel (1975) found that very attractive women were judged as being egotistic, vain, materialistic, snobbish and likely to have unsuccessful marriages.

---

❷ Race and ethnic group.   Similar to nationality. Prejudice based on race is called **racism**.

RESEARCH EXAMPLE | **Katz and Braly (1933) Racial stereotypes of one hundred college students**

PARTICIPANTS: 100 Princeton University students

METHOD: Experiment. Participants were asked to characterise 12 ethnic groups from a list of traits.

RESULTS: There was considerable agreement from people in the 1930s, for example some of the more positive traits were:

Americans	industrious, intelligent, materialistic
English	sportsmanlike, intelligent, conventional
Japanese	intelligent, industrious, progressive

INTERPRETATION: People clearly hold highly racist stereotypes of ethnic groups. They may not *act* on these stereotypes but the fact that there is high agreement demonstrates the *existence* of such stereotypes.

EVALUATION:
1 **Demand characteristics**: participants have no other information and therefore the task 'demands' a response drawn from stereotypes. The participants are asked to describe an ethnic group in terms of a 'typical' member. It is really the same as asking them to write down their stereotype.
2 The results demonstrate attitudes, but does this mean that people *behave* in this way? People may recognise that prejudice is 'wrong' and therefore control their behaviour.

RELATED STUDIES: The study was replicated by two later studies:

Gilbert (1951) found that, thirty years later, students were far less willing to generalise about ethnic groups. Some rejected the task and others qualified their answers by saying they were reporting 'what people think' rather than what they thought. All 10 stereotypes declined in uniformity.

Karlins *et al.* (1969) found that the stereotypes were again as uniform as they had been in 1933. However, the content had changed.

APPLICATION: If we ignore the fact that stereotypes exist, the situation will not change. However, if we accept that people do have some racist stereotypes then the problem can be tackled.

③ Gender. Gender stereotypes and their effects on behaviour are discussed in Unit 9.2. Prejudice based on gender is called **sexism**.

RESEARCH EXAMPLE | **Fidell (1970) Sex discrimination in hiring practices**

RESEARCH QUESTION: Men and women are different. Therefore, it is natural that people hold gender stereotypes. But are women necessarily inferior?

PARTICIPANTS: 228 administrators in psychology departments, involved with hiring new staff.

METHOD: Field experiment. The administrators received 10 profiles of Ph.D students. They were asked for their professional opinion on the likelihood of the person getting a full-time post and at what level. They were also asked to rank the 10 profiles. For example:

Dr. Patrick (or Patricia) Clavel received his (her) doctorate in clinical psychology from Western Reserve University. He (she) is considered both highly intelligent and very serious about his (her) academic goals … He (she) is married.

Some participants received the male version, others received the female version. In all each participant received five male and five female profiles.

RESULTS: The administrators favoured men, who were placed in higher positions and rated more highly overall than women.

INTERPRETATION: People who might have been expected to know better show sexual discrimination in their hiring practices. Such discrimination is based on gender stereotypes.

RELATED STUDIES: Smith and Lloyd (1978), Mischel (1974) (see Unit 9.2).

④ Other sources of bias:
- *Ageism* applies to adolescents (**juvenile ageism**) as well as persons in late adulthood. We picture adolescents as 'troubled' and the over 60s as 'declining in mental ability'.
- *Disability*: People make assumptions, drawn from stereotypes, about the ability of the disabled to control their own lives.
- *Dress* and *appearance* are nonverbal means of communicating a wealth of information about yourself.
- Also: *manners, accent, social class, profession.*

Quick test 5.2

1 Give **one** example of a positive gender stereotype.
2 How could a stereotype be changed? (*NEAB, 1993*)
3 Lynne says she works in a bank. Why do many people assume she is a cashier? (*MEG, 1991*)
4 What is *sexism*?
5 What is **one** advantage of stereotypes?

Summary

FACTORS WHICH AROUSE STEREOTYPES	1 Physical attractiveness (Dion *et al.*) 2 Race and ethnic group (Katz and Braly) 3 Gender (Fidell) 4 Ageism (Linville *et al.*) 5 Disability 6 Dress and appearance 7 Manners, accent, social class, profession

5.3 Prejudice and discrimination

THE ROBBERS' CAVE EXPERIMENT, PART I

What are the conditions which lead to friction between groups of people? Sherif *et al.* (1961) conducted a classic field experiment to show how prejudice forms as a result of ingroup and outgroup behaviour.

He selected 22 White, middle-class, well-adjusted 11-year-old boys to go on a summer camp at Robbers Cave (a Jesse James hideaway). Parents were informed that the aim of the study was to observe co-operative behaviour. The camp counsellors were psychologists. The boys arrived in two separate groups of eleven. They were matched so that each group contained similar boys.

Stage 1, the ingroup develops. For most of the first week, the groups didn't know of the other group's existence. Their activities were aimed at developing a sense of group belonging. They involved co-operation, such as hiking, pitching tents and a treasure hunt. The counsellors observed typical group-defining behaviours. For example, adopting a group name (one was the Rattlers, the other the Eagles), using nicknames and developing group norms. In one group it became the norm to act tough, not complaining about small injuries, and to swear a lot. Each boy was given caps and t-shirts with their group name to increase this sense of group identity.

Stage 2, introducing competition. As soon as the groups were aware of each other, they showed signs of territoriality. For example, being watchful that *they* were not sharing *our* swimming hole. This sense of competition was brought out in the open with a grand tournament.

In a bean pickup game, ingroup preferences were displayed. The game involved an individual picking up as many beans as they could in a set time. The group was shown each competitor's collection, and asked to rate individual performance. They consistently rated their group members higher than the outgroup even though there were always 35 beans.

Hostile, prejudiced behaviour had been created by:

1 *Ethnocentrism*: the boys identified with their ingroup.
2 *Stereotypes*: recognition of in- and outgroups through superficial characteristics.
3 The final ingredient was *competition*. Before this prejudice was only expressed in terms of them and us. Competition brought open hostility.

For **stage 3, resolution** see Unit 5.4.

DEFINITIONS		
prejudice	Literally, a pre-judgement, a bias.	
	• It is an *attitude* held prior to direct experience towards a group or individual simply because he is a member of the group.	
	• It is drawn from a *stereotype*, disregarding individual attributes.	
	• It is usually *extreme* and *hostile*, though it can be positive as in ingroup favouritism.	
	• It also tends to be *inflexible* and *resistant* to logical argument.	
	• It is an integral part of intergroup behaviour.	
attitude	A liking or disliking of an object based on beliefs (cognitions) about that object. It leads to a readiness to behave in a particular way.	
discrimination	Literally means to distinguish between. The *behaviour* arising from a prejudice. The unequal treatment of individuals or groups based on arbitrary characteristics such as race, sex, ethnicity.	
ingroup	Any social group to which you belong. Everything else is **outgroup**.	

ingroup favouritism	A positive bias favouring members of your group.
minority groups	Not necessarily fewer in number, it may help to think of 'psychological' minorities.
ethnocentrism	The belief that one's own group, nation, religion, gender, etc. is superior to all other cultures. This arises through a sense of social identity and ingroup favouritism.
superordinate goal	A goal which is shared by all. It is more important than individual desires.
scapegoat	Any powerless person or group who is given the blame for a problem. Traditionally it was a goat, who was driven into the wilds after a religious leader recited the sins of the community over its head. Its escape symbolically took their problems with it.

Behaviours which arise from prejudice

1 <u>Intergroup conflict</u>.   Conflict is an expression of prejudice, as shown by Sherif. It is also a cause (see the beginning of this unit).

2 <u>Discrimination</u>.   Most of the studies already reported demonstrate discrimination: subjects distinguishing between people on the basis of limited characteristics and *acting* on this in the way they treat the individuals.

RESEARCH EXAMPLE   **Elliott (1977) Discrimination: Are blue or brown eyes better?**

RESEARCH QUESTION: Can the process of discrimination be easily simulated using an arbitrary basis for prejudice?

PARTICIPANTS: A class of third graders.

METHOD: Field experiment, deception. Pupils were told by their class teacher that those with brown eyes (the minority group) were 'better' and more intelligent. The teacher backed this up by treating this group of pupils more favourably, for example seating them at the front and giving them extra privileges. The blue-eyed children were given less play time and had to be last in any queue.

RESULTS: In a short time, the blue-eyed children were performing less well, became depressed and angry. They described themselves in more negative terms. The brown-eyed children's behaviour also changed, they made derogatory statements about the other group and ordered them about.

INTERPRETATION: The teacher's behaviour was discriminatory. The brown-eyed children learned her prejudices and also showed discrimination in their behaviour.

EVALUATION: The fact that this research involved the deliberate manipulation of participants' interpersonal and personal attitudes raises serious ethical questions, particularly as it used children. Oprah Winfrey, the American talk show hostess, conducted a similar 'experiment' with a studio audience, some of whom were most indignant about being manipulated in such a way.
  Elliott, the class teacher, debriefed the children by talking to them about prejudice and the importance of empathy.

RELATED STUDIES: Rosenthal and Jacobsen (1968), see Unit 8.2, showed how expectations of performance can influence subsequent behaviour.

Causes of prejudice

Explanations of prejudiced behaviour can be grouped in several ways.
Theoretical approaches:
- *Psychodynamic*: Frustrations are projected onto outgroups and expressed as hostility.
- *Social learning*: We learn particular prejudices through conditioning and imitation from parents, the media and our culture generally.
- *Cognitive-informational*: Prejudices arise from stereotypes which are cognitive schemas.

Approaches which emphasise different aspects of prejudice:

- *Individual* approach: Emphasises *individual* personality or emotional state.
- *Interpersonal* approach: Emphasises what goes on *within* a social group.
- *Intergroup* approach: Emphasises the relationships *between* groups of people.

Causes of prejudice: the individual approach

1 The prejudiced personality:
  - There may be a type of personality which tends to be prejudiced, for example, the 'authoritarian' personality described below. Eysenck (1954) suggested a 'tough-minded' personality (as opposed to 'tender-minded'). Another view is of open versus closed mindedness.
  - The development of such personalities might be associated with certain child-rearing styles.

RESEARCH EXAMPLE   **Adorno *et al.* (1950) The authoritarian personality**

RESEARCH QUESTION: Are some people more likely to be prejudiced than others? Why?
  This research grew out of a desire to understand the anti-Semitism of the 1930s and was funded by the American Jewish Society.

PARTICIPANTS: The questionnaires were given to a wide range of people: university and school students, nurses, prison inmates, psychiatric patients, union members and so on. In all, about 2,000 people answered who were White, middle-class, non-Jewish, native-born Americans.

METHOD: Questionnaire and interview.
1 *Questionnaire*: The researchers developed several scales. The potentiality for Fascism (F) scale is a measure of authoritarianism. There were also anti-Semitism (A-S), ethnocentrism (E), and Political and Economic Conservative (PEC) scales.
  The F-scale questionnaire was a list of statements, such as:
    Sex crimes, such as rape and attacks on children, deserve more than mere imprisonment, such criminals ought to be publicly whipped.
    Most people don't realise how much of our lives are controlled by plots hatched in secret places.
    Familiarity breeds contempt.
  For each statement participants were asked to indicate slight / moderate / strong support or slight / moderate / strong opposition.
2 *Interview*. To assess how such personalities may have developed, they selected and interviewed 80 of the most prejudiced respondents about their parents' child-rearing styles.

RESULTS:
1 The F-scale showed that certain characteristics were associated with a prejudiced-type personality. Such a person:
  - *Self-concept*: Had a more favourable impression of themselves.
  - *Cognitive style*: Tended to be rigid.
  - *Moral view*: Favoured law and order, and tradition.
  - *Values*: Was more concerned with status and success rather than solidarity.
  - *Personal style*: Was not interested in psychological interpretations.
2 Prejudiced-type people tended to have parents who:
  - Used strict discipline and severe punishment.
  - Expected unquestioning loyalty.
  - Were insensitive to or intolerant of the child's needs.
3 The E-scale found that people who tended to be prejudiced against Jews, were the same towards Negroes and foreigners generally. They placed their national and racial group above others (ethnocentric).

INTERPRETATION:
1 The authoritarian personality finds it hard to cope with *ambiguity*. Therefore they seek simplistic solutions which ignore any inconsistent information. Stereotypes are a simple formula for dealing with ambiguous data about people.
2 People who lack personal insight often have *repressed feelings*. A person with repressed feelings will project these onto scapegoats (see 'The Scapegoat Theory' below).
3 Parents who use *severe discipline* create an insecure adult who respects authority and power (see Unit 9.1). Such individuals conform more readily to group norms (see conformity, below) and may increase their self-esteem through ingroup favouritism (see social identity theory, below).
4 This accounts for both the existence of prejudices and the hostility element often present.

EVALUATION:
1 Biased population.   The study only concerned itself with a particular group of Americans. Therefore the results can't be generalised to all people.

2 Response set.   The F-scale is worded so that agreement leads to authoritarian-type answers. Participants who prefer to agree will be classed as authoritarian.

3 Unreliable data.   The data concerning upbringing came from retrospective questioning and therefore may be inaccurate.

4 Correlation.   The study was correlational and therefore causal inferences are unjustified. Other factors such as little education and low social class could be more plausible explanations.

RELATED STUDIES: Christie and Cook (1958) reviewed 230 similar studies and concluded that there was general support for the existence of an authoritarian-prejudiced type.

② Frustration.   Frustration arises from many situations, including economic ones or overcrowding. This in turn may lead to aggression (see Unit 7.1) which we then project onto other, less powerful, people or objects rather than blame ourselves. This **scapegoat** is usually a socially-determined group.

Freud explained this in terms of **displacement**. When direct action against a frustrator is not possible, it is redirected through the outgroup. This is the same process as ego defence mechanisms – conflicts are repressed and expressed through other channels (see Unit 8.3)

RESEARCH EXAMPLE   **Weatherly (1961) The Scapegoat Theory**

RESEARCH QUESTION: Does frustration increase hostility towards a group of people?

PARTICIPANTS: Non-Jewish male college students.

METHOD: Questionnaire and experiment.
1 Participants filled in an anti-Semitism scale, to assess their prejudice towards Jews.
2 Participants completed another questionnaire. During this, half of the participants (group A) were exposed to some extremely insulting comments.
3 All participants were asked to write short stories about some pictures of men. Two of the men were given Jewish names.

RESULTS:
1 All participants who expressed anti-Semitic tendencies in the first questionnaire, showed more hostility towards Jews in the picture story task than those with no bias.
2 Those participants in group A were even more extreme in their negative attitudes.
3 Both groups showed the same amount of aggression towards the non-Jewish pictures.

INTERPRETATION: Frustration makes existing prejudices worse, in terms of the hostility expressed.

EVALUATION: This does not explain why prejudices occur but it does account for strength of feeling.

RELATED STUDIES: Miller and Bugelski (1948) assessed participants' attitudes towards ethnic minorities. Some participants were then shown a film (no frustration) while others were given a mildly frustrating task. When they re-tested attitudes, those who had experienced frustration showed increases in prejudice, unlike the other participants.

Causes of prejudice: the interpersonal approach

① Stereotypes.   Stereotypes are a means of classifying groups of people and therefore they explain an aspect of interpersonal behaviour. Every stereotype is associated with an attitude or prejudice. This explanation accounts for discrimination but not hostility.

② Conformity: group processes.   People conform to group norms. If one of those norms is that prejudiced behaviour towards certain groups is acceptable, then people will behave in that way. Conformity is an important part of group processes (see Unit 6.1).

RESEARCH EXAMPLE   **Pettigrew (1959) Comparing different cultures**

RESEARCH QUESTION: White Southerners are regarded as more prejudiced against Blacks than are the Whites in the Northern United States. Is this because Southerners are generally more prejudiced personalities or is it an effect of different cultural norms?

PARTICIPANTS: 8 towns were selected, 4 from the south and 4 from the north. White adults were randomly chosen from town directories.

METHOD: Questionnaire. Participants were assessed using an authoritarianism (F) scale, anti-Semitism (A-S) scale and anti-Negro prejudice (N) scale. There were also many 'filler' questions to distract participants.

RESULTS:

1 Levels of prejudice against Negroes were much higher in the south.
2 The number of prejudiced-type personalities was not greater in the south than the north.
3 The White northerners who were most conformist were *least* prejudiced. Conformist White southerners were *most* prejudiced.
4 Women were more anti-Negro in the south than men. The difference in male and female Northerners was not significant.

INTERPRETATION: The same personality type behaves differently depending on the attitude of their culture towards Blacks. Conformists were conforming to their group norms.

RELATED STUDIES:
Bagley and Verma (1979) compared levels of racial discrimination in Britain and Holland. Both countries have similar proportions of Black and White residents but Dutch culture disapproves of prejudice more strongly. They found that levels of prejudice are lower in Holland. This suggests that the cultural norm, disapproving of prejudice, lowers the amount of discrimination.

Causes of prejudice: the intergroup approach

1 Realistic conflict theory. Prejudice stems from direct competition between social groups over scarce and valued resources. For example, unequal distribution of wealth, unemployment or disputes over territory. Pre-existing prejudices are turned into hostilities. The outgroup is a scapegoat for the economic problems. Sherif's study of intergroup conflict (see the beginning of this unit) showed how competition over scarce resources turned ingroup and outgroup attitudes into hostility.

Prejudice may exist but it is not expressed until conflict occurs. Therefore conflict is not a primary cause of prejudice but it is a necessary part of intergroup hostility.

RESEARCH EXAMPLE | **Hovland and Sears (1940) Lynching and economic indices**

RESEARCH QUESTION: Are people motivated to behave aggressively because they are frustrated in their attempts to get what they want?

PARTICIPANTS: Official records from 1882 to 1930, relating to the southern United States.

METHOD: Retrospective observation.

1 The measure of aggression used was the number of lynchings, 4,761 cases; 71% were Negroes. Aggression towards Negroes is a product of prejudice.
2 Level of frustration was assessed using the price of cotton. In times when the price of cotton is low there will be fewer jobs and greater hardship.
3 Frustration was also assessed using a more general index (Ayres' Index) of economic factors, which covers consumption, production, imports, exports, construction and prices.

RESULTS:

1 The number of Negro lynchings was negatively correlated with the price of cotton, −0.70.
2 The number of lynchings was negatively correlated with the Ayres' Index, −0.61.

Examiner's tip

This study illustrates discrimination as well as prejudice. Many studies are concerned with prejudice only. It is important to be able to distinguish between these two concepts.

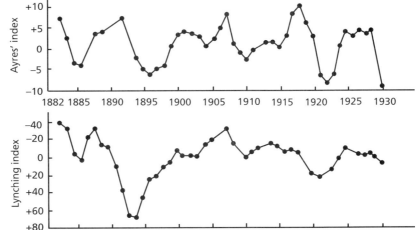

Fig. 5.1 Lynchings increased at times when the Ayres' index was low

INTERPRETATION: When social and economic threats are greatest, prejudice and aggression are more widely expressed.

② Social identity theory: ethnocentrism.   A person's self-image has two components: personal identity and social identity. Social identity is determined by the various social groups to which you belong: your family, school, 'gang', town, football club, race and so on.

- Ingroup favouritism enhances self-esteem by raising social identity.
- A negative bias towards the outgroup achieves the same and further defines the ingroup.
- Stereotypes are used to identify group members.
- Prejudiced and ethnocentric behaviour is rooted in the basic human tendency to categorise things (cognitive), form groups (social) and then favour one's own group over all others (personal).

This account does not fully explain the violence of feeling associated with some prejudices, but it does explain negative and positive prejudices.

RESEARCH EXAMPLE   **Tajfel *et al.* (1971) The minimal group experiment**

RESEARCH QUESTION: Could ingroup behaviour be created even when there is no competition?

PARTICIPANTS: 14–15-year-old schoolboys from Bristol.

METHOD: Experiment, deception.
Task 1: Participants were asked to estimate the number of dots shown on a screen for a fraction of a second. The participants were given false feedback about whether they were over- or under-estimators. It was emphasised that neither was preferable. The boys were divided into two groups according to their supposed initial performance (allocation was in fact, random).
Task 2: Each boy had to sit alone and assess the performance of the others on a task. For each assessment they were only told whether the performer was an over- and under-estimator.

RESULTS: Boys gave higher estimates when the performer was a member of their own group.

INTERPRETATION: Ingroup favouritism occurs even when the group is defined in terms almost nothing (*minimal*). Later experiments by Billig and Tajfel (1973) involved *telling* the participants that group membership was determined randomly. Even then participants showed ingroup favouritism. This suggests that group identity is a very basic tendency.
   The experiment also demonstrates positive discrimination.

EVALUATION: It may be that the results are due to **demand characteristics**. In the absence of any other information, ingroup favouritism had to be produced. But the same may be true of real-life, we often have little other basis for determining our behaviour.

A summary

The various explanations do not individually explain both the existence of prejudice *and* hostility. It is the combination of:

cognitive processes + a pressure factor = hostile behaviour.

The concept of ethnocentrism

Ethnocentrism arises as an inevitable product of group processes and social identity. It leads to:

① The positive side:
- Ingroup pride.
- Group cohesion.

② The negative side:
- Discrimination against outgroups.
- A sense of moral, intellectual and general superiority.
- A conviction that ingroup beliefs are held by everyone (i.e. universal).

EXAMPLE   **Nobles (1976) Psychology and ethnocentrism**

Nineteenth century colonialism was the domination of Third World peoples by Europeans. Nobles argues that Western psychology dominates the world today in a similar way. It is therefore a tool of oppression and domination.
   The most obvious examples are Western views of:
Intelligence: Some psychologists have suggested that Blacks are naturally intellectual inferior to

Whites (see Jensen, Unit 4.3). This judgement is based on assessing intelligence with intelligence tests devised by White, middle-class Americans.

The self-concept: A great deal of psychology is based on the Western view of the self which emphasises individuality, uniqueness, independence, survival of the fittest and control over nature. Nobles claims that Africans have an opposite view. They value co-operation, similarity, survival of the group and oneness with nature. Therefore it is inappropriate to generalise about human nature on the basis of our own culture.

Analysis of real life situations

RESEARCH EXAMPLE **Abeles (1976) Black militancy: Intergroup causes of hostility**

RESEARCH QUESTION: In America in the 1960s, socio-economic conditions were improving for Blacks and the civil rights movement showed that many Whites were on their side. Why, then, were there still so many urban riots?

PARTICIPANTS: 400 Black males and females over 21 living in Cleveland's 'poverty zones', plus 530 Black adults from Miami.

METHOD: Questionnaire. They assessed:

1 Attitudes towards militancy: the rejection of the traditional, subordinate Negro role and demands for greater self-control.
2 Feelings of relative deprivation: the extent to which Black people feel better or worse off *compared* with White counterparts.
3 Feelings of rising expectations: as conditions of life improve, so too do desires. If desires grow faster this leads to dissatisfaction and rebellion.

RESULTS: Respondents who had a militant outlook also tended to feel relatively deprived and had rising expectations.

INTERPRETATION: The sense of dissatisfaction and militancy, despite improved absolute conditions, may be understood by the following:

1 The average family income of Blacks has increased, but it has increased even more for White families. The 'dollar gap' has got larger.
2 Even though some Blacks are doing better, the group as a whole continues to do less well than White counterparts.
3 A new generation of Blacks are being socialised to new racial norms which teach a militant world view.

RELATED STUDIES:

Reicher (1984) analysed the behaviour of a mainly Black crowd in the St. Paul's Riots in Bristol, 1980. He concluded that behaviour which seemed unruly was in fact highly controlled. Aggression was directed only at the police, against whom there were existing negative feelings. A minor event turned a passive attitude into open hostility.

Langford and Ponting (1992) were interested in why Canadians resist attempts to assist their aboriginal population (those people who are native inhabitants of Canada). He found support for Realistic Conflict Theory in that negative attitudes were strongly related to perceived conflict.

Quick test 5.3

1 In Sherif's classic study of prejudice, how did he create an *ingroup*?
2 Give **one** ethical criticism of Sherif's study.
3 What is the difference between *prejudice* and *discrimination*?
4 Give **two** characteristics of an Authoritarian Personality. (*MEG, sample Foundation*)
5 In what way can conformity increase prejudice?

Summary

THE INDIVIDUAL APPROACH	THE INTERPERSONAL APPROACH	THE INTERGROUP APPROACH
1 The prejudiced personality 2 Frustration	1 Stereotypes 2 Conformity	1 Realistic conflict theory 2 Social identity theory
COGNITIVE-INFORMATIONAL MODEL	SOCIAL LEARNING MODEL	PSYCHODYNAMIC MODEL
stereotypes	conditioning, imitation, modelling	frustration

5.4 Reduction of prejudice

THE ROBBERS' CAVE EXPERIMENT, PART II

Stage 3, resolving the conflict. The experimenters first tried equal contact as a means of reducing the conflict they had created. For example, the children filled out questionnaires together, watched movies, had a Fourth of July party and took meals together. Such occasions only served as opportunities to continue their fighting.

The second method was to introduce **superordinate** goals that could only be achieved through joint co-operation. For example, the tank for their drinking water sprung a leak and they all assisted in the repair. Also, on the way to a special overnight camp one of the buses broke down and they all had to help push.

By the end of the three weeks, friendships were again assessed. This time ingroup choices were still more frequent than outgroup ones but no longer 100%. More importantly, they no longer expressed *hostile* attitudes towards the outgroup.

Methods of reducing prejudice

Prejudice is an *attitude* whereas discrimination is *behaviour*. Psychological explanations of the process of *attitude* change highlight:

- All attitudes are *learned*. Therefore attitude change can involve conditioning, imitation or reasoned argument.
- People are *resistant* to attitude change. Your attitudes are a fundamental part of your personality. To change an attitude may require a massive overall of your self-image including your social identity.
- A person may be *persuaded* to change their attitude. Some 'messages' are more persuasive than others.
- People prefer to maintain a sense of *balance* in their attitudes. Therefore, if someone you like expresses a positive attitude towards an outgroup, this will increase your liking of the outgroup.

❶ Increasing social contact.   If a person is given an opportunity to learn more about an outgroup, this will lead to greater differentiation of their stereotypes (reduce the illusion of outgroup homogeneity, see beginning of Unit 5.2). They will see that members of the group are not all the same and become less prejudiced.

RESEARCH EXAMPLE   **Deutsch and Collins (1951) Interracial housing: Enforced contact**

RESEARCH QUESTION: One of the most prominent solutions to the racial problems in America was to bus children to different schools so that a better racial mix would be obtained. Does this enforced contact lead to reductions in prejudice?

PARTICIPANTS: White housewives who lived in bi-racial housing projects. A 'project' is an American term for a housing estate with blocks of flats.
1 Two projects were *integrated*: the families were randomly assigned apartments regardless of race and therefore Whites and Blacks lived in relatively close proximity.
2 Two of the projects were *segregated*: Black and White families were assigned to different buildings.

METHOD: Interview. A sample of housewives were interviewed about their attitudes towards Blacks.

RESULTS:
1 Those women in integrated flats showed decreases in prejudice.
2 Where housing was segregated, there was little attitude change and often increases in prejudice.

INTERPRETATION: When Whites were forced to make close contact, they found that Black individuals did not conform to their racial stereotypes and therefore changed their attitudes. When Blacks were observed from a reasonable distance, stereotypes, if anything, were confirmed and conflict remained.

EVALUATION: The degree of contact seems to be crucial. The desegregation of the American south by extensive bussing, did not lessen prejudice. In fact it led to increased tension and resentment (see Aronson, below).

RELATED STUDIES: See Sherif, above.

---

❷ <u>Co-operation</u>.   Contact alone is probably not sufficient to create attitude change because people are resistant to change. Sherif found that **superordinate** cooperative tasks enabled individuals to see each others as individuals rather than group members.

RESEARCH EXAMPLE | **Aronson *et al*. (1978) The jigsaw method**

RESEARCH QUESTION: Aronson, a well-known social psychologist working at the University of Texas, was approached by the superintendent of Austin schools to give advice about the violence erupting in his schools as a result of the bussing policies. Could he provide a solution?

Aronson's view was that the conflict was due to fierce competition between persons of unequal status. He felt that high school students were too old to benefit from prevention programs, so he concentrated on primary schools.

PARTICIPANTS: 53 groups from 7 schools met three days a week for six weeks. The classes contained White, Black and Hispanic students.

METHOD: Field experiment. The team developed an approach to learning which involved mutual interdependence. The class was divided, irrespective of ethnic origins, into groups of six children. Each group was given a project, broken down into six pieces. Each member of the group was given a piece of this 'puzzle' to research and must then report back to the other group members. At the end, everyone was tested on their knowledge of their project. Each individual's test performance was dependent on the help of the rest of the group. This is co-operation in pursuit of a superordinate goal.

Control groups received six weeks of traditional teaching methods.

RESULTS: Those children using the jigsaw methods showed increases in their self-esteem, academic performance and liking for their classmates. They also held less intergroup prejudices at the end of the experiment.

INTERPRETATION: The effects were positive but small.

EVALUATION: One of the drawbacks may be that the method does not eliminate competition. When non-White students work with more advanced White pupils it only confirms both ingroup and outgroup stereotypes held by both groups.

---

❸ <u>Challenging stereotypes</u>.   Schemas (stereotypes) resist change for a number of reasons (see Unit 5.2). Making direct and explicit statements which challenge existing stereotypes may be more effective than simply increasing contact.
   ● Pressure groups for minorities run campaigns to change attitudes. For example, 'Black is beautiful' or changing the label of a group from 'queer' to 'gay', 'Black' rather than 'Negro' or 'disabled' instead of 'handicapped'. Such labels change regularly to avoid the negative stereotype which inevitably catches up.
   ● Media policies which deliberately cast actors against 'type' (stereotype). For example, showing a Black women as a judge or a man looking after his children. Legislation was used in America to force all advertisements to represent ethnic groups equally.

❹ <u>Promoting positive images</u>.   The process of selling or persuasion relies on classical conditioning. For example, a poster showing an attractive man smoking a French cigarette leads us unconsciously to associate the unconditioned response (feelings of desire) with the conditioned stimulus (the cigarette). This increases our liking for the image of smoking.

❺ <u>Direct instruction</u>.   All attitudes are learned, therefore new attitudes can be taught. Children are relatively free of prejudices and therefore a preventative measure may be to 'inoculate' them against prejudices. This is an educational technique aiming to provide children with counter-arguments to protect them against attitudes and behaviours they may meet later in life, in the same way that a measles vaccine prevents them from getting measles.

❻ <u>Legislation</u>.   US segregation was seriously challenged in 1954 when the Supreme Court declared it was unconstitutional in a case 'Brown vs. the Board of Education of Topeka'. Amongst those who testified were a number of social psychologists who argued that equal status is necessary to eliminate false stereotypes. Initially change was slow and in some cases it aggravated racial tension. Ultimately great change has taken place though conflict still exists.

Legislation in this country has tried to help prevent race and gender discrimination. For example, the Equal Pay Act (1970), the Sex Discrimination Act (1975) and the Race Relations Act (1976).

7 <u>Social and political change</u>.   The element of hostility depends on a sense of frustration or inequity. Therefore, to reduce conflict there must be improved social conditions for the outgroups and a fair distribution of resources. This *sense* of equity is very hard to achieve.

Why are such attempts not completely successful?

1 <u>Prejudice is inevitable</u>.   Both stereotype formation and social identity are processes basic to human nature and therefore inevitable. The hostility factor is introduced by intergroup conflicts which may also be inevitable or would require massive political change.

2 <u>Holding prejudices has benefits</u>:
- Positive discrimination for the ingroup increases self-esteem.
- Prejudices provide a means of displacing aggression.
- The ready-made aspect of stereotypes and prejudices makes the world more manageable.

3 <u>Resistance to attitude change</u>.   People need to have a sufficiently strong reason to change their attitudes.

4 <u>Generalising from the particular</u>.   It is quite common for people to like *individual* members of an outgroup, but still feel prejudiced towards the *group* as a whole. For example, Stouffer *et al.* (1949) found that racial prejudice amongst soldiers diminished in battle but did not extend to relations back at base.

5 <u>Increased contact increases conflict</u>.   First hand knowledge may even increase aggression through resentment. For the minority group, integration may lead to lowered self-esteem because it emphasises their inferior position, thus creating stronger hostilities. To be successful contact should be under conditions of roughly equal status and a friendly context.

6 <u>It doesn't always fail</u>.   It's a slow process, and requires attacks at all sources of prejudice. It may seem unchanging because old prejudices are replaced by new ones.

Quick test 5.4

1 Describe **one** way in which a psychologist might try and reduce sexism. (*MEG, 1991*)
2 How do superordinate goals help to reduce prejudice?
3 What is the *jigsaw technique*?
4 Give **two** reasons why attempts to reduce prejudice might fail.
5 Describe **one** way that a psychologist might assess whether people had become less prejudiced.

Summary

METHODS OF REDUCING PREJUDICE	WHY SUCH ATTEMPTS FAIL
1 Increasing social contact (Deutsch and Collins, Sherif)	1 An inevitable process
2 Co-operation (Aronson *et al.*, Sherif)	2 Prejudices have advantages
3 Challenging stereotypes	3 Resistance to attitude change
4 Promoting positive images	4 People make exceptions, but hold to generalised view
5 Direct instruction	5 Increased contact may increase conflict
6 Legislation	6 It doesn't always fail
7 Social and political change	

Chapter 6
Social influence

Ancient astrologers believed that human behaviour could be explained in terms of an airy fluid flowing down from the heavenly bodies. This fluid exerted a force called *influentia*, a term which developed into the concept of 'influences'. They are invisible yet powerful.

Social influences are the forces exerted by other people which affect your behaviour. Such behaviours could be classed as 'good' or 'bad', prosocial or antisocial.

This chapter explains how others can affect you through their behaviour, their mere presence or just the thought of them.

6.1 Group norms, conformity and obedience

WOULD YOU HAVE OBEYED?

RESEARCH EXAMPLE

Milgram's (1963) studies of obedience are extremely well known. There are two reasons for this:
- The results are disturbing and surprising.
- His methods have been seen as unethical.

The study is relevant to obedience especially, but also to norms and conformity: The participants were *conforming* to a cultural *norm* that says we should *obey* authority figures.

THE RESEARCH QUESTION: Will people inflict great harm simply because they are ordered to do so? History provides much evidence to suggest that they will, most infamously the behaviour of some Germans in response to their Nazi leaders. Would ordinary Americans behave in the same way?

PARTICIPANTS: Forty males, aged between 20 and 50, whose jobs ranged from unskilled to professional. The participants were all volunteers, recruited through newspaper advertisements or flyers through the post. When they arrived for the supposed memory experiment they were paid $4.50 at the onset and introduced to another participant, a confederate of the experimenter. They drew lots for their roles, though the confederate always ended up as the 'learner' while the true participant was the 'teacher'. There was also an 'experimenter' dressed in a grey lab coat, played by an actor.

THE EXPERIMENT: The 'learner' was strapped in a chair in another room and wired with electrodes. The 'teacher' was told to administer an electric shock every time the 'learner' made a mistake, increasing the level of shock each time. There were 30 switches on the shock generator marked from 15 volts (slight shock) to 450 volts (danger – severe shock).

As the shock level increased, the 'learner' expressed his discomfort. The choice of phrases was predetermined, including one that his heart was bothering him. The 'experimenter' also had some predetermined phrases to use if the 'teacher' sought guidance about whether to continue. For example, 'Please continue' or 'It is absolutely essential that you must continue.'

RESULTS: No one stopped below the level of intense shock; 65% of the 'teachers' continued to the highest level of 450 volts.

LEVEL OF SHOCK (shown on generator)	VOLTS	NUMBER OF PARTICIPANTS WHO REFUSED TO CONTINUE AT THIS LEVEL
Intense shock	300	5
Extreme intensity shock	315	4
	330	2
	345	1
	360	1
Danger: severe shock	375	1
	390	0
	405	0
	420	0
XXX	435	0
	450	0
Number of participants who continued to the end		26

LATER VARIATIONS (he conducted 21 in all):
- *Proximity of 'learner'*, if the 'teacher' was placed in the same room as the 'learner' and had to press the learner's hand on the shock plate, obedience fell to 30%.
- *Proximity of experimenter*, when instructions were given over the phone the 'teacher' often said they were giving the shocks when they weren't. Overall, 21% of 'teachers' continued to obey.
- *Perceived authority*, when the experiment was conducted in a run-down building rather than a prestigious university setting, obedience fell to 47.5%.
- *Individual differences*, the experiment was repeated with over 1,000 participants from all walks of life. It was found that educated participants were less obedient, and military participants were more obedient. This may be related to their group norms.
- *Social support*, if the 'teacher' was paired with other two other 'teachers' (confederates) who dissented, then only 10% of the real participants continued to 450 volts.
- *Female participants* were equally obedient.
- *Deindividuation* increases obedience, see Unit 6.3.

Examiner's tip

This is an extremely well known piece of research and in order to demonstrate a good understanding you should be familiar with the variations, and with both positive and negative criticisms.

EVALUATION: The experimental set-up may not represent obedience in real life. The participants were in an unfamiliar situation, the norms were set by the 'experimenter'. (See also the evaluation of all studies of conformity and obedience later in this unit.)

DEBRIEFING PARTICIPANTS: After the experiment all participants were told the real details of the experiment and had a 'friendly reconciliation' with the 'learner'. The experimenter reassured the participants that their obedient behaviour was entirely normal. Later, Milgram sent out a questionnaire to give further support to participants. Only 1% said they were sorry to have participated. Some felt the experience had been worthwhile, even if only to warn them about blind obedience in the future.

WOULD YOU HAVE OBEYED? Most people think not. Before the experiment, Milgram asked various people to predict how his participants would behave. On average they thought participants would stop at 150 volts (a strong shock). They thought that at most only 3% of the participants might go as far as 450 volts.

People often express surprise at the unexpected results of these studies because people appear to be much more obedient than we expect. *This* is the result that is often overlooked: the surprise is that *we are surprised by human behaviour*. This is the value of psychological *research* compared with reasoned argument.

DO THE ENDS JUSTIFY THE MEANS?
- *Ethics*: Participants were placed under extraordinary tension and emotional strain. Afterwards many said that they had not suffered, but this may be because they were ashamed of their behaviour and were rationalising what they had done.
- *Artificial*: Research conducted in a laboratory may not generalise to real life.
- *Interpretation of findings*: The persistent efforts to discredit these experiments in terms of ethics may reflect the fact that people feel uneasy about the findings. It is easier to blame inhuman behaviour on evil personalities than to accept that it may be part of the human psyche and group processes.

norms	A norm is any pattern of behaviour which is typical or representative of a group. There are norms for intelligence tests or for physical development. Abnormal behaviour is that which is not typical. Group or social norms are the rules established by a group to regulate the behaviour of its members.
role	A social position that is governed by a set of norms about how to behave.
conformity	A change in behaviour as a result of *group* pressure or norms. This usually involves a change of personal opinions as well.
obedience	Behaving as instructed but *not necessarily* changing your opinions. Usually in response to *individual* rather than group pressure, though you might obey group norms.
compliance	Similar to conformity, because you go along with other people, but to comply does not involve a change of personal opinion. Similar to obedience, because it is can be a response to an explicit request, but to comply suggests some willingness.
identification	Establishing a link between oneself and another person or group. It is the first step leading to opinion change and conformity.
internalisation	Making group beliefs, values, attitudes, etc. your own. This is the second step in the process of conforming. Group or social identity becomes personal identity.
deindividuation	Losing any sense of individuality (see Unit 6.3).

Norms

Norms are rules which guide your behaviour. They underlie the processes of conformity and obedience. Their *influence* can be explained in various ways:

1 Ingratiational social influence.   Conforming to group norms is a sign of membership. (To ingratiate is to try to gain favour.)

2 Normative social influence.   Norms regulate the behaviour of groups and individuals. It is important to comply with norms such as driving on the left or to follow agreed rules of spelling so that we can understand each other.

3 Informational social influence.   In some situations there is no clear answer, therefore you rely on norms for 'social reality'. For example, what cutlery to use or judging a beauty contest.

Some examples of different norms:

1 Group norms.   Ingroup values. Each group establishes particular norms of behaviour as part of their group identity (see Sherif's study, Unit 5.3).

2 Personal norms.   Personal values and beliefs. For example, some people believe in giving to charity or not eating meat. Such norms may be learned through imitation (see social learning, Unit 3.2) or may be the product of independent thinking.

3 An equity norm.   A norm of justice. A relationship is fair if those involved receive rewards that are in relation to what they have invested (see interpersonal attraction, Unit 9.2).

4 Prosocial norms.   Social values. The norm to be responsible towards others, a moral outlook (see Unit 7.2).

Studies of group norms

❶ Norm formation.   The behaviour of a group leads to the formation of norms.

RESEARCH EXAMPLE   Sherif (1935) The autokinetic effect

RESEARCH QUESTION: In some psychology experiments group members are told to make a group decision. When this decision has an affect on their subsequent behaviour, the group agreement is acting as a norm (a group-determined rule of behaviour) which then creates pressure to conform. Do norms form even when a group is not told they have to agree?

PARTICIPANTS: Forty male students not majoring in psychology.

METHOD: Experiment. The autokinetic effect is a visual illusion created when you view a point of light in total darkness. The light appears to move around erratically because there are no points of reference.

1 Participants were shown the light individually and asked to estimate how far and in which direction it moved. For each participant an average was calculated and participants were grouped in twos or threes so that they were as different as possible.
2 Each group member continued to be asked to give individual estimates aloud. They were not told to reach a group decision.
3 Individuals were again tested on their own (conforming to a personal norm).

RESULTS:

1 At first each participant's estimates varied widely, but over 100 trials they settled down to a narrow range with a consistent central value.
2 After a few exposures the judgements of the group tended to converge.
3 When participants again gave their individual estimates their judgements were now more like the group norm.

INTERPRETATION: The mere presence of others is sufficient to lead to norm formation. We look to others to provide a social standard or norm in ambiguous situations (informational social influence). This study shows the experimental creation of a social norm which then acts as a pressure towards conformity.

RELATED STUDIES: The evidence related to **social facilitation** (see Unit 6.2) also shows how the presence of another establishes norms for expected productivity.

 Normative social influence.   The existence of social norms influences the way you behave in social situations.

RESEARCH EXAMPLE   **Zimbardo (1975) The Stanford Prison Study**

RESEARCH QUESTION: In the US, in 1975, there had been much alleged brutality by prison guards. Zimbardo questioned whether such behaviour was caused by the situation, or by the personality of the guards.

PARTICIPANTS: Zimbardo selected 21 healthy, intelligent, psychologically 'normal' male volunteers to serve as either prisoners or guards in a simulated prison set up in the basement of the psychology department at Stanford University. Roles were decided by the toss of a coin. Each participant was paid $15 a day.

METHOD: Observation. The 'prisoners' were unexpectedly 'arrested' at home, sometimes while neighbours looked on. On entry to 'prison' they were put through a delousing procedure, searched, given a prison uniform with ID number, nylon stocking caps (to make their hair look short), and an ankle chain. They were told to refer to each other only by number. They were in prison 24 hours a day.

The guards had uniforms, clubs, whistles, handcuffs and reflective sunglasses (to prevent eye contact).

Deindividuation was an important part of the process, encouraged for example by wearing uniforms.

RESULTS: It was intended that the study should last for two weeks but Zimbardo was forced to abandon it after six days because the participants had become too involved in their roles. The guards grew increasingly tyrannical. They woke prisoners in the night, locked them in a closet and got them to clean the toilet with their bare hands. The prisoners also changed their behaviour. One went on a hunger strike, and those who broke down asked to be paroled not simply to quit. On day 3 one prisoner was released because of 'acute emotional disturbance', the next day another prisoner broke down and cried hysterically.

Zimbardo tested the participants' personality and found no differences between the prisoners and guards. He did find that the participants who left early tended to have less conforming personalities.

INTERPRETATION: This was a remarkable demonstration of the strength of social norms and people's reluctance to 'disobey' them. In this case the norms dictated what behaviour was appropriate for specific roles (normative social influence). It is most accurate to say that the participants *obeyed* rather than *conformed* since they probably did not change their personal beliefs.

EVALUATION:

1 Ethics: Involvement in this study must have caused all participants emotional distress. One defence is that the extremes of behaviour could not have been anticipated at the outset.

2 Artificial: It is possible that participants took on very specific role behaviours because that is what they were asked to do (**demand characteristics**). In real life a person might adapt a role to suit their personal beliefs and the requirements of the situation.

Studies of conformity

RESEARCH EXAMPLE | **Asch (1955) Opinions and social pressure**

RESEARCH QUESTION: It is possible that informational social influence only occurs in ambiguous situations, as in Sherif's study of the autokinetic effect. How do people behave when there is clearly no doubt about the correct answer?

PARTICIPANTS: 123 male college students, paid $3.

METHOD: Experiment, deception. Participants were asked to be in a study of visual perception. They were tested in groups of seven to nine participants. The group was shown two pieces of card. One had a 'standard' line on it, the other card had three lines of varying length. Each member of the group was asked to say aloud which line they thought was the same length as the standard.

In fact, apart from the participant, all the members of the group were confederates. The true participant was the last but one to answer. On each trial the answer is clear. On the third trial and several later ones, the confederates unanimously give the wrong answer. There were 12 trials in all, half of which were 'critical' (the confederates gave wrong answers).

RESULTS: Approximately 75% of the participants conformed at least once, 5% conformed all of the time, 24% never conformed. The average rate was 37%.

INTERPRETATION: This was astonishing evidence that some people are extremely willing to conform with group norms.

1 Why did the participants give the wrong answer? During debriefing, most participants said they thought their answer was wrong but they went along with the rest. Therefore the results might be more accurately described as **compliance** rather than conformity.

2 Participants who did go against the majority reported feeling like a 'misfit' or 'crazy'. This demonstrates the pressure which exists towards complying with group norms.

3 There were important individual differences. Some people are less compliant or conformist than others.

EVALUATION:

1 Artificial: The consequences of complying were not harmful and the pressure to comply was great. In some real life situations this would not be true.

2 Ingrational normative influence: In a group of strangers, the need to establish social contact is greater than the need to be correct. The same would not be true for established groups, though there may be other pressures to conform.

LATER VARIATIONS:

- A group of three was sufficient to create the effect, larger numbers did not increase conformity.
- The presence of a second dissenter cut conformity rates by 25%, even when the dissenter disagreed with the participant as well as with the group.
- Conformity increased if the group members were regarded as of high status.
- Conformity decreased if the participants were not face-to-face.

RELATED STUDIES:

Crutchfield (1955) used a more efficient method than Asch, testing 600 participants. He designed the **Crutchfield apparatus** consisting of a cubicle with a series of switches and lights. A participant is given a question and can see the selection made by other (non-existent) participants. The participant then registers their own choice. Participants were tested on up to 50 different items. When the question was clear-cut, 30% conformed. If the question was an insoluble mathematical one (therefore ambiguous), conformity was 80%. If the question asked for agreement or disagreement with a statement of opinion, 58% conformed.

Pettigrew (1959) has shown how conformity to social norms can explain why some groups are prejudiced (see Unit 5.3).

Studies of obedience

Milgram's study is the the one most associated with obedience (see the beginning of this unit).

RESEARCH EXAMPLE   **Hofling *et al.* (1966) Obedience in nurses**

RESEARCH QUESTION: Would a real life situation produce evidence to support Milgram's findings about obedience?

PARTICIPANTS: 22 staff nurses on night duty in public and private psychiatric hospitals in the US.

METHOD: Field experiment, deception. An unknown doctor (a confederate) telephones the staff nurse and asks her to check the medicine cabinet for 'Astroten'. The bottles were labelled *Normal dose 5 mg., maximum daily dose 10 mg.* They in fact contained a harmless substance.

The doctor tells the nurse to give 20 mg. to his patient, Mr. Jones, because the patient needs it. 'When I get to the hospital I will sign the necessary authorisation papers'.

To comply with this request, the nurse broke four rules. They must not accept instructions:

- Over the telephone.
- From an unknown doctor.
- For a dose in excess of the safe amount.
- For a drug not on the ward list of permitted drugs.

RESULTS: 21 out of 22 (95%) of the nurses obeyed the order.

INTERPRETATION: The nurses defended themselves by saying it often happens, a doctor would be annoyed if they refused. Part of the nurses role is to obey the higher authority of a doctor without question.

EVALUATION:
1 Were they *conforming* to expected role behaviour rather than being obedient?
2 When other nurses were asked what they would do, they said they would not give the drug. This is a similar result to Milgram's. People do not think they are as obedient as psychologists have shown that they are.

Evaluation of empirical studies of conformity and obedience

All of the studies which have been described should be considered in the light of the following criticisms:

❶ Demand characteristics.   Participants' behaviour may be due to the fact that features of the experiment *demand* a certain typical response rather than because people would normally behave in this way. For example:
- Participants want to *please the experimenter*. Crutchfield asked his participants for feedback after the experiment, many of them said they didn't want to spoil the results so they had gone along with the others. The experiments largely used *paid volunteers*. This means that the participants had entered into a social contract to behave in line with what the experimenter wanted.
- The psychology experiment is a *social situation*. In Asch's study the participants expressed how much of an outsider they felt by dissenting. Belonging to the group is more important than being correct.
- The psychology experiment is a *role playing game*. The experimenter is perceived as being in charge and bearing responsibility. The participant's role is to obey.

❷ Are the results a *child of the times*? Some more recent studies have found less conformity and obedience. It is possible that today's norms are for less conformity.

❸ Were the results evidence of conformity, obedience or compliance? It is not clear to what extent *private opinion* changed.

❹ What do the results tell us about *real life*?
- In real life people sometimes have the option to simply do nothing, which may not be possible in an experiment.
- Many of the experimental situations were *oversimplified*.
- *Anxiety* or *ambiguity* foster conformity and obedience. Both of these feature in the experiments and increase the pressure to conform or obey thus exaggerating human behaviour.
- All of the experiments involved *strangers*. We may behave differently with individuals or groups who know us and we know them.
- Conformity and obedience are a problem when their consequences lead to *harm*. Some of the experiments did *not* have harmful consequences, therefore conformity/obedience is more understandable.

Factors which affect conformity and obedience

1 Gradual changes.   A person can be unaware of complying before it's too late and they've already committed themselves. Future behaviour persists as a justification for behaviour up to that point. For example, in the Milgram study, the shocks increased by only 15 volts each time. The subject might argue, 'What does one more step matter, I've harmed him already?'

2 Deindividuation.   Obedience is increased when the target is anonymous (Zimbardo) or out of the room (Milgram). Conformity is decreased by anonymity (Asch).

3 Size of group.   Obedience decreases with group size (Gamson *et al.*). Conformity increases with group size though three may be sufficient (Asch). One dissenter is sufficient to alter conformity.

4 Fear of dissent.   There is much pressure to comply with group norms. This pressure comes from our inherent drive to be part of a group.

5 Personality.   Some people are more likely to be conformist or obedient. Affiliators need social approval more than others (see Unit 9.3). Crutchfield found that nonconformists tended to be self-reliant, expressive, unpretentious, and lacked feelings of inferiority. Conformists respect authority, are submissive, inhibited, lacking in insight and overly accepting.

6 Situational factors.   There may be situations in which we all conform rather than there being a conformist personality (see Mischel's situational theory of personality, Unit 8.3). There may be aspects of a situation which encourage conformity, such as being an outsider or nervousness. Similarly, obedience may be related to the figure in authority.

7 Gender.   There has been evidence that women tend to be more conformist, Eagly (1978) suggests that women may be more oriented towards interpersonal goals and thus appear more conformist.

Ethical issues

In all the experiments there were certain infringements of personal rights:

1 Deception.   Ideally experimental participants should give their informed consent. Since many of these experiments would not work without deception, the only alternative was to debrief the participants, telling them the true nature of the research afterwards. They should be offered the chance to withdraw their data at this point.

2 Emotional distress.   This may occur:
- During an experiment. In Milgram's or Hofling's study the participant thought they might cause harm to another. In Asch's study the participant was either aware of lying or made to feel an outcast.
- During debriefing. The participant realises the extent to which they have conformed or obeyed. People find this fact about themselves disturbing because they would not expect it from themselves.

3 Means versus ends.   All ethics are a judgement of whether the means justify the ends. The findings of theses studies demonstrate an important aspect of human behaviour and social influence that was not previously expected.

RESEARCH EXAMPLE | **Gamson *et al.* (1982) A deceptive sleight of hand**

Gamson's study involved a trick so that, theoretically at least, participants weren't deceived. When participants volunteered, they were asked if they would participate in any of the following studies:
- Research in brand recognition of commercial products.
- Research on product safety.
- Research in which you will be misled about the purpose until afterwards.
- Research involving group standards.
When the participants had agreed to being involved in all of the studies, they were told that only the last kind was in progress currently. Therefore they had agreed to be deceived!

Applications

Juries are a special and important example of a small group. When the US Supreme Court considered the matter of reducing jury size to six just men, it turned to evidence from social psychologists, in particular Asch's work on group size and conformity. The court concluded that juries of six took less time to deliberate, cost less money and were sufficiently representative of the population. A sample of less than six is likely to experience unjust pressures to conform when the jury is split because a minority of one could well be critical.

Quick test 6.1

1 Compliance, conformity and obedience are closely related. Which involves a change of behaviour *and* of opinions?
2 If you give the same answer as other people in a discussion group, even though you know it to be wrong, what kind of conformity is this called?
3 Name **two** factors which might increase your willingness to conform to majority opinion.
4 Give **one** advantage and **one** disadvantage of people's tendency to conform to social pressure.
5 What is the main reason given for why people conform in ambiguous situations?
6 Describe **two** problems with measuring conformity in a laboratory environment. (*MEG, 1991*)
7 Give **one** example from everyday life when obedience to authority would be useful. (*MEG sample Foundation*)
8 Why are studies of obedience likely to raise ethical objections?
9 What is *deindividuation*?
10 Why is it important to conduct cross-cultural studies of conformity and obedience?

Summary

STUDIES OF GROUP NORMS	STUDIES OF CONFORMITY	STUDIES OF OBEDIENCE

1 Norm formation (Sherif)
2 Normative social influence (Zimbardo)

1 Asch
2 Crutchfield

1 Milgram
2 Hofling *et al.*
3 Gamson *et al.*

EVALUATION OF EMPIRICAL STUDIES	FACTORS WHICH AFFECT CONFORMITY	ETHICAL ISSUES

1 Demand characteristics
2 A 'child of the times'
3 No change in private opinion
4 Not true to real life

1 Gradual changes
2 Deindividuation
3 Size of group
4 Fear dissent
5 Personality
6 Situational factors
7 Gender

1 Deception
2 Emotional distress
3 Means vs. ends

6.2 The presence of others

DO PEOPLE WORK BETTER ON THEIR OWN?

Triplett (1897) was intrigued by the fact that cyclists performed better when in a race or with a pacemaker than when they practised on their own. He examined the various theories put forward to explain this. The 'suction theory' proposed that the cyclists created a vacuum which helped pull each other along. The 'shelter theory' suggested that they sheltered each other from the wind. Alternatively, it might be that the cyclists encouraged each other and each person came to expect a better performance of themselves.

Triplett offered his own explanation. The presence of others might be psychologically stimulating because of the sense of competition. This stimulation would release energy not previously available. He designed an experiment to test his hypothesis. The participant had to turn a reel as fast as possible so that a flag sewn to a thread made four circuits of a four metre course. Participants did this on their own or **coacting** (working side-by-side with another participant performing the same task independently). Each participant performed six trials, alternating between the two conditions. In all he tested 225 people of all ages.

The participants who were coacting performed faster than those working alone. This supports the hypothesis. Triplett acknowledged that other factors are important, to a lesser extent. For example seeing another person work apparently faster probably increases your self-expectations.

The result was replicated in a number of experiments using different tasks and even with animals.

Allport (1920) compared the performance of participants doing a variety of tasks such as multiplication problems, word associations, and debating. Participants worked faster when they were coacting than when they were alone.

Zajonc *et al.* (1969) placed a bright light at the start of a maze, if the cockroaches were in pairs they ran away faster. Performance was also increased when an audience of four cockroaches watched! Caution should be exercised in making inferences about human behaviour.

This research has an application in examination practices. Do people revise better on their own or when in a library? Do students perform better in an exam when in a crowded room or when alone?

DEFINITIONS

social facilitation	The enhancement of an individual's performance when working in the presence of other people (an audience). Also called the **audience effect**. This is true for only certain kinds of tasks, those involving a dominant response. On other kinds of tasks an audience may be inhibiting. There are individual differences.
social inhibition	Individual performance decreases in the presence of others. This is true for nondominant responses or when considering quantity rather than quality. See also **social loafing**.
audience effect	See **social facilitation**. Audience effects may occur even if members of the audience are blindfolded and wearing headphones.
coaction	Activity where two or more people are performing side-by-side but not interacting.
dominant responses	Performance on well-learned, instinctive, often simple motor tasks.
nondominant responses	Performance on conceptual, novel, complicated or untried tasks.

social loafing	The reduction of individual effort when people work in groups compared with when they work alone. Unlike **social inhibition**, individuals are not affected by arousal so much as deindividuation.
The Ringlemann effect	The tendency for group members to become progressively less productive as the size of the group increases. Part of the reason is due to co-ordination losses rather than just social loafing.

Indirect social influence

This whole chapter is related to *indirect* social influences. Another person may influence your behaviour just because they are there not because of what they say or do.

❶ Conformity (Unit 6.1): People are strongly affected by group norms, even when the group is not present.

❷ The bystander effect (Unit 7.2): A group of onlookers may resist helping because of a diffusion of responsibility.

❸ Crowding and density (Unit 6.3): The arousal created by the closeness of others leads to antisocial behaviours.

❹ Self-fulfilling prophecy (Unit 8.2): A person's behaviour is influenced by the expectations communicated from another person. The behaviour now confirms the original expectations.

❺ Social facilitation (below): Performance is better on simple (dominant) tasks when an audience is present. It is worse on complicated, novel (nondominance) tasks.

❻ Social loafing (below): Individuals make a greater effort when on their own than when they are part of a group effort.

Social facilitation

❶ Mere presence.   The presence of an audience may lead to improved performance just because the others are there. Triplett (see the beginning of this unit) first observed this social facilitation. Many studies supported his findings, but found that an audience does not always facilitate performance.

❷ Quality versus quantity.   Speed may be increased by the presence of others but errors may also increase.
   ● Quantity improves when people are coacting.
   ● Quality improves when people are working alone.
   For example:
   Dashiell (1930) found that participants may be faster at multiplication when coacting but they also made more errors.
   Pessin (1933) arranged for participants to learn a set of nonsense syllables, a novel task. Those who worked in front of an audience rather than alone took longer and made more errors.

❸ Dominant and nondominant responses.   Zajonc suggested the idea that there are different kinds of task:
   ● Tasks requiring dominant responses. These are improved by the presence of others.
   ● Tasks requiring nondominant responses. Performance is depressed by the presence of an audience.

RESEARCH EXAMPLE   **Schmitt *et al.* (1986) Mere presence and social facilitation**

RESEARCH QUESTION: Does the presence of others help or hinder our performance? Does it depend on the nature of the task?

PARTICIPANTS: Forty-five college undergraduates.

METHOD: Experiment, deception. Participants were asked to perform two tasks:
- A *simple, well-learned* task: typing their name into a computer.
- A *difficult, novel* task: type their name backwards with ascending numbers placed between each letter.

This task was performed in one of three conditions:
1 *Alone, no audience.*
2 *Audience, mere presence.* The experimenter wore a blindfold and earphones.
3 *Audience, evaluation apprehension.* The experimenter assessed the participant's performance.

The participants thought the task was a prelude to the experiment rather than experiment itself, so it was followed by several filler questions to complete the deception.

RESULTS:
1 Participants performed the simple task faster under both audience conditions than when alone.
2 Participants performed the difficult task slower under both audience conditions.
3 When the audience created 'evaluation apprehension' the participants were faster still on the simple task.

Mean time in seconds for participants to complete both tasks

	Alone	Mere presence	Evaluation apprehension
Simple task	15	10	7
Difficult task	52	73	63

INTERPRETATION:
1 An audience speeds up the performance of a well-learned task but slows down performance of a novel task.
2 If the audience is evaluating performance this lessens the social facilitation effect. The stress created by evaluation apprehension will depress performance.

RELATED STUDIES:
Markus (1978) asked participants, prior to the supposed experiment, to take off their shoes (dominant response) and put on a lab coat, some large socks and shoes (nondominant response) so that they were dressed identically. This was done either alone, while an observer watched or while the observer had their back turned. They recorded the time taken to do this. The results showed the same order as above.

Zajonc *et al.* (1969) found task effects in their cockroaches (as mentioned at the beginning of this unit). If the maze task was made more complex, by adding a right turn, the lone cockroaches did better.

4 Explanations:
Why does an audience lead to *improved* performance on *dominant* tasks?
- *Increased arousal* is created by evaluation apprehension or competition. Greater arousal leads to faster performance as long as the task is not complicated.
- The desire to present a *favourable image* to self and others increases motivation and effort.

Why does an audience lead to *depressed* performance on *nondominant* tasks?
- *Increased arousal* will depress performance on a complicated task and lead to more errors being made.
- The desire to present a *favourable image* may take attention away from the task. Complicated tasks require the extra attention.
- Other people may be *distracting*, also dividing attention and reducing concentration.

This relationship between changes in arousal and performance levels is illustrated by the Yerkes-Dodson effect, see Unit 10.2 for a graph of this.

Social loafing

The *interaction* of individuals, rather than their mere presence or coaction, may lead to depressed performance.

The Ringlemann effect

A German agricultural engineer was intrigued by the way group behaviour affected physical performance. He questioned whether tug-of-war teams exerted the same pull as the sum of the individual's best efforts. To test this he attached a rope to a pressure gauge and measured the group and individual pulls. He found that individual performance decreased as the size of the group increased.

Number of people	Kg. of pressure exerted	Comparison with a single individual	'Pull' per person in kg.	% decrease of individual effort
1	63		$\frac{63}{1} = 63$	
2	118	1.9 times	$\frac{118}{2} = 56$	11%
3	160	2.5 times	$\frac{160}{3} = 53$	16%
8	248	3.9 times	$\frac{248}{8} = 31$	51%

Latané *et al.* (1979) suggest that the presence of others leads to depressed performance because of:

1 *Co-ordination losses*: Poorer performance in condition 1 shows that there is some loss of output due to lack of co-ordination of effort.

2 *Social loafing*: Each member is making less effort because they feel their lack of effort will not be detected and others will take up the slack.

APPLICATIONS: The factory production line is a place where management wish to maximise production. There are various methods for doing this:

1 Making each person's effort readily identifiable. This can be done by marking each piece of work with the workers' name.

2 Increasing the sense of competition between group members. Rewards might be offered for the best production levels.

3 Making opportunities for individuals to evaluate their own performance.

RELATED STUDIES: Shaw (1932) set 'eureka' type problems such as the missionaries and the cannibals who are trying to cross a river, however at no time can there be more cannibals than missionaries on either bank or in the boat. Four-person groups were able to solve such problems faster than individuals. Social loafing is less of a problem in creative tasks which depend on interaction to produce unusual solutions. **Brainstorming** is an example of this approach.

Quick test 6.2

1 What term is used to describe performance on novel or complicated tasks?
2 What are *coaction* effects?
3 Give an example of social facilitation from everyday life.
4 In some situations the presence of others leads to depressed performance. Give **two** psychological terms used to describe this negative effect.
5 A particular factory finds performance on the assembly line has got worse since they increased the numbers working there. What **two** ideas might a psychologist suggest for improving production?

Summary

Sources of indirect social influence

CONFORMITY	THE BYSTANDER EFFECT	SOCIAL FACILITATION (INCREASED ACTIVITY)	SOCIAL LOAFING (DECREASED ACTIVITY)
See Unit 5.1	See Unit 7.2	1 Mere presence 2 Quality versus quantity 3 Dominant *vs* nondominant responses (Schmitt *et al.*)	1 Ringlemann effect 2 Latané *et al.* 3 Social impact theory
CROWDING AND DENSITY	THE SELF-FULFILLING PROPHECY		
See Unit 6.3	See Unit 8.2		

APPLICATIONS:
1 Audience effects: Revision and examination/testing related to task difficulty.
2 Social loafing: Work groups, e.g. factory assembly line.

6.3 Crowds, crowding and territorial behaviour

OVERCROWDING AND POPULATION CONTROL

A classic study by Calhoun (1962) showed how overcrowding could cause more than simply antisocial behaviour. He called this pathological behaviour **behavioural sink**.

Calhoun established a population of rats in a quarter of an acre enclosure. They had plenty of food, no predators and little disease. After two years the population stabilised at 150 adults. The only thing which regulated the size of the population was the behaviour of the animals themselves. He concluded that stress from social interactions disrupted maternal behaviour leading to a high infant mortality rate and population control.

To confirm this, Calhoun designed several experiments. In each experiment a population of rats was placed in a room divided into four interconnected pens, comfortably housing about 50 rats. They were observed over 16 months. The experimenters kept the population steady at about 80 rats by removing any who survived past weaning. Food and water were in plentiful supply.

Observed behaviours:

- *Probers* were hyperactive and hypersexual males who constantly sought sexually receptive females. They attacked females in their burrows and became cannibalistic, eating baby rats.
- Females became *poor mothers*. They frequently died giving birth, failed to build nests for their young, to feed them or to protect them from danger. In one experiment 95% of the young died before reaching maturity.
- The *dominant males* behaved oddly, ignoring their females and offspring and biting off the tails of other rats.
- There were also increases in *aggression* and *physical illness*.
- In the two end pens, the dominant male protected his territory, maintaining a normal level of population density. Here breeding and mothering were normal.
- Those young rats who were removed to keep the population steady, were placed in normal cages. However, their experiences of overcrowding continued to influence their behaviour. They produced smaller litters than normal and their young failed to survive to maturity.

There are three concluding points to be made:

1 The fact that many of the abnormal or 'pathological' behaviours were related to *reproduction* suggests an innate mechanism to prevent overpopulation. Population density may act as a social pressure which breaks down those social structures which have evolved as a means of ensuring the group's survival.

2 The experiment also showed how establishing a *territory* is a means of avoiding the harmful effects of overcrowding. This was only possible in end pens.

3 What does this study tell us about *human* responses to overcrowding? The results of animal studies don't always apply to humans. See Unit 11.1 for arguments for and against using animals.

NOTE: The terms 'crowd' and 'crowding' refer to two very different aspects of social influence.

DEFINITIONS

crowd	A large but temporary gathering of persons with a common focus. A number of persons or things closely pressed together.
crowd behaviour	The influence of others in a crowd.
crowding	A psychological response to *some* situations of population density. Also called **overcrowding**.
population density	The number of individuals in a particular space.
social contagion	Transmission of social behaviour from one person to another, in the same way that a physical disease is spread.

deindividuation	Losing a sense of individual identity. This affects both the individual's self-perceptions and the attitudes of others towards the deindividuated person.
personal space	An area individuals maintain around themselves. Inappropriate intrusions lead to discomfort.
proxemics	The study of how people use interpersonal distance to convey social information.
territory	A portion of land belonging specifically to a person or group. It is for their exclusive use and can be defended by them. It is important to distinguish the concept of territory from personal space, both are defensible and exclusive areas but one is land. All animals have a personal space but only some are territorial.
privacy	Your primary territory. A place where you can control your social interactions and information about yourself.
defensible space	Secondary territories or semi-public areas around private dwellings which people can defend. It is associated with a better quality of life.

Crowd behaviour

Individuals in crowds sometimes behave differently from when they are on their own. Crowd behaviour may lack personal control and may be antisocial. How do social psychologists explain this behaviour?

1. Bystander apathy.   The presence of the crowd leads to inaction in situations requiring help. Diffusion of responsibility means that each member of a crowd feels less responsibility towards helping a victim. The bystander effect is explained in detail in Unit 7.2.

2. Deindividuation.   The presence of a crowd leads individual members to feel anonymous and act according to a different set of rules than they would normally. Zimbardo (1969) first described the term in detail:
   1. *Individuated behaviour*: Rational, consistent with personal norms, controlled.
   2. *Deindividuated behaviour*: Unrestrained, acting on primitive impulses, free to commit antisocial acts. It can be caused by being a member of a crowd, but can also occur when an individual puts on a uniform.

RESEARCH EXAMPLE | **Diener *et al.* (1976) Trick or treat: Effects of deindividuation on stealing**

RESEARCH QUESTION: What forces change a socialised individual into an uninhibited person who will commit antisocial acts?

PARTICIPANTS: 1,352 children who visited one of 27 homes on a Hallowe'en night in Seattle.

METHOD: Field experiment. In each home there was a table just inside the front door on which was a large bowl of fun-sized chocolate bars and another bowl of small change. There was a decorative backdrop behind which an observer could watch through a peephole.

As each child arrived, the experimenter told them to take *one* of the chocolate bars and then said, 'I'm going to return to work in another room'. Each observer recorded the number of children present and what they took.

1. *Anonymity* condition. No attempt was made to identify the children and the experimenter was a stranger to the house. The children were in fancy dress.
2. *Non-anonymous*. The experimenter asked all the childrens' names and address. She told them her name and described where she lived.
3. *Altered responsibility*. The experimenter asked the youngest child to make sure that everyone took only one chocolate. She also asked the child's name and address. The youngest child was used because of their low status. Therefore, they should exert the least influence on the group.

RESULTS: 'Transgressing' was defined as taking money, extra chocolate or both.

Percentage of children transgressing

	Alone	Group
Anonymous	21%	57%
Non-anonymous	8%	21%
Altered responsibility		27%

1 Anonymity led to more antisocial behaviour.
2 The effects of anonymity were strongest when a child was in a group rather than alone.
3 The presence of one non-anonymous person reduced antisocial behaviour considerably.

INTERPRETATION: Deindividuation leads to antisocial behaviour.

RELATED STUDIES:
Zimbardo (1969) tested the effects of deindividuation on obedience using Milgram's experimental design (see Unit 6.1). For one group the 'learner' was introduced to the participant and wore a name tag (individuated condition). In another group, the 'learner' was disguised in lab coat and hood (like a Ku Klux Klan member). This 'deindividuated' confederate received more electric shocks.

Zimbardo's (1975) prison study (see Unit 6.1) showed how deindividuation acts both on the individual and on the perceptions of the individual. Both prisoners and guards wore appropriate uniforms. These made each participant lose their own sense of individuality and to perceive other participants not as individuals but as members of a group (guards or prisoners).

3 Social contagion.   Once antisocial behaviour has emerged it is catching or contagious. Individuals in the crowd *imitate* the behaviour of others and it becomes a *norm* of the crowd.

A harmless example is when a person stops and looks at the top floor of a high-rise building. Soon others stop and look up too. The larger the number who are in the crowd, the larger the percentage of passersby who join the crowd.

4 Positive effects.   In some situations a crowd may be associated with enjoyment, as in a rock concert or football match. The influence of the crowd is to increase whatever the general mood is (see 'density–intensity hypothesis', below).

5 Explanations of uncontrolled crowd or mob behaviour:
- Deindividuation and a focus on external events decrease self-awareness. Intense activity and overcrowding lead to arousal. This brings the wild, antisocial behaviour associated with a mob. It can also lead to ecstatic behaviour.
- The social cognitive view is that crowds are not unruly (without rules). They are obeying a different set norms appropriate to the situation (see Reicher, see Unit 5.3).

Density versus crowding

Crowding is not the same as crowd behaviour. To be in a crowd does not necessarily mean that you feel crowded or overcrowded. To feel crowded you don't have to be in a group of people, it is enough to sense their nearness.

To understand crowding, it is important to distinguish the physical from the psychological problem:
- *Density* (population density) is the objective or physical measure.
- *Crowding* is the subjective or psychological response.
The same population density may be felt as crowding at an airport but not at a football match. Only when we experience a sense of crowding is there a negative effect.

The effects of crowding

Population density leads to sensory stimulation (because of all the people) and therefore physiological arousal. What are the effects of this arousal?

1 Social pathology hypothesis.   Calhoun (see the beginning of this unit) suggested that arousal creates stress which leads to social abnormality, in other words, pathology. The effects of stress are described in Unit 10.2.

Freedman (1973) gives the following representative correlations between urban density and symptoms of social pathology:

Symptom	Correlation
Incidence of venereal disease	0.83
Admissions to mental hospitals	0.74
Incidence of tuberculosis	0.70
Juvenile delinquency	0.63
Illegitimate birth rate	0.50
Welfare rates	0.37
Infant mortality rate	0.32
Suicide	0.04

2 Arguments against the social pathology hypothesis:
- Freedman argues that the existence of a positive a correlation does not mean that overcrowding has *caused* the social pathologies. One explanation may be the high migration rates associated with urban areas. People are attracted to cities in search of 'better lives'. Many of those who can afford to leave, do. Leaving an aged, deprived and jobless population in densely populated, urban areas. Other explanations include noise and pollution.
- The fact that there are *cultural differences* also suggests that density does not necessarily lead to social pathology. Asians in Hong Kong have lower levels of pathology than Westerners living in less densely populated cities such as Los Angeles.
- Some studies have looked at situations of residential crowding where the irrelevant factors can be eliminated. For example in prisons, hospitals, naval ships, dormitories and laboratory groups. In these situations high density is not always tied to a sense of crowding or social pathology.

Conclusion: The social pathology hypothesis is probably an exaggeration.

3 Density-intensity hypothesis. Freedman also suggests that situations of high density only intensify what is happening already. The physiological arousal heightens the mood you are in.

For example, at a football match or a party, you enjoy the high density. However, if you are not enjoying yourself, you might begin to feel stressed and want to leave. Arousal may also improve performance of dominant responses, and not others (see Unit 6.2).

This should encourage urban planners to make cities more pleasant and trouble-free environments. Then high density would lead to an even greater sense of pleasure.

Control of crowding: territories and privacy

Personal space and territories act as social organisers. They control population density and social behaviour. Too much contact with others leads to aggression and stress. Too little contact leads to a sense of isolation.

1 Personal space. Personal or body space is the most intimate territory. Hall (1966) called this **proxemics**. He suggested that personal space can be divided into four zones, which vary from culture to culture. The norms we are familiar with are:
1 Intimate distance (0 to 50cms)   Close contact: lovers, family or fighting.
2 Personal distance (50cms to 1.5m)   Everyday interactions between familiar people.
3 Social distance (1.5m to 3.5m)   Impersonal transactions, as in business.
4 Public distance (over 3.5m)   Formal settings, such as addressing an audience.

These norms act as a channel for nonverbal communication. You communicate your relationship to others in terms of personal distance. Any intrusion is felt as a threat.

The degree of comfort or discomfort you feel varies with:
- Personal characteristics (such as age, gender, culture, personality).
- Characteristics of the other person (such as their nonverbal behaviours, similarity, gender).
- Interpersonal relations (such as status, degree of friendship, family membership).
- Situational factors (such as being indoors or outdoors, size of room).

RESEARCH EXAMPLE | **Felipe and Sommer (1966) Invasions of personal space**

RESEARCH QUESTION: What are the effects of norm violation, in this case the invasion of personal space?

PARTICIPANTS: 188 female students, an opportunity sample.

METHOD: Field experiment. The experimenter (E) located a 'victim' (participant, P) in a university library. Each P was the first female sitting alone in the library with at least one book in front of her and an empty chair either side of her. The second female filling the same criteria served as a control. E had a book and appeared to be making notes. In fact she was recording the time and any relevant behaviour of P, such as moving books or her chair.

Condition I E invaded P's personal space, moving her chair so she was 7cms away and maintaining a shoulder distance of 30cms despite any adjustments made by P.

Condition II E sat at a 'normal' distance away. Their chairs were about 40cms apart and shoulder distance about 60cms.

RESULTS: Some participants usually built some kind of physical barrier to mark their space or territory. Some signalled with body posture, such as turning their back. Some actually left. One asked for more space.

INTERPRETATION: Spatial invasions result in flight, defensive behaviour or the use of markers to establish territory.

APPLICATIONS: An understanding of the cultural differences in appropriate body space is important in international diplomacy. Arabs tend to have less personal space and interpret our distance as a sign of disliking.

❷ The concept of territoriality in animals.   Territories assist the survival of the individual and the species.
  1 They are a means of managing *food* supplies. This is not true for all territorial animals. For example, sea birds have cliff territories, but search for food elsewhere
  2 They aid *breeding* success by ensuring sufficient food for the young, providing a protected place for rearing the young and regulating population size (see Calhoun, at the beginning of this unit). Most animals will not breed until they have a nest site. This also helps population control.
  3 They reduce the amount of *aggression* within a species. There is a social convention that the owner of a territory invariably wins. This is not because the owner is stronger, but because a species which practices this kind of social contract has a better chance of survival than one which has constant skirmishes (see Unit 7.1).
  Territorial behaviour involves three processes:
  ● Control of access.
  ● Marking the boundaries.
  ● Defending against intruders.

❸ Human territories.   Altman (1975) distinguished three types of territory:
  ● *Primary* territories: Private places where you have a sense of ownership rather than simply using it a lot. For example a named car parking space rather than one you use frequently.
  ● *Secondary* territories: Available to many but not all people, established through regular use. For example, where you sit in class, or stand at the local pub. These territories are only available to your classmates or the pub regulars.
  ● *Public* territories: Available to everyone, yours only while you use it. For example, a telephone box or public toilet.
  Even though humans have evolved considerably from their animal ancestors, *some* human societies remain territorial. Why? Territories continue to have social importance.
  ● They are an extension of your personal and group *identity*. People seek to identify with a physical space defined as theirs or belonging to their group.
  ● They are a means of establishing and maintaining *privacy*.
  ● They are a means of reducing *aggression*.
  ● They may be related to *reproduction*. Many people feel a need to have a home before they start a family.

RESEARCH EXAMPLE | **Sundstrom and Altman (1974) Settled territories as a means of reducing aggression**

RESEARCH QUESTION: How is territorial behaviour in humans related to dominance and levels of aggression?

PARTICIPANTS: A group of 23 delinquent boys, aged between 12 and 15, in an institutional 'cottage'.

METHOD: Observation, natural experiment. The boys' use of space was systematically observed for a 10-week period. The observer walked through the cottage along a predetermined route and recorded the location of each boy. This was done, on average three times each day.

RESULTS: The study could be divided into 3 periods:

Period 1: During the first five weeks of the study, the boys maintained fairly well-defined territories. The dominant boys controlled the most desirable areas, leaving the less dominant boys with the lower quality areas. During this time disruptive and aggressive behaviour was at a minimum.

Period 2: Two of the most dominant boys were transferred and two new members added. Orderly space-use patterns broke down. For the next three weeks disruptive behaviour increased dramatically as the boys fought for the best territories.

Period 3: In the final few weeks of the study, territories became re-established. Conflict and misbehaviour was reduced.

INTERPRETATION: Settled territories act as a means of reducing aggression. They are a means of social control.

APPLICATIONS: The **home field advantage** describes the phenomenon that the home team is more likely to win (a rule which prevents the need for aggression). Other examples: gangs usually win on their home turf, and people are less influenced by salespersons in their own homes. The basis for this is that a sense of territory provides confidence for the owner and insecurity for the intruder.

RELATED STUDIES: The same behaviour can be observed in animals. Yasukawa (1979) formed two separate hierarchies of junco birds and placed one group in the others' cage. In this case the 'intruders' took their place at the bottom of the hierarchy with little fighting. However, if both groups were placed in a completely new cage they engaged in much more fighting while establishing a new hierarchy.

④ <u>Privacy</u>. Altman suggests that privacy is a matter of regulating the amount of contact with people. Every person has a desired level of contact and an actual level of contact. When the latter becomes too great, the individual experiences a need for privacy.
- *Establishing* privacy is a matter of marking out a primary territory. This is the place where you can avoid or regulate contact with others.
  - Marking can be done with decorations for a room or cultivating your garden.
  - Barriers may be erected, such as a pile of books on a library table or fences around the garden.
  - Regular use acts as a sign of ownership.
- *Maintaining* privacy is a matter of controlling access. Privacy can be invaded by any unwelcome stimuli, such as noise as well as other people. Therefore control must extend to the social and physical environment. Unless you have this control, the space can not be felt as truly yours. Examples of privacy control are:
  - Closed doors or other barriers.
  - Threatening behaviour, such as staring or verbal requests to leave.
- The effects of *lack* of privacy
  - Some institutions are designed to encourage social interactions between residents. For example in a nursing home. However, a communal dormitory may provide too much interaction and insufficient privacy, resulting in discontented residents.
  - In burglaries people often suffer more from the sense that their primary territory has been invaded than from any physical losses.

⑤ <u>Defensible space</u>. A sense of privacy also extends to secondary territories. People are not content unless these can be defended too.

RESEARCH EXAMPLE   **Newman (1972) Housing design**

RESEARCH QUESTION: Newman was an architect and urban planner. The 1950s and 60s were a time of high-rise apartment blocks, much admired architecturally, but disasters socially. A notable example was the Pruitt-Igoe public housing project in St. Louis. It was an award-winning complex of 33 11-storey buildings with 3,000 apartments. Within three years of its construction, many of the apartments had become vacant, crime and vandalism were rampant and the residents were very unhappy. Ultimately it was demolished.

What aspects of high-rise apartment blocks might cause such antisocial behaviour?

METHOD: Observation using records. Newman looked at two housing projects in New York which were next door to each other.

- The *Van Dyke* project consisted of many 14-storey buildings separated by open spaces.
- The *Brownsville* project was eight years older. It had 6-storey X-shaped buildings with some 3-storey wings.

RESULTS: He assessed satisfaction in terms of crime rates and building damage.

Incident	Van Dyke	Brownsville
Crimes	1,189	790
Maintenance jobs	3,301	2,376

INTERPRETATION: Both projects provided residents with primary territories. However, the Brownsville project provided residents with secondary territories which were defensible. The buildings had central entrances which were overlooked by a number of windows. Not many families used each entrance and anyone entering would feel watched.

The Van Dyke buildings had such a large population that residents couldn't be distinguished from outsiders. The stairwells were isolated and the open spaces between the buildings had no markings or barriers to create a sense of territory.

EVALUATION: The data used is correlational. Therefore you cannot be sure that the housing design *caused* positive or negative attitudes.

APPLICATIONS: Providing project residents with defensible spaces will foster positive attitudes. Newman recommended that:

- Boundaries should be established both inside and outside the buildings.
- Residents must be able to watch over these secondary territories.
- It helps to build projects in low crime areas!

RELATED STUDIES: Baum and Valins (1977) compared traditional and suite-style student dormitories. Traditional dorms have a long corridor with bedrooms, toilets and kitchens off it. Suite-style dorms consist of a few bedrooms clustered round a central, communal area. The students in traditional dorms tend to feel crowded and lacking in privacy, whereas suite-style dorms facilitates good friendships. This is explained in terms of the secondary territories which are provided in suite-style dorms but not in an isolated and indefensible communal hallway.

Quick test 6.3

1 It is sometimes said that the police try and create a sense of deindividuation when they enrol a new recruit. Give **two** advantages to the Police Force of creating a sense of deindividuation when someone joins. (*MEG, 1992*)

2 People often seek out crowds, and some people choose to shop at the busiest times. Give **two** positive effects of crowding. (*MEG, 1992*)

3 Give **two** brief suggestions that a large shop could use to reduce the negative effects of crowding on shoppers. (*MEG, 1992*)

4 What are **two** factors that influence how we experience crowding. (*MEG, sample Higher*)

5 Describe **two** factors which might affect the amount of personal space that we maintain between ourselves and others. (*MEG, 1992*)

Summary

Crowd behaviour is not the same as crowding.

CROWD BEHAVIOUR	THE EFFECTS OF CROWDING	TERRITORIES AND PRIVACY (control of crowding)
1 Bystander apathy 2 Deindividuation (Zimbardo, Diener *et al.*) 3 Social contagion 4 Positive effects 5 Mob behaviour	1 Social pathology hypothesis (Calhoun) 2 Counter-argument (Freedman) 3 Density-intensity hypothesis (Freedman)	1 Personal space (Hall) 2 Territoriality 3 Human territories (Altman) 4 Privacy 5 Defensible space (Newman)

APPLICATIONS: crowd control, urban planning, building design, international relations.

Chapter 7
Social behaviours

Any situation involving more than one person is a social one. We can distinguish between antisocial and prosocial behaviours according to the effects a person has on others. The key question is why some people in some situations behave antisocially or prosocially.

7.1 Antisocial behaviour: Aggression

'WHAT U LOOKING AT?'

I'm in a train going from Birmingham to Coventry with my family, and a woman got upset because I'd sat in a seat on the train that had been booked, but no one was going to be sitting on the seat. She was getting rather stuck up about it and I dragged her out of the chair and gobbed in her face. I said, 'Listen, my wife will sit wherever she wants. I'm not having you telling her where she's sitting.' My wife was carrying a baby at the time. I was rather upset about that as well, but then it was crazy, you know, it was just over-reacting. There was no need for it. But she got up my nose and I just reacted violently.

[from BBC Horizon, 24 May 1993]

Psychology is the business of accounting for why certain people, in certain situations, behave as they do. In this case, there are many factors at work:
- *Anger*, both with the stranger and with his wife.
- *Prejudice*, the woman's way of speech aroused hostility.
- *Personality*, the man may have been born with an aggressive temperament.
- *Home background*, he may have learned to express his anger in this way.
- *Protective response*, he may have been feeling oversensitive because his wife was pregnant.

The behaviour described here highlights two features of aggression: the emotional state and the expression of it. He felt angered and the woman's behaviour triggered an inevitable response. Is there some way that he could learn to react differently?

This unit looks at the reasons why people are aggressive and how their behaviour might be controlled.

DEFINITIONS		
antisocial behaviour	Behaviour which is harmful to others.	
aggression	A first act of hostility with the deliberate intention of harming another or of achieving a goal. Self-assertiveness can be an example of aggression in pursuit of an objective when it imposes on others.	
anger	Hot displeasure. A state of physiological arousal. It is the emotional side of *some* aggressive acts.	
hostility	Similar to anger but implies a longer-lasting and less intense state.	

violence	Unrestrained, excessive or unjustified force.
adaptive response	Behaviour which contributes to the individual's and species' survival.
ethology	The study of behaviour in terms of its survival value and function.
gene	A physical unit which contains DNA. It records the inherited aspects of an individual's makeup.
ritualised fighting	A fixed set of behaviours which communicate aggression. They aim to prevent aggressive escalation and reduce actual injury. They are often innately-determined.
appeasement behaviour	A ritualised behaviour which tries to reduce aggression in another animal.
threat display	A ritualised behaviour which communicates the intention to be aggressive.
dominance hierarchy	A social group where one member is dominant in terms of choice of food, mate and other important resources. The other members of the group occupy varying positions of subordinance.
type A personality	A particular disposition to be competitive, ambitious, impatient and so on. It is controversially linked with an increased likelihood of heart disease and other physical disorders (see Unit 10.2).
prefrontal lobotomy or leucotomy	A surgical procedure to cut the connections between the frontal lobes of the brain and other areas of the cortex. It was introduced in the 1930s as a means of controlling antisocial behaviour, but was not wholly effective and was certainly objectionable.
limbic leucotomy	Another form of psychosurgery, in this case connections to the limbic system are severed.

The nature of aggression

1. What is aggression?
   - *Action*. It is not just thinking about being aggressive.
   - *Intention*. Accidental harm is not aggression.
   - *Emotion*. The stages of aggression are autonomic arousal, cognitive appraisal and emotional expression. This is the same as for all emotions (see Unit 10.1).

2. Hostile and instrumental aggression:
   - Hostile aggression: aggression for the purpose of causing harm.
   - Instrumental aggression: aggression for the purpose of achieving a goal.
   A child who hits another child may do so out of jealousy (hostile) or to get the other's toy (instrumental).

3. Legitimate versus illegitimate aggression:
   - Legitimate aggression: a harmful action may be justified by the need to protect another from harm (a mother attacking an intruder to defend her young) or by a person's role (a policeman arresting members of a violent mob).
   - Illegitimate aggression: where there is no reason for harmful or assertive behaviour (a policeman forcefully arresting a peaceful demonstrator).

4. Cultural differences. There are examples of both aggressive and nonaggressive human societies. This is evidence that some aspects of aggressive behaviour are not universal or innate.
   - Nonaggressive. The *Arapesh* tribe of New Guinea and the *Pygmies* of Africa use weapons to hunt but rarely show any interpersonal aggression. The *Amish* of Eastern America and people of the *Quaker* faith refuse to take part in aggressive

encounters. In World War II the *Swiss* refused to fight on either side, though they are a fairly militaristic nation.

● Aggressive. The *Mundugumour* of New Guinea are extremely aggressive and raise their children with these values (see Unit 9.2). The dominant culture in *America* is one of assertiveness and aggression.

⑤ Human versus animal aggression.   In animals aggression is important for survival. At the same time aggression must be regulated or it will threaten survival.

● Aggression between species (**interspecies**): either for predation (which ends in death), defence against predation or competition over shared resources/territory. Even in predation there is a balance to be struck because it is not in the interest of the predator to wipe out all of its prey.

● Aggression within a species (**intraspecies**): related to mating as in male rivalry, or parenting. A species whose individuals threaten aggression successfully but avoid unrestrained battles is more likely to survive in the long run.

Animals have evolved behaviours which keep intraspecies aggression to optimum levels. These natural regulators may be missing in the case of some human aggression.

● **Ritualised fighting**. For example, threat displays, appeasement, submission, and displacement gestures all stop opponents being injured. One participant backs off before it's too late. Modern warfare in humans prevents such nonverbal signals being used. It is also possible that violent people are less sensitive to such signals.

● **Dominance hierarchies.** Such a system means that subordinate individuals know their place and don't engage in aggressive encounters. In some species, the dominant male polices any fighting. Humans also develop hierarchies (see Unit 6.3).

● **Territories.** Many species operate a strategy where the owner of a territory always wins, this reduces territorial disputes and aggression. Modern housing estates do not provide for the territorial needs of humans (see Unit 6.3).

RESEARCH EXAMPLE | **Clutton–Brock and Albon (1979) The behaviour of the red deer**

METHOD: Naturalistic observation of red deer on the island of Rhum off Scotland.

RESULTS: In the autumn rutting season the stags challenge each other for ownership of females. Clutton-Brock and Albon observed three main stages of ritualised fighting.
1 *Roar contest.* A stag in good condition will roar better. A male with an inferior roar will probably give up now.
2 *Parallel walk.* A kind of broadside display where two males walk back and forth alongside each other. This enables them to assess each other more closely, particularly with respect to body size. A smaller animal may decide to back down at this stage.
3 *Antler clashes.* Proper fighting, the stags interlock antlers and push against each other. Only 25% of the contests reach this stage, and about 25% result in injury, most of it short-term. Usually the larger stag wins.

INTERPRETATION: Animals that avoid unnecessary fighting are at an evolutionary advantage (an adaptive response). An animal who fights risks losing the females to other opportunistic males who may take them while they are fighting or the male may be injured and therefore unable to mate.

Therefore most species have evolved some simple, quick means of assessing their rivals and avoiding aggressive encounters.

This system benefits the species as a whole because it should ensure that the 'best' male mates with the females.

Explanations of aggression and violence

Are some people born aggressive or is their aggression a product of their experience? Is it nature or nurture?

Biological perspective

E xaminer's tip

You should be familiar with the theories specified in your examination syllabus and be able to answer questions on all of them and not on any others which have not been specifically mentioned.

Argument: The fact that some people are more aggressive than others is due to their biological makeup. This may be genetically determined or the effect of diet or other environmental factors.

❶ Hormones.   Aggression may result from high levels of the male hormone, **testosterone**. This would also explain why men are generally more aggressive than women.

In women, there is evidence that pre-menstrual tension is correlated with increases in irritability, hostility, child abuse and crime (Floody, 1968). Levels of **progesterone** increase at this time. This may prepare mothers for parental aggressiveness.

A state of physiological arousal is associated with the release of certain hormones. This 'fight or flight' response is related to **adrenalin** (also called epinephrine).

2 <u>Genes.</u>   Jacobs *et al.* (1965) examined the chromosomes of men in prison. They found a surprising number of men who had XYY sex chromosomes. Normal men are XY and women are XX. They supposed that the extra Y chromosome might make the men more aggressive. Later studies have found that such genetic abnormalities are in fact widespread throughout the general population and therefore can't explain aggression.

Mednick and Hutchings (1978) found that adopted children with biological fathers who were criminals were more likely to become criminals themselves. Some personality disorders may have a genetic origin but are also moderated by the effects of experience.

3 <u>Brain differences.</u>   Bard (1929) found that if parts of the cortex are removed cats display 'sham rage', purring and hissing simultaneously. His conclusion was that the cortex normally inhibits the the **limbic system** (see Unit 10.3), thus preventing aggression. In humans there is some evidence that limbic tumours are associated with aggressive behaviour. In addition, prefrontal or limbic leucotomies sometimes result in reduced aggression. Therefore brain differences might explain individual differences in aggression.

4 <u>Brain chemistry.</u>   Low amounts of the neurochemical **serotonin** have been associated with excessive violence, alcoholism, fire-setting and suicide (see below).

5 <u>Evaluation of the biological perspective</u>
- This approach does not explain *cultural differences*.
- All of these factors are *correlated* with aggression but they may not be the cause of it. In fact, some of them might be an *effect* of being aggressive. For example, hormones might be released as the result of feeling angry (see Unit 10.1).
- Aggression may be influenced by biological factors though they are probably *not the sole determinants*. For example, the fact that men are more aggressive may be due to social norms and child-rearing practices as much as hormones.

RESEARCH EXAMPLE | **Brown *et al.* (1979) The effects of serotonin on aggression**

RESEARCH QUESTION: Are there neurochemical differences between aggressive and nonaggressive people? A neurochemical is a substance found in the nervous system. It is associated with regulating mood and arousal. High levels of serotonin are associated with sleep, low arousal and the inhibition of certain behaviours.

PARTICIPANTS: Twenty-six marines who had been diagnosed as suffering from a personality disorder. They had no history of mental illness. There was also a control group of twenty-six normal males.

METHOD: Correlation.
1 Biochemical data: samples of cerebrospinal fluid (which bathes the brain) were tested for levels of various neurochemicals.
2 Behavioural data: participants were asked about previous episodes of aggression, for example fighting, temper tantrums, school discipline, response to authority. Each participant received a total aggression score.

RESULTS:
1 The experimental group had higher aggression scores than the control group.
2 Within the experimental group, there was a significant negative correlation between aggression and levels of **serotonin**. The violent participants had a lower turnover of the neurochemical than normal.

INTERPRETATION: Low levels of serotonin are related to aggression. High levels of serotonin have been related to sleep. This suggests that serotonin raises or lowers arousal.

It is possible that some people are born with lower production of serotonin and are therefore inclined to greater aggression.

EVALUATION: Since this is a correlation study, it is not clear whether serotonin is a cause or an effect of aggression.

RELATED STUDIES:
Valzelli and Bernasconi (1979) found that a decrease in serotonin turnover was associated with an increase in aggressive behaviour in male rats.

Mawson and Jacobs (1978) found that murder rates are highest in those countries which eat most corn. Corn contains a substance important in the production of serotonin.

Mednick and Hutchings (1978) found that adopted children with biological fathers who were criminals, were more likely to become criminals themselves. This supports a genetic link.

Ethological perspective

Argument: Aggression must be understood in terms of its natural function. Animals, especially males, are biologically programmed to fight over sources of food, territories and members of the opposite sex.

1 One of the classic ethological accounts was from Lorenz (1966). His conclusions were based on observations of animals in their natural environment. He felt that his view was equally applicable to humans because they are governed by the same laws of natural selection. His conclusions were:

- Aggression is an *innate tendency* which is triggered by environmental signals. For example, the male stickleback will behave aggressively when it sees anything red (see Unit 3.3).
- Aggression is a highly *adaptive response*. An individual who is aggressive controls the food, territory and mating. It is the one most likely to survive to reproduce.
- Aggression is *not harmful* behaviour. Any species where aggression leads to death or serious injury will eventually become extinct unless it evolves a form of natural regulation.

2 Evaluation of the ethological perspective:

- This approach is similar to the biological one because it suggests that aggression is *inevitable*.
- The belief that animals have *effective signals* to turn aggression off has been challenged by a number of studies. For example, Goodall (1978) noted that appeasement gestures did not stop fighting amongst a troop of chimpanzees.
- Human aggression is affected by *learning* as much as any innate factors. Therefore any parallels between man and animals may be oversimplified.
- This approach does not account for *cultural differences*.

Social learning perspective

Argument: Experience explains aggressive behaviour. If an aggressive act is positively reinforced, it is more likely to be repeated. A person can be directly or indirectly reinforced. (See Units 3.1 and 3.2 for an explanation of learning and social learning theory, and Unit 9.1 for evidence about the effectiveness of punishment.)

1 Modelling: imitating specific acts.   Bandura *et al.* (1963) showed that, if children watched someone else behave aggressively towards Bobo the doll, they were more likely to do the same themselves (see Unit 3.2). Imitation was even more likely if:

- The model was *rewarded*.
- The model had high *status*. For example, a favourite hero or heroine on TV.
- The child *identified* with the model. For example, the same sex.
- The observer had low *self-esteem*.

2 Learning to be more aggressive.   Watching violence on TV may affect aggression because:

- It presents us with social *norms* which suggest that certain levels of violence are common and acceptable.
- Exposure to violence may *desensitise* us so that we tolerate it more easily.
- It *exaggerates* aggression in people who already have aggressive tendencies. Such people may choose to watch more violent TV programmes.

RESEARCH EXAMPLE   **Eron *et al.* (1972) A longitudinal study of the effects of watching violence on TV**

RESEARCH QUESTION: Can violence on TV be associated with aggressive behaviour?

PARTICIPANTS: 9-year-olds, followed up 10 years later at age 19.

METHOD: Longitudinal, interview and questionnaire.

1 The researchers determined the extent of an 9-year-old's exposure to violence by asking their parents what their favourite television programmes were.

2 They asked peers to rate the participants for aggressiveness.

RESULTS:

1 At age 9 there was a high correlation between aggression and violent television watching.

2 At age 19, boys showed a correlation between violent television at age 9 and peer-rated aggression at 19, but peer-rated aggression at age 9 was not correlated with watching violent television at 19.

3 The findings for girls, if anything, went in the reverse direction.

INTERPRETATION:

1 The findings for boys suggest that watching violent television leads to aggression rather than vice versa.

2 The lack of effect for girls may be because there are fewer aggressive female role models.

EVALUATION:

1 Many studies have found an effect but this does mean that it affects all people in the same way.

2 Violence has always been part of fairy tales, myths and books. Therefore *media* violence is not new. Television and film violence may be different because it is realistic, but lacing in an important emotional element. This may mean that the cause and effects of violence are not learned together.

RELATED STUDIES:

Friedrich and Stein (1973) observed children in a nursery school for three weeks to establish how aggressive they were. After this initial period of observation, the children were shown either aggressive cartoons, prosocial or neutral films. In the final two weeks behaviour was again observed. Children who were above average in aggression initially were affected by the violent cartoons, those who were neutral did not react to either type of programme. This suggests an interaction between personality and the effects of violent programs.

Gerbner and Gross (1976) found that people who watched a lot of television rated the outside world as being more dangerous and threatening than it actually is. They overestimate the occurrence of crimes such as rapes and muggings. This is called **deviance amplification** (see Unit 5.1).

See also Williams, in Unit 9.2.

---

3 <u>Child-rearing</u>.   The most significant learning influence in a child's life is their parents. Particular styles of parenting or child-rearing may lead to higher levels of aggression in later life.

RESEARCH EXAMPLE   **Patterson *et al.* (1989) A developmental perspective on antisocial behaviour**

RESEARCH QUESTION: Is it possible to identify reliable developmental experiences which can be associated with later delinquency?

PARTICIPANTS: 200 families of normal boys aged between 8 an 16.

METHOD: Natural experiment, survey, observation, correlation. The researchers compared families having at least one highly aggressive child with other families of the same size and socio-economic status who had no problem children. Assessments were made through questionnaires and interviews with children, parents, peers and teachers, as well as home observations.

RESULTS: They identified **coercive home environments**. These are families where little affection is shown, family members are constantly struggling with each other, and using aggressive tactics to cope. Parents rarely use social reinforcement or approval as a means of behaviour control. Instead they use physical punishment, nagging, shouting, teasing. The children in such families are typically manipulative and difficult to discipline.

INTERPRETATION: The coercive home environment may create aggressiveness in a number of ways:

1 *Control theory*. Harsh discipline and lack of supervision results in disrupted bonding between parent and child, and lack of identification.

2 The parental behaviours *provoke* aggressiveness in the children. For example, through nagging.

3 *Modelling*. The children are experiencing aggressive means of solving disputes at home and not being given clear examples of alternative methods.

4 Such children become *resistant* to punishment, and progressively harder to restrain.

5 This aggressive behaviour leads them to be *rejected* by their peers, join deviant peer groups and to fail at school.

APPLICATIONS: The way to prevent this is to teach parents alternative skills, and give antisocial children social skills training to prevent rejection and remedial help to help their failure at school.

RELATED STUDIES:
Mead (1935) observed the Arapesh tribe of New Guinea and thought that their child-rearing practices encouraged gentle and nonaggressive behaviour in both boys and girls (see Unit 9.2).

4 Evaluation of the social learning perspective:
- It is an *oversimplified* account of behaviour. People are *not* consistently rewarded for aggression. Often they are punished.
- This approach *can* account for *cross-cultural* and individual differences between people.
- It also explains the fact that people *imitate* specific acts of violence.

Motivational perspective

Argument: Individuals are driven or motivated to behave in an aggressive manner because of being physiologically aroused and because of the presence of specific cues.

1 The frustration–aggression hypothesis.   Dollard *et al.* (1939) suggested that frustration always leads to some form of aggression and aggression is always the result of frustration. Aggression motivates us to do something. We then *learn* ways to express our aggression.

2 The arousal–aggression hypothesis.   The more general state of physiological arousal may be a better explanation for aggression than frustration. Arousal can come from a number of sources, such as anger, happiness, pain or overcrowding (see Unit 6.3).

3 Evaluation of the motivational perspective:
- Arousal doesn't always lead to aggression.
- And aggression may arise before arousal.
- This approach doesn't explain *cultural* or individual differences.
- Arousal is related to the presence of certain *hormones* (biological explanation).

RESEARCH EXAMPLE   **Geen and Berkowitz (1967) Conditions which facilitate aggression**

RESEARCH QUESTION: Frustration leads to emotional arousal. When a person is in an aroused state, will they be more likely to respond to an aggressive attack on a third party by behaving aggressively themselves?

PARTICIPANTS: 108 male college students.

METHOD: Experiment. Each participant worked alongside a confederate in one of 12 experimental conditions:
- Group 1: Task frustration: given an insoluble puzzle. The confederate solved his.
- Group 2: Insult: not only did the participant fail to complete his puzzle but the confederate made remarks about the participant's stupidity.
- Group 3: Control: participant had an easily soluble puzzle and the confederate remained neutral.

All participants viewed one of two films:
- Film 1: An aggressive film, Kirk Douglas in *The Champion*, a film about boxing.
- Film 2: A nonaggressive but physically active film about an foot race.

Finally all participants were placed in a learning experiment. The confederate introduced himself as 'Kirk' or 'Bob'. The participants were told to give electric shocks to the learner (the confederate) every time he made a mistake.

RESULTS: Intensity of shocks delivered by participants:

	Boxing film		Track film	
Treatment	Kirk	Bob	Kirk	Bob
Control	3.07	2.60	3.34	3.01
Task frustration	4.49	3.84	3.91	2.98
Insult	6.20	5.41	3.99	4.23

1 The frustrated participants gave more shocks to the 'learner'.
2 Participants who watched an aggressive film gave more shocks.
3 Participants gave most shocks to a 'learner' in some way associated with the aggression they viewed. ('Kirk' was associated with the Kirk Douglas film).

INTERPRETATION: The aggressive scenes acted as a trigger for already frustrated participants. People are most willing to vent their aggression on a person in some way associated with the source of their aggressive feelings.

RELATED STUDIES:

Berkowitz *et al.* (1981) created a state of general arousal by using pain. Participants' hands were placed in cold or warm water while they delivered rewards or punishments to a partner (not shocks). The cold water condition produced greater harm to their partner.

Calhoun's (1962) study of overcrowding (see Unit 6.3) showed a link between arousal and aggressive behaviours.

Psychodynamic perspective

Argument: Aggression comes from unconscious, instinctive drives. Freud (1920) called it **Thanatos**, after the Greek God of Death. It works in opposition to the life-force, **Eros**.

1 Freud's conclusions were:
- Aggression is naturally produced and *builds up* until it is released.
- This may be achieved either through violent behaviour or channelled into more socially acceptable forms such as sport. The act of release is called **catharsis**.
- If the energy remains pent-up this will cause *psychological disorders*. For example, depression, suicide or masochism.

2 Evaluation of the psychodynamic perspective:
- Freud's views are not supported by *empirical evidence*. For example, sports activity is often associated more with increased rather than decreased aggression.
- This approach does not account for *cultural differences*.

A conclusion: Nature versus nurture

The truth is that each approach explains part of the story.
- Biological: Aggression levels are affected by hormones and neurochemicals.
- Ethology: Aggression serves important survival functions.
- Social Learning: Aggression is learned through imitation and child-rearing styles.
- Motivation: Arousal and appropriate cues trigger an aggressive response.
- Psychodynamic: The release of aggressive energies is cathartic.

Aggressive behaviour is caused by innate, biological factors which are modified by cultural norms and personal experiences.

EXAMPLE **Human violence**

Violence is an extreme form of aggression, not just harm but great harm. Why do some people commit violent crimes yet not all crime is violent?
1 They are imitating the behaviour of others.
2 They are positively reinforced in their actions. For example, a wife beater might find that his wife is more obedient.
3 The presence of aversive stimuli, frustration and other unpleasant stimuli, motivate aggressive behaviour.

Application: How to cope with human aggression

Solutions are related to cause. If aggression is caused by biological factors, then it needs to be redirected or treated. If the cause is environmental or learned, then relearning or social change is necessary.

1 Unlearning aggression.   In the same way that aggression is learned it can be unlearned. For example, providing nonaggressive models, or models who are negatively reinforced (or punished), or rewarding nonaggressive behaviour.

2 Removing aggressive cues.   Reducing violence in the media so that individuals with a tendency to be aggressive are not triggered to commit violent acts or imitate what they see. Reducing violence in the media may also alter social norms about the acceptability of aggression in certain situations.

3 Teaching nonaggressive skills.   Prisons might train people who had violent tendencies to find ways of redirecting their emotions.

Parents can be taught technique. For example, the **time-out technique** uses methods which withdraw attention from a naughty child. The child is sent to their room or sat in a chair facing the wall. A parent using physical punishment is serving as an aggressive model in their hostile action and rewarding the child with attention. The time-out technique works best when the child is also rewarded for cooperative behaviour.

4 Socially acceptable ways of channelling aggression.   We can learn to express our aggression verbally, channel it into other activity such as sport, or fantasise about violent action while never doing anything. Suitable facilities should be provided for children and adults in areas where violence is high.

5 Undoing aggressive motives.   A tense situation might be diffused through incompatible responses, such as tickling someone who's angry or offering apologies (a form of submission). If you know mitigating circumstances, such as hearing that someone was late because their dog was run over, it reduces feelings of anger.

6 Ritualising aggression.   Encouraging people to express angry feelings in fixed, more acceptable ways to prevent escalation. For example, learning appropriate appeasement gestures or effective threat displays which stop further aggression.

7 Chemical means.   Giving drugs to counteract hormones in cases of excessive aggression. In some cases it is thought that certain food substances may lead to aggression, therefore a change of diet might be tried.

8 Psychosurgery.   Lobotomy is a controversial method used in the past. Recent use is very rare and not related to aggression, where drugs are a more suitable method of control. Ethical objections include possible side effects, lack of consent and irreversibility.

9 Encouraging prosocial behaviour.   Discourages and controls antisocial behaviour.

Examiner's tip

Make sure you relate suggestions about reducing aggression to psychological explanations rather than using anecdotal material.

Quick test 7.1

1 What is the function of the *parallel walk*? (*MEG, 1993*)
2 State **one** reason why members of the same species might be involved in physical conflict. (*MEG, 1994*)
3 Give **one** advantage to animals of avoiding physical fighting. (*MEG, 1993*)
4 Describe **one** way that animals and humans differ in their aggressive behaviour. (*MEG, 1993*)
5 Male violence is a serious social problem. Different solutions might be suggested depending on whether male aggression is due to social or biological influences. Give a suggestion of how male violence might be reduced (a) using a biological method, and (b) using a social method. (*MEG, 1992*)

Summary

BIOLOGICAL PERSPECTIVE	ETHOLOGICAL PERSPECTIVE	SOCIAL LEARNING PERSPECTIVE	MOTIVATIONAL PERSPECTIVE	PSYCHODYNAMIC PERSPECTIVE
1 Hormones 2 Genes 3 Brain differences 4 Brain chemistry	1 Innate tendency 2 Adaptive response 3 Not harmful	1 Modelling (Bandura *et al.*) 2 Learning to be more aggressive (Eron *et al.*) 3 Child-rearing (Patterson *et al.*)	1 Frustration-aggression hypothesis 2 Arousal-aggression hypothesis	1 Naturally-produced 2 Released by catharsis 3 Pent-up aggression causes disorder

APPLICATIONS: Coping with human aggression.

7.2 Prosocial behaviour

THIRTY-EIGHT SILENT WITNESSES

On 13 March 1964, a young woman, named Kitty Genovese, was stabbed in New York. There is, unfortunately, nothing remarkable about this, *except* in this instance there turned out to be 38 people who watched what happened and did nothing. Such apathy deeply troubled many people.

The woman was returning from work as the manageress of a bar at around 3 a.m. She parked her car and, as she got out, she noticed a man in the parking lot. She headed along the street towards a police telephone box. The man caught her and she screamed 'Oh, my god, he stabbed me! Please help me!' Many lights came on in nearby apartments. One person shouted from his window, 'Let that girl alone'. The attacker walked away, but no one appeared so, as she struggled towards her home, he attacked again. She screamed 'I'm dying'. Again lights went on and the man got into his car and drove away. The woman once more staggered to her feet and got as far as a doorway near her apartment. The assailant returned a final time and stabbed her to death. The first and only call the police received was at 3.50 a.m. and they arrived at the scene two minutes later.

Why were her pleas met with such apathy? The police were puzzled that so many people did not even pick up their telephones from the safety of their own apartments. The witnesses said they didn't want to get involved or they thought it was a lover's quarrel. They also blamed the police because, on previous occasions, others had shown little interest in calls to such crimes.

Who do we blame? Is it the fault of the witnesses that she died, or her attacker? Some people felt, at the time, that the apathetic onlookers should be punished because people should feel a moral obligation to help.

There are other kinds of bystander behaviour. In some situations people *are* helpful, and *some* people are more helpful or altruistic.

In the midst of a heavy snowstorm a jet took off from Washington airport. Almost immediately it stalled and plunged into the icy waters of the Potomac river, hitting several vehicles on a bridge which were stopped in rush hour traffic. Many members of the rescue service risked their lives in pulling survivors out of the water. The greatest altruism was shown by one nameless passenger.

THE 'REAL HERO OF THIS'

WASHINGTON, Jan 13 – There was a hero, name unknown, in today's plane crash into the iced-over waters of the Potomac River.

To the rescuers in the helicopter, he was only a head in the water, a balding man, perhaps in his mid-50s, with a heavy mustache.

He was clinging with five others to the tail section of the Air Florida 737, the only part of the plane still afloat. The helicopter crew, Donald W. Usher and M. Eugene Windsor of the Federal Park Police, threw down a yellow ring life preserver attached to a rope.

Passed Preserver to Others

'He could have gone on the first trip,' said the pilot, Officer Usher. 'We threw the ring to him first, but he passed it to somebody else,' a man who was bleeding badly from a head injury.

'We went back five times, and each time he kept passing the ring to someone else, including three ladies who were hanging onto the tail section,' Mr Usher said.

Finally, after making several trips and plucking everyone else from the water, the helicopter returned to pick up the man who had put the others first.

'We flew back out to get him but he was gone,' Officer Usher said.

'The Real Hero of This'

'We really want to know who he was. That gentleman put everyone else ahead of himself. He is the real hero of this whole thing,' Mr Usher continued: 'There's no doubt about it. You have to ask yourself the question: If you were in his situation, a hundred yards from shore and knowing that every minute you were closer to freezing to death, could you do it? I really don't think I could.'

The officers said that when they failed to find the man in the water near the wreckage, they began circling the area to see if he had drifted away from the tail section, but they saw nothing.

'I cried when I did not see him,' Officer Windsor said, biting his lip and fighting back tears again as he told reporters about the man late tonight. 'If I could have seen him under the water, I would have jumped in myself to try to pull him out, dead or alive.'

DEFINITIONS	**prosocial behaviour**	Behaviour which benefits others, and may or may not benefit the helper. It is a basic social value.
	altruism	Behaviour when you put the interests of others before the interests of yourself. An altruistic act may involve some cost or risk to the altruist.
	helping behaviour	Providing assistance to someone in need. Unlike altruism, there is no personal sacrifice.
	co-operation	To work together for mutual benefits.
	bystander effect [bystander apathy]	The presence of others decreases the likelihood that anyone will offer help.
	empathy	A person's ability to experience the emotions of other people.

Prosocial behaviour

Psychologists are often asked to explain why people are antisocial. However, *lack* of prosocial behaviour can equally explain some of today's problems.

❶ Altruism.   Selfless behaviour with the *sole* motive of someone else's good, not your own personal satisfaction, and sometimes at considerable personal cost. For example, jumping in to save a drowning man. Other examples, such as donating blood or Japanese kamikaze pilots, can be understood in terms of more than altruism.

❷ Helping behaviour.   A psychological concept to describe the more commonplace behaviour which requires little or no 'cost' with some 'reward', even if it's only feeling good.

❸ Co-operation.   Helping behaviour which has mutual benefits.

❹ Routine courtesies.   There are many other behaviours which smooth the wheels of social interaction. They are not helping someone in need. For example, allowing another to go through a door first or making a guest feel comfortable.

EXAMPLE   **Altruism in the animal world**

The question for ethologists is why altruism exists at all? It makes more sense to expect that selfish animals will be the ones who survive rather than those who sacrifice themselves for the sake of another. Dawkins (1976) proposed the idea of the **selfish gene**. A parent might sacrifice themselves for the sake of their offspring to ensure the survival of their genes (the ultimate purpose of all life is to reproduce itself). The same argument applies to **kinship**. Animals promote the survival of any of their kin and thus protect their **gene pool**. The notion of kin can extend to the whole species. This is called the **paradox of selfish altruism** or **kin selection**.

Altruism in humans usually involves an element of choice. A person can weigh up alternatives and decide on one that favours others rather than oneself. Human altruism is also guided by their culture: moral, religious or political values. Animal altruism does not appear to involve choice or culture.

RESEARCH EXAMPLE   **Lerner and Lichtman (1968) Altruistic behaviour in humans**

RESEARCH QUESTION: How do people respond to victims? How are the norms of self-interest adapted to cope with pleas for assistance from another?

PARTICIPANTS: 140 female student volunteers, who participated as part of their college course requirement. Data from 26 participants was excluded because they appeared to see through the deception.

METHOD: Experiment, deception. Participants were told they would work in pairs in a learning experiment. One participant (the learner) would receive negative reinforcement (painful electric shocks) when mistakes were made. The other participant was to be a control, receiving no negative reinforcement. They were told that they would each be given a random number which would indicate which partner got to choose whether to be learner or control.

Each participant was in one of six experimental conditions:
1 Justified self-interest: Told that her random number meant that the choice was hers.
2 Gracious act: Told that the other participant had been given the free choice but had said the choice was up to her partner.
3 Plea for help: Told that the choice was hers but also told that the other girl wished it to be known that she was really scared and would prefer to be the control.
4 Illicit gracious act: Told the other participant hadn't even drawn the random number but wanted her partner to make the choice even though it would probably mean ending up as the learner.
5 Illicit plea for help: Told that the choice was hers but, when the other participant heard this, she said she'd leave the experiment. Therefore the experimenter said the partner could be the control 'if that's OK'.

After each participant stated her choice they were told the true nature of the experiment.

RESULTS: The vast majority of participants behaved altruistically, except when they received no information about their partner or were led to believe that the partner behaved selfishly.

Experimental condition	% choosing shock
1	9%
2	88%
3	72%
4	22%
5	86%

INTERPRETATION: This shows that self-interest isn't the only factor which determines behaviour. Most people take responsibility for their own and an unknown other's fate, given appropriate information.

The Development of prosocial behaviour

Much of prosocial behaviour is governed by a sense of morals, but it is different from morality. Moral development is described in Unit 9.1.

1 Empathy.   Prosocial behaviour depends on the ability to comprehend what someone else is feeling. It is a natural ability, but experience may lead some people to be more or less empathetic. It is possible that aggressive individuals lack empathy. For example, there are schemes to rehabilitate prisoners through talking with their victims and learning to see the crime from the victim's point of view. This should prevent them re-offending.

There is a description of the development of empathy in Unit 9.1.

2 Social norms.   Group norms (see Unit 6.1) instruct us to behave in certain ways. These norms are passed on through our moral, religious and political systems. Some examples:
- The norm of *social responsibility*: we feel a duty to help those who are dependent or more needy.
- The norm of *social justice*: we help others who do not deserve their suffering.
- The norm of *reciprocity*: if we help another, we are more likely to be helped ourselves when the need arises.
- Helping behaviour wins *social approval*.
- *Group* norms: some groups have particularly strong prosocial norms. For example, people in the French resistance or the Civil Rights movement in America. Individuals are affected by group norms even when the group is not present.

3 Social learning.   Like antisocial behaviour, prosocial behaviour can be learned.
- *Positive reinforcement*: praise, respect of others or increased liking.
- *Modelling* prosocial behaviour in others.

RESEARCH EXAMPLE | **Beaman *et al*. (1978) Increasing helping rates through imitation**

RESEARCH QUESTION: Are people more likely to help if they know about the psychology of helping behaviour?
PARTICIPANTS: Sixty psychology students.

METHOD: Experiment, deception. Session 1:

Group 1: The experimental group received a lecture or a film about helping behaviour.

Group 2: The control group had a lecture on obesity and emotions.

All participants were asked to report to the experimenter's office (session 2). They were then asked to report to another room and, en route encountered a confederate sprawled against the corridor wall. The experimenter secretly observed the participant's behaviour.

RESULTS: 43% of the experimental group offered to help compared with 25% of those in the control group. There was no difference between whether they had seen a film or lecture.

INTERPRETATION: Prosocial behaviour can be learned, in this case through explicit teaching.

RELATED STUDIES: Bryan and Test (1967), see Unit 9.1, showed how people were more likely to help a stranded motorist if they had just seen someone doing the same thing. The model may act as a cue to helpfulness.

---

❹ <u>Child-rearing practices</u>.   Various aspects of parental behaviour will encourage prosocial behaviour. This is essentially another form of social learning.

RESEARCH EXAMPLE   **Rosenhan (1970) Parents as prosocial models**

RESEARCH QUESTION: Why do some people engage in acts which are altruistic? For example, working in the French resistance during World War II.

PARTICIPANTS: Sixty-eight Black and White adults who had contributed financially or who participated in US civil rights activities in the 1960s.

METHOD: Interview, correlation, natural experiment. Participants were interviewed for as long as 12 hours about their involvement in the movement (why, how, where) and about their personal history. The data revealed two subgroups among the active volunteers:

1 The *fully committed* who were involved in more than a few 'freedom rides' and were active for more than a year. They gave up homes and careers to work for the movement.

2 The *partially committed* who did not sacrifice important aspects of their lives. (Strictly, this is not altruism but rather, helping behaviour).

RESULTS:

1 The fully committed had warmer relations with their parents. Their parents were liberals who expressed outrage about moral issues *and* did something about it.

2 The partially committed described their parents in negative or ambivalent terms. Some of them had run away from home, or were openly hostile. Their parents were also liberals, but they did not practice what they preached in terms of moral behaviour.

3 The financial contributors tended to be involved because it was a socially approved activity.

4 There was very little difference between Black and White civil rights workers.

INTERPRETATION: Models who do rather than say are more effective.

EVALUATION:

1 Parental behaviour came from unreliable retrospective reports.

2 Correlations do not identify a cause.

RELATED STUDIES:

Zahn-Waxler *et al.* (1979) found that parents who deal with wrongdoing by punishing and giving no explanation inhibit the development of helpful and altruistic behaviour in their children. This may be because they do not encourage the development of empathy.

The bystander effect

❶ <u>Demonstrating the effect</u>.

RESEARCH EXAMPLE   **Darley and Latané (1968) Bystander intervention in emergencies**

RESEARCH QUESTION: Darley and Latané responded to the tragic case of Kitty Genovese (see beginning of this unit) with a desire to find out what had prevented her neighbours from helping. Was it because the large number of bystanders has an inverse effect on the motivation to help? One might think that the more people there are, the more help there would be. Darley and Latané proposed that the opposite is true. The larger the number of people, the less responsibility each person feels. They called this the **diffusion of responsibility**.

PARTICIPANTS: Seventy-two mainly female undergraduates on an introductory psychology course.

METHOD: Experiment, deception. They asked students to discuss any personal problems they were having with other students. To avoid any embarrassment they arranged for each participant to be in a separate cubicle and to talk over an intercom. Of course, the other participants were non-existent.
- Group 1 thought they were talking with one other student.
- Group 2 believed there were two other people.
- Group 3 were told there were five other participants.

During the conversation, an emergency situation is created when one 'student' complains of feeling unwell. He had previously mentioned that he is prone to epileptic seizures. Over the intercom you can hear that the student is clearly having a seizure and then he becomes silent.

RESULTS:

Condition	% who sought help before silence	% who eventually sought help	Average time delay
Group 1, no bystanders	85%	100%	52 seconds
Group 2, one bystander	62%	85%	93 seconds
Group 3, four bystanders	31%	62%	166 seconds

INTERPRETATION: Group size is related to helping behaviour. The larger the group of bystanders the less likely each individual is to offer help, and help will be slower.

Latané and Darley (1970) suggested that there are five steps in responding to an emergency. At any stage helping behaviour may be prevented.
1 You must *notice* the event.
2 You must *interpret* that the event does require help.
3 You must take personal *responsibility*.
4 You must decide what *action* to take.
5 Do it.

EVALUATION: The lack of help may be because the participants couldn't see whether anyone else was helping.

RELATED STUDIES:
Latané and Darley (1968) arranged for participants to fill out a fake questionnaire. During this activity the room filled with white smoke. If the participant was alone 75% reported the emergency within four minutes. If two other participants were present this dropped to 12%. The participants persisted with the questionnaire despite rubbing their eyes and choking on the smoke.

---

② Characteristics of the *situation* which lead to the bystander effect.

RESEARCH EXAMPLE **Clark and Word (1972) Why don't bystanders help? Because of ambiguity?**

RESEARCH QUESTION: Is the bystander effect due to the fact that the presence of others increases the ambiguity of the situation? For example, 'Why isn't anyone else helping, maybe there's something I haven't realised?'

PARTICIPANTS: 150 naive male undergraduates.

METHOD: Experiment, deception. Participants were asked to fill out a questionnaire in a lab. While they are doing this, a maintenance worker (confederate) walked through the room to an adjacent room carrying a ladder and a Venetian blind. Three minutes later the ladder and blind crashed to the floor:
- Condition 1: *Low ambiguity*: the crash was followed by groans and an exclamation, 'Oh my back, I can't move' .
- Condition 2: *High ambiguity*: they heard nothing after the crash.

Participants were either alone, in a two person or five person group.

RESULTS:

Mean reaction times (in seconds) and percentage of helping:

Condition	Low ambiguity	High ambiguity
Alone	6.97 (100%)	55.67 (30%)
One bystander	7.74 (100%)	61.59 (20%)
Four bystanders	10.39 (100%)	52.18 (40%)

1 Participants are more willing to help in a less ambiguous situation.
2 Ambiguity has a much stronger effect than the number of bystanders.

INTERPRETATION: Ambiguity of a situation decreases the likelihood of helping.

③ Characteristics of the *victim* which lead to the bystander effect. Certain personal characteristics of the victim may increase or decrease the likelihood of helping behaviour:

- *Victim's appearance.* Many instances of helping require immediate assessment and therefore it is not surprising that we use superficial clues to enable us to decide on appropriate action.
- *Victim's behaviour.* We may mistake what we interpret as the cause. For example, thinking that the victim is drunk or that the couple struggling are having an argument. We are less likely to help if the person doesn't seem to deserve it (the norm of social justice).

RESEARCH EXAMPLE | **Piliavin *et al.* (1969) Good Samaritanism: An underground phenomenon?**

RESEARCH QUESTION: People who are partly responsible for their plight should receive less help. In addition, if the victim is drunk, he might become disgusting, embarrassing and/or violent. How do bystanders respond to such aspects of a victim's behaviour in a natural setting?

PARTICIPANTS: Four teams of psychology students (two males and two females, both Black and White) acted as victims and observers. The true participants of the experiment were over 4,000 people travelling on the New York subway.

METHOD: Field experiment (a classic). The male 'victim' boarded the train and, as it pulled out of the station, staggered and collapsed.
1 The *drunk condition*: the victim smelled of liquor and carried a liquor bottle wrapped in a brown bag.
2 The *cane condition*: the victim appeared sober and carried a black cane.
The observers noted the race, sex and location of all passengers and helpers. They timed how long help was in coming. After 70 seconds, a confederate stepped in to help.

RESULTS:
1 The cane victim received immediate help on 95% of the trials (there were 65 in all).
2 The drunk victim was helped spontaneously 50% of the time (38 trials in all).
3 Black victims were less likely to receive help in the drunk condition.
4 The *more* passengers in the immediate vicinity of the victim, the *more* likely help would be given.

INTERPRETATION:
1 Characteristics of the victim influence the willingness of bystanders to help.
2 This study found a reversal of the 'diffusion of responsibility'. More bystanders meant more help. Why?

- *Ambiguity*: It was clearly an emergency.
- *Responsibility*: with the immediate presence of others it was clear that no one else was helping. It was impossible to ignore.
- *Costs*: The costs of helping were low and of not helping were high.
- *Ecological validity*: 'Diffusion of responsibility' may be a laboratory phenomenon. In real situations people do feel personal responsibility.

RELATED STUDIES:
Bickman (1974) left a dime in a telephone box. If the experimenter was dressed in a suit he got the dime back 77% of the time, if he was wearing unkempt work clothes there was a 38% return rate.
    Benson *et al.* (1976) (described at the beginning of Chapter 5) demonstrated that physical attractiveness is associated with increased helping behaviour, even more so than race or gender.

---

④ Characteristics of the *bystander* which lead to the bystander effect.

- Bystander's *gender*. Piliavin *et al.* (1969) found that men are more likely to help than women, but this is probably because women feel more open to attack and also have less confidence in their ability to help. For example, where a car has broken down.
- Bystander's *race*. Piliavin *et al.* (1969) found more helping between members of the same race.
- Bystander's *personality*. Is there such a thing as a 'helpful person'? Most people help in some situations and not others. The evidence on child–rearing suggests that some people are generally more helpful than others (see 'Development of prosocial behaviour', earlier in this unit).

RESEARCH EXAMPLE | **Hartshorne and May (1928) Are some people generally more helpful?**

RESEARCH AIM: The Character Education Inquiry was undertaken to evaluate moral and religious education, and its association with moral behaviours such as helping. In order to do this the researchers developed methods by which they could measure moral behaviour and attitudes.

PARTICIPANTS: Over 10,000 children between the ages of 8 and 16.

METHOD: Experiment, survey. This was an enormous project, lasting five years. The researchers developed 33 ways to measure anti- and prosocial behaviours in a variety of situations (school classroom, athletic contests, parties and at home). The measures were either directly of behaviour or using tests to establish moral attitudes.

The direct measures were ones that tempted the children to lie, cheat, steal or to demonstrate their honesty or helpfulness. For example:

● The Planted Dime Test: pupils were given a little box containing several puzzles. There was a dime in the box belonging to a puzzle which wasn't used and the tester never referred to it. Which pupils took the dime before returning the box?

● Children were given classroom tests and assessed for cheating in terms of whether they copied from an answer sheet which was available or added their scores incorrectly.

Examples of test questions:

● Do you usually pick up papers and trash that others have thrown on the schoolroom floor?

● Do you usually report the number of a car you see speeding?

● Did you ever act greedily by taking more than your share of anything?

● Did you ever pretend to understand a thing when you really did not understand it?

● Have you ever disobeyed any law of your country or rule of your school?

RESULTS: They found that children were not always honest or helpful. A child would behave prosocially in some situations but not others. The correlation between different situations was very low, 0.23.

They also found that methods of direct moral instruction, such as Sunday Schools, if anything made children less rather than more honest.

INTERPRETATION: The fact that people are honest in some situations and not others seems obvious, but it goes against the idea of a general trait of honesty. Mischel's situational theory of personality (see Unit 9.3) suggests that all personal traits are responses to certain *situations* rather than *consistent* personality features.

APPLICATIONS: Hartshorne and May suggest that deceit as a social problem can best be tackled by controlling the child's experiences in such a way as to make deception unnecessary and, at the same time, building up a series of behaviour habits which are honest.

RELATED STUDIES: See Unit 9.1, 'Moral inconsistency'
Rushton (1980) found that children who help or share in one situation are more likely to do the same in *similar* situations. This suggests that there is some consistency.

---

⑤ <u>A summary.</u>   When and why does bystander apathy occur?

● *Diffusion of responsibility* (lack of personal responsibility). Everyone thinks that someone else in the group may be in a better or more qualified position to help. The psychology of the crowd encourages deindividuation and antisocial norms. However, even when a participant is alone there is not a 100% rate of helping so this is not the only explanation.

● *Attention.* The bystander may simply not notice the victim.

● *Informational influence.* In ambiguous or novel situations we look to others to tell us what to do. Each non-responding bystander sends the same message to the others, 'It's OK, no action needs to be taken'. This is sometimes called **pluralistic ignorance**.

● *Ambiguity.* The circumstances surrounding an emergency are often confused. For example, is the woman being attacked or is she arguing with her boyfriend? By the time the confusion is resolved other factors have come into play.

● *Evaluation apprehension.* The bystander fears that he may do something inappropriate or actually wrong, and wants to avoid looking foolish. The larger the audience the more inhibited we feel.

● *Confusion of responsibility.* If you help, other bystanders may mistake your involvement for actually being responsible for the victim's suffering or that you know the victim.

● *Costs of intervening.* Helping behaviour is moderated by any 'costs'. There may be real costs in terms of physical danger or long term matters, such as court appearances, which make people feel that they don't want to get involved.

Practical applications

An understanding of the bystander effect might be used to increase prosocial behaviour:

1 <u>Assigning responsibility</u>.   One social psychologist, Cialdini (1985) was involved in a car accident. He watched as other cars passed by without stopping.

> *I remember thinking, 'Oh no, it's happening just like the research says. They're all passing by!' I consider it fortunate as a social psychologist, I knew exactly what to do. Pulling myself up so I could be seen clearly, I pointed at the driver of one car: 'Call the police'. To a second and third driver, pointing directly each time: 'Pull over we need help'. The responses were instantaneous. (p. 118)*

2 <u>Teaching</u>.   The research by Beaman *et al.* (earlier in this unit) suggests that knowing about the bystander effect may make people less likely to be affected by it.

3 <u>Prosocial television</u>.   There is some evidence that prosocial television influences behaviour in a positive direction (research tends to concentrate on the effects of antisocial television). For example, Forge and Phemister (1987) found that the behaviour of preschool children was influenced by prosocial cartoons.

Quick test 7.2

1 What is *altruism*?

2 How can parents help their children develop prosocial behaviour?

3 Children learn prosocial behaviour through their parents. Describe **two** other ways that people develop prosocial behaviour.

4 Why is a bystander less likely to help when other people are about?

5 A person might not offer to help even when they are alone. Why might that be?

6 Could the study by Piliavin *et al.* be called an experiment?

7 Suggest **one** ethical problem with this study.

8 Give **one** example of how psychologists measure helping behaviour.

9 Give **two** problems with studying bystander behaviour in a laboratory. (*MEG, 1991*)

10

| A | → | B | → | C | → | D |

| Noticing | Deciding whether or not it is an emergency | Taking personal responsibility | Giving help |

People often give different reasons for not helping in an emergency situation. For each reason given below, indicate which stage of the decision-making process it is concerned with by writing the letter of the stage in the space provided.

Reason given	Stage of decision-making process
(i) It's not my problem.	....
(ii) It didn't look serious.	.... (*MEG, 1993*)

(Adapted from Latané and Darley)

Summary

TYPES OF PROSOCIAL BEHAVIOUR	DEVELOPMENT OF PROSOCIAL BEHAVIOUR	THE BYSTANDER EFFECT
1 Altruism	1 Empathy	1 Demonstrating the effect (Darley and Latané)
2 Helping behaviour	2 Social norms	2 Characteristics of the situation (Clark and Word)
3 Co-operation	3 Social learning	3 Characteristics of the victim (Piliavin *et al.*)
4 Routine courtesies	4 Child-rearing practices	4 Characteristics of the bystander (Hartshorne and May)

APPLICATIONS:

1 Coping with situations where help is needed.

2 Teaching prosocial behaviour.

3 Prosocial television programmes.

Chapter 8
Personal development

Development is the sequence of changes which occur over a person's lifetime. Many of the changes are due to inherited factors and maturation (nature). At least as much is due to the influence of other people and the physical environment (nurture).

8.1 Attachment and separation

THE IMPORTANCE OF LOVE

Bowlby (1951) said 'mother love in infancy and childhood is as important for mental health as are vitamins and proteins for physical health' At the time he wrote this, people were amazed. No one had considered that emotional health might be so important.

Widdowson (1951) studied a group of orphanage children who were showing signs of malnutrition. They were given dietary supplements but this didn't help. Their harsh and unsympathetic supervisor was replaced. After this the children's weight improved.

It is possible that the harsh supervisor might have harassed them during eating so that they never finished their meal. Alternatively, it may be that they were underdeveloped because they lacked affection and emotional security. Food alone was not enough.

This condition is called **deprivation dwarfism**: psychological problems accompanied by physical under-development. The physiological explanation for this would be that stress causes certain hormones to be produced which affect physical health (see Unit 10.2). Such an association between emotion and under-development can also be seen in **anorexia nervosa**.

In this chapter, the relationship between early emotional development and later consequences is examined.

DEFINITIONS	attachment	An intense emotional relationship between two people that endures over time. In infancy, it is the mutual bond between the infant and its caregiver(s): 1 It makes sure that the caretaker is near for safety and feeding. 2 It is a model for healthy emotional relationships later in life.
	monotropy	Bowlby's concept that there is one main attachment bond which differs in strength and quality from all other bonds.
	sociability	The willingness to interact with others. This is different from **socialisation**. In infants, it ensures the involvement of people who will take care of the infant. In adults, it is important for mating.
	socialisation	The process of learning what is right and wrong in your culture.

Examiner's tip

'Socialisation' is not the same as 'socialising'.

reciprocal behaviour	Responding appropriately to the behaviour of another.
social referencing	Using other people's emotional expressions to resolve ambiguous situations.
critical period	An innately determined period of time during which the infant is most ready to learn certain behaviours (see Unit 3.3).
innate	Inherited.
privation	*Lack* of attachments, having formed no attachments.
deprivation	*Loss* of attachments. The loss of maternal care but *not necessarily* the mother-figure.
separation	The physical loss of the mother-figure though not maternal care, as others may continue to provide 'mothering'.
separation anxiety	Distress shown when a child's attachment figure leaves the room. There are three stages of separation anxiety: 1 *Protest.* Crying but able to be comforted, inwardly angry and fearful. 2 *Despair.* Calmer, apathetic, no longer looking for caregiver, self-comfort e.g. thumb-sucking or rocking. 3 *Detachment.* Appears to be OK but unresponsive, return of caregiver may be ignored.
affectionless psychopathy	An inability to form emotional relationships, linked to separation experiences in early childhood.

The development of reciprocal behaviour

A baby who *makes* adults feel interest and affection has a greater chance of survival. This is an ethological explanation because it accounts for a behaviour in terms of its survival value (see Unit 3.3).

Some examples of nonverbal behaviours in the infants' repertoire: smiling, imitation, crying, etc.

RESEARCH EXAMPLE   **Brazelton *et al.* (1975) Mother-infant reciprocity**

RESEARCH QUESTION: By the age of 3 weeks an infant behaves differently with an object than with a human. Caretaker-infant interactions can be described as a dance. To what extent is the infant an active participant in the 'dance'? What happens when there are distortions of this normal interaction?

PARTICIPANTS: Twelve mother–infant pairs were studied over the first five months of their lives.

METHOD: Observation. Each study session was recorded by two video cameras, one for the infant's face and one for the mother's face. The videotapes could then be viewed simultaneously to relate the effects each participant had on the other. The sessions were conducted when the infant was alert and active.
1 Mother plays for 3 minutes.
2 Mother leaves for 30 seconds.
3 Mother returns for 3 minutes play.
In a second experiment they deliberately distorted the normal interaction, asking mothers to behave unresponsively, as a means of testing whether the infant is behaving intentionally.

RESULTS:
1 The interaction showed cycles: attention phase and build up to mother's cues, turning away and recovery phase. A rhythm of attention and non-attention, occurring several times a minute.
2 The infant's response to an unresponsive face was to become visibly concerned, trying to get the mother's attention. Finally the infant withdraws into an attitude of helplessness: face averted, body curled up and motionless.

INTERPRETATION: This shows that very young infants are responsive to adult signals and are active participants.

Such attentional cycles allow the infant to learn important emotional and cognitive information from their caregiver, otherwise they would be overwhelmed by information. This **interactional synchrony** is critical for positive development.

RELATED STUDIES:
Seligman (1975) suggests that the infant who finds no response to his behaviour learns **helplessness**. In the same way that an adult does, the infant learns to stop responding. (Helplessness is discussed in Unit 10.2.)

The development of attachment

Who does an infant become attached to?

❶ Feeding.   Mother love is established through feeding the infant at the breast.
- Freud suggested that the origins of love lie in satisfaction of the infant's hunger drive.
- Behaviourists argue that, the infant should come to associate the hand that feeds it with satisfaction of a need. The feeder becomes a conditioned stimulus associated with satisfaction.
- Lorenz (1952) found that goslings became attached to him through mere exposure regardless of whether he fed them or not (see Unit 3.3).

❷ Physical contact.   The person who feeds the infant is also physically close to the infant, spends time with them and interacts socially. Perhaps some of these things are more important than feeding itself.

RESEARCH EXAMPLE | **Harlow (1959) Love in infant monkeys**

RESEARCH QUESTION: Harlow and his associates worked with rhesus monkeys. They reared monkeys apart from their mothers because they could be fed and protected from disease, and therefore more survived. They noticed that their separated monkeys became very attached to the cotton nappy pads at the bottom of their cages and were distressed when their cages were cleaned. This led Harlow to question the relative importance of feeding and bodily contact in the formation of attachment bonds. Is there a basic need for close contact with something soft? Is this stronger than the primary biological need of feeding?

PARTICIPANTS: Eight rhesus monkeys, separated from their mothers a few hours after birth.

METHOD: Experiment. Each monkey was given two 'mothers', a wire one and a cloth one. Milk was provided through a nipple in one of the mothers. Half of the monkeys received milk from the wire mother, the other half from the cloth mother.

RESULTS:
1 All of the monkeys spent more time with the cloth mother and, when frightened, went to the cloth mother.
2 Later these monkeys were unsuccessful at mating, and those females who did become pregnant were poor mothers.

INTERPRETATION: Physical contact appears to be more important than feeding in the development of emotional bonds. Harlow terms this 'love'. Such early deprivation affects later sociability and reproductive success.

APPLICATIONS: These findings influenced the kind of care offered to children in institutions and hospitals. More attention was paid to physical contact.

EVALUATION:
1 With hindsight, these experiments may appear unethical. At the time, however, no one expected that the experiments would cause such distress. This might excuse the early experiments at least.
2 This is a study of *animal* behaviour. Human infants may not be affected in the same way.

RELATED STUDIES:
Klaus and Kennell (1976) found that early contact with newborn babies increased the attachment of the mothers, this included skin-to-skin contact within three hours of birth. The effects were still apparent a year later.

❸ Time.

RESEARCH EXAMPLE | **Fox (1977) Cross-cultural study of attachment on Kibbutzim**

RESEARCH QUESTION: Does the person who spends most time with an infant become their main attachment figure?

PARTICIPANTS: 122 children born and reared on a kibbutzim. In Israel about 4% of the people live in kibbutzim where everything is shared, including childminding. Mothers return to work a few weeks after giving birth. A **metapelet** or nurse looks after the child. By the age of one, the children all live in the Children's House. They spend a few hours each evening with their parents but sleep at the Children's House. They spend the greater amount of time with the metapelet.

METHOD: Cross-cultural observation. Fox observed infant attachment behaviours in a variation of the Ainsworth Strange Situation (described later in this unit): both the natural mother and the metapelet took the role of parent.

RESULTS:
1 The children protested equally when either mother or metapelet left.
2 Behaviour at reunion showed some difference, favouring the mother. Some children sought their mother and were more comforted by her.

INTERPRETATION: Time alone cannot account for strong attachment. The mothers are able to offer quality time. The metapelet spends much of her time in routine childminding activity rather than focusing attention on the child.

EVALUATION:
1 The metapelet with the child at the time of assessment was not a permanent figure. There is quite a high turnover rate on kibbutzim. In this study they found that the minimum length of employment was four months. Where the metapelet is a more permanent figure, attachment might be stronger.
2 Any study which is cross-cultural is prone to bias.

APPLICATIONS: This is particularly important with respect to child care arrangements. The fact that a child spends more time away from their main caregiver may not affect their mutual attachment.

④ Critical period:
  ● Bowlby suggested that children who did not have an attachment by the age of two would never recover.
  ● Attachments form at about the same time as infants start to understand object permanence (Piaget, see Unit 4.4). This suggests that attachment is related to biological processes of maturation.
  ● It may be preferable to talk about a **sensitive period** instead of a critical period. This means that there are times when the infant is more *likely* to learn something. Learning, however, may take place at any time and therefore recovery is always possible.

RESEARCH EXAMPLE **Hodges and Tizard (1989) The effect of early institutional rearing**

RESEARCH QUESTION: What are the long-term effects of early institutionalisation?

PARTICIPANTS: Sixty-five children placed in an institution before the age of four months.

METHOD: Natural experiment, longitudnal study, psychometric, interviews.
There was an explicit policy in the institution against staff forming strong attachments with the children. Before the age of four, an average of 50 different caretakers had looked after the children for at least a week. By the age of four, 24 were adopted and 15 had returned home, often to single parents. The rest remained in the institution.

RESULTS: A study of these children at age eight and at sixteen showed that:
1 Those who were adopted were able to form close bonds with their adoptive parents. However, they showed signs of emotional and attentional problems in school.
2 Those who remained in the institution had similar problems in school.
3 Those children who were restored to their natural homes did less well on almost every measure than those who were adopted.

INTERPRETATION: The children were able to form attachments after the age of four, which is well past the critical age of two suggested by Bowlby. However, the affects of early deprivation seem to be long term.
  Bowlby (1951) claimed that even a bad home is preferable to any institutional upbringing *provided* the maternal bond remains unbroken. These findings suggest that home is not always best.

EVALUATION: The results may be explained in other ways:
1 The adoptive families tended to be of higher social class than the original homes.
2 Restored children went home to difficult relationships and poor conditions.
3 Children who suffer early deprivation are also likely to continue to experience disruption. Their problems maybe due to the continued disruption rather than the effects of early experience alone.

RELATED STUDIES: Pringle and Bossio (1960) compared a group of severely maladjusted children in care with ones who were 'notably stable'. The most marked difference between the two groups was the amount of contact maintained with parents or parent substitutes. *All the* stable children had a lasting relationship, whereas this was true for only *one* of the maladjusted group. Those children who were maladjusted seemed unable to make lasting relationships with other children or adults.

⑤ <u>Sensitivity and responsiveness.</u>   The idea of 'quality time' is that a caregiver gives the infant attention and is responsive to the infant's needs. The person who feeds and cares for the infant is most likely to provide such sensitive social interaction.

RESEARCH EXAMPLE   **Ainsworth (1979) Quality rather than quantity counts**

RESEARCH QUESTION: Ainsworth studied babies in Baltimore and noted one important feature of mother–infant interaction. The mother is used as a secure base for exploration. Is this related to attachment?

PARTICIPANTS: Mothers and babies.

METHOD: Experiment, observation. Ainsworth developed the **Strange Situation** as a standardised means of assessing strength or quality of attachment. The procedure consists of seven three-minute episodes.

The most important thing is what the child does when the parent leaves and when the parent returns. This behaviour is classified as:

- Type A *anxious – avoidant*. No protest when parent leaves, ignores parent's return.
- Type B *securely attached*. Mild protest, on return seeks parent and is easily comforted.
- Type C *anxious – resistant*. Seriously distressed, when parent returns alternatively clings and pushes away.

RESULTS: Ainsworth found that 10% are Type A, 70% Type B and 20% Type C. When children are tested in other cultures, the distribution varies. For example, a German study found 40% of Type A, and a Japanese study found 35% Type C.

Type B is universally the largest group. Such children have been found to be more socially outgoing, independent, cooperative, compliant and curious, and better able to cope with stress.

INTERPRETATION: Ainsworth proposed that it is the quality not quantity of interaction that counts.

Anxious attachment results from mothers who respond less readily to a child's needs. Secure attachment occurs when a mother is sensitive, sees things from infant's viewpoint and is accepting. Ainsworth called this the **caregiving hypothesis**.

APPLICATION: The Strange Situation has become a very popular way of testing the strength of a child's attachment.

RELATED STUDIES: Vaughn *et al.* (1979) studied economically disadvantaged mothers for six months. They found that some of the young children changed from being securely attached to anxious or vice versa in line with changing stress-states in the mother. This suggests that attachment is not a fixed part of the mother–infant relationship.

---

⑥ <u>Individual differences.</u>   Different children may respond to different aspects of their caregiver's behaviour. For example, Schaffer and Emerson (1964, see below) found that some children like cuddling while others don't. Such differences appeared very early on and are therefore not related to how the mothers handled the infant, but must be a matter of innate individual preference (see 'Temperament', Unit 8.4).

⑦ <u>One or more attachments?</u>   The possibilities are:
- An infant needs mother love, or
- A child develops many different attachments, or
- An infant needs one primary attachment, not necessarily the mother. Bowlby called this **monotropy**.

Mothers' love. Attachments need not be just to a mother-figure, it can be to a father, other sibling, grandparent or adoptive/foster family. In Freud and Dann's study (see Unit 9.3) the infants acted as attachment figures for each other.

Different attachments. There are different *kinds* of attachment and each kind is important for healthy development. For example, fathers' style of play is more often physically stimulating and unpredictable, whereas mothers are more likely to hold their infants, soothe them, attend to their needs and read stories. Many societies rely on multiple attachments. For example, Ainsworth (1967) studied the Ganda tribe of Uganda, where most infants were cared for by several adults and formed multiple attachments.

> *Monotropy.* Infants may form many attachments, yet there is still one primary attachment bond which is stronger and offers a different kind of emotional support.

RESEARCH EXAMPLE   **Schaffer and Emerson (1964) The development of social attachments**

RESEARCH AIM: The aim was to explore the nature of attachment behaviour. Some specific questions were asked about the age of onset, the intensity and the objects of attachment, plus any individual differences.

PARTICIPANTS: Sixty babies from a largely working-class area of Glasgow.

METHOD: Survey, naturalistic observation, longitudinal. The infants were observed every four weeks from the age of 0 to 18 months. Attachment was measured in terms of separation protest in seven everyday situations. For example, infant left in pram outside a shop, or passed by while in cot or chair.

RESULTS:
1 *Age* of onset: at about 6-9 months.
2 *Intensity*: this peaked in the month after its first appearance. It was measured by the strength of separation protest. However there were large individual differences. Intensely attached infants had mothers who responded quickly to their demands (high responsiveness) and who offered the child the most interaction. Infants who were weakly attached had mothers who failed to interact.
3 *Objects* of attachment: soon after one main attachment was formed, the infants also became attached to other people. By 18 months very few (13%) were attached to only one person. 31% had five or more, such as the father, grandparent or older sibling.
4 *Time* spent with infant: in 39% of the cases the person who usually fed, bathed and changed the child was *not* the child's primary attachment object.

INTERPRETATION: This indicates that the infant's emotional dependence on a caretaker is *not* related to filling physiological needs. Instead, attachment can be best understood in terms of the various relationships that an infant forms with those who stimulate and respond to it.

Effects of breaking attachment bonds

RESEARCH EXAMPLE   **Bowlby (1946) Forty-four juvenile thieves**

RESEARCH QUESTION: What are the causes of habitual delinquency? Can it be explained in terms of early emotional traumas, particularly disturbance of the mother–child relationship?

PARTICIPANTS: Forty-four 'thieves' or delinquents, children referred to a Child Guidance Clinic who had been involved in stealing. There was a control group of forty-four emotionally-disturbed teenagers, also seen at the Child Guidance Clinic. Their ages ranged from 5 to 16 years. The 'thieves' presumably lacked a social conscience whereas the control group were disturbed but remained emotionally functional.

METHOD: Retrospective observation, psychometric. Bowlby recorded details of their early lives and obtained measures of their present adjustment.

RESULTS: There were two distinctive features of the children studied.
1 Some displayed an 'affectionless' character. This is a lack of normal affection, shame or sense of responsibility.
2 Some of the children had suffered 'early and prolonged separations from their mothers'. In practice this meant that, at least before the age of two, these children had continually or repeatedly been in foster homes or hospitals, often not visited by their families. It does not include those children who were adopted early and therefore had a stable maternal relationship in early life.

Type of case	Separated from mother	Not separated	Total
Affectionless thieves	12	2	14
Other thieves	5	25	30
All thieves	17	27	44
Control cases	2★	42	44

★ Both of these control cases became schizophrenic.

INTERPRETATION: Bowlby termed this disaffected state **affectionless psychopathy** and concluded that it was caused by attachment bonds being disturbed in early life. (See Bowlby's theoretical view, later in this unit).

APPLICATIONS: This is potentially of profound importance for fostering, adoption and day care.

EVALUATION: Bowlby's concept of maternal deprivation had a major impact on post-war parenting. However, the evidence is *flawed* in several respects:

1 It is *retrospective* and unreliable.
2 Some children had in fact been separated from their mothers for *very short* periods.
3 The diagnosis 'affectionless' may not have been reliable.
4 It is *correlational*, we cannot be certain that the *cause* was maternal separation. In fact the children were not just separated from their mothers but experienced traumatic disruptions of their early years. Rutter (1981) suggested that maladjustment could be due to family discord rather than disrupted attachments (see later in this unit).

It is important to distinguish between **deprivation**, **privation** and **separation**. Bowlby originally suggested that deprivation led to affectionless psychopathy. Rutter criticised this, saying that privation may cause emotional maladjustment but deprivation is different.

❶ Privation (lack).   The evidence comes from two sources:
Case histories of children raised in isolation. Notable cases include: Genie (described in Unit 4.5), Isabelle, Anna, the Czech twins P.M. and J.M., sisters Mary and Louise, and a Japanese brother and sister. Such children show enormous developmental and social retardation, however they were mostly very keen to interact and form relationships. When they have been followed up years later their *social* recovery is only partial, inevitably held back by poor linguistic skills. Most of them also suffered permanent *cognitive* deficits. It is difficult to really draw any conclusions from these cases because:
1 They are small samples.
2 The data about their early childhood were collected retrospectively and was anecdotal.
3 There is no way of knowing whether the children had at any time formed attachment bonds. If they *did* have attachments they would be deprived rather than privated.
4 Any lack of social development might be due innate backwardness, or cognitive as well as emotional deprivation.
Studies of institutional care. The study by Hodges and Tizard (earlier in this unit) indicated that children who had formed no attachment bonds until relatively late (aged four), were never able to completely recover. Pringle and Bossio's (1960) study indicates that a child who is rejected and *remains* unwanted is likely to become maladjusted. This supports the view that *privation* leads to permanent emotional damage, whereas *deprivation* can be recovered from.

❷ Deprivation (loss).   Permanent deprivation occurs when a parent dies. For example, Bifulco *et al.* (1992) found that women who had lost their mothers, through prolonged separation or death, before they were 17 were twice as likely to suffer from depressive and anxiety disorders as adults. There was a particularly high rate of adult depression among those whose mothers had died before the age of six. This was not true where *separation* occurred before the age of six. It should be remembered that maternal death has many other consequences aside from maternal deprivation, such as any replacement figure and the ability of the rest of the family to cope.

❸ Separation.   When a child is separated from its caregiver, even for a short while, the attachment bonds are disturbed. Is this deprivation?

RESEARCH EXAMPLE **Robertson and Robertson (1968) Young children in brief separation**

RESEARCH QUESTION: Is **separation anxiety** caused by the loss of the mother-figure (separation) or the loss of maternal care (deprivation)?

PARTICIPANTS: Children between one and two who had to spend time away from their mothers.

METHOD: Case studies, observation. In all cases the children continued to receive maternal care.
1 Loss of mother-figure (bond disruption). Filmed a two-year-old being admitted to hospital. Also filmed John, a seventeen-month-old boy, who stayed in a residential nursery for a short time.

2 Loss of mother-figure but some substitute provided (no bond disruption). Filmed Kate and Jane, who came to stay in the Robertsons' home. The girls met the Robertsons briefly a few weeks before they came to stay. The Robertsons tried to follow the usual daily routine of the girls and to talk to the children about their mothers.

RESULTS:
1 The boys showed clear signs of acute distress.
2 The girls showed signs of mild stress or insecurity but essentially adapted well.

INTERPRETATION: The Robertsons distinguished between bond disruption and separation. The boys suffered both separation and bond disruption because they had no substitute mother-figure though adequate maternal care was provided. The girls only experienced separation.

Therefore it is the bond disruption (deprivation) rather than separation which causes distress.

APPLICATIONS:
1 Hospitals have developed the policy of encouraging parents to stay with young patients to prevent separation anxiety and bond disruption.
2 The same syndrome of distress can be observed in adults. For example, in bereavement and divorce.

EVALUATION: This was not methodical research.
1 The conditions were not equivalent, for example, the child in hospital were in a more threatening situation regardless of the maternal care.
2 The records kept were not systematic.
3 The sample is very small.
4 The children studied were at a critical age, the same might not be true of older children.

RELATED STUDIES
Douglas (1975) studied all the children born in Great Britain during one week in 1946 (excluding illegitimate births and twins). The children were contacted every two years over the next 26 years. They kept a record of preschool hospitalisation and assessed behaviour in adolescence. They found strong evidence that a hospital admission of more than a week or repeated admission in a child under four was associated with an increased risk of behaviour disturbance and poor reading in adolescence.

Clarke and Clarke (1976) re-analysed Douglas' data and found that the reason for this apparent association was because many of the children were in hospital because of problems associated with disadvantaged homes. Social rather than maternal deprivation was the main cause delinquency.

④ Short-term separation – day care.

RESEARCH EXAMPLE **Kagan *et al.* (1980) A longitudinal study of children in day care**

RESEARCH QUESTION: During the late 1960s, people in the US became aware of the large number of mothers who were working or wanted to work. Many parents and psychologists felt concerned about the effect day care would have on preschool children. Most believed that the mother was the best source of consistent physical care, emotional security and cognitive challenge. While this might be true for middle-class children, there was some feeling that lower-class children might benefit from day care to enrich their lives. This suggests a dual standard where privileged children have access to their own mothers while the poor have substitutes. Is day care a poor substitute?

PARTICIPANTS: The research team set up a day care centre in a working-class area of Boston, the Treemont Street Infant Centre. The staff at the school had special responsibility for a small group of children, thus ensuring close emotional contact.

The children came from middle and lower-class families and various ethnic groups (White, Chinese, and Black). Some members of the Black community did not want the Black children evaluated so they were excluded from the study.

METHOD: Longitudinal field experiment.
1 *Day care subjects*: 33 infants aged between $3\frac{1}{2}$ and $5\frac{1}{2}$ months. None of the children had any particular personal or home problems.
2 *Home control group*: 67 infants of whom 32 were matched with the day care group in terms of demographic factors (age, sex, ethnicity, social class) and psychological factors (language development, quality of attachment to the mother, separation anxiety).
The children were followed until they were $2\frac{1}{2}$ years old. The researchers selected certain qualities to assess:
- *Temperamental traits*: attentiveness, excitability, reactivity to others.
- *Other behaviours*: attachment and later cognitive functioning.
They then decided on specific methods to test these qualities. For example:
- Free play with an unfamiliar peer, a variation of the strange situation.

- Social interactions.
- Questionnaire to mother regarding child's characteristics.
- Cognitive measures: memory test, tests of attentiveness, Bayley Infant Scales of developmental landmarks.

RESULTS: They found no consistently large differences between the two groups of children. There was large variability among all the children, but it was not related to the form of care.

INTERPRETATION: They concluded that day care and home-reared children developed similarly with respect to cognitive, social and emotional qualities during the first three years.

EVALUATION: It is important to distinguish two separate issues:
1 The effects of care arrangements on emotional development. Studies of childminding rather than day care (see below) suggest that this is no better than day care as a means of providing a mother substitute.
2 The effects on cognitive development. Tizard (1979) looked at children talking with their mothers and their nursery school teachers. Irrespective of social class the conversations between mother and child were more complex, had more exchanges and elicited more from the children. This is in part due to a teacher's lack of time and divided attention but also because they inevitably know the children less well.

RELATED STUDIES: Bryant *et al.* (1980) examined the quality of care provided by childminders. They observed 98 children and their mothers and childminders. They found that at least a third of the children were 'failing to thrive' and some were actually disturbed. Many minders felt that they did not have to form emotional bonds with the children nor did they have to stimulate them. In fact, minders rewarded quiet behaviour. They concluded that 'minding is thought to be a good form of care because it approximates more closely to being at home, but this may be a government-sponsored myth because childminding is a cheap form of care'.

Examiner's tip

Beware of offering anecdotal or commonsense evidence. You must present psychologically informed answers.

⑤ Prolonged separation – divorce. Divorce disrupts attachment bonds. Does this cause emotional disturbance? This is a difficult question to assess because:
- Other factors may cause the emotional disturbance. For example, family discord both before and after the divorce, and financial hardship.
- Divorce will affect each child differently, depending on: their age, their attachment to the parent who leaves, the extent of their continuing relationship with the absent parent.
- Some divorces result in deprivation, the total loss of the attachment figure. Other divorces result in separation, only the physical loss of an attachment object. This might explain why some children in divorced families suffer emotional disturbance.

RESEARCH EXAMPLE | **Cockett and Tripp (1994) The Exeter Family Study: Children living in reordered families**

RESEARCH QUESTION: It has been the popular belief that a good divorce is better than an unhappy home. The stress caused by family rows may be worse than problems created by divorce. Is this true?

PARTICIPANTS: 152 children in late childhood and early adolescence, and their parents.

METHOD: Interview, natural experiment. The participants belonged to one of five sets:
Group 1: 'Experimental' children from 'reordered families': those who had experienced parental separation or divorce. This group was subdivided into:
- Set 1: Those who had been living with one parent since the other left home.
- Set 2: Those who had experienced a second change, becoming part of a step-family.
- Set 3: Those who had experienced multiple changes.
Group 2: 'Control' children had lived with both their natural parents since birth. These were matched to the experimental children on key variables such as age, sex, mother's educational background, socio-economic status. This group was subdivided into:
- Set 4: Those whose parents had regular conflict.
- Set 5: Those whose parents had no serious rows.

RESULTS:
1 Children from *reordered* families were more likely to have encountered health problems, needed extra help at school, experienced friendship difficulties and to suffer from low self-esteem.
2 Those who had experienced *multiple changes* were worse off than those with a one-parent or step-family.
3 Those children living in intact families where there was marital *discord* did less well than other control children but were better off than those from reordered families.

INTERPRETATION: Marital breakdown causes more problems for children than discord alone. The more disruption a child suffers, the worse it is.

EVALUATION: Reordered families were also more likely to be receiving social security benefits, had moved house more often and were less likely to own a car. Therefore, the differences between reordered and intact families may be due to other factors in addition to change.

Theories of attachment and separation

BOWLBY

❶ <u>The theory</u>.
- *Psychoanalytic influence.* Bowlby was trained as a psychoanalyst. Freud claimed that an infant who is denied oral satisfaction will suffer later consequences (see Unit 9.3). Similarly, Bowlby (1951) suggested that the child who experiences maternal loss will suffer irreparable consequences, namely **maternal deprivation** and **affectionless psychopathy**. He claimed that the effects of maternal deprivation were equivalent to malnutrition in both their duration and seriousness.
- *Ethological influence.* Bowlby (1969) suggested a **critical period**, up to the age of two, for children to form attachments. After this, recovery should be rare. Attachment can be understood in terms of *survival value*, the infant's attachment to its mother is vital for safety and food. Attachment also serves as the basis for all later emotional and social relationships which affect reproductive success. (See Unit 3.3 on ethological concepts)
- *Monotropy.* Bowlby first talked of a *maternal* bond, but later widened this to allow for any caregiver. However, he felt that there is *primary* bond which is different in strength and quality to all others.

❷ <u>Supporting evidence</u>.   Bowlby's forty-four thieves, the Robertsons' filmed studies (both reported earlier in this unit).

❸ <u>Evaluation</u>.
- The evidence against Bowlby suggests that some aspects of his theory are wrong. For example the concept of a critical period is probably too strong. The idea of sensitive periods is preferable.
- Bowlby initially wrote about the *loss* of a mother figure, which may not have such permanent consequences as he thought. Privation, on the other hand, may have long-term consequences (Rutter).
- There are be different *kinds* of attachment, such as secure or anxious. Quality rather than quantity counts. (Ainsworth).
- A child may form *multiple* attachments (Shaffer and Emerson).
- There are *individual* and *cultural differences* in the way attachments are formed.
- Bowlby's theory has had an enormous impact, particularly in influencing the way we see the relationship between children and their caregivers.

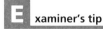

E xaminer's tip

This is a key theory. Make sure you are familiar with the arguments, evidence and counter-evidence.

RUTTER

❶ <u>Criticisms of Bowlby</u>.   Rutter (1972) wrote *Maternal Deprivation Reassessed*. He felt that Bowlby's work was flawed in certain respects:
- It is wrong to claim that separation causes emotional disturbances. These may be due to a history of family *discord* rather than the final separation.
- The *primary attachment bond* does not differ in kind and quality from all other bonds.
- *Individual differences* should be taken into account. Many children are not damaged by deprivation.

❷ <u>Conclusions</u>.   Rutter (1981) produced a second edition of his book *Maternal Deprivation Reassessed*. He emphasised the view that Bowlby was right, but other factors are important too.
- Bowlby's original views on the importance of deprivation have been amply confirmed.
- The single concept of *early deprivation* is misleading. There are many factors at work and many effects. Experiences during the first few years do have special importance, however experiences at all ages are important.
- The *reciprocal* nature of infant–caregiver interactions is important in the development of attachment bonds (see Brazelton *et al.*, earlier in this unit).

- *Importance of other factors*: such as different types of parenting behaviour and the influence of school.

❸ <u>Supporting evidence</u>.   Rutter *et al.* (below), Fox, Hodges and Tizard, Pringle and Bossio (all earlier in this unit).

RESEARCH EXAMPLE | **Rutter *et al.* (1976) The Isle of Wight study**

RESEARCH QUESTION: What causes anti-social behaviour and adolescent turmoil?

PARTICIPANTS: 2,300 9–12 year olds living on the Isle of Wight

METHOD: Questionnaire, interview. The sample was divided into good, fair and poor families. A good family was defined as one with warm, loving and secure relationships.

RESULTS: They looked at instances of separation and found:
1 In good and fair homes, separation did not lead to delinquency.
2 The cause of the separation is important. If separation was due to illness, it was not related to delinquency. Those separations due to stress in the home were four times more likely to become delinquent.
3 Recovery from deprivation is possible, especially in 'good' families.

INTERPRETATION: It is not separation itself which leads to antisocial behaviour, but the stress which often surrounds separation.

EVALUATION:
1 The study was correlational. Therefore any statement about stress *causing* antisocial behaviour is not justified.
2 The study used retrospective data. Memory is never perfect.

Quick test 8.1

1 What is *attachment*?
2 What is meant by the term *reciprocal behaviour*?
3 Name **two** factors which may prevent attachment between children and their parents.
4 Give **one** reason why psychologists suggest that pre-school children should remain with their mothers in prison. (*NEAB, 1992*)
5 Describe **two** problems that researchers may have in trying to study the effects of adoption and/or divorce. Suggest how **one** of these problems may be overcome. (*SEG, 1990*)

Summary

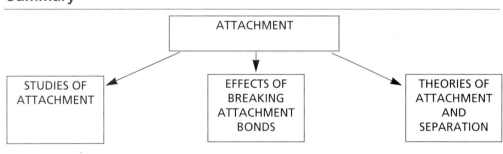

1 Feeding (Lorenz)
2 Physical contact (Harlow)
3 Time (Fox)
4 Critical period (Hodges and Tizard)
5 Sensitivity and responsiveness (Ainsworth)
6 Individual differences (Schaffer and Emerson)
7 One or more attachments? (Schaffer and Emerson)

1 Privation (Pringle and Bossio)
2 Deprivation (Bifulco *et al.*)
3 Separation (Robertson and Robertson)
4 Day care (Kagan *et al.*)
5 Divorce (Cockett and Tripp)

1 Bowlby
2 Rutter

APPLICATIONS: Institutional care, hospitalisation of children, day care, parenting.

8.2 Self-concepts and the role of expectations

PYGMALION IN THE CLASSROOM

A classic experiment by Rosenthal and Jacobsen (1968) indicated that expectations may have a critical effect on what you feel about yourself, and on your behaviour.

Rosenthal and Fode (1963), demonstrated an **expectancy effect** when working with rats. They told one set of college students that their experimental rats were specially bred for high intelligence and could learn mazes very quickly. A different group of students were told that their rats were bred for dullness. The rats were actually randomly assigned to the students, who trained the rats to perform various skills including maze learning. It was found that the 'maze-bright' rats were significantly faster than the 'maze-dull' ones in learning a T-maze. The critical conclusion was that the students had unintentionally and unconsciously influenced their participants. This is relevant for any experimental situation and is referred to as **experimenter bias**.

Rosenthal and Jacobsen (1968) extended this to the behaviour of teachers. Traditionally, it is argued that disadvantaged children perform poorly at school because of their background or innate ability. Rosenthal and Jacobsen felt that such children may be affected by the expectations of their teachers and this alone might explain their lack of scholastic success.

The researchers selected a primary school in a run-down section of San Francisco. They called it 'Oak School'. The students were mainly lower-class and some were immigrant. In all there were 18 teachers and 18 first to sixth grade classes. The researchers told the teachers that they were validating a new kind of intelligence test which would identify children who were 'academic bloomers'. These are children who currently weren't doing especially well but had the potential to improve.

They tested the children's IQ and randomly selected 20% to be 'bloomers'. The teachers were given information about 'bloomers' at the beginning of the academic year, in a casual manner so as not to arouse suspicions.

The children were retested three times, after four months, at the end of the school year and finally a year later. The effects of expectations were particularly strong in the younger children, and virtually non-existent in older children. On average however, the experimental group (bloomers) showed greater IQ gains than the control group. However, a year later the gains had disappeared.

The interested public regarded these results as highly significant and crucial in understanding why disadvantaged children fail in school. Psychologists were less happy with the results. One critic commented that the study was 'so defective that one can only regret that it ever got beyond the eyes of the original investigators.' (Thorndike, 1968)

Some comments:

1 The IQ test that was used was not standardised for the younger participants and was not administered under the same conditions by each teacher. This might explain why there were some very large IQ gains. For example, one student showed an improvement of 40 points, a change from nearly subnormal to above average.

2 The results were not consistent. For example, why did IQ gains disappear after a year?

3 Later studies were unable to produce significant effects on IQ, though other aspects of performance were affected by expectations. Brophy and Good (1974) reviewed 60 attempted replications and concluded that there were consistent expectation effects, but not as strong as was first suggested. The effects are probably linked to self-esteem rather than directly to performance.

4 If you accept that expectations have a profound affect, and if some teacher expectations are based on IQ test scores, then we must be especially careful about such tests.

Someone could be feeling unwell on the day of a test. More seriously, most tests have some culture bias, questions are inevitably related to learned behaviour (see Unit 4.3).

In this unit, other evidence will be explored relating to the effect of expectations on self-image and behaviour.

DEFINITIONS	
self	A sense of your unique existence, an inner agent.
self-concepts	Self-concepts are attitudes that we hold about ourselves.

self-image	The image you have of yourself, the id plus the ego.
ideal self	The super-ego, the self you would like to be.
self-esteem	The evaluation you have of yourself, largely determined by the distance between your self-image and your ideal self. If this gap is large, your self-esteem will be low.
self-fulfilling prophecy	A has beliefs about B. These change B's self-concepts and behaviour. B's behaviour confirms A's beliefs. One person's prediction about another person's behaviour comes to be realised *because* of their expectation. This realisation then *confirms* the original expectancy.
expectancy effect	The effect of a person's expectations on another person's behaviour.
labelling	A label is a word or phrase which is associated with a number of other characteristics. Labels such as 'mentally retarded' or 'dwarf' conjure up a stereotype, prejudices and expectations. The principle of a 'self-fulfilling prophecy' suggests that, once a label is attached, its effects are inevitable.
self-efficacy	The *belief* in your abilities as distinct from the abilities themselves.
self-actualisation	The motive to realise your full potential..
self-perception	A special case of person perception (see Unit 5.1), we only know ourselves through observation.

The self-fulfilling prophecy, labelling and expectations

The self-fulfilling prophecy, labelling and expectations are all aspects of the same thing.

Expectations do not *always* cause changes in the thing you are observing. If you expect a flower to bloom today, this belief will not affect the blossom's appearance.

Some things *are* influenced by our beliefs. Perception is altered by expectations (see Unit 2.2). Interpersonal perception, the way we see ourselves and others, is also affected by beliefs.

EXAMPLE **Guthrie (1938) A nice trick**

A group of students played a trick on an unattractive female classmate. They pretended that she was the most desirable girl in the college and took turns asking her out. By the sixth date, the general opinion was that she had actually become more attractive. Presumably this was because her self-image changed and this led her to behave differently.

A model of the self-fulfilling prophecy. This model is based around teacher-pupil performance, but can be used for all situations of self-fulfilling prophecy.
1 Teachers form an initial impression for each pupil, some are inappropriate or resistant to change.
2 Teachers begin to treat pupils differently in line with their expectations in (1). Their behaviour will be subtly different, often using nonverbal signals.
3 Students are affected by such treatment, probably it influences their self-image or it may lead them to feel greater anxiety about their performance.
4 The students' performance is affected by their altered self-expectations and/or anxiety.
5 The teachers' initial expectations are reinforced.
6 This process continues over time so that the teacher's expectations and student's behaviour gradually become the same.
Points to consider:
1 Expectations are not abnormal or illogical. They are common, everyday experiences and are an example of the way we think about all things.

2 The problem with expectations arises when they are inaccurate and resistant to change (see 'prejudice', Unit 5.3).

Learning the self-concept

We learn to know ourselves through experience.

❶ Self-observation.   We learn about ourselves in the same way as we learn about other people, by observing behaviour. For example, you come to view yourself as an emotional creature because you cry when reading a sad book.

❷ Comparisons with others.   Many self-concepts are comparative terms, such as tall or clever, and therefore require the standards to be set by others. We make comparisons with particular reference groups or peer groups. One of the reasons people may seek the company of others is to make such comparisons.

❸ The reactions of others.   You see yourself as others see you. Cooley (1902) called this the **looking-glass self**. It again means that we need social interaction to gain self-knowledge.

These perceptions do not just provide a picture of yourself, but also convey expectations. If your parents tell you that you are clever, you come to believe that yourself. It makes you work harder and therefore do well. Their expectations are self-fulfilling.

❹ Identification with models.   Both social learning and psychoanalytic theories suggest how models act as a means of developing a self-image (see Units 3.2 and 8.3 respectively). People with lower self-esteem are most ready to imitate others.

❺ Social roles.   Part of your self-concept is determined by your social role. Each role has a set of role-behaviours which generate a set of expectations for the performer and for the perceiver. For example, you expect your mother to behave in accord with her role as a mother and she also expects to behave according to her concept 'mother' when she's 'playing' that role. Goffman (1959) suggested that life is a series of theatrical performances, each role is acted out in accordance with expectations about what is appropriate.

Evidence related to the self-fulfilling prophecy

❶ The effect of low self-esteem.   Research generally finds that low self-esteem is associated with poor performance. The presumed connection is that people of low self-esteem *expect* to do less well, and this expectation might be the cause of their failure. When they do fail, this confirms their expectation, therefore becoming self-fulfilling.

People with low self-esteem are also more likely to be affected by other people's expectations.

RESEARCH EXAMPLE   **Coopersmith (1968) Studies in self-esteem**

RESEARCH QUESTION: How is self-esteem related to performance?

PARTICIPANTS: A 'representative sample of normal boys' were followed from pre-adolescence to early adulthood.

METHOD: Longitudinal, interview. Each boy was tested and then categorised as being high, medium or low in self-esteem. They used teachers' reports and psychological tests such as the Rorschach Ink Blot test.

To assess the behavioural differences between participants they tested, for example, the boys' memory, responses to stress, personality, attitudes. An interesting aspect of behaviour was their level of aspiration. This was tested using the 'beanbag experiment'. A boy has to throw a bean bag at a selection of targets, some closer than others. More distant targets give a higher score. He must select his target before throwing. The boys were asked the *ideal* score they would like to get, and the score they *expected* to get.

Examiner's tip

Descriptions of empirical studies can include comments on practical and ethical limitations.

RESULTS: Those boys high in self-esteem had higher goals and were more successful in achieving these goals. Those low in self-esteem had lower ambition and also did less well.

INTERPRETATION: This shows how self-esteem can determine how well someone does. If you expect not to succeed you won't, thus confirming your expectation.

---

② The effect of your own expectations.   Bandura (1976) introduced the concept of **self-efficacy** to more precisely describe that aspect of the self-concept which is related to expectation.

RESEARCH EXAMPLE | **Weinberg *et al*. (1979) Self-efficacy, expectations and performance**

RESEARCH QUESTION: Are feelings of self-efficacy associated with how well you perform in a competition?

PARTICIPANTS: Thirty male and thirty female university students.

METHOD: Experiment. Participants were assessed on:
1 A leg strength machine which gave false feedback about their leg strength.
2 A muscular endurance task: Sitting down and extending their leg in a horizontal position as long as possible. This task was performed with both legs (trial 1 and 2).
Participants were assigned to one of two experimental conditions:
1 They performed the task in the presence of a confederate who was said to have strained knee ligaments. The participant was led to believe that their leg strength was greater than the confederate (*high self-efficacy condition*).
2 The confederate was said to be a member of the college track team and a weight lifter. The participant performed less well on the leg strength machine than the confederate (*low self-efficacy*).
The competitions between participant and confederate were rigged so that the participant always lost.

RESULTS:
1 The low self-efficacy participants did less well and their performance deteriorated on trial 2.
2 Females participants did as well as males if they were given raised expectations and male participants' expectations were lowered.

INTERPRETATION: Expectations affect subsequent performance. This can be used to explain observed sex differences. Females may learn lower levels of self-efficacy which contributes to their poorer performance.

RELATED STUDIES:
Baron and Byrne (1991) report that Russian athletes are shown films of their performance, edited to make it look better. This is meant to create higher self-efficacy and improved performance.

---

③ The effect of others' expectations.   The self-fulfilling prophecy explains how others' expectations may affect your own expectations and behaviour. Coopersmith (1968) found that boys who had high self-esteem had parents who showed greater interest/respect than low self-esteem boys.

④ The affect of prejudices and stereotypes.   People's prejudices and stereotypes serve to organise their attitudes and generate expectations. Such expectations inevitably lead to a confirmation of the stereotype.

RESEARCH EXAMPLE | **Word *et al*. (1974) Self-fulfilling prophecies in interracial interaction**

RESEARCH QUESTION: Racial prejudices generate expectations. Do these beliefs come true *because* these expectations determine the behaviour of others?

METHOD: Experiment, deception. White college students were hired to act as interviewers. They were carefully trained for the task. The interviewees were both Black and White adolescents who were 'confederates'. They were not real job applicants, but had been trained to respond identically. The interview was recorded and analysed.
   In a later experiment, the interviewers were told to behave either in a friendly, relaxed manner or a relatively distant manner. This time the job candidates (again confederates) were all White.

RESULTS:
1 When interviewing a Black candidate the interviewer was more negative, sat further away, displayed signs of nervousness and finished the interview sooner.
2 In the second experiment, independent judges looked at the performance of the confederates. When the interviewer was friendly, the applicant's behaviour was judged as better than when the interviewer was hostile.

INTERPRETATION: Stereotypes may in themselves cause the behaviour they predict, they are self-fulfilling.

RELATED STUDIES: Snyder *et al*. (1977) showed men a photograph supposedly of the woman to whom they were conversing on the telephone. If they thought they were talking to an attractive woman they behaved differently, *and* the women responded by behaving 'more attractively'.

⑤ <u>The affects of labels</u>.   A label is a means of conveying a stereotype and a set of expectations, using only a word or phrase.

For example, Rolison and Medway (1985) gave teachers a booklet of information about a hypothetical student named Bob, who was described either as 'a *learning-disabled* boy' (LD), 'an *educably mentally retarded* boy' (EMR) or simply 'a 10-year-old boy' (no label). The booklet showed that Bob had performed better than average on half of the achievement tests last year. The teachers rated the IQ of the EMR students as lower than the LD or no label students. Harari and McDavid (1973) compared the effects of attaching different first names to essays and found that 'attractive' ones (David, Michael, Karen and Lisa) did better than less favourable ones (Elmer, Hubert, Bertha and Albert).

This research suggests that labels may have an important and detrimental influence. On the other hand, labels may sometimes have a positive effect. For example, a diagnostic label such as 'autistic' may avoid a child being seen as naughty or disturbed.

⑥ <u>The communication of expectations</u>.   To what extent are we aware of our expectations and, more importantly, aware that we are showing them to the target person?

RESEARCH EXAMPLE | **Adair and Epstein (1968) Non-verbal leakage**

RESEARCH QUESTION: How are biased expectations transmitted?

PARTICIPANTS: 120 female students.

METHOD: Experiment. The task that the participants had to perform was to judge a series of 10 photographs in terms of whether the person in the photograph had experienced success or failure.
1 *Visual condition.* Sixty participants were given instructions by an experimenter, face-to-face. The experimenter had been told either that the participant would positively evaluate the photographs or would negatively evaluate them (positive and negative expectancy).
2 *Non-visual condition.* Tape recordings were made of the experimenter giving instructions to the first 60 participants. These were played to the other participants who then judged the photographs.

RESULTS: In *both* conditions, participants' behaviour was influenced in the expected direction.

INTERPRETATION: This indicates that verbal cues alone, such as intonation, inflection and emphasis, are sufficient to create the expectancy effect. Such cues are vocal but considered nonverbal behaviour. They are difficult to control and therefore a person unconsciously conveys expectancy through this channel. This is called **nonverbal leakage** (see Unit 10.1).

EVALUATION: The experiment lacks realism. In the classroom, teachers' expectations are also affected by real achievement. Though this may, of course, have been determined by previous expectations.

---

⑦ <u>Confirmatory bias</u>.   Stereotypes are perpetuated partly because of their self-fulfilling nature, but also because people prefer information which is consistent with the attitudes they already have. Therefore we ignore inconsistent information and welcome that which confirms our beliefs. See Cohen (1981) described in Unit 5.1.

⑧ <u>Individual differences</u>:

Differences in the receiver:
- Some people are better at picking up nonverbal signals and therefore more susceptible to the expectations of others.
- Some people are more affected by the attitudes of others, such as people low in self-esteem or those have unstable self-concepts (children).
- Some people find another's expectations are a challenge, they make a greater effort to disprove low expectations.

Differences in the sender:
- Some people are more likely to have stereotypes, which automatically generate expectations, i.e. they are less open-minded.
- Some people are more inflexible, i.e. resistant to change in the light of new information.

How to manage the effects of negative expectations

① <u>Positive thinking</u>.   Learning to focus on the things you are good at to increase your self-esteem, learning to believe in yourself.

② Changing stereotypes:
- Counter-stereotypes in the media (see Unit 5.1).
- Being more aware of the stereotypes you hold and being more willing to change them.
- Assigning new labels which are related to different and more positive stereotypes and expectations. For example, using 'visually impaired' instead of 'blind'.
- High profile activities, such as disabled Olympics, which improve self-image and the image others have.

③ Using better interpersonal techniques.   Useful in situations where expectations may be particularly influential, such as an interview or in teaching.

④ Recognising your own negative expectations.   Seligman (1978) found that people with low self-esteem tend to explain any success in terms of external factors (such as luck or a good teacher) and failure to internal factors (for example, lack of ability). The outcome of this is that such people lack *control* over their failure and learn to be *helpless*. This **learned helplessness** (see Unit 10.2) is similar to the self-fulfilling prophecy: A person fails, which lowers self-esteem, any success is explained in terms of external factors and the person comes to believe there is nothing they can do to change things, thus perpetuating their low self-esteem.

However, there are individual differences. Not everyone *allows* information about failure to influence their self-esteem. Other people, such as those prone to depression, do appear to be more affected by failure.

Quick test 8.2

1 Use your knowledge of psychology to explain how a *self-fulfilling prophecy* occurs. (*NEAB, sample Higher*)
2 Give an example of a *self-fulfilling prophecy* from everyday life.
3 In what way do friends *and* teachers affect how well someone does at school? (*SEG, 1991*)
4 How can *labelling* affect an individual's behaviour?
5 An organisation concerned with children suffering from cerebral palsy wants to change the negative stereotype that most people have. Give **one** suggestion that a psychologist might offer.

Summary

LEARNING THE SELF-CONCEPT	EVIDENCE RELATING TO THE SELF-FULFILLING PROPHECY	MANAGING THE EFFECTS OF NEGATIVE EXPECTATIONS
1 Self-observation 2 Comparisons with others 3 The reactions of others 4 Identification with models 5 Social roles	1 Low self-esteem 2 Your own expectations 3 Others' expectations 4 Prejudices and stereotypes 5 Labels 6 Communicating expectations 7 Confirmatory bias 8 Individual differences	1 Positive thinking 2 Changing stereotypes 3 Interpersonal techniques 4 Self-awareness

8.3 Personality

A SENSE OF HUMOUR

The earliest approach to personality was Hippocrates (400 BC) who claimed that it was body fluids or, what he called 'humours', which caused different people to have different personalities. Too much of a particular fluid would produce a particular personality type.

PERSONALITY TYPE	FLUID	LATIN or GREEK	DESCRIPTION
sanguine	blood	sanguis	optimistic, hopeful
melancholic	black bile	melan coln	sad, depressed
choleric	bile	coln	irritable
phlegmatic	phlegm	flegma	apathetic

His theory may at first seem laughable. But the labels have had lasting value. For example, we still use the terms 'good-humoured', melancholic and phlegmatic.

More recently, Sheldon *et al.* (1940) also investigated the link between biology and temperament. Sheldon spent most of his working life photographing thousands of naked men to identify body types (somatotype) and tried to establish correlations between these and temperament.

BODY TYPE	BODY SHAPE	TEMPERAMENT
endomorph	short, plump	sociable, relaxed, even-tempered
mesomorph	heavy-set, muscular	noisy, callous, fond of physical activity
ectomorph	tall, thin	restrained, self-conscious, fond of solitude

Many other people have conducted similar research. In general, there seems to be some support for a relationship between physique and personality (Hall and Lindzey, 1970).

The link between personality and biology continues to be of interest. Some psychologists are interested in the link between certain temperaments (type A, B or C), stress and illness, particularly heart disease or cancer. This is discussed in Unit 10.2.

Some developmental psychologists regard early temperamental differences in infant behaviour as due to inherited factors. Such characteristics may form the basis of later personality. This research is described in Unit 8.4.

Most personality theorists describe personality as a characteristic set of behaviours which are both learned and biologically based. Except Mischel, whose views are explained in this unit, along with all major theorists.

DEFINITIONS		
personality	Those relatively enduring aspects of an individual which distinguish them from others (individual differences), and which make them unique.
personality theory	A systematic account of the ways that people differ.
radical behaviourism	A phrase used to distinguish this from more moderate forms of behaviourism, which do not take the extreme position that only observable behaviour should be studied rather than any internal state such as thought or feelings.
self-actualisation	The motive to achieve all of one's potentials.
idiographic	An approach based on individuals. It emphasises uniqueness.
nomothetic	An approach which tries to summarise the differences between people by making generalisations based on large amounts of data.

What is personality?

Personality comes from the Latin *persona* meaning an actor's mask. It is:
- A characteristic pattern of behaviours, attitudes, interests, capabilities.
- An integrated set of traits.
- Unique (a means of differentiating individuals).
- Relatively stable (though there is some disagreement about this).
- It forms a basis for predicting future behaviour.

The concept of personality is important in several ways:
- *Personally.* It enables each of us to form a coherent view of our self, and form expectations about what we might do in future situations.
- *Interpersonally.* Another individual's behaviour is also viewed as a coherent set of traits which enable future predictions to be made (implicit personality theories, see Unit 5.1).
- *Psychologically.* Explicit personality theories are the basis for:
  - Personality tests, which are important for job selection and psychiatric assessment.
  - Theories of psychiatric disorders and treatment.

Personality theories

The general approaches to personality theory are:

1 The trait approach. Expresses differences between individuals in terms of selected traits. Traits are essentially adjectives such as 'serious' or 'trusting'. They are tendencies to act in a particular way.
For example: Catell
Evaluation:
- Reflects natural tendency to categorise people using traits, such as talkative or shy.
- Useful for developing personality tests based on a list of adjectives.
- Not very sophisticated, little more than a list of adjectives which describe, but do not explain how behaviour develops.

2 The type approach. Each person fits into a broad, emotional category. Each type is qualitatively different from other types.
For example: Eysenck, Freud
Evaluation:
- A very similar approach to trait theory, a type is a cluster of traits.
- Like trait theory, it is useful for testing but over-simplistic.
- Personality type may be linked to biological differences.

3 The psychoanalytic approach. In the course of early development some biological urges are not satisfied. They are repressed, and act as unconscious motives which affect personality development.
For example: Freud
Evaluation:
- The theory has continuing popular appeal. It is sensational, sensual, dreamlike, and represents the complexity and uniqueness of human nature.
- It is a theory which was developed from dealing with disturbed individuals, therefore may not truly represent normal development.
- Some aspects of the theory are valid, such as the importance of early experiences and the influence of the unconscious.
- It is not really a scientific theory because it is not easily testable.

4 Self theory. The development of self and self-attitudes are critically important. An individual's personality only makes sense in terms of how *they* experience it rather than how an a psychologist might interpret it.
For example: Rogers, Kelly
Evaluation:
- They stress uniqueness of the individual, free-will and potential for change.
- They do not account for the unconscious.

5 Radical behaviourist approach. All behaviour is learned through selective reinforcement. It is not necessary to understand why certain traits emerge, only to observe them and their effects.
For example: Skinner, Eysenck

Evaluation:

- It is an objective theory which is easy to test.
- It has led to behaviour therapy, a successful form of treatment for some mental illnesses.
- It is a simplistic view of human behaviour, derived largely from the study of animals and therefore may be inappropriate in explaining human behaviour.
- It is an extreme form of learning theory, social learning offers a more moderate view.

6 Social learning theory.   Explains behaviour in terms of reinforcement and modelling. Mischel's **situationalism** is a startling departure from all other theories in suggesting that personality is not consistent. People behave differently in different situations. Any seeming consistency is due to the fact that we are often in similar situations.

For example: Bandura, Mischel

Evaluation:

- Such theories combine elements from all other approaches. For example, accounting for both internal (personal control) and external (reinforcement) factors.
- The situational view is an extreme one. It assumes that we are completely controlled by situations rather than our own free will. Nevertheless it raises serious questions for all other theories.

Some theories in detail

1 CATTELL (1965) A Trait Theory

Cattell held the view that all personality could be expressed in terms of a select number of traits. He used three sources of data:

- **L–data** (life). Cattell identified about 4500 adjectives or trait names. After removing any synonyms, they were used to rate a group of participants. The results were factor analysed, so that adjectives which essentially referred to the same trait could be identified. This left 15 first-order or **source** traits.
- **Q–data** (questionnaire). The 15 source traits were presented to large numbers of participants and their results factor analysed. This produced a slightly different set of 16 source traits.
- **T–data** (test). Objective tests of personality, such as GSR, reaction time, and body sway, yielded 21 factors.
- The final result of 16 source traits, expressed as opposites, makes up the 16PF questionnaire.

reserved	outgoing
less intelligent	more intelligent
affected by feelings	emotionally stable
submissive	dominant
serious	happy-go-lucky
expedient	conscientious
shy	venturesome
tough-minded	tender-minded
trusting	suspicious
practical	imaginative
forthright	shrewd
self-assured	apprehensive
conservative	experimenting
group-dependent	self-sufficient
undisciplined self-conflict	controlled
relaxed	tense

- Later, Cattell added eight **surface** traits, such as exvia (like extroversion), anxiety, depression, arousal, and fatigue. These are produced through combinations of source traits and represent more general **mood**. These surface traits are similar to Eysenck's personality types (see opposite).

- Behaviour is motivated by **ergs**, biological factors such as food-seeking, mating and affiliation.

Test: Cattell's 16 Personality Factor Questionnaire (16 PF) is taken directly from the list of traits above, and has proved very popular.

② EYSENCK (1963): A Behaviourist Type Theory

Eysenck (1947) based his early work on personality ratings made of 700 servicemen by observers. Like Cattell, he factor analysed his data. However Eysenck found that people tend to have many of the traits belonging to one cluster, therefore it is more appropriate to refer to them as this *type* of person, rather than the individual *traits*. These personality types or dimensions were:

extrovert − introvert, and neurotic − stable.

Later he added the third dimension, intelligence − psychoticism.

- Eysenck emphasised the role of *learning* (Behaviourism).
- Eysenck also suggested that personality is based on *biological* differences. He proposed that extroverts have lower **cortical arousal** than introverts. That is, their brain runs at a lower level of excitement and therefore they need greater external stimulation to experience the same 'excitement' as introverts. This leads to some predictions about extroverts and introverts:
  - *Extroverts* should be 'stimulus hungry', seek greater excitement and more dangerous pastimes. They are not easily conditioned, a fact which may lead to a less developed conscience and a greater likelihood of criminal and antisocial behaviour.
  - *Introverts* should be more easily conditioned, more socially conforming, able to concentrate longer and have lower sensory thresholds which would mean that they feel pain more acutely.

Tests: Eysenck Personality Questionnaire (EPQ) and Inventory (EPI)

Note: This theory has proved very popular, and led to a lot of research.

Psychologists now suggest that there are five dimensions of personality, referred to as **The Big Five Factors**: extroversion, agreeableness, conscientiousness, neuroticism, openness or intellect. Eysenck and Cattell's work was important in introducing the idea of traits or dimensions of personality.

③ FREUD (1890 onwards) Psychoanalytic Theory

This is a *dynamic* view of personality, because it focuses on how personality develops rather than just describing what is there. Individual differences in adult personalities can be traced back to the specific way that *early conflicts* were handled. These conflicts are between *biological* drives, such as aggression and sex, and higher intellectual functioning. Freud's theory describes personality *types*, and is therefore in a sense a type theory.

Freud's theories are also described in Units 9.1 and 9.2.

THE STRUCTURE OF PERSONALITY

id	The primitive, instinctive, unconscious part. Demands immediate satisfaction. Governed by the pleasure principle.
ego	The conscious and intellectual part. It regulates the id. Governed by the reality principle, the need to behave in acceptable ways.
super ego	The ethical and moral component, learned from others particularly parents. It gives rise to a conscience.

THE UNCONSCIOUS IS REVEALED THROUGH:

ego defence mechanisms	Protect the ego from reality when necessary. For example: sublimation, repression, denial, displacement, projection.
neurotic symptoms	Appear when desires have become repressed.
Freudian slips (parapraxes)	Everyday forgetfulness, such as slips of the tongue, forgotten names or appointments.

PSYCHOSEXUAL STAGES (sexual means physically pleasurable)

oral stage	In the first year the id is dominant, tension is reduced through satisfying basic needs. Pleasure is gained through sucking and body stimulation. Any disturbance of this may result in a permanent fixation on the oral channel for gratification, for example smoking, overeating, thumb-sucking, pencil chewing. Certain personality traits may be related to such fixations, such as impatience, passivity, greediness, dependence, preoccupation with issues of giving and taking.
anal stage	At the age of about two, the anus becomes the favoured pleasure zone. Pleasure is derived from expelling and withholding faeces. Fixations may be caused by either exceptionally strict toilet training or intense pleasure associated with taboos such as smearing faeces on the wall. The anal/obsessive character wants to make a terrible mess and therefore must build defences against this, for example orderliness, rigidity, hatred of waste. Associated personality traits are obstinacy, stinginess, punctuality, possessiveness. The opposite would be untidiness, hot-temper or destructiveness.
phallic stage	Around the age of three, children's sexual interest focuses on their genitalia and their opposite-sex parent. Resolution is through identification with the same-sex parent and is important for an appropriate gender concept and a conscience (see Units 9.1 and 9.2). The conflicts may result in homosexuality, authority problems, and rejection of appropriate gender roles if not resolved.
latency period	Up to the start of puberty little development takes place.
genital stage	The final stage of personality development, the development of independence. If some issues remain unresolved, the individual can't shift focus from their immediate needs to larger responsibilities involving others.

Therapy: Psychoanalysis. The treatment relies on the therapist's ability to make the unconscious conscious and guide the patient in resolving the conflicts. Diagnosis occurs alongside treatment. The techniques used are:

- **Free association.** The therapist introduces a topic and client talks about anything that comes into his mind.
- **Rich interpretation.** The therapist uses his knowledge of the dynamics of personality development to explain causes.
- **Analysis of dreams.** The expression of the innermost workings of the mind, particularly repressed desires.
- **Transference.** The patient transfers his feelings about others on to the therapist. The therapist then has to work through these new feelings.

Note: This was quite a remarkable theory for its time, introducing novel concepts such as the unconscious and sexuality. Many theorists have adapted Freud's ideas (the Neo-Freudians), lessening the importance of biological desires and substituting social factors. Psychoanalytic theory is a major psychological perspective and has been applied to understanding prejudice, aggression, attachment, dreams and normal, abnormal, moral and gender development.

❹ **ROGERS (1959) Self-theory**
Rogers' approach is an example of a *humanist* theory. It emphasises the whole rather than the individual parts, and values the uniqueness of each individual, their capacity for self-actualisation and self-determination (free will).

- **Unconditional positive regard** from significant others (generally, parental love) enables healthy personality development, particularly high self-esteem and self-acceptance. It frees the individual from striving for social approval and enables him/her to seek **self-actualisation**.
- **Conditional love** leads to maladjustment because the **self** and **ideal self** are in conflict. The individual feels they must be someone else in order to receive love.

Therapy: Rogers founded non-directive therapy (counselling). The non-directive therapist practices unconditional positive regard to enable self-actualisation.
Note: Non-directive therapy has been very successful and led to many related forms such as group therapy, co-counselling and telephone support services.

⑤ KELLY (1955) Personal Construct Theory

Kelly's approach also stresses the uniqueness of the individual and the view that personality only makes sense in terms of the person who is experiencing it. His theory is strongly tied to the test he developed and its use in treating emotionally disturbed individuals.

- Each person is a **personal scientist**. They hold theories about the world, these lead to hypotheses (expectations) which are tested and modified as a result.
- Personality is a set of **constructs**: Bipolar (two-ended) dimensions such as loving-unloving, or open-minded-dogmatic. These are organised into hierarchies of broader constructs such as good-bad and these broader constructs are somewhat like personality types.
- The constructs are *personal*. The meaning for a particular trait varies from person to person. For example, 'loving' does not mean the same thing to you as it does to me.

Test: Repertory grid. The participant is asked to name the important figures in their life. They are then given three of them and asked to say in what way two are alike and the third is different, for example 'my father and brother are funny and my mother is serious'. This continues with different threesomes, each time the answer produces a bipolar personal construct, such as 'funny-serious'. At the end, all the names are arranged along the top of a grid and the constructs (no more than 25) down the side. Ticks and crosses represent relations between elements (people or almost anything) and constructs. The grid allows a participant to show reality as they see it, and gives the therapist a view of this reality.
Note: This is regarded as one of the most systematic and clearly formulated theories. The repetory grid is well used.

⑥ SKINNER (1938) Operant Reinforcement Theory

Skinner's personality theory is essentially an extension of his behaviourist approach (see Unit 3.1). Personality is learned as a result of **shaping**. Positive reinforcement or reward makes it more likely that the same behaviour will be repeated, punishment makes a behaviour less likely.

- All traits are learned, for example encountering bullies at school might led a child to develop shyness, or generosity might arise through the positive reinforcement of being liked by others.
- **Functional analysis** is a means of looking at a person's *observable* behaviour and identifying what things act as *discriminative stimuli* and *reinforcers*.

Therapy: Behaviour modification is based on operant conditioning (see Unit 3.1).
Note: The particular value of this theory lies in the successful therapies it has generated.

⑦ BANDURA (1977) Social Learning Theory

The main difference between social learning theory and behaviourism is the suggestion that people can learn by *indirect observation*, imitation and modelling.

- Development proceeds through *reinforcement*, both direct and indirect.
- Behaviour can be reinforced by one of three factors: past experience, the environment and the individual themselves. The individual is controlled by and controls their environment, called **reciprocal determinism**.
- A person's sense of **self-efficacy** (their belief about what they can do) has a major influence over what they actually achieve.
- Therefore a person has the potential to control their environment (reciprocal determinism), whether they do or not depends on whether they expect to succeed (self-efficacy).

Therapy: Behaviour therapies. For example: *modelling*, a patient who has a phobia first watches the therapist experiencing the phobic situation calmly, then the patient does the same.
Note: This approach combines many different features: learning theory, modelling, self-determination and situational control. It lacks detail and cohesiveness, it is more a collection of diverse ideas.

8 **MISCHEL (1968) Situational Theory**

The very core of most personality theories is the idea that traits are lasting features. In other words, by saying that someone is shy we expect that this trait will persist, they will probably be shy next year and in five years time. However, people may not be so consistent now or in the future. Mischel and Peake (1982) asked family, friends and unknown observers to rate 63 students in several situations involving conscientiousness. They found almost no correlation (0.08).

- Any *regularity* of behaviour is due to the fact that we tend to find ourselves in similar situations. For example, someone may be shy in class but quite extrovert amongst close friends. You might regard them as shy because you rarely see them outside of class.
- The notion of consistency is a useful tool in *organising our perceptions* about ourselves and others. But this is the way we *think* about personality, which doesn't really exist.
- We learn, through selective *reinforcement*, what behaviours are appropriate in what situations.

Note: The idea of situationalism is a challenge to all other theories and to personality tests. If personality is situationally determined, tests cannot accurately predict behaviour.

Quick test 8.3

1 What do personality theorists mean by the term 'trait'?
2 According to Eysenck, why are introverts better at vigilance tasks? (*MEG, sample Higher*)
3 What is meant by a 'humanistic approach' to personality? (*MEG, sample Foundation*)
4 Which of Freud's personality structures, the id, ego or superego, is associated with the pleasure principle?
5 How does the *superego* develop? (*SEG, 1992*)
6 What does Kelly mean when he says that people are like 'scientists'? (*MEG, 1992*)
7 An *idiographic approach* to personality focuses on the individual. A *nomothetic approach* focuses on groups of people. Which of these approaches does Kelly use? (*MEG, 1992*)
8 (a) What is meant by the term *unconditional positive regard*?
   (b) Why is it important to the development of self-concept? (*MEG, 1991*)
9 According to Rogers, what is the difference between the *self* and the *ideal self*? (*MEG, 1991*)
10 Many personality theories have been developed out of the theorists' experience with patients in therapy. What is **one** problem with developing a theory in this way?

Summary

Personality is personal, interpersonal, psychological. It is a pattern, integrated, unique, stable, predictable.

PERSONALITY THEORIES		
	1 Trait approach	Cattell
	2 Type approach	Eysenck
	3 Psychoanalytic approach	Freud
	4 Self theory	Rogers, Kelly
	5 Radical behaviourist	Skinner, Eysenck
	6 Social learning theory	Bandura, Mischel

8.4 Temperament

THE ORIGINS OF PERSONALITY

Thomas *et al.* (1968) observed that, where some problem children develop emotional problems, other children in the same family do not. Psychological explanations which explain development in terms of child-rearing style or environmental influences can't account for this. The factor that is missing from these explanations is the child's own temperament, his/her individual style of responding to the environment.

Thomas *et al.* collected detailed descriptions of children's behaviour and identified nine common characteristics, some of these are listed later in this unit. A child could be rated as high, medium or low on each characteristic and a *behavioural profile* constructed. Thomas *et al.* used this scheme of classification to assess the emotional development of a group of children, called the New York Longitudinal Study. They used a sample of 141 children from 85 highly educated professional or business families. The mothers were interviewed every three months for the first two years of the child's life. There have been numerous subsequent follow ups of the children for more than twenty years (Thomas and Chess, 1986).

The data collected could be regarded as unreliable since it relies on mothers' own interpretations. However, the evidence has had an enormous impact. There were two main findings:

1 The characteristics tended to cluster together. There were three temperamental types: the easy, difficult and slow-to-warm-up child (these are described later in this unit).
2 In some children, temperament remains constant as they get older. But this is not necessarily true. Life experiences, in particular the way that parents handle problems, either help or hinder difficult traits.

Temperament may be *inherited* but this does not mean it can't be *altered* by a person's life experiences or by their own will. Therefore studies of temperament represent nature *interacting* with nurture and support the view that a child is an *active* participant.

DEFINITIONS	**temperament**	A person's characteristic modes of emotional response. Such tendencies are associated with biological factors, which may be modified by experience.
	behavioural inhibition	The tendency to withdraw from unfamiliar situations or people.

What is temperament?

Temperament is an aspect of personality. The essence of developmental research into temperament is:

- *Nature.* Infants seem to have consistent individual behaviour patterns. Some cry a lot, others are more sleepy. Are these patterns inherited?
- *Nurture.* To what extent do initial innate temperamental differences persist? Do social, chiefly parental, influences make all the difference?
- *Interaction.* Both nature and nurture views describe the child as a passive participant in their development, either they inherit certain characteristics or they are influenced by social forces. Research into temperament has shown how the process is bidirectional. The parent-child relationship goes two ways: parents influence children and the child's temperament alters parental behaviours.

❶ Temperamental traits.   Research into temperament has focused on five major dimensions. They are chosen because they appear early, continue to be expressed in later behaviour and are easy to study (Goldsmith *et al.*, 1987)
   - *Activity* level.
   - *Emotionality* (how easily or intensely upset).
   - *Soothability* (how easily the infant can calm down).
   - *Fearfulness.*
   - *Sociability* (receptiveness to social stimulation).

2 Temperamental profiles.   Certain temperamental characteristics tend to cluster together forming broader temperamental profiles which may also persist over time.
- The *easy child*. Even tempered, positive, adaptable, predictable. Found in 75% of Thomas and Chess' (1968) original sample.
- The *difficult child*. Active, irritable, irregular, finds newness distressing and responds by withdrawing or being slow to adapt. Found in 10% of their sample.
- The *slow-to-warm-up child*. Inactive, moody, slow to adapt but puts up passive resistance rather than crying like the difficult child.

EXAMPLE | **The difficult child**

'Difficultness' is the most widely agreed upon category. It is measured through parental reports. Typical comments, in addition to those characteristics listed above, are that daily care routines are hard to manage, the child may have many expressions of intense negative mood and behaviour is different from other siblings.

It is a normal form of behavioural individuality, though such children have a high risk for behavioural problems later in life. This outcome may occur because parents find it hard to manage such children and this makes their problems worse. It also may reflect our culture which has particular expectations of children.

Treatment and prevention is possible as the case of Carl, described below, shows.

Nature, nurture or goodness of fit?

1 Nature.   Evidence comes from many sources:
- *Twin studies*. These suggest that at least some components of temperament are influenced by genes. For example, Goldsmith and Gottesman (1981) conducted the Collaborative Perinatal Project where 350 pairs of twins were observed at birth, 8 months, 4 and 7 years of age. Half were monozygotic or MZ (genetically identical) and half were dizygotic or DZ (non–identical). Trained observers rated their behaviour for activity level, sociability, irritability and other temperamental characteristics. The MZ twins were more similar at 8 months than the DZ twins but not at 4 or 7 years, therefore suggesting a moderate genetic contribution up to the age of 8 months but not thereafter.
- *Selective breeding with animals*. When rearing livestock, it is useful to be able to breed in positive behavioural traits. Such work has shown that activity, fearfulness and sociability are inherited.
- *Cross-cultural studies*. Freedman (1979) found newborn Caucasian babies were more irritable than Chinese–American ones, despite the same prenatal care. This suggests a genetic difference.
- *Physiological basis*. Research might show that a particular trait is shown at the same time as there are physiological changes in the body.

RESEARCH EXAMPLE | **Kagan (1989) Behavioural inhibition**

RESEARCH QUESTION: Are there consistent biological states associated with **behavioural inhibition**?

PARTICIPANTS: 21-month-old children, retested at 4, $5\frac{1}{2}$ and $7\frac{1}{2}$ years.

METHOD: Longitudinal, observation. Children were filmed in situations designed to provoke uncertainty. Observers used the films to rate behaviour as inhibited or not. Signs of inhibition were: withdrawal, staying close or clinging to mother, crying, failure to play.

Those children who were most and least inhibited were later observed for their responses to new situations (pictures or spoken phrases which were difficult to understand) and their heart rates and other measures of arousal were recorded.

RESULTS:
1 They found that inhibited children had a higher average level of physiological arousal of the autonomic nervous system (for example, heart rate, respiration) and higher levels of cortisol (indicating more stress).
2 These traits persisted when retested in later childhood. Such children were shy with peers and adults, more cautious in physical activity, in new situations and playing with novel toys.

INTERPRETATION: These findings support an inherited view because:
1 They show a link between behavioural inhibition and physiological arousal.

2 The persistence of behavioural inhibition from early to later childhood.

3 There are distinct behavioural *types* rather than just children who are more or less inhibited.

RELATED STUDIES:

Eysenck (see Unit 9.3) found that introverts are more cortically aroused and therefore prefer lower levels of stimulation.

② <u>Nurture</u>.   A behaviour shown at birth may not be due to inherited factors. The prenatal environment (which is nurture not nature) must be considered. Carey and McDevitt (1980) suggested that a difficult temperament may be due to hormones produced by a mother in a highly emotional state during pregnancy.

However, Vaughn *et al.* (1987) found a correlation between maternal distress in late pregnancy and infant temperament at 6 months. They did not find any correlation between hormones in the intrauterine environment and later temperament, which suggests that infant temperament is not due to prenatal experience but rather to postnatal mothering.

③ <u>Persistence</u>.   Are early temperamental profiles unchangeable? In what way is the parent-child relationship *bidirectional* (parent influences child and child influences parent)? Irritable or overactive babies do not necessarily grow into difficult children.

- Some traits may be due to *temporary problems*. For example, irritability may be caused by physical problems in infancy such as colic. When the colic stops so does the irritability.
- Some parents or cultures may be better able to manage a 'difficult' child. This is called the **fit** between parent and child.

EXAMPLE   **Thomas and Chess (1986) Goodness of fit**

Personality development is a result of both nature and nurture, and also the interaction between both of these elements. When a person's environment is suited to their particular temperament, this is considered a **good fit**. The result is a well-adjusted individual. If the fit is not good, then early, 'difficult' traits may be amplified into troublesome maladaptive behaviours.

One of Thomas and Chess' most extreme cases was a boy named Carl. He had a difficult temperament from the beginning. However, the fact that he didn't develop a behaviour disorder was mainly due to optimal handling by his parents and the stability of his environment. Carl's father was easy going, took delight in his sons 'lusty' characteristics, recognised his son's negative reactions to new experiences and had the patience to wait for his eventual maturing to occur. His father felt that his son's difficultness was not due to himself or his wife. His wife was anxious and self-accusatory over her son's tempestuousness but her husband was supportive and reassuring.

New demands on Carl always restarted his intense negative responses. When he went off to college he was faced simultaneously with a host of new situations and demands. Within a few weeks his temperamentally difficult traits reappeared. He felt negative, couldn't motivate himself to study and was constantly irritable. The doctors Chess and Thomas advised a coping strategy which meant dropping some extracurricular activities and limiting social contacts. Once he felt more positive, he was able to take on these additional demands.

Quick test 8.4

1 Name **two** emotional traits which are thought to be present early in life and form the basis of later behaviour.

2 List **four** characteristic traits of a *difficult child*.

3 In order to determine whether temperament is due to nature or nurture psychologists study very young children. Describe **one** problem with this approach.

4 What is *behavioural inhibition*?

5 How do parents influence the development of temperament in their children?

Summary

Adult personality can be understood in terms of an interaction between nature (temperamental traits) and nuture (goodness of fit).

Chapter 9
Social development

It is a basic human need to be social. If we weren't, it would be difficult to find a mate and reproduce. Certain behaviours are a key part of this: moral behaviour is a means of policing our interactions, gender awareness is critical for mate selection, and the formation of relationships is the basis of it all.

9.1 Moral development

A MORAL DILEMMA

John is seven and has recently been beaten up by an older boy who attends his brother Alan's school. Alan is a very protective older brother and they are very close. Alan decides to avenge John's victimisation and to beat up the older boy. But his parents strongly disapprove of physical aggression and he could get into serious trouble with them (as well as the school authorities). One day after school, Alan waited for the boy and gave him a thorough beating. Should he have done that? Why?

Kohlberg wrote dilemmas like this to try to understand how people think about moral issues. He classified the answers and developed a scale of moral development related to age.

There are many questions about moral principles and moral behaviour. Does moral behaviour change as people get older? Is it different in different situations? Do people practice what they preach? Is someone who works for the good of others morally 'better' than another person? Are men morally superior to women? Are there universal morals? Are they innate? If not, how do we learn right and wrong?

DEFINITIONS		
morality	A sense of right and wrong, within a particular moral code or society. Morals guide behaviour.
social	Any situation involving two or more members of the same species.
moral behaviour	The presumed outcome of morals. Some examples: behavioural conformity, perception of authority as rational, impulse inhibition and consideration for others.
conscience	A reasonably coherent set of internalised moral principles.
empathy	An understanding of the emotions and feelings of another person.

pro-social behaviour	Those social behaviours which are cooperative in nature, therefore they are judged as 'beneficial to others' rather than 'right'. There is much overlap between the concepts 'prosocial' and 'moral'.
ethics	A code of acceptable conduct.

The development of empathy

Emotions, prosocial behaviour and morals all have one thing in common: empathy. The development of prosocial behaviour (see Unit 7.2) and morals depends on an understanding of the feelings of others. People who lack empathy, tend also to be amoral (sociopathic personalities).

The development of empathy:

1 Emotional responsiveness in infants.   Infants signal their own emotional state through smiling, cooing or crying. They can respond to the emotional states of others, called **social referencing** (see Unit 8.1). Infants also exhibit global empathy, becoming distressed when they hear another child crying.

2 Attachment.   The process of attachment is critical for later emotional stability (see Unit 8.1). It signals the start of emotional relationships and starts around 7 months.

3 Egocentric empathy.   Children presume that another person feels the same as they do. By the age of 3 this changes and children become capable of understanding that another person is feeling different.

4 Self-definition.   Understanding your own emotions and interacting with others is part of the process of self-definition. Self-esteem is the emotion you feel about yourself and seems to develop after the age of 7.

5 Friendships.   Up until the age of 4, children do not *interact* with other children when they play together. After the age of 7, when the child has passed the egocentric stage, they form their first real friendships. Only then can they really understand the emotions of others and respond to the other's needs. Friends give comfort and support and further the emotional development of the child (see Unit 9.3).

Theories of moral and social development

There are three major psychological approaches to explaining moral development. Since morals are intimately associated with social awareness, they are also theories of social development.

1 Learning.   Explanations based on Behaviourist concepts of conditioning, reinforcement, rewards and punishment, and the social learning notion of modelling.

2 Psychoanalytic.   Explanations based on Freud's description of the development of personality.

3 Cognitive-developmental.   Explanations based on the idea that mental (cognitive) abilities change as children get older and therefore there are *stages* of moral development.

Learning and social learning explanations

Behaviourists explain all behaviour, including making moral judgements, in terms of learning. See Units 3.1 and 3.2 for a description of learning and social learning theory.

1 Punishment.   The most obvious way that children learn right and wrong is to be punished. Questions about whether it is effective and how effectiveness can be increased are answered in Unit 3.1.

RESEARCH EXAMPLE   **Hoffman (1970) Discipline style and moral development**

RESEARCH QUESTION: What kind of discipline is most effective?

METHOD: A literature review of correlational studies. Hoffman identified three major approaches to child-rearing:

1 *Love withdrawal*. Withholding attention, affection or approval when the child misbehaves, which creates anxiety over loss of love.
2 *Power assertion*. Using superior power such as forceful comments, physical restraint, spanking or withdrawing privileges. May lead to fear, anger, resentment.
3 *Induction*. Explaining why a behaviour is wrong, emphasising how it affects others and suggesting ways to make amends.

RESULTS: Few parents used one approach exclusively, however most had a dominant approach. There was a high correlation between more mature moral development and the use of induction, whereas the opposite was true for power assertion.

The table shows the number of studies reporting positive or negative correlations with a particular disciplinary strategy.

Type of parental discipline	Correlation with moral development	
	Positive correlation	Negative correlation
Power assertion	7	32
Love withdrawal	8	11
Induction	38	6

INTERPRETATION: Induction allows children to develop their own moral reasoning rather than to obey instructions mindlessly.

EVALUATION: The data is *correlational*, therefore you can't say for sure that parental style *caused* more mature moral development. It could be that the child's level of moral development dictates the kind of punishment their parents use. For example, children who are morally less well-developed, need more coercive forms of punishment. Whereas children who are already morally sophisticated can be reasoned with.

APPLICATIONS: The same principles may be applied to education and teachers' disciplinary strategies.

RELATED STUDIES:
Baumrind (1971) suggested three parenting styles: authoritarian, authoritative and permissive. She found that authoritative parenting was correlated with many desirable behaviours in children. It is a form of firm control, rather than power, which allows the child to be an active agent rather than an obedient one.

---

❷ Rewards.   Many parents and teachers offer rewards as an incentive for good behaviour. Are rewards an effective means of teaching?

RESEARCH EXAMPLE **Lepper *et al*. (1973) Undermining interest with rewards**

RESEARCH QUESTION: Schoolchildren may do their work in order to get good grades, gold stars or other external (*extrinsic*) rewards. Alternatively they may do it because it gives them pleasure or satisfaction, an *intrinsic* reward. Are people's intrinsic interests undermined by offering them extrinsic rewards?

PARTICIPANTS: Fifty-five nursery school children, aged 3 to 5.

METHOD: Field experiment, undisclosed observation. Participants were selected from the nursery school population on the basis of those who showed the greatest intrinsic interest in drawing. Some selected participants refused to take part, leaving the final 55 participants. The participants were placed in one of three experimental conditions, and taken to a separate room for a drawing session. The experimenter did not know the experimental condition for the group until after they did their drawing (double-blind).

1 *Expected-award*: Participants agreed to do some drawing in order to get a 'Good Player Award', the extrinsic reward.
2 *Unexpected award*: The participants received the same reward but didn't know about it until after doing their drawing. Their work was not motivated by extrinsic rewards.
3 *No award*: The participants neither expected nor received any reward.

A few weeks later the researchers assessed interest by asking the children to draw while observing them through a one-way mirror.

RESULTS:

Experimental condition	Percentage of free-choice time spent drawing
Expected award Unexpected award No award	8.6% 10.7% 18.1%

INTERPRETATION: Extrinsic rewards appear to destroy intrinsic motivation.

APPLICATIONS: This has an important message for parents and teachers: offering extrinsic rewards may be permanently damaging. Ultimately a child needs to develop their own, intrinsic sense of control.

---

❸ Modelling.   Social learning theory extends the principles of behaviourism to include the effects of observation. You don't have to be punished or rewarded yourself, you might learn from seeing what happens to other people. The question 'who is likely to be imitated?' is answered in Unit 3.2.

RESEARCH EXAMPLE | **Bryan and Test (1967) Learning to help**

RESEARCH QUESTION: To what extent does the presence of a model in a natural setting affect helping behaviour? The researchers specifically set out to use participants *other* than students in a context *other* than a school or college.

PARTICIPANTS: An opportunity sample of 4,000 cars which passed the control car, located on a main road in a residential section of Los Angeles.

METHOD: Field experiment, deception.
1 *No model condition.* A young female stood by her 1964 Ford Mustang (the control car) with a flat tyre.
2 *Model condition.* A 1965 Oldsmobile was located about $\frac{1}{4}$ mile from the control car. This car was raised on a jack and a woman was watching a man change the tyre.
Any individual who stopped to help was told that she had already arranged for help and told the nature of the experiment.

RESULTS:

	No model	Model present
Cars who stopped	35 (nearly 1%)	58 (1.5%)

INTERPRETATION: Models act as a means of learning moral and prosocial behaviour. This is a form of social learning.

RELATED STUDIES: Beaman *et al.* (1978) also showed how direct instruction increases prosocial behaviour (see Unit 7.2).

---

❹ Evaluation:

Advantages:
- Some moral behaviour is obviously learned through reinforcement and modelling.
- It can explain how moral behaviour is related to particular *situations* rather than to principles (see 'Moral inconsistency', later in this unit)
- It has stimulated a lot of *research* because it makes clear predictions.

Criticisms:
- Some moral behaviour will be the result of *conscious decisions* rather than conditioned responses. For example, a decision to become a vegetarian or to truant from school.
- Behaviourist theory is based on the results of *animal* and laboratory experiments. It is wrong to assume that the same laws apply to everyday human behaviour.
- Does not account for the fact that children seem to pass through different *stages* of moral behaviour.

Psychodynamic explanations

Freud's view of moral development grew out of his psychoanalytic theory (see Unit 8.3).

xaminer's tip

If you are describing Freud's theory of moral development do not spend time on the earlier stages of personality development.

① The phallic stage and the superego.   Moral behaviour is controlled by the superego, which develops during the phallic stage.
- Around the age of 3 a child's sexual interest focuses on their genitalia and they feel desire for their opposite-sex parent.
- This makes them see their same-sex parent as a rival. The child feels unconscious hostility, resulting in guilt. The child also feels anxiety and fear of punishment should his true desires be discovered.
- Resolution occurs through identification with the same-sex parent. Identification is the process of 'taking' on the attitudes and ideas of another person.
- This identification results in the formation of the conscience and ego-ideal, which embody the moral values of the same-sex parent.
- Identification is also important for gender identity and attitudes towards authority.
- Unsatisfactory resolution results in problems such as amorality, homosexuality or rebelliousness.

Freud described this process in boys as the **Oedipus complex**. Oedipus was a figure in Greek mythology who loved his mother and killed his father. Freud described the phallic stage for boys as a time when they want their mother and therefore feel jealous of their father, wanting to remove him. The fear that the father will discover these feelings is expressed as a fear of castration, but eventually is resolved through identifying with the father.

In girls, the same process is termed the **Electra complex**. Electra urged her brother to kill her mother. The young girl has 'penis envy' and resents her mother for not providing her with one. A girl does not resolve this through identification, therefore girls should not reach moral maturity.

② The conscience.   Your conscience punishes you when you do something wrong. It is an internal representation of the 'punishing' parent. The conscience appears at age 5 or 6. It is composed of prohibitions imposed on us by parents and is a source of guilt feelings.
- Freud predicted an inverse relationship between guilt and wrongdoing, the more guilt a person experiences the less likely they are to do wrong. This is because a child raised leniently should have a strong conscience and vice versa.
- Freud also explained the strong bonds between dominant parents and their children. A more threatening parent will produce a greater fear of punishment, which therefore leads to a stronger sense of identification.

③ The ego-ideal.   Your ego-ideal rewards you when you behave in accordance with parental moral values, acting as the 'rewarding' parent. The ego-ideal is a source of feelings of pride and self-satisfaction.

④ Evaluation:
Advantages:
- Emphasised the importance of *early childhood*, which has had an enormous impact.
- Can account for moral *inconsistency*, behaviour would be different when governed by either the irrational or rational self.
- Relates to *personal experience* of guilt and the internal sensor.
Criticisms:
- There is little *evidence* to support his theories.
- This view can't explain how children from *one parent* families generally manage to develop a sense of morals and gender identity.
- Assumes that morals are *unconscious*.
- The concepts of reward and punishment are also used by behaviourists, and cannot *totally* explain behaviour.

Cognitive-developmental explanations: Piaget (1932)

All cognitive developmental theories have certain features in common:
- *Stages.* They describe moral development in terms of a series of fixed stages.
- *Consistency.* They assume that people always behave according to moral principles.
- *Universal.* Moral behaviour is essentially the same the world over and develops as a result of cognitive maturity.

Piaget's views are closely related to his description of cognitive development (see Unit 4.4).

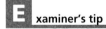

xaminer's tip

Piaget's theory of moral development is related to his theory of cognitive development but do not offer one explanation as a substitute for the other.

AGE (approximate)	0–5 years	5–8+	9+
STAGE	PREMORAL JUDGEMENT	MORAL REALISM *Heteronomous* morals (controlled by others).	MORAL SUBJECTIVISM/ RELATIVITY *Autonomous* morals (controlled by oneself).
RULES	Rules not understood.	Rules exist as 'things', (*realism*).	Rules mutually agreed and can be changed by mutual consent (*relativism*).
CHILD EVALUATES ACTIONS BY		*Consequences.*	*Intentions.*
PUNISHMENT		Make up for the damage done, to make *atonement.*	Punishment to fit the crime, principle of *reciprocity.*
EQUIVALENT STAGE OF COGNITIVE DEVELOPMENT	Pre-operational, egocentric.	Intuitive, inability to conserve.	Concrete and formal operations.

 Evidence:

Piaget (1932) A Game of marbles: Realism versus relativism

RESEARCH QUESTION: When children play marbles, how will their use of rules change with their age and cognitive development?

PARTICIPANTS: An opportunity sample including Piaget's own children.

METHOD: Observation, interview. When children were playing marbles, he asked them questions such as: 'Who made the rules?', 'Can we change them?'.

RESULTS:
1 2–3-year-olds used no rules at all.
2 By the age of 5, children were using rules, which were seen as absolute law and unchangeable. They saw the rules as coming from some semi-mystical authority.
3 Children of 10 understood that people had invented the rules. They could be changed, but in principle, only if all the players agreed. In practice some children changed the rules to their own advantage.

INTERPRETATION: Children of 5 had a sense of moral *realism*, older children understood moral *relativism*.

EVALUATION: The game of marbles is a rather insignificant example of understanding rules and morals. Even very young children have a more complex understanding of rules such as when certain behaviours are permitted.

Piaget (1932) Moral stories: Intentions versus consequences

RESEARCH QUESTION: Do children differ in their focus on intentions or consequences? Are some 'wrongs' made right because the person didn't intend to be naughty?

METHOD: Experiment. Piaget presented children with pairs of stories and asked 'are these children equally guilty?' and 'which of the two is naughtiest?' For each pair of stories (A) has a greater consequence but the intentions are good, (B) has smaller consequences but bad intentions. For example:

(A) *Albertine had a little friend who kept a bird in a cage. Albertine thought the bird was very unhappy, and she was always asking to let him out. But her friend wouldn't. So one day when her friend wasn't there, Albertine went and stole the bird. She let it fly away and hid the cage in her attic so the bird should never be shut up again.*

(B) *Juliet stole some sweeties from her mother one day when her mother was not there, and she hid and ate them up.*

Albertine is not intentionally doing wrong, her intentions are to protect the bird. Juliet is intentionally doing wrong.

RESULTS:

1 The *heteronomous* younger child could distinguish between intentional and unintentional actions, but based their judgement on the severity of outcome. This is using objective or external responsibility as the basis for morality.

2 The *autonomous* older child used the motive/intention as the means for judgement. This is using internal responsibility as the basis for morality.

INTERPRETATION: Younger children evaluate guilt in terms of consequences whereas older children take intention into account.

EVALUATION:

1 The moral stories are poorly designed and they demand that certain inferences are made.

2 The younger children may not have understood the stories and were only able to pick out the consequences.

2 Evaluation:

Advantages:

- Piaget's work introduced the idea of *stages* of moral development which are dependent on stages of cognitive maturity.

Criticisms:

- Piaget's *empirical methods* are not rigidly controlled and therefore his evidence may be influenced by experimenter bias.
- He probably *underestimated* children's moral sophistication in some situations.
- His account does not explain moral *inconsistency*, the lack of relationship between moral attitudes and moral behaviour.
- His account ignores the *emotional, spiritual* and *political factors* which are involved in behavioural choice.

Cognitive-developmental explanations: Kohlberg (1966)

Kohlberg elaborated Piaget's theory and extended the scope right through to middle age. He attempted to account for moral reasoning rather than behaviour.

LEVEL	AGE (approx.)		STAGE
I Pre-conventional	6–13	1 2	Deference to authority, heteronomous. Doing good to serve one's own interests, egocentric.
II Conventional	13–16	3 4	Care for the other, interpersonal conformity, 'good boy/girl'. The primacy of social order, conscience, unquestioning acceptance of authority.
III Post-conventional or principled	16–20	5 6	Creation of social order, individual rights, questioning the law and authority to ensure justice. Universal, ethical principles (later dropped because rarely, if ever exhibited except by e.g. Gandhi).

1 Evidence:

RESEARCH EXAMPLE   **Colby, Kohlberg *et al.* (1983) Moral dilemmas**

RESEARCH AIM: The aim of the research was to find out *how* people think rather than *what* they think.

PARTICIPANTS: Followed 58 US males over 20 years. They were aged between 10 and 16 at the start of the study.

METHOD: Questionnaire. Kohlberg developed a set of moral dilemmas, based on 10 moral issues/values: punishment, property, law, roles and concerns of affection, authority, life, liberty, distributive justice, truth and sex. An example is given at the beginning of this unit.

RESULTS: Children and adults at different stages of moral development produce significantly different answers.

INTERPRETATION: The results confirm Kohlberg's stages.

APPLICATIONS: The results have been influential in education and criminology.

RELATED STUDIES:

Gilligan (1982) noted that women are most often scored at stage 3 (see more later in this unit).

Colby and Kohlberg (1987) performed a more careful analysis of the original data and found only 15% reached stage 5 and there was no evidence whatsoever of stage 6 judgements.

Fodor (1972) found that delinquents operate at a much lower level on the Kohlberg scales than non–delinquents.

E **xaminer's tip**

It is important to be able to offer both positive and negative criticism of any theory as well as being able to describe it.

2 Evaluation:

Advantages:
- The notion of 'dilemmas' recognises the fact that people behave differently in different situations (see 'Moral inconsistency')
- It may be the *best available* approach and has generated much empirical interest, despite the criticisms below.

Criticisms:
- This is a theory of moral *principles*, it doesn't mean that people will *behave* in the same way. To be fair, Kohlberg never claimed to predict behaviour, his interest was in moral reasoning.
- Stages 5 and 6 may be *moral ideals*, never achieved by some people.
- *Gender bias.* The theory is biased towards male morality as the participants were male.
- *Culture bias.* Kohlberg claimed that the moral stages are universal. In fact the stages reflect Western values of democracy and the assumption that such systems are more morally advanced that other social systems (see Nobles, Unit 5.3).
- *Age bias.* The dilemmas are biased towards older participants, some of them are irrelevant to children. For example: 'What would you do if you were in the war …?' This would mean that Kohlberg underestimated the moral development of some children.

A combined conclusion

Hoffman (1970) presented an overview of moral development which uses all three approaches. He suggests that moral development proceeds along four tracks:

1 Social learning.   The beginnings of moral behaviour are learned through reward and punishment.

2 Psychoanalytic.   Learning to tame irrational impulses and feeling anxiety for wrongdoing.

3 Cognitive control.   The child takes on the role of control, making his/her own rationalisations rather than being controlled.

4 Empathy.   Becoming aware of how other's feel.

Types of morality

1 Intentions versus consequences.   Kohlberg's dilemmas focused on whether an action was immoral if the result was bad though the intentions were good.

2 Behaviour versus principles: Moral inconsistency.   A major problem for theories of moral development is that people don't always behave in accordance with their beliefs. For example, Hartshorne and May (1928) found little consistency in moral behaviour. A child who cheated in one situation didn't in another. They also found that immoral behaviour was more governed by the probability of being caught than any principles of morality (see details in Unit 7.2).

Gilligan (1982) distinguished between hypothetical and real moral dilemmas. For example, she interviewed 29 women attending an abortion and pregnancy counselling service. Faced with a very real moral dilemma she found that they focused lesson the 'justice' dimension as suggested by Kohlberg and more on 'responsibility'. Gilligan also argued that Gandhi, Kohlberg's example of ultimate morality, was callous to his family and personal followers. Most people practice different 'moralities' in different spheres.

3. Ethnocentrism.   Are morals universal? Psychology tends to be dominated by a European perspective of human behaviour. Nobles (1976), see Unit 5.3, made the following distinction:

- The Western world view emphasises individuality, uniqueness, independence, survival of the fittest and control over nature.
- Africans value commonality, co-operation, similarity, survival of the tribe and oneness with nature. They do not have a sense of 'me' but of 'we'.
- Therefore, it would be wrong to suggest that the two communities would have the same sense of morals.

4. Gender differences.   Gilligan (1982) criticised Kohlberg for promoting a 'male' morality. Gilligan and Attanucci (1988) asked a group of men and women to produce accounts of their own moral dilemmas. These were analysed and scored according to whether they emphasised the moral principle of care or justice. Overall men favoured a justice orientation and women favoured a care orientation.

Assuming that gender differences are learned, then morals must be too, and will not be universal.

Quick test 9.1

1 What is meant by the term *socialisation*. (*NEAB,1993*)
2 How is empathy important in the development of morals?
3 According to psychological studies, what are the effects on children of punishment like smacking likely to be? (*SEG, 1991*)
4 Social learning and cognitive-developmental theorists offer **two** explanations of moral development. Outline **one** difference between these explanations.
5 According to Freud, what is the key stage in moral development?
6 Give **one** way that Piaget's theory of moral development differs from Freud's theory. (*MEG, sample Higher*)
7 According to Piaget, how is the moral reasoning of most 5-year-old and 9-year-old children different? (*SEG, 1993*)
8 Give **one** criticism of the use of moral stories to investigate morals.
9 How do friends affect the ways in which children learn right from wrong? (*SEG, 1992*)
10 What is the relationship between morals and behaviour?

Summary

	LEARNING THEORY	PSYCHODYNAMIC	COGNITIVE
ACTIVE OR PASSIVE	The child is passive, influenced by the environment	The child is passive, influenced by inner drives.	The child is active in controlling the world.
CAUSE OF DEVELOPMENT	Morals are learned through reward/punishment and experience.		Cognitive maturation controls the level of moral development.
PEER VS. ADULT INFLUENCES	Adults, particularly parents, are important in teaching morals, consciously or unconsciously.		Peers are important.
GUILT AND EMOTION	Painful anxiety states are associated with wrongdoing (conditioning).		Not mentioned.
STAGES OF MORAL DEVELOPMENT	Not mentioned.	In early childhood.	Throughout childhood and possibly later.
MORAL INCONSISTENCY	Predicted by situational conditioning.	Can be explained by the split between rational/ irrational behaviour.	A problem for stage theories

APPLICATIONS: Educational implications, criminology, child-rearing techniques.

9.2 Gender development

AN ACCIDENTAL CASTRATION AND OTHER CASES

A pair of identical twin boys were circumcised at 7 months. The physician accidentally used too high an electric current to cut the tissue and more or less burned off one of their penises. Ten months later the parents decided that the best course of action was to raise the child as a female. 'She' was given female hormones and had a vagina constructed. The parents promoted feminine-type behaviour in the female twin so that the only difference between the twins was one of hormones and social influence. Genetically they were identical.

When 'she' was older she was more feminine than her brother but had some social problems and found it difficult to accept her female role.

In another case a 17-month-old boy who was born with no penis was given corrective surgery to make him into a girl. 'Her' parents and an older brother felt their behaviour changed towards the child. 'She' soon showed signs of feminine behaviour, such as wanting Cinderella slippers for Christmas. (Money and Ehrhardt, 1972)

The importance of these case histories is that they strongly support the view that gender identity is related to the sex of rearing rather than being a genetic fact. However, hormones probably play a significant role.

The Batista's had 10 children, 4 of whom were born with normal female genitalia and grew up as girls. At puberty their vaginas healed over, testicles descended and they grew full-sized penises. The same thing had happened to other families in their remote village in the Caribbean. They all had a common ancestor who had a mutant gene. This gene caused a lack of male hormone during embryonic development so that the external male genitalia did not develop, though the male organs were present internally. During puberty, massive amounts of male hormone are produced and this caused the male genitalia to appear. The girls seemed to accept their change of sex without much difficulty (boys might not have accepted such a change so easily) (Imperato-McGinley *et al.*, 1974).

In this case biological sex (genetic and hormonal) seems to have had a greater effect than sex of rearing. It is possible that their trouble-free transition was helped by a culture which made relatively little fuss of gender identity.

The debate is whether nature (genes and hormones) or nurture (social factors) makes the more significant contribution, and how.

DEFINITIONS		
sex	Male or female, usually associated with biological difference.	
sex typing	Differential treatment of children according to sex.	
gender	Psychological/social aspects of maleness or femaleness.	
gender role	Masculine or feminine, the behaviour expected from an individual on the basis of their (perceived) biological sex.	
chromosomes	X-shaped bodies which carry all the genetic information (DNA) for an organism. In humans there are 46 chromosomes arranged in pairs, one member of each pair comes from the mother, the other from the father.	
embryo	The organism during the earliest stages of development. In humans the **embryonic** period lasts for the first 7 weeks, after which it is properly called a **foetus**.	
hormones	Chemical substances produced by certain glands in order to trigger a specific response in some other part of the body. Sex hormones are largely produced in the pituitary gland in the brain and affect the sex organs as well as certain behaviours, such as aggression, fertility and arousal.	
sexual dimorphism	Two distinct forms of a species. These different forms may be based on sex (males and females look different) or age (as in juveniles and adults having different markings).	

| androgyny | A concept introduced by Bem, who argued that a person can be both masculine *and* feminine. |

XX

XY

Sex development

One pair of chromosomes determine the sex of an individual. The pair can be XX or XY, so-called because of their shapes. The Y chromosome carries very little genetic material and is why males are more likely to suffer from recessive disorders. In females, a pair of genes are present so you would need two recessive genes, one from each chromosome. Whereas in males only one gene of the pair is present.

Nature's impulse is to create a female. *All* embryos start developing the same genital structures, then the production of male hormones causes the female parts to be absorbed and the male parts to develop. Without the hormone the embryo will remain externally female. The chromosomes determine the sex but most sexual development and activity is governed by hormones.

	MALE	FEMALE
chromosomal sex	XY	XX
gonadal sex	testes	ovaries
hormonal sex	androgens, mainly testosterone	oestrogen, progesterone
internal organs	prostate gland, sperm ducts, seminal vesicles, testes	womb, fallopian tubes, vagina, ovaries
external genitalia	penis and scrotum	outer lips of vagina (labia majora)

RESEARCH EXAMPLE   **Testicular Feminising Syndrome (TFS): The influence of hormones on sexual development**

RESEARCH QUESTION: This rare condition is a result of a normal XY embryo having an insensitivity to testosterone and therefore failing to develop testes in early development. Such an individual appears to be female externally but internally is essentially male. What sex and gender do such individuals have?

PARTICIPANT: Goldwyn (1979) described the case of Daphne Went. She was a married woman who sought help because she could not become pregnant. Examination revealed that she was in fact a male. Since she was content with her female role, she continued to live happily as a woman and adopted two children.

INTERPRETATION: Gender is a result of rearing.

EVALUATION:
1 Any conclusion drawn from a single case history must be treated with caution as other unique factors may be involved.
2 Hormones affect behaviour. Therefore Mrs. Went's insensitivity to male hormones may explain why she behaved in a more feminine than masculine fashion.

RELATED STUDIES: See 'Androgenital syndrome', described later in this unit.

How gender is determined

① <u>Sex typing</u>.   The key event in gender development is the sex given at birth (sex typing). This is obviously based on the external genitals. In rare cases, such as TFS (see above) the practice is generally to go with external appearance. Such individuals are usually infertile so they will never be able to reproduce. What they actually look like matters most.

EXAMPLE   **Hermaphroditism**

True cases are extremely rare. Like **Hermaphrodite**, the mythical Greek god/goddess, they must have both sex organs. Mr. Blackwell (Goldwyn, 1979) was the 303rd ever to be recorded.

He was a Bantu 'boy' who developed breasts at puberty. Medical examination revealed that 'he' had an active ovary on one side and an active testes on the other. He elected to have the female parts removed, remaining with his original gender identity. If his tubes had been connected differently he might have been able to fertilise himself. There is a case of this happening to a hermaphrodite (*Sunday Times*, June 1992).

❷ <u>Stages of gender development</u>. Gender is cognitive rather than physical. *Cognitive-developmental* theorists describe gender development in relation to cognitive development generally, as a series of stages linked to cognitive maturation. *Cognitive schema* theory describes development as the formation of schemas which organise attitudes about gender-appropriate behaviour. A person is motivated to behave in a way which is consistent with cognitive concepts or schemas.

	Development of gender identity [Knowing what sex you are and that it is fixed.]	Development of sex-role stereotypes [Knowing what a boy or girl should be like.]	Development of sex-typed patterns of behaviour [Tendency to prefer activities associated with your sex.]
2-3 years	Child can say whether they are male or female, but not aware that this is fixed.	Tolerant of doing things which are not gender-appropriate, e.g. play with opposite-sex toys.	Prefer playing with same sex and gender-appropriate toys.
3-7 years	**Gender stability:** Awareness that gender is fixed.	Rigid and intolerant of violations, e.g. boys should not play with girls' toys or have long hair.	Girls are more likely to have an interest in masculine things, possible because such behaviour is more highly valued. At the same time girls are freer than boys in being able to engage in all types of behaviour.
7-12 years	**Gender consistency:** Using gender schema, have learned to 'conserve' gender.	More flexible, gender violations seen as less serious than moral ones. Similar to moral relativism rather than realism.	
12+ years		Adolescents become more intolerant of cross-sex behaviours again, reflecting the need to recognise the opposite sex.	

❸ <u>Androgyny rather than gender development</u>. Traditional views assume that masculinity and femininity are separate dimensions of personality. Bem suggested that it is possible for a person to be androgynous, they can be both masculine and feminine.

RESEARCH EXAMPLE **Bem (1974) Measuring androgyny**

RESEARCH QUESTION: Traditionally it is assumed that rigid sex-role definition leads to mental health. Bem suggests that this view may have outlived its usefulness. An androgynous approach is more flexible, allowing a person to select the best and most appropriate behaviours for them. Is there a positive relationship between androgyny and psychological health?

METHOD: Psychometric, correlation. Bem designed an inventory, the Bem Sex Role Inventory (BSRI) which would make it possible to test for masculinity and femininity independently rather than setting them against each other. In traditional tests, if you selected a masculine item you couldn't select a feminine one.

RESULTS: Researchers who have used the BSRI and other measures have found that androgynous participants are more adaptable in different situations, have higher self-esteem and a greater sense of emotional well-being.

INTERPRETATION: Bem (1983) reformulated her approach in terms of gender schema theory. She suggests that the difference between an androgynous and a traditionally sex-typed person is one of cognitive style. An androgynous person, when faced with a decision as to how to behave in a particular situation, responds independently of any gender concepts. Whereas a traditionally sex-typed person, determines what would be appropriate for their gender using gender schemas. A person who has a 'freer' cognitive style will be psychologically healthier.

EVALUATION:

1 Psychological health is associated with high self-esteem. All the test items were socially desirable, therefore someone who scored high on both masculine *and* feminine traits (i.e. androgynous) would be higher in self esteem than someone who choose only male *or* female items.

2 Spence *et al.* (1975) devised the Personal Attributes Questionnaire (PAQ). They showed that Bem had not distinguished between persons who are androgynous (*high* in both masculine and feminine traits) and a different kind of androgyny, where a person is neither masculine nor feminine (*low* in both traits).

APPLICATIONS: Children who are encouraged to adopt a more androgynous approach to their gender should develop a more adaptable, and mentally healthier, cognitive style.

Influences on gender identity

❶ <u>Biological influences</u>

- Gender is usually determined by *sex typing* at birth, based on physical characteristics. The first question new parents are usually asked is 'What sex is it?'.
- *Hormones* influence the development of sex and later sexual behaviour. For example, ovulation, pregnancy, birth and aspects of parenting are naturally or artificially controlled by the release of various hormones.
- The manipulation of hormones in *animal studies* has shown how gender behaviours can be controlled. For example, giving a female rat male hormones results in male behaviours. However, the effects are not the same in different species, particularly primates. Studies of non-human primates have shown how social conditions, such as the presence or absence of the opposite sex, will alter the results of such studies.

RESEARCH EXAMPLE   **Money and Ehrhardt (1972) The role of hormones in gender-appropriate behaviour**

Androgenital Syndrome is the reverse of TFS. An XX individual (normal chromosomal female) receives an excess of male hormones during embryonic development. This causes external male genitalia to develop, though internally the individual remains female. Corrective surgery can remove the penis, but the brain's exposure to male hormones may have permanent consequences.

PARTICIPANTS: A group of 25 **androgenised** girls, aged 4 to 16. Their mothers had been prescribed male hormones during pregnancy to prevent miscarriage. There was a control group of 25 normal girls matched in terms of age, IQ, race and socio-economic level. The androgenised girls had received corrective surgery where necessary.

METHOD: Interview. The girls and their mothers were interviewed on various topics and the girls were tested for gender-role preferences.

RESULTS:

1 None of the androgenised girls wished to change sex.

2 The androgenised girls were not more aggressive than the control group but preferred vigorous outdoor activity and boys' sports. They had less interest in playing with dolls, dressing with adornment or playing games involving mothering-roles.

3 In a follow up study, the girls at 16 were found to be at least three years behind their peers in sexual activities.

INTERPRETATION: The 'tomboyishness' of androgenised girls may be due to the effects of male hormones on the infant's brain before birth. This suggests that hormones may cause gender behaviours in humans as well as animals.

EVALUATION: The girls, their parents and teachers all knew of their problem condition and therefore expectations may have led to different development and different perceptions of behaviour.

---

❷ <u>Parental influences:</u>

RESEARCH EXAMPLE   **Smith and Lloyd (1978) Maternal behaviour and perceived sex of infant**

RESEARCH QUESTION: Do mothers treat boy and girl infants differently?

PARTICIPANTS: Thirty-two mothers and four six-month-old babies, two boys and two girls.

METHOD: Experiment, observation, deception. The mothers were told that the study was concerned with analysing play. They were videotaped while playing with the 'actor baby' for 10 minutes. Seven toys were present: a squeaky hammer and stuffed rabbit in trousers (masculine); a doll and squeaky bambi (feminine); a squeaky pig, a ball and a rattle (neutral). The babies were dressed either as boys or girls and introduced with an appropriate name. These labels were not always consistent with the real sex.

At the end the mothers were debriefed.

RESULTS: If a mother thought she was playing with a boy, she verbally encouraged more motor activity and offered gender-appropriate toys.

INTERPRETATION: Mothers responded to the perceived sex of the infant, in line with typical gender expectations.

EVALUATION: There may have been some tendency for mothers to behave differently in front of video cameras than they would at home.

RELATED STUDIES: Condry and Condry (1976) showed male and female participants a 10-minute video of a 9-month-old infant taken through a one-way mirror. Four toys: a teddy bear, a jack-in-the-box, a doll and a buzzer, were pushed towards the child and pulled back five times. Participants were then asked to rate the infant's emotional response on a 10-point scale in terms of pleasure, anger, fear, and intensity of emotion. The participants were tested in a group and given written instructions which said whether the infant was a male or female. The same infant was seen as displaying different emotions and different levels of arousal depending on the sex attributed to the infant.

3 <u>Other social influences</u>.   Many adults will reinforce gender-appropriate behaviours as well as acting as models for children to imitate. Peers have a strong influence.

RESEARCH EXAMPLE | **Lamb and Roopnarine (1979) Peer influence on sex-role development**

RESEARCH QUESTION: Do peer responses to sex-stereotyped activities affect their occurrence?

PARTICIPANTS: Thirty-two boys and girls in a nursery school, aged 3–5 years old. This age group is used because they are in the process of acquiring gender concepts.

METHOD: Naturalistic observation for 2–3 weeks during free play periods. There were three observers. Their time sampled observations were based on:
1 Target activities. Thirteen were selected representing male and female type activities.
2 Response behaviours. Five were positively reinforcing (e.g. praise, imitate), four were negative (e.g. criticise, stop play), two were neutral.

RESULTS:
1 Children generally reinforced peers for sex-appropriate play and were quick to criticise sex-inappropriate play.
2 Children respond more readily to reinforcement by the same sex rather than opposite sex peers. This suggests that children already know what is sex-appropriate, their peers are just reinforcing that knowledge.

INTERPRETATION: Reinforcement and punishment seem to have direct effects on preschool children's behaviour. Peer behaviour is probably reinforcing rather than informative.

---

4 <u>Persistent stereotypes</u>.   Others around us reinforce gender-appropriate behaviours on the basis of stereotypes. The problem is that stereotypes are very resistant to change and they are self-perpetuating (see Unit 5.2). Do stereotypes *cause* gender-appropriate behaviour or do observed sex differences *cause* gender stereotypes?

RESEARCH EXAMPLE | **Mischel (1974) Sex bias**

RESEARCH QUESTION: Are differences between male and female abilities innate, or are they the result of social learning? Do we assess a piece of work differently if we know the sex of the author, in other words, on the basis of a common stereotype?

PARTICIPANTS: US male and female high school and college students.

METHOD: Experiment, deception. Participants were asked to rate four articles, each on a different topic. Two were in about masculine-type topics, two were feminine-type topics. Two were supposedly written by men and two by women. The authors' names were varied between participants as a control. In each case only the first name was changed, e.g. Joan R. Simpson or John R. Simpson.

RESULTS:

1 If the article was about a feminine-type pursuit, such as dietetics or primary education, judges rated articles by female authors more highly.

2 If the field was masculine, such as law or city planning, the male authors were judged more able.

INTERPRETATION: The author's perceived sex leads to a different assessment of ability, particularly in relation to commonly held stereotypes.

EVALUATION: When participants are given limited information on which to base their judgements they have to use cues such as gender. This may not truly reflect the real world.

APPLICATION: This should be considered in relation to the practice of students putting their first names one examination papers.

RELATED STUDIES:

Fidell (1970), see Unit 5.2, sent personal profiles about a Dr. Patrick or Patricia Clavel to over 200 psychology professors, people who might have been expected to know better. They favoured the man when assessing the candidate for an academic post.

5 <u>The influence of the media</u>. 'Media' includes: books, magazines, films and television. It is responsible for perpetuating stereotypes, but it is also a means of changing stereotypes by presenting men or women in unusual roles (counter-stereotyping). Are efforts to change stereotypes effective, or desirable?

- People tend to impose their existing stereotypes on what they watch and this moderates any influence counter-stereotypes might have.
- There are individual differences in the way people respond to counter-stereotypes.
- The ethics of such manipulations are open to question. Should a TV producer deliberately manipulate our stereotypes?

RESEARCH EXAMPLE | **Williams (1985) The effects of television on sex stereotypes**

RESEARCH QUESTION: Does watching TV affect levels of aggression and sex-role stereotypes?

PARTICIPANTS: Residents in three Canadian towns were studied over two years. One town (Notel) was located in a valley and had no television, another (Unitel) had one television channel and the other (Multitel) had four channels. During the period of the study Notel finally received one channel and Unitel got another one. The towns were similar in terms of population (about 3,000 people), ethnic mix, socio-economic factors and nearness to urban areas.

METHOD: Naturalistic experiment, cross-cultural. They assessed the effect of television content on children's aggression and sex roles.

RESULTS:

1 Children's aggressive behaviour, as observed in the school playground, increased in Notel.

2 Notel children's sex role attitudes became more traditional and sex-stereotyped.

INTERPRETATION: Cultures vary considerably in what is considered sex-appropriate behaviour. American television portrays men and women in traditional roles. This may considerably influence sex-attitudes in other cultures. Williams felt that the effects of television are stronger in developing countries where children have relatively less information, which affects their attitudes, compared with children in the developed world.

EVALUATION: The study showed *attitude* change, but sex role *behaviour* may not necessarily change.

RELATED STUDIES:

Manstead and McCulloch (1981) used the content analysis technique to look for sex stereotyping in British commercials, and found that men and women continue to be portrayed in traditional roles. Males have expertise and authority, women are shown as consumers and unknowledgeable about the reasons for buying a particular product.

Collins *et al.* (1984) found that preschool picture books *did* reflect changes in women's work roles. This was based on a sample of 16 award-winning books.

6 <u>Cultural influences</u>. If research shows that there are cultural differences in gender behaviours, this suggests that stereotypes are based on learning rather than innate sex differences.

Mead (1935) Cross-cultural studies of gender role behaviour

RESEARCH AIM: Mead's interests, as an anthropologist, were to record the behaviour of other cultures as a means of exposing the importance of culture as opposed to genetic inheritance.

METHOD and RESULTS: Cross-cultural observation of tribes from New Guinea.

1 The **Mundugumour** tribe were all aggressive (masculine quality) regardless of sex. Pregnancy and child-rearing were unwelcome activities for men and women, children had to fight for any attention and thus also became equally as aggressive as the adults. At one time the tribe had been cannibals.

2 The **Arapesh** were all warm, emotional and nonaggressive (feminine qualities). Husbands and wives shared everything, including pregnancy. The men took to bed during childbirth. Acts of aggression were rare and sex was associated with gentleness.

3 The **Tchambuli** exhibited a reversal of our own gender roles. Women reared the children but also looked after commerce outside the tribe, they made things which were useful and took the lead in sexual matters. The men spent their time in social activities, were more emotional and artistic.

INTERPRETATION: This evidence shows that there are very different male/female roles in different societies. Mead called this **cultural determinism**, the position that gender roles are entirely a result of learning from cultural attitudes and completely unrelated to biological sex.

EVALUATION: Cross-cultural observations require cautious interpretation (see Unit 11.1) and these results are almost too neat to be believed. It is possible that Mead was selective in reporting her results. Others have pointed out that in all three tribes men seemed to show the most violent behaviour and men did the hunting. In other words, men were more aggressive in *comparative* terms, supporting the idea of universal gender-related tendencies.

Mead later adopted a less extreme view of **cultural relativism**: There are cultural differences and these can be explained in terms of different cultural practices. There are also some universal gender behaviours which are innately-determined.

Observed sex differences

❶ <u>Sexual differences</u>.   There are many ways that boys and girls, men and women are physically different:
- At *birth* there are differences in external genitalia.
- At *puberty*, there are differences related to secondary sexual characteristics, such as breast and facial hair, menstruation and development of testicles.

❷ <u>Biological differences</u>.
- *Size*: Through childhood boys are generally bigger but not especially stronger. Girls have a growth spurt at puberty.
- *Metabolic rate:* Higher in boys from birth, which means they can expend more energy and burn calories faster.
- *Motor skills:* Developed earlier in girls. This might explain the fact that they have fewer problems with bedwetting than boys.
- *Vulnerability:* Boys are more likely to become ill early in life, and also more likely to have reading disabilities, speech defects, emotional disorders and some forms of mental retardation. This may be because of the lack of genetic information on the Y chromosome which allows recessive genes on the X chromosome to be expressed.

❸ <u>Psychological differences</u>.   There are certain roles that can be related to biological differences. Most notably child-bearing in women might be expected to be related to certain personality traits such as being caring. It has been observed that:
- Women are more oriented towards interpersonal goals whereas men function on a level of principles.
- Girls are more cautious, compliant and conformist.
- Girls are more emotionally sensitive than boys from the age of about four.
- Cognitive differences.

Maccoby and Jacklin (1974) A review of sex difference studies

RESEARCH QUESTION: What are the overall conclusions from studies of sex differences?

PARTICIPANTS: Children under the age of 12

METHOD: Reviewed more than 1,500 studies of gender differences.

RESULTS:

1 Girls are marginally superior on tests of verbal ability.

2 Boys are marginally better on tests of visual/spatial ability, for example identifying the same figure from different angles.

3 Boys are marginally better on tests of arithmetic reasoning, especially in adolescence.

4 Boys are physically and verbally more aggressive than girls, from the age of two.

5 Considering overall intelligence, 10 studies favoured girls, one favoured boys and 18 found no difference.

INTERPRETATION: Maccoby and Jacklin concluded that the sex differences observed were minimal. They suggest that most popular sex-role stereotypes are 'cultural myths' that have no basis in fact. They are perpetuated by expectations arising from gender stereotypes.

EVALUATION:

1 This review may *underestimate* sex differences because it pools results from studies which used different tests, methods, sample sizes, and so on.

2 On the other hand, studies of sex differences tend to *overestimate* sex differences, because those studies which failed to find any differences tend not to get published!

RELATED STUDIES:

Weinberg *et al.* (1979) see Unit 8.2, found that sex differences disappeared if girls were given raised expectations and boys given lowered ones. This also suggests that socialisation is responsible for sex differences.

Theoretical accounts of gender development

❶ The Biological Approach. *For example:* Hutt (1972), Money and Ehrhardt (1972)
Argument: Genetic and hormonal factors cause gender-appropriate behaviours.
Advantages:
- Some sex differences are clearly biological, therefore the biological approach must be part of any account.
Criticisms:
- Case histories show that genetic *sex* and *gender* need not correspond. Therefore biological explanations are not sufficient on their own.
- There is *cross-cultural* evidence for different as well as similar male/female roles, supporting the role of social learning.

❷ Psychoanalytic. *For example:* Freud (1905)
Argument: Gender-appropriate attitudes become internalised from identifying with the same sex parent (see Unit 9.1). This must be achieved during a critical period.
Advantages:
- Freud was probably correct in identifying the age of four as a time of gender awareness and in drawing attention to the child's sexual awareness of his parents. Children do have to cope with sexual feelings towards parents.
- Explains identification with *role models*.
Criticisms:
- *One-parent* and *homosexual* families raise questions. Children in such families appear to follow typical psychosexual development.
- *Gender bias*. Freud said women were sexually inferior, they have to make do with babies as a poor substitute for a penis. A more modern interpretation is that envy is about status, the penis is a symbol of men's superior status.
- There is no evidence to support this view.

❸ Social Learning Theory. *For example:* Bandura (1977)
Argument: Gender identity and sex-appropriate behaviours are learned through direct or indirect reward and punishment, imitation and modelling.
Advantages:
- Explains *cultural differences*, which are learned from the cultural practices.
- There is evidence that adults do *reinforce* gender-appropriate behaviours.
Criticisms:
- Reinforcements are not sufficiently *consistent* to explain observed differences.
- Lacks account of *biological* factors, such as hormones, which moderate the influence of social factors.
- Does not account for normal gender development in *homosexual* or *one-parent* families.

❹ Cognitive-Developmental Theory. *For example:* Kohlberg (1966)
Argument: Gender identity is a combination of social learning plus maturational and

cognitive factors. The ability to form coherent, consistent thought (maturation) is necessary for the formation of gender concepts. The child actively organises its own identity (cognitive).

Advantages:
- Combines a *social learning* approach with some aspects of *biological* development.
- Basic gender identity does appear between 2 and 5, in line with *cognitive development.*

Criticisms:
- This view assumes that development proceeds in *stages*, and that gender identity is mediated by *cognitive factors.* This may not universally be true.
- Does not account for the fact that some gender behaviours occur *before* the age of four.

⑤ Gender-schema Theory. *For example:* Martin and Halverson (1981), Bem (1984)
Argument: Once a child has a basic gender identity they are motivated to learn more about the sexes and incorporate this information into a gender schema. Like all schemas, this serves to organise relevant information and attitudes and will influence behaviour.

Advantages:
- Offers a *middle ground* between social learning and cognitive-developmental explanations.
- Explains how *gender stereotypes* persist, because people are more likely to remember information which is consistent with their schemas and to ignore inconsistent information (see Unit 5.1).
- Explains how gender behaviours occur *before* gender identity.

Criticisms:
- The same criticisms mentioned with respect to social learning and cognitive-developmental theories apply here.

Quick test 9.2

1 Give an example of the use of sex-role stereotyping in advertising.
2 How might sex-role stereotyping be reduced?
3 What is *gender stability*?
4 What have psychologists discovered about cultural differences in sex roles?
5 In what ways do psychologists believe that parents encourage gender differences? (*SEG, 1992*)
6 What is meant by the term *androgyny*?
7 Describe how Freud believed sex-role behaviour develops in boys. (*NEAB, 1993*)
8 How do magazines and television encourage gender stereotypes? (*SEG, sample Foundation*)
9 Suggest **two** aspects of behaviour or experience which might show **no** difference between the sexes. (*MEG, 1993*)
10 Men have better visual spatial ability. Using your psychological knowledge, suggest **two** reasons why this might be.

Summary

HOW SEX IS DETERMINED	HOW GENDER IS DETERMINED	INFLUENCES ON GENDER IDENTITY	OBSERVED SEX DIFFERENCES	THEORIES OF GENDER DEVELOPMENT
1 Chromosomes	1 Sex typing	1 Biological	1 Sexual	1 Biological
2 Hormones	2 Stages	2 Parental	2 Biological	2 Psychoanalytic
	3 Androgyny	3 Other social	3 Psychological	3 Social learning
		4 Stereotypes		4 Cognitive-developmental
		5 The media		5 Gender-schema
		6 Cultural		

9.3 Attraction and friendships

ALPHABET AND ATTRACTION

What factors influence our selection of friends? A study by Segal (1974) found that people who sat close together in class were likely to become friends, regardless of other factors such as having similar interests.

A group of 44 male police cadets were given a questionnaire to assess their attitudes and social characteristics. They were also asked to list their three closest friends on the force. In class, they were seated alphabetically and, as the researchers expected, it turned out that 45% of their named friends had surnames adjacent in the alphabet. Therefore nearness acted as a cause of friendship.

This factor showed greater correlation than other characteristics, such as religion, age, marital status, ethnic background, parents' education, leisure activity preferences or certain attitudes

Is this result reasonable? Surely people are more discerning in their friendships than to select the 'girl next door'? There are some flaws with the study. For example, the population studied was relatively similar in terms of age, background and interests. In a group of people who were more different, other factors such as similar attitudes might be more important than nearness.

However, most groups of people who spend a lot of time together *are* relatively similar. So physical nearness maybe one of the key factors in who becomes friends with who. This chapter looks at some other factors as well as the development and importance of friendship.

DEFINITIONS		
interpersonal attraction	The ways in which people come to like each other.
peer	One that has equal standing with another. 'Equality' can be in terms of age or skill.
friendship	An intimate acquaintance, attachment from mutual esteem and trust.
affiliation	Bringing into close contact or association.
self-disclosure	Revealing things about yourself.

Interpersonal attraction: Initial attraction

Why do some people become friends, and not others? Some factors can account for *initial* attraction. Other factors are important in the *maintenance* of a relationship (see later in this unit).

Kerckhoff and Davis (1962) used the term **filter** to describe how superficial characteristics are used initially in selecting friends.

A list of filters:

1 Physical attractiveness.   The **matching hypothesis** suggests that people select partners whose social desirability matches that of their own. Realistic desires are compromise between objective desirability (status, power, physical attractiveness) and the perceived possibility of attainment.

This compromise is necessary because of a fear of rejection (a more attractive person might reject your advances) and/or to achieve a set of balance between partners.

RESEARCH EXAMPLE   **Walster *et al.* (1966) The computer dance**

RESEARCH QUESTION: Do people select partners whose attractiveness approximately matches their own social desirability?

PARTICIPANTS: A computer dance was advertised in a freshers week handbook. The first 376 male and 376 female volunteers were allowed in at $1.00 a piece.

METHOD: Field experiment, deception.

1 When the students arrived to sign up for the dance, four independent judges assessed each student's physical attractiveness as a measure of social desirability.
2 The participants were seated upstairs and asked to fill in a lengthy questionnaire, ostensibly for use in the computer pairing. In fact the questionnaire was used to provide data about similarity and the pairing was done randomly (except no man was assigned to a taller woman).
3 The dance was held two days later, before which the students were given their dates' names. 44 couples did not attend.
4 During the dance, participants were asked to complete a questionnaire about the dance and their dates.
5 All participants were contacted after four months to see if they had continued dating.

RESULTS:

1 Physical attractiveness proved to be the most important factor in liking, above such qualities as intelligence and personality.
2 Liking was not affected by how attracted the other person felt towards the subject.
3 Physical attractiveness was also the best predictor of the likelihood that they would see each other again, though it assumed less importance.

INTERPRETATION: Sheer physical attractiveness appears to be the overriding determinant of liking. The **matching hypothesis** did not receive support.

EVALUATION: Not a very realistic test because:

1 The date was assigned, and assessments were made before any rejection could have taken place.
2 The interaction was very brief and therefore interpersonal assessments had to be based on superficial characteristics.
3 The measure of physical attractiveness may not be reliable.
4 The results may only apply to a youthful population who are not making long-term romantic choices.

RELATED STUDIES:

Murstein (1972) assessed whether existing couples were similar in terms of attractiveness. Independent judges rated photographs in random order. The photograph's attractiveness, as judged independently, was closer for real couples than random pairs.

Silverman (1971) in a field study, observed couples and rated their attractiveness, confirming Murstein's findings and also noting that the greater the degree of physical attractiveness the more physical intimacy was displayed.

---

2 Proximity. The people you sit next to in class or who you work with or who live in your neighbourhood, are the people you are most likely to talk to. Therefore you will select your friends from this population. The closer they are, the more you'll have an opportunity to get to know them better.

RESEARCH EXAMPLE **Festinger *et al.* (1950) Human factors in housing**

RESEARCH QUESTION: How does spatial distribution affect the formation and structure of social groups? Festinger *et al.* refer to this as **human ecology**.

PARTICIPANTS: The residents of two adjoining housing projects, Westgate and Westgate West in Boston, Massachusetts. Westgate consisted of 100 single-storey housing units, arranged in groups of between 7 to 13 to form a U-shape. Westgate West consisted of 17 two-floor buildings with 10 apartments. All residents worked at the Massachusetts Institute of Technology, in other words they were well-educated. Some had families.

METHOD: Observation, survey.

1 *Sociometric data* was gathered from all residents by asking 'What three people in Westgate or Westgate West do you see most of socially?'
2 Observations were made about the amount of *passive contact* between residents. Such contacts are determined by the routes you have to take when going to and from your house. It can be measured in terms of:
   - *Physical* distance between residents.
   - *Functional* distance, the design of a building or positional relationships between houses will determine specific paths people have to take. For example those residents in end positions had more passive contacts than those living in the middle.

RESULTS:

1 The greatest number of sociometric choices were given for next-door neighbours. Therefore physical proximity is a major determinant of friendship.

2 The people living in the end apartments of Westgate West were chosen more often than any other apartment position. This is because they are at the foot of the stairways connecting the two floors and therefore all residents must pass by frequently, thus increasing their passive contacts.

INTERPRETATION: The more people you meet, the more opportunity you have to make friendships. Environmental (ecological) factors affect passive contacts and therefore the friendships you make.

APPLICATIONS: Demonstrates one of the ways that urban planning influences our lives.

RELATED STUDIES:
Segal's (1974) study is described at the beginning of this unit.
Hargreaves' (1967) study of schoolboys (described later in this Unit) found that boys were more likely to form relationships within their form because they interact more frequently.

③ <u>Familiarity</u>.   Familiarity is related to proximity, people like things which are familiar and when you see someone often they become familiar. Why do people like things which are familiar? It may be that people (or things) who are known to us become more predictable, which makes them preferable to the unknown and unpredictable.

RESEARCH EXAMPLE   **Zajonc (1968) The effects of mere exposure**

RESEARCH QUESTION: Zajonc quotes the following press clipping dated 27 February 1967:

A mysterious student has been attending a class at Oregon State University for the past two months enveloped in a big black bag. Only his bare feet show. Each Monday, Wednesday and Friday at 11.00 a.m. the Black Bag sits on a small table at the back of the classroom. The class is … basic persuasion … Goetzinger, professor of the class, knows the identity of the person inside. None of the 20 students in the class do. Goetzinger said the students' attitude changed from hostility towards the Black Bag to curiosity and finally friendship.

Is simply 'being there' enough to change a person's attitude towards something?

METHOD: Experiment, deception.
Experiment I. Participants were shown nonsense words on cards (such as 'iktitaf' and 'enanwal') and asked to say them over 86 trials. Some words occurred more frequently than others, either 0, 1, 2, 5, 10 or 25 times. At the end they were told that the words were Turkish adjectives, and were asked to guess how pleasant or unpleasant they thought their meaning was.
Experiment II. The same but with Chinese characters.
Experiment III. Used photographs of men (faces only) from a college yearbook. Again frequency was varied and participants asked to say how much they might like each photograph.
Experiment IV. Galvanic skin response (GSR) was measured towards words in experiment I to assess their 'emotionality'. (GSR is explained in Unit 10.1)

RESULTS:
1 The more frequent a word, character or photograph, the more positively it was assessed.
2 A low GSR was associated with increased familiarity, suggesting that such words became less threatening.

INTERPRETATION: Exposure alone increases liking, which goes against the saying 'familiarity breeds contempt'.

APPLICATIONS: Such principles are used to good effect in advertising so that, when faced with an array of unknown soap powders, you choose the name that appears most familiar and therefore pleasant.

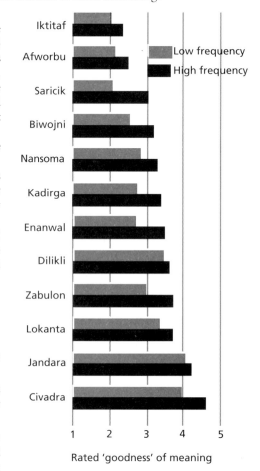

Fig. 9.1 The relationship between frequency and perceived 'goodness' of meaning

4 <u>Reciprocity</u>.   You are more likely to like someone who likes you. You reciprocate their feelings. However, it is not always straightforward. Hewitt (1972) found that we like those who evaluate us positively, but only if it is deserved. Otherwise it is seen as unfounded flattery (the **ingratiation effect**) and results in decreased liking. The opposite (the **extra credit effect**) occurs when we receive deserved criticism. We admire the honesty and increase our liking.

5 <u>Similarity</u>.   Similarity may be shown in terms of having similar attitudes or interests, agreeing with each other, or being the same race or gender. Why do we prefer such friends?
- It is *rewarding* and *comforting* to spend time with people who support our own attitudes (an example of the confirmatory bias, see Unit 5.1).
- One of the reasons to seek friendships is for *social comparison* and self-knowledge (see Unit 8.2), such comparisons are made in terms of similarity.
- Similarity may be a useful initial filter ('birds of a feather flock together'), whereas *complementarity* may be more significant later.

RESEARCH EXAMPLE   **Newcomb (1961) The acquaintance process**

RESEARCH QUESTION: How do stable interpersonal relationships develop?

PARTICIPANTS: A number of new students were invited to volunteer for rent-free accommodation in a lodging house in return for 4–5 hours of work per week as informants and experimental participants during the autumn term (15 weeks). From this volunteer sample, 17 men were selected who were all strangers. The following year (Year II), another group of 17 were selected to match the first group as closely as possible on selected demographic variables.

METHOD: Experiment, psychometric. Collected information about the students' likes and dislikes.
1 Year I were assigned rooms by drawing a number from a hat. They were told they could change room at any time (no one did).
2 Year II had prearranged room assignments, so that some students were given roommates who had similar attitudes, whereas other students had roommates who were most dissimilar.
  The participants were asked to rate each other every week, by sorting cards with names on them into three piles 'prefer', 'do not prefer' and 'undecided'.
  Attitudes were measured with a set of 175 statements and personality tests were used.

RESULTS:
1 Where roommates had similar views, 58% developed good friendships whereas only 25% of those with dissimilar views did.
2 Individuals expressed greatest attraction for those individuals with whom they were in close agreement. The relationship between pair *attraction* and pair *agreement* was greater by the end of the study. It increased from about 0.20 in the first week to 0.50 by the end for both year groups. This means that those who had more similar attitudes became more attractive to each other.
3 In Year II, proximity was a major factor, overriding attitude similarity: 80% of roommates (including those who were most similar or most dissimilar to each other) ended up at high attraction levels. However, the results for Year I were totally different, therefore proximity *alone* is not responsible.

INTERPRETATION:
1 Similarity and proximity are related to interpersonal attraction.
2 The relationship between similarity and friendship may be two-way. People who are similar become friends, and people who become friends increase their agreement.
3 Being roommates provides opportunities for the exchange of intimacies which increase trust, and this leads to the formation of friendship.

RELATED STUDIES:
Kandel (1978) surveyed 2000 teenagers and found that best friends tended to be similar in terms of age, ethnic group and class at school. This result could also be interpreted as evidence for proximity.
  Schachter (1951) found that, in group discussions, a stooge who seemed to agree with everyone else in the room was later rated as more likeable than one who went against the group's beliefs.

---

6 <u>Complementarity</u>.   Do opposites attract each other? Some people seek a partner who fills in the gaps in their own personality or complements their temperament, as in the case of dominant and submissive partners. This may be useful in avoiding stormy relationships.

7 <u>Perceived competence</u>.   People who are capable, intelligent, knowledgeable or have power appear more attractive. Henry Kissinger, an American diplomat, said that power is the world's greatest aphrodisiac.

The importance of perceived competence may be due to the operation of a **halo effect** (see Unit 5.1).

RESEARCH EXAMPLE   **Aronson *et al.* (1966) The effect of a pratfall**

RESEARCH QUESTION: A superior person is seen as superhuman and less likeable. If they blunder, does this humanise them and increase their attractiveness?

PARTICIPANTS: Forty-eight male psychology undergraduates.

METHOD: Experiment. Participants were assigned to one of four experimental conditions. In all conditions the participants heard a tape recording of a student trying out for the College Quiz Bowl team. After hearing the tape participants were asked to rate the student's attractiveness and intelligence. The four versions of the tape were:
1 Average ability student, answered 30% of the questions correctly.
2 Superior ability student, answered 92% of the questions correctly.
3 Superior ability student who committed a blunder: near the end of the interview the student spilled a cup of coffee all over himself, followed by much noise and clatter.
4 Average ability student who committed an identical blunder.

RESULTS: The most attractive was the intelligent but clumsy one. The least attractive was the average but clumsy one.

Mean attraction scores

	Pratfall	No pratfall
Superior ability	30.2	20.8
Average ability	−2.5	17.8

INTERPRETATION: The researchers termed this the **pratfall effect**. A blunder committed by a person who is very able is seen as making him more human and likeable, whereas a blunder by a mediocre person only serves to make him less attractive.

APPLICATIONS: Don't blunder unless you can be sure of your status.

---

8 <u>Emotional state</u>.   Liking for another may be increased when you are feeling positive. For example, Veitch and Griffitt (1976) found that participants who evaluated the work of another, hypothetical student while they listened to a 'good' news broadcast gave more positive evaluations than those who listened to 'bad' news.

9 <u>Individual differences</u>:
- Much of the above depends on individual abilities to *communicate*, to code and decode nonverbal messages and to make conversation. These are skills that some people lack, particularly children and the mentally ill.
- Different people have different *values*. If you ask people to order a list of the features they look for in a mate, such as physical attraction, similar interests, intelligence and personality, each person will do it differently.
- Some people have a greater *need* for friends (called **nAffiliation**) than others and therefore proximity may have a stronger influence.
- Some people *like* people more, whereas others are more self-contained.

Interpersonal attraction: Maintenance

Once initial selection has taken place, what determines the likelihood of a relationship continuing or deepening?

1 <u>A sense of reward or equity</u>.   This is a more general application of the **matching hypothesis**. Relationships should continue to offer both partners the same 'rewards'. A stable relationship is one where both partners feel they are getting what they deserve.

2 <u>Reinforcement</u>.   We learn to associate positive feelings with people or situations which reward us (reinforcement), therefore liking someone may be due to the fact that we associate them with positive feelings, rather than any personal attributes. This is described by the Byrne-Clore **reinforcement-affect model**. (See also Veitch and Griffitt, above).

3 <u>Self-Disclosure</u>.   By sharing information about yourself you are showing someone that you trust them. This trust is the basis of friendship. As friendship deepens, people

progressively share more intimate secrets. However, unless the friend 'matches' such behaviour the disclosure will stop.

4 <u>Dormant relationships</u>.   There are many relationships which continue despite little contact. The bond once formed remains, for example, distant friends or parent-child relationships.

5 <u>Daily routine</u>.   Relationships are buried in daily routines, and offer comfortable predictability. They continue until there is a reason for breakdown.

6 <u>Why do relationships break down</u>?   For example:
- *Conflict:* Too much disagreement or disrespect, though some pairs are locked into a love-hate relationship.
- *Deception:* The betrayal of trust.
- *Boredom:* A relationship that is not going anywhere or has run out of mutual interest, passionate love may have cooled off.
- *Relocation:* One partner moves away, so reversing the initial factors of proximity and exposure.
- *Change:* Partners' interests or attitudes change, situations change, a better alternative presents itself.

A developmental view of friendship

1 <u>What is friendship?</u>   Certain characteristics distinguish between casual acquaintances and friends, such as enjoyment, trust, mutual assistance, respect, understanding and intimacy.

RESEARCH EXAMPLE   **Argyle and Henderson (1984) The rules of friendship**

RESEARCH QUESTION: Relationships, like games, are social systems. Games have formal rules. In our society there are no *formal* rules for friendship, are there *informal* rules which govern the formation and maintenance of friendship? Are there cultural differences in these rules?

PARTICIPANTS: Thirty male and thirty female participants from two age groups, 18 to 25 and 30 to 60. They comprised an opportunity sample covering many educational and socio-economic backgrounds.

The study was repeated in Italy, Japan and Hong Kong with another 270 participants.

METHOD: Questionnaire, cross-cultural. Participants rated a list of 43 rules for interpersonal relationships in terms of their importance in friendship. The list of 43 rules was constructed from previous research as well as a pilot study with six participants.

RESULTS:
1 There were some cross-cultural differences. For example, Japanese attached less importance to rules about emotional support.
2 High and low intimacy friendships have some rule differences. Closer friends have 'quality rules' which were related more to rewards.
3 Females endorsed rules concerned with intimacy and emotion more than men did.
4 Age differences were small, though older people were more concerned over privacy.

The most important rules of friendship	
Rules of exchange • Share news of success with the other. • Show emotional support. • Volunteer help in time of need.★ • Strive to make him/her happy while in each other's company. • Repay debts and favours.	Rules related to a third party • Stand up for the other person in their absence. • Be tolerant of other friends. • Don't criticise in public. • Keep confidences. • Don't be jealous or critical of other relationships.★
Rules of intimacy • Trust and confide in the other.★	Rules to co-ordinate activity • Don't nag. • Respect privacy.★

★ Highly endorsed across all cultures.

INTERPRETATION: Such rules are needed to keep up the rewards and minimise inevitable conflicts in friendships.

---

2 <u>Stages of friendship</u>.   As children grow older, the type of friendships they have change. The changes can be related to general cognitive maturity. For example, a child needs to have empathy before a mutually-caring relationship can form.

AGE approx.	DESCRIPTION
0–2	Infants show an interest in peers from an early age.
2–4	By the age of 2, children are ready for nursery school and activities involving their peers, though much of it is *parallel* not cooperative play. They have very little understanding of another's feelings. 'Friends' are not necessarily the same sex.
4–7	First mutual friendships, play with friends is different from that with acquaintances. Friends show each other affection and approval, but the relationship still lacks empathy. Friendship is largely based on common activity, proximity, and sharing things.
8–11	More genuine friendships, based on trust and empathy. Friends have psychological similarity, shared interests, traits and motives. Emergence of the peer group and loosely formed gangs. These gradually become more elaborate involving membership requirements.
10–12	Reciprocal emotional commitment. Deeper, more enduring friendships, sharing thoughts, feelings and secrets. Friends give comfort and support, act as confidants and therapists.
12+	Relationships incorporate the conventions of the society.

3 Individual differences in popularity.   Who becomes 'liked'?
  ● *Status:* For example, academic success or success at sports.
  ● *Physical features:* Those who mature early or physical attractiveness.
  ● *Later-born children* who must learn to negotiate with older, more powerful siblings tend to be more popular than first-borns.
  ● *Interpersonal skills:* Some children have better social problem-solving skills.

RESEARCH EXAMPLE | **Hargreaves (1967) Social relations in a secondary school**

RESEARCH AIM: To study the social relations between pupils and teachers and among pupils themselves in a secondary modern school.

PARTICIPANTS: 14–15-year-old-boys (Year 10) in a secondary modern school in the north of England.

METHOD: Sociograms (diagrams showing the interrelationships between classmates). Boys were asked to name their *preferred* (rather than actual) friends within their own class. There were four classes, A, B, C and D, streamed according to academic ability.

RESULTS: The most popular clique varied depending on the dominant subculture of the group. There were two opposed subcultures:
1 The *academic high streams*. In stream 'A' the most popular boys were those who were more academically successful. They were also the ones most liked by the teachers and were often prefects.
2 The *'delinquescent' low streams*. Popularity was not related to academic success but instead to delinquent behaviour. Boys conformed to the antisocial norms of the group in order to gain popularity.

INTERPRETATION: Popularity varies according to characteristics of the individual. There are no general rules for friendship.

---

4 Individual differences in making friends.   Children can be grouped according to their friendship skills:
  ● *Popular* (socially-accepted) children tend to watch and wait, gradually joining a group by making group-oriented statements. They are cooperative and very good at social problem-solving skills.
  ● *Neglected* children tend to hover around the edge of groups, and shy away from attempts to engage them.

- *Rejected* children tend to be highly active and aggressive. They disrupt play and are uncooperative, self-serving and critical.

RESEARCH EXAMPLE

Oden and Asher (1977) Skills important in friendship

RESEARCH QUESTION: Do socially isolated children lack the necessary social skills for making friendships?

PARTICIPANTS: Socially rejected or neglected 8 and 9-year-old children.

METHOD: Experiment. The researchers coached the children on skills such as how to participate in groups, how to communicate and cooperate with peers. They did this in special play sessions with one other child present, acting as a peer.

RESULTS: These children improved in terms of peer ratings more than a control group who only had play sessions without coaching. The effects were still present after a year.

INTERPRETATION: Interpersonal skills can be learned, and may well be the product of early socialisation experiences. Training can remedy such problems.

RELATED STUDIES: Coie and Kupersmidt (1983) put children in play groups with unfamiliar peers. The children soon achieved the same status as they normally had. This suggests that friendship skills are the *cause* of social acceptance rather than social acceptance leading to certain the behaviours listed earlier.

The importance of friendship

Friendship serves many purposes:

1. <u>A basic human need</u>.   Humans are social animals. This 'socialness' helps the process of finding a mate for reproduction.

2. <u>Self-knowledge and development</u>.   Relating to others is a means of learning about yourself, through social comparison and the reflection of yourself in others (see Unit 8.2).

3. <u>Emotional support</u>:
   - Emotional safety: children are bolder in the presence of friends.
   - Emotional support: children confide in friends about their problems with parents or boyfriends, taking a therapeutic role.

RESEARCH EXAMPLE

Freud and Dann (1951) The Bulldogs Bank study: An experiment in group upbringing

RESEARCH QUESTION: A group of extremely deprived children were placed in the care of Freud and Dann. How would they cope with their first experiences of relatively normal life?

PARTICIPANTS: Six children, four were orphaned at birth or immediately afterwards. They were together from the age of 1 in the Terezin concentration camp during World War II, cared for by other inmates. After the war they came to England, first to the Lake District and later to a children's home, Bulldogs Bank, in Sussex. At this time they were all three years old, knew no permanent home or sense of family except among themselves and they were devoted to each other, with the usual sibling-type rivalries.

METHOD: Case study, natural experiment, observation. Sophie Freud and Gertrud Dann were in charge of the home. They kept a record of what the children said and did during their year at Bulldogs Bank.

RESULTS: Their initial condition was one of developmental emotional and intellectual retardation. They had little language, were fairly hostile and aggressive towards adults, and held little interest in others. However, over a period of one year, they gradually were able to form emotional relationships with some of the staff and to make normal developmental progress.

INTERPRETATION: The fact that they did not appear to suffer permanent retardation as a result of emotional and physical deprivation may be due to the lasting emotional support they had gained from each other during those vital early years. Friends had acted as attachment figures.

EVALUATION: It is a limited sample in special circumstances.

---

4. <u>Emotional development</u>:
   - Through friendships children learn to understand the feelings of others: *empathy*.
   - The friendship relationship serves as a *model* for adult relationships with a husband/wife.
   - The lack of friends may lead to *social* and *emotional* problems in childhood.

RESEARCH EXAMPLE **Cowen *et al.* (1973) Long-term follow-up of negative peer ratings**

RESEARCH QUESTION: What behaviours early in childhood predict later psychological problems? If these can be found, it might be possible to intervene and prevent later difficulties.

PARTICIPANTS: Over 800 schoolchildren living in Monroe County, New York. They were first assessed at the age of 8. Eleven years later the county psychiatric record was examined to see who had developed psychological problems, 60 of the original children appeared on this register.

METHOD: Longitudinal observation using records, interview, observation. The researchers used data from two sources:

1   Their own Primary Mental Health Project, started in 1958, which assessed 8-year-olds in Monroe County in terms of achievement and behaviour measures. The data was collected through interviews with mothers, psychometric testing, classroom observation, attendance registers, peer ratings and teacher report.
2   The Monroe County Psychiatric Register which kept a record of almost all patients receiving psychiatric care in the county, including children, from 1960.

RESULTS: Eleven years later, the researchers found that those who had negative peer ratings at age 8 were three times more likely to have sought psychiatric help than those children who had positive peer ratings.

INTERPRETATION: Low peer acceptance is related to maladjustment.

EVALUATION: This data is correlational. Lack of friendships may be a *cause* of later maladjustment. Equally, lack of friendship *and* maladjustment may be caused by other factors.

RELATED STUDIES: The cycle, once begun, may be self-perpetuating. Dishion *et al.* (1991) studied children from parents who lacked social skills. The children follow these patterns and become rejected by their peers. Such a 'rejected' status leads similar children to band together and form deviant cliques

⑤   A socialising agent:
- Provides practice in interpersonal interactions, such as resolving squabbles, coping with forming and breaking-up relationships.
- Reinforcement of gender-appropriate and other social behaviours (see Unit 9.2).
- Peers act as models for social behaviour.

Quick test 9.3

1   Explain the *matching hypothesis*.
2   The computer dance study assessed attraction using a questionnaire. Give **one** other way that psychologists have measured attraction.
3   There is a saying that 'opposites attract'. Some psychologists disagree. Give **two** reasons to support their view.
4   What have psychological studies found are the changes to friendships of most children between 7 and 14 years? (*SEG, 1991*)
5   What factors are likely to influence a young child's choice of friends?

Summary

INITIAL ATTRACTION	INTERPERSONAL ATTRACTION: MAINTENANCE	DEVELOPMENTAL VIEW OF FRIENDSHIP	THE IMPORTANCE OF FRIENDSHIP
1 Physical attractiveness	1 Sense of equity	1 What is friendship?	1 Basic human need
2 Proximity	2 Reinforcement	2 Stages of friendship	2 Self-knowledge
3 Familiarity	3 Self-Disclosure	3 Popularity	3 Emotional support
4 Reciprocity	4 Dormant relationships	4 Making friends	4 Emotional competence
5 Similarity	5 Daily routine		5 Socialising agent
6 Complementarity	6 Why do relationships break down?		
7 Competence			
8 Emotional states			
9 Individual differences			

9.4 Parenting

In this chapter, and previous chapters, there is advice for good parenting practices:

1 <u>Cognitive development</u> (Units 4.3 and 4.4):
- Parental attention is associated with higher IQ (Zajonc and Markus).
- Teaching new skills should rely on a child's readiness (Piaget).

2 <u>Prejudice</u> (Units 5.3 and 5.4):
- Authoritarian parents produce children with a rigid cognitive style who are more likely to hold prejudiced opinions (Adorno *et al.*).

3 <u>Aggression</u> (Unit 7.1)
- The way that parents resolve conflict or behave aggressively acts as a model for their children (Patterson *et al.*).

4 <u>Prosocial behaviour</u> (Unit 7.2):
- Parents who actually engage in prosocial activities are better models (Rosenhan).

5 <u>From studies of attachment</u> (Unit 8.1):
- Emotional responsiveness will lead to strong attachments (Brazelton *et al.*).
- Attachment is critical for healthy emotional development (Bowlby).
- Where a child must be separated from a parent, separation anxiety can be prevented by maintaining contact with the parent, explaining the absence, having a strong attachment and/or suitable substitute care (Robertson and Robertson).
- Good parenting is a way of teaching your children how to become good parents (Harlow).

6 <u>Self-concepts and the role of expectations</u> (Unit 8.2):
- High self-esteem in children is associated with affectionate family relationships, consistent discipline, interest and respect from parents (Coopersmith).
- A parents' expectations will affect the child's self-concept, self-esteem and self-expectations, eventually enhancing or depressing their performance (Bandura).

7 <u>Personality</u> (Unit 8.3):
- Parents help the child resolve psychosexual stages and serve as models (Freud).
- Positive unconditional regard fosters healthy development (Rogers).

8 <u>Temperament</u> (Unit 8.4):
- A 'difficult' infant may not become a maladjusted child if parents are able to handle the infant in a way that minimises the conflicts (Thomas and Chess).

9 <u>Moral development</u>
- Parents who explain why a behaviour is wrong, how it affects others and how to make amends allow children to develop moral reasoning (Hoffman).
- Identification with parents is important for internalising moral standards (Freud).

10 <u>Gender development</u>:
- Children who are encouraged to adopt a more androgynous approach to their gender will develop a mentally healthier cognitive style (Bem).
- Parents unconsciously pass on their gender expectations (Smith and Lloyd).

11 <u>Attraction and friendship</u>:
- If parents lack social skills, their children tend to follow these patterns and become rejected by their peers (Dishion *et al.*).

Quick test 9.4

1 Describe an *authoritative* style of parenting.
2 Imagine that you are a social worker choosing a family to be a foster family. State **two** characteristics that you might look for. (*MEG, 1994*)
3 How might a social learning theorist explain the role that parents play in their children's development?

Summary

The work of psychologists, such as Piaget, Bowlby and Freud, has profoundly altered child-rearing practices.

Chapter 10
Biological psychology

PLEASURE CENTRES IN THE BRAIN

Olds and Milner (1954) made a discovery which changed the way psychologists viewed pleasure. They placed electrodes in various places in a rat's brain and stimulated that part of the brain by running a small electric current into it. In this way they could find out the function of different parts of the brain because the electrical current acts like a nervous signal. When they stimulated parts of the hypothalamus the rat sat up, looked around and sniffed. Rats who had received this stimulation always returned to the part of the pen where they'd experienced it. If the rat was taught to press a lever to deliver stimulation to its own brain, it did this for long periods, in some cases over 2,000 presses per hour, until it collapsed exhausted.

In a sense the rats were getting something which might be called pleasure. There has also been support for this in human studies of brain stimulation. Campbell (1963) placed electrodes in the hypothalamus of patients suffering from severe pain as a way to relieve it. The patients could press a button to stimulate themselves. They did this for the maximum amount of time permitted.

This is certainly a remarkable view of human experience, pleasure is simply the result of an electrical charge to a specific part of the brain. It is a **reductionist** view because it explains behaviour and experience only in terms of a simple set of activities, activity of nerve cells. Reductionism means reducing a complex thing to simple units. Other examples of reductionism: bottom–up perception, behaviourism, and ethology.

It is possible to explain behaviour in biological terms but this leaves out many important factors, perhaps most importantly subjective experience and the fact that we have cognitive control over much of our biological system.

10.1 Emotion

CUPID IS NOT SO WIDE OF HIS MARK

The Romans told the story of Cupid, who roamed around with a quiver full of arrows. He shot unsuspecting victims who then became passionately aroused and fell in love with the next person they saw.

This story may not be as foolish as it seems. What is love? Some psychologists suggest that what happens is that feelings of sexual arousal towards an attractive person are mentally interpreted as a state of high emotion. The next step is to label this emotion. You have learned that 'love' is a combination of physiological sensations (increased heart rate, muscular tension and so on) and the presence of someone likely to be a love object.

In another situation, intense arousal might be interpreted differently. You are walking down a dark street and hear footsteps behind you. Your heart beats rapidly, your muscles tense, you feel fear. What causes the emotion? The arousal or the arousing stimulus? Can we separate emotion and arousal?

DEFINITIONS	emotion	The word comes from the Latin *emotio* and *motum* meaning 'to move, excite, stir up or agitate'. It is a state of physiological arousal. It has important motivational properties, it drives the individual to behave in a certain way.
	two-factor theory of emotion or cognitive labelling theory	An emotional experience depends on the occurrence of two factors: 1 Physiological arousal. 2 Situational cues which provide expectations which are cognitive.
	cognitive appraisal	Literally, mental assessment. A theoretical approach to understanding emotion which places greatest importance on a person's immediate assessment of a situation, which then leads to a coping response. It is an extension of cognitive labelling theory.
	hormone	Biochemical substances produced by one part of the body and released into the blood. Their presence affects target organs and, ultimately, behaviour.
	galvanic skin response (GSR)	The presence of water (sweating) increases electrical conductivity. Electrodes placed on the skin detect this. Emotion is associated with increased sweating as well as other signs of ANS (autonomic nervous system) arousal (increased heart rate, heavy breathing).

Aspects of emotion

An emotional experience has three elements:
- *Physiological* state: Hormones produce a state of physiological arousal.
- *Subjective* experience: A person is aware of feelings such as sadness or elation.
- *Behaviour*: The objective result. For example, crying or running out of the room.

① Physiological arousal:
- Hormones. **Adrenalin** (also called **epinephrine**) is a hormone. It is largely produced by the kidneys. Its overall effect is to activate the internal organs for vigorous activity. In other words, to *arouse* an organism. Its precise *physiological* effects are: increasing the heart beat and rate of breathing, releasing sugar from the liver, inhibiting digestion and saliva (mouth feels dry), dilating the pupils, and activating sweat to cool the body temperature. Its *behavioural* effects are increased attention and improved performance on cognitive tasks. If arousal becomes too great performance become depressed (see Yerkes-Dodson Law, in Unit 10.2).
- The ANS. The **autonomic nervous system** (autonomic means 'self-governing') controls the system of arousal and relaxation. The ANS is largely controlled by the hypothalamus. The nerves of the ANS stimulate production and release of various hormones into the blood. It is divided into two branches, **sympathetic** and **parasympathetic**. Sympathetic nervous activity leads to arousal. Parasympathetic activity regulates the relaxed state of digestion and normal heart rate, etc. An external or internal stimulus activates the sympathetic ANS. The animal is now in a state of arousal or readiness for fight or flight.
- The **fight or flight response**. It is an adaptive response because it is important for survival. How does the animal 'choose' which response, fight or flight, is most appropriate? Cognitive or situational factors influence the emotional behaviour. For example, if a male sees another male the owner of the territory will prepare to fight but the intruder will flee (see Unit 3.3).
- Physiological arousal is not *necessary* for the subjective experience of emotion (see Valins, below).

② Subjective experience of emotion.   The cognitive experience of an emotion may be based on physiological sensations (*primary*) or may be related to situational cues and past experience (*secondary*).

- *Primary* emotions are universally experienced, for example: fear, anger, sadness, joy and disgust (see Schwartz *et al.* later in this Unit).
- *Secondary* emotions are learned blends of primary ones. For example, contempt is a blend of anger and disgust. Secondary emotions are specific to certain cultures. For example, *hagaii* means helpless anguish tinged with remorse for the Japanese, an emotion not experienced in the Western world.
- The same emotion can be innate or learned. For example, anger in response to a threat from someone is innate, anger as a response to someone smoking nearby may be learned.

3 Emotional behaviour.   Each emotion can have a great range of expressions. This range varies between individuals and cultures.
- *Nature:* Some emotional expressions are *innate* and universal. For example, the crying of an infant or expressions of pain which might be important for survival. For these expressions to be effective our understanding of these expressions must also be innate.
- *Nurture:* Children learn **display rules**, the social norms which are learned about what behaviours are acceptable in particular situations and cultures.
- *Nonverbal communication:* Most emotions are shown nonverbally, using facial expressions and body language. We often show our emotions without conscious awareness. This is called **nonverbal leakage** (see Unit 8.2). Customs officers are able to detect lying by looking at a person's body language. Some people are better than others at controlling this channel and it is possible to train it to a certain extent.
- *Other behavioural effects:* Emotional arousal may lead to repressed memories or depressed performance (anxiety leads some people to do worse, while others do better).

RESEARCH EXAMPLE   **Ekman *et al.* (1971) Constants across cultures in the face and emotion**

RESEARCH QUESTION: Are facial expressions of emotion universal?

PARTICIPANTS: To test this, it is necessary to have participants who have had minimal visual contact with Western culture so that we can be certain their interpretations are due to innate rather than learned factors.

The researchers used people from the South East Highlands of New Guinea, who spoke *Fore*. Until 1960 they had led an isolated, Neolithic existence.

METHOD: Cross–cultural, field experiment. The experimental group consisted of 189 adults and 130 children. The control group, 23 male adults, spoke English and had had much contact with Western people and culture (e.g. movies).

Six emotions were selected for study: happiness, sadness, anger, surprise, disgust and fear. A pilot study indicated that each of these had a clear equivalent in the Fore culture.

A participant was shown three photographs of Europeans and read a short passage describing an emotion. For example 'His (her) child has died, and he (she) feels very sad'. Only one photograph showed the Western expression of sadness. The participant was asked to identify the most appropriate face. A member of the tribe read the stories to the participants.

RESULTS:

1 Both children and adults were very accurate in recognising Western expressions of emotion. They were better than 80% correct for happiness, sadness, anger and disgust. The results were no different from the control group.

2 Ekman *et al.* (1987) studied over 500 participants from 10 cultures: Estonia, Germany, Greece, Hong Kong, Italy, Japan, Scotland, Sumatra, Turkey and the US. Cross-cultural agreement was highly significant.

INTERPRETATION: Facial behaviours are universally associated with particular emotions.

Measuring emotional states

Studies of emotion often need to measure emotional states. The same methods apply for studies of aggression and stress, which are also emotional states.

1 Self-report.   Some studies rely on participants imagining that they are experiencing certain emotional states. They rely on the participant's own report (for example, Marañon, Hohmann, Schwartz *et al.*).

2 Observation.   A participant might judge emotions from observing facial expressions (for example, Ekman *et al.*). Or, as in Schachter and Singer's experiment, the researchers judged emotional state from observations of the participants' behaviour.

RESEARCH EXAMPLE | **Ekman *et al.* (1971) Facial affect scoring technique (FAST)**

Independent judges were asked to score facial expressions from slowed down videotapes. Three areas of the face were used:
- 8 positions of the brows and forehead,
- 17 for the eyes and lids,
- 45 for the lower face.

Ekman later developed a more sophisticated scheme (FACS, Facial Affect Coding Scheme) based on small facial movements or action units (AUs). Eighty facial muscles can be identified, and their effects are visible to an observer and can be discriminated between.

Using these, one can build up precise descriptions of emotional expressions. These can then help in presenting stimulus material to participants or in evaluating the emotional state of participants.

Ekman *et al.* (1983) has also used this information for **facial feedback**. If he told participants to tense certain muscles and then measured physiological response, these corresponded to the appropriate emotion (see below).

❸ Physiological measures:
- *Autonomic arousal* can be measured in terms of increased heart rate, blood pressure, respiration, etc. (see above).
- The *galvanic skin response* (GSR) is a measure of sweating, a sign of ANS arousal.
- The *polygraph* (also known as the lie detector) is a machine which records signs of ANS arousal plus brain activity. The assumption is that lying or deception is accompanied by increases in ANS arousal. The problem is that fear of being tested may also lead to ANS arousal.

Theories of emotion

A theory of emotion must explain the relationship between the subjective experience, the physiological state and the expression of the emotion.

The James–Lange Theory

Argument: Physiological arousal comes first and forms the basis of an emotional experience. For each emotional state there must be a different physiological state. This is the reverse of the common sense view that the mental state triggers the emotional response.

James (1884) and Lange (1887) independently proposed this view. James said you are frightened when you see a bear *because* you run, not the reverse, that you run because you are frightened. 'We feel sorry because we cry, angry because we strike, afraid because we tremble.'

Evidence for the James–Lange view:

❶ For each emotion there is a different physiological state. For a long time it was thought that this was not true. Recently a few studies have found evidence for at least some different physiological states.

RESEARCH EXAMPLE | **Schwartz *et al.* (1981) Cardiovascular differences in happiness, sadness, anger and fear**

RESEARCH QUESTION: Are emotional experiences and their facial expressions universal?

PARTICIPANTS: Thirty-two healthy college paid volunteers. They must have had some prior acting experience.

METHOD: Experiment. Each participant was asked to close their eyes and imagine a situation from their past or future which would evoke a named emotional state. The emotions were: happiness, sadness, anger and fear. They should try to recreate the feelings and physical sensations associated with the scene. There was also a control imagery condition.

The researchers measured heart rate and blood pressure.

RESULTS: Each emotion produced a different physiological 'signature'. For example:
- Heart rate and blood pressure were lowest during happiness and highest during anger.
- Sadness had a higher heart rate than happiness, but lower blood pressure.

INTERPRETATION: Primary emotions, at least, appear to have individual physiological states.

EVALUATION: While this supports one aspect of James' theory, it also indicates that physiological changes can be *caused* by the subjective experience, rather than vice versa.

RELATED STUDIES:

Ekman *et al.* (1983) asked participants (mainly actors) to show surprise, anger, disgust, sadness, fear and happiness using the facial muscles which they watched in a mirror. They measured heart rate, skin temperature and other measures of autonomic arousal and found that each emotion did have a different 'signature'.

Laird (1974) told participants that he was measuring activity of facial muscles using electrodes and instructed them to relax and contract muscles, eliciting smiles and frowns presumably without their conscious awareness. Cartoons viewed when 'smiling' where rated as funnier. Participants were amused because they were smiling, not smiling because they were amused.

❷ The more intense the arousal the greater the emotion.   If subjective emotion is based on arousal, the strength of the experience should be related to the strength of arousal.

White *et al.* (1981) asked male college students to run on the spot and then showed videos of some women they would meet later. Those who ran for 120 seconds found videos of attractive women more attractive than those who ran for only 15 seconds, whereas the opposite was true if the woman was unattractive, suggesting that arousal enhances existing emotional states.

Evidence against the James-Lange view. Cannon (1927) presented the following objections:

❶ Each emotion needs a corresponding physiological state. Even if there are different physiological states, there are not as many as there are emotions. Therefore some aspects of emotion *are* determined by mental state. Schachter and Singer (see below) showed that one state alone can produce different emotional experiences.

❷ It is very difficult to perceive different physiological states accurately. People are not very good at saying whether their blood pressure has increased or decreased (see Valins, below).

❸ Emotional experiences occur quite rapidly, yet the autonomic nervous system is slow to react.

❹ You can feel aroused but not feel any emotion. Marañon (1924) injected his patients with adrenalin and asked them to report what they experienced, 71% reported physical sensations with no emotional overtones, the rest used phrases like 'it's *as if* I was afraid'. Hohmann's participants (see below) also reported 'as if' experiences and they lacked the physiological arousal.

❺ You can experience an emotional state without any physiological changes. This is the key problem for James' theory and Schachter's theory as well (see below).

RESEARCH EXAMPLE   **Valins (1966) The Valins Effect**

RESEARCH QUESTION: Is a state of physiological arousal necessary for an emotional experience? For example, an increase in your heart rate. Or is it sufficient just to *think* it has increased (cognitive awareness)?

PARTICIPANTS: Volunteer male introductory psychology students.

METHOD: Experiment, deception. The participants were shown slides of semi-nude women while their physiological reactions were supposedly recorded.
Group 1 False-feedback, the participants were told that the sounds they heard were their own heart beats. In fact they heard a tape where the heart beats were either increased or decreased for particular 'critical' slides.
Group 2 Heard the same sounds but were told to ignore them.
Perceived attractiveness was measured by:
1 Asking the participants to rate the slides for attractiveness.
2 At the end of the experiment asking if there were any slides they would like to keep.
3 Four weeks later, asking participants to rate a set of photos including the experimental ones.

RESULTS:
1 The slides accompanied by supposedly increased heart beat were rated as more attractive.
2 Where heart beat supposedly decreased there was less effect on attractiveness rating.

INTERPRETATION: This supports Cannon's objections in two ways:
1 Subjective emotional states exist without any real physiological change.
2 Subjects are relatively unaware of their actual physiological state, otherwise the tape recordings would not have been believed.

RELATED STUDIES:
Hohmann (1966) interviewed patients with spinal-cord injuries which severely limited the information the brain received from the ANS. They said they still felt emotions but not to same extent as before. They reported 'as if' experiences when in presence of appropriate cognitive stimulus.

Evaluation of the James-Lange view:
- It offers a reasonable account of some of the evidence, but it cannot explain emotion before or without any arousal.
- There is no room for *learning* or cognitive control.
- It is therefore not a wholly satisfactory account.

Cognitive Labelling Theory

Argument: All emotional experiences are preceded by a state of arousal, but the nature of the subjective experience is determined by the individual's cognitive assessment, not the particular physiological state. Cognitions may come from external, situational cues or internal ones such as imagination.

Like the James-Lange view, this suggests that emotion is based on arousal. However, Schachter's cognitive view is that there is only one physiological state rather than a separate one for each emotion. Different subjective experiences arise not from physiological differences, but because an arousal state is *labelled* using situational cues and past experience. The state of arousal demands an explanation. The mind provides one.

Evidence for the Cognitive Labelling Theory:

❶ One state can produce more than one emotion.

RESEARCH EXAMPLE | **Schachter and Singer (1962) Cognitive, social and physiological determinants of emotional state**

RESEARCH QUESTION: James' view of emotion can be understood by supposing that the physiological state is first and leads to *evaluative needs* to understand and label the physiological sensations. This is done by using situational cues and past experience. Can it be shown that the same state of arousal will lead to different subjective reports in different situations?

PARTICIPANTS: 185 male undergraduates who agreed to having an injection.

METHOD: Experiment, deception. They asked participants to help test a new vitamin, Suproxin, which was thought to affect visual skills. The injection was in fact adrenalin, the hormone naturally produced at moments of intense emotion, or it was a placebo. Participants were either:
1 *Correctly informed*: Told the correct side effects.
2 *Misinformed:* Told that the vitamin would cause numbness of the feet.
3 *Uninformed*: Given no extra information.
4 *Placebo:* Given a placebo and uninformed.
After the injection, the participants were placed in a room with a confederate who supposedly had also received the injection. They were both asked to fill out a questionnaire. The confederate was either:
1 *Euphoric*: Making paper airplanes, laughing and playing waste paper basketball.
2 *Angry:* Becoming increasingly critical of the questionnaire, finally ripping it up and storming out of the room.

RESULTS:
1 Those correctly informed were least affected by the stooge's behaviour. They could unconsciously 'explain' the emotional sensations in terms of the drug.
2 The misinformed and uninformed groups mimicked the emotional behaviour of the stooge. They were experiencing a state of arousal but had no ready explanation for this. Therefore they used situational cues (the confederate's behaviour) to label their arousal state.
3 Some placebo participants also mimicked the stooges' behaviour. This may be because they had experienced some arousal through anxiety.

INTERPRETATION: Therefore one physiological state (adrenalin arousal) can lead to varying emotional states depending on the contextual cues.

EVALUATION:
1 Can you compare arousal states created by drugs with real-life emotions? In any case, adrenalin does not have the same effect on all people.
2 The researchers excluded some participants who did not report any physiological sensations. If their data had been included the results may not have been so significant.

3 Some studies have failed to replicate these findings (for example, Marshall and Zimbardo, 1979).
4 Criticisms of the theory are given below.

Evidence against the Cognitive Labelling Theory:

1 Cognition can occur before or without arousal (see the Valins Effect).

2 There is evidence that there are different physiological states (see Schwartz *et al.*).

3 You can have an emotional response with no cognitive awareness McGinnies' (1949) research on 'perceptual defence' (see Unit 2.2) showed that participants produced a GSR when shown taboo words. This demonstrates an emotional response in response to an arousing stimulus, but with no cognitive awareness.

Evaluation of the Cognitive Labelling Theory:
- This view can explain how emotions are *learned*. The emotional 'label' is derived from previous experience of emotion in a similar situation.
- It has stimulated a lot of *research*. A good recommendation for any theory.
- It offers the *best account* of the available evidence.

Theories of emotion: A conclusion

The evidence consists of the following:
- Physiological arousal *alone* can be sufficient
- Physiological arousal is *not* always necessary.
- *Arousal* may come first, and then receives an appropriate label.
- The *cognition* (label) may come first and lead to arousal.
- You can have an emotional response with *no* cognitive awareness.

Both factors, arousal and cognitive appraisal, are sufficient but not necessary conditions. The contradictions can be understood in terms of different kinds of emotional experience, some are more physiological, others are more cognitive. For example:
- *A physiological experience:* A jet screams over your head, you duck and experience a tightness in your chest. Past experience and individual differences will determine the emotion you might report feeling – fear, surprise, elation. For each of us it will be different, but the basis will be arousal. Such responses are more related to emotion as an adaptive response.
- *A cognitive experience:* You hear that you have passed GCSE psychology and feel ecstatic, which may lead to physiological sensations.

Quick test 10.1

1 What reason would a psychologist give for the difficulty children have in matching named emotions to pictures of faces showing the emotions? *(MEG, 1992)*
2 State **two** bodily changes associated with activity of the ANS.
3 What is GSR and how is it associated with emotion?
4 Put **one** letter in each box so that the diagram below describes the James-Lange theory of emotion.

☐ ⟶ ☐ ⟶ ☐

A – physiological response
B – perception of emotional stimulus
C – perception of emotion   *(NEAB, 1988)*
5 Name **one** study which shows how interpretation of a situation affects emotional experience.
6 What is the difference between the James-Lange view and the Cognitive Labelling Theory?

Summary

Measurement of emotional states: self report, observation, physiological means.
Theories of emotion: James-Lange (each emotion has a specific arousal state). Cognitive labelling (arousal is labelled according to cognitive cues).

10.2 Stress

PSYCHOSOMATIC ILLNESS AND STRESS

Your state of mind can *cause* physical illness. Psychological and physiological stress has been shown to be a major factor in this relationship.

Holmes and Rahe (1967) worked as doctors. They observed during their work that certain **life events** seemed to be associated with stress and poor health. The key thing about such life events is that they involve *change*. It is change from a steady state which leads to stress, even when the change is for the better.

To test this relationship between life events and illness, they first needed to develop a means of measuring life events. Holmes and Rahe examined 5,000 patient records and made a list of 43 life events which seemed to precede illness. Next, they asked nearly 400 participants to rate each item in terms of the amount of stress it produced. Specifically they asked for the 'average degree of adjustment for each event'. They assigned an arbitrary value of 500 to marriage as a reference point. At the end they averaged everyone's results.

The result was the Social Readjustment Rating Scale (SRRS)

RANK	LIFE EVENT	MEAN VALUE
1	Death of spouse	100
2	Divorce	73
3	Marital separation	65
4	Jail term	63
5	Death of close family member	63
6	Personal injury or illness	53
7	Marriage	50
8	Fired at work	47
9	Marital reconciliation	45
10	Retirement	45
–	–	–
–	–	–
41	Vacation	13
42	Christmas	12
43	Minor violations of the law	11

They compared various subgroups to see if the ratings were consistent. For example, male vs. female, single vs. married, White vs. Black, younger vs. older. There was strong agreement.

To use the scale, you should circle events which have happened to you in the last 12 months. Each event is awarded a value measured in **life change units** (LCUs). Your LCU total is an estimate of the amount of life stress you have experienced.

*Criticism*s of the SRRS:
- The scale *muddles* different kinds of life events, most particularly those which you have some control over and those which you haven't. It is these latter events which may be most stressful (see below).
- The scale does not allow for the fact that *dissimilar* people interpret the same event differently, and therefore a single value cannot be assigned for stress.
- Studies using the scale have found only a *small correlation* between life events and illness. It cannot be used to predict who will become ill and who won't (see below).
- The importance of this scale is not in its usefulness but in its status as a breakthrough. It triggered off a wealth of research and efforts to develop a more effective tool.

DEFINITIONS		
	stressor	A physical or psychological stimulus which threatens an individual's psychological and/or physiological well-being. In humans this extends to any situation which disrupts normal functioning and threatens personal goals or one's ability to cope.

stress	An emotion. A state of psychological tension and physiological arousal produced by physical or psychological pressures. The arousal makes the individual ready to respond in situations which threaten well-being. It does not necessarily result in a response. [In engineering terms, stress is any force which causes some significant modification of form, usually a distortion, to a system.]
stress response	An innate, defensive reaction to promote survival. If stress is long-term or beyond control, the stress response becomes undesirable. In this case health may suffer.
coping responses	Deliberate techniques for reducing stress or the effects of stress. The methods are aimed at the problem (reduces the stress) or the emotion (reduces the effects).
life events	A time of external change which requires major internal, psychological adjustments. For example, marriage, divorce, parenthood, employment or unemployment, retirement and bereavement.
anxiety	A vague, unpleasant, emotional state of tension or stress. It is distinct from fear which is both situation-specific and more short term.
psychosomatic illness	The causes are primarily psychological rather than physical. The illness is not imaginary, the person suffers real pain and infection.
hassles	Irritants, things that annoy or bother you. They can make you upset or angry.
uplifts	Events that make you feel good, they make you feel joyful or satisfied.
psychic energy	A person's mental resources which are available to cope with external and internal stimuli. If there is too much demand on these resources it leaves less for coping with physical defence against illness.

xaminer's tip

Distinguish between physical and psychological responses.

Sources of stress

1. <u>Life events.</u>   Physical illness may be caused by social events which involve change. The link is stress, caused by change.

RESEARCH EXAMPLE   **Rahe *et al.* (1970) Using the SRRS**

RESEARCH QUESTION: Life events create stress. Does this lead to physical illness?

PARTICIPANTS: 2,500 naval personnel on a six-month tour of duty.

METHOD: Questionnaire. Holmes and Rahe developed the SRRS (see beginning of this unit) to test the link between stress and physical illness.
1 Just before a tour of duty, participants were asked to fill in a questionnaire relating to significant changes in their life over the past six months. This meant that a LCU (life change unit) value could be calculated for each participant.
2 A health record was kept for each participant during the six months tour of duty by the ship's physician.

RESULTS: There was a significant correlation of 0.118 between LCUs and illness.

INTERPRETATION: LCUs are positively correlated with illness, though the correlation is small. Changes associated with major life events absorb 'psychic energy', leaving less available for other matters such as physical defence against illness.

EVALUATION:
1 The results of all such studies are *correlational*. It does not mean that stress *caused* illness.

2 The data about LCUs was *retrospective*.

3 The concept of 'life events' should be questioned. Individual differences, such as your coping skills, past experiences and your physical strength, all moderate the extent to which a potentially stressful event will affect you (see DeLongis *et al.*, 1988, below).

❷ Daily events.   Most people do not often experience major life events. Therefore strains of everyday life might be a better measure of stress and predictor of physical illness.

RESEARCH EXAMPLE   **DeLongis *et al.* (1982) Hassles and uplifts**

RESEARCH QUESTION: Are daily hassles more strongly related to physical health than major life events have been found to be?

PARTICIPANTS: 100 people living near San Francisco. The sample was obtained through probability techniques (see Unit 11.2). They were aged between 45 and 64, and were predominantly well-educated and high income. They were paid $8 per month.

METHOD: Questionnaire. The assessment spanned a period of one year. Four questionnaires (scales) were filled in each month.

● *Hassles Scale:* Rating the frequency and intensity of 117 hassles. Typical hassles include: concerns about weight, rising prices, home maintenance, losing things, crime and physical appearance.

● *Uplifts Scale:* Rating the frequency and intensity of 135 uplifts. Later these were combined into one Hassles and Uplifts Scale. The authors felt that some events can be both a hassle and an uplift simultaneously. Typical uplifts include: recreation, relations with friends, good weather, job promotion.

● *Life Events Questionnaire:* 24 undesirable major events.

● *Health Status Questionnaire:* Questions on overall health status, bodily symptoms and energy levels.

RESULTS:

1 The frequency and intensity of hassles were significantly correlated with overall health status and bodily symptoms.

2 Daily uplifts had little effect on health.

3 There was no relationship between life events and health during the study, though there was a relationship for life events recorded for the $2\frac{1}{2}$ years before the study.

INTERPRETATION: Hassles appear to have a significant influence. DeLongis *et al.* point out:

1 Hassles are an additional factor to major life events.

2 There is not a simple causal relationship between hassles and illness. Since they are usually repeated events, it is a circular model: hassles affect health and health affects the subjective experience of hassles.

EVALUATION:

1 You should also consider chronic sources of stress. These are more general, ongoing life difficulties such as poor housing, low incomes, strains of family life, unsatisfying work and so on. Health is affected by all three: hassles, chronic situations and life changes.

2 Individual differences affect the degree of stress experienced. This explains why correlations between life events, hassles and physical illness are not as high as might be expected.

3 The same hassle can be experienced in different ways on different occasions. For example, a traffic jam may sometimes give you time to relax whereas at other times it seems highly stressful.

RELATED STUDIES: DeLongis *et al.* (1988) studied married couples over a period of six months and found a significant relationship between hassles and health problems. They also found important individual differences in stress responses. People high in self-esteem and social support were not as affected by stress. People who are low in psychosocial resources are more vulnerable to illness and mood disturbance when exposed to stress.

---

❸ Environmental stimuli.   Factors such as noise or temperature increase general arousal and therefore increase any stress already felt. For example, Baron and Ransberger (1978) looked at incidences of collective violence in the US between 1967 and 1971, and checked the weather records for these dates. They found that, when the temperature was moderately hot, incidence of riot and civil disturbance was greatest, with a peak around 84°F. When the temperature rose further and become extremely hot, aggression declined.

Other environmental stimuli include pollution, poor architecture, overcrowding and the urban environment generally (see Unit 6.3). The effects are lessened if such stimuli are: ● Predictable   ● Controllable

---

RESEARCH EXAMPLE   **Glass *et al.* (1969) Predictable and unpredictable noise**

RESEARCH QUESTION: Earlier experiments indicated that people adapt to noise even when it is unpredictable. Does this process of adaptation have a 'psychic cost'? In other words, individuals may adapt *physiologically* but their *performance* may suffer.

PARTICIPANTS: Two groups of 48 and 18 female undergraduates, paid $3.40.

EXPERIMENT I
METHOD: Experiment. Participants were asked to complete a number of cognitive tasks, such as number work and letter searches, as fast and accurately as possible. While doing this for 23 minutes a tape was played:
1 Loud or soft *random* intermittent noise (LRI or SRI).
2 Loud or soft *fixed* intermittent noise (LFI or SFI).
3 No noise (control).
The noise was a collection of different sounds, superimposed: two people speaking Spanish, one person speaking Armenian, a copying machine, a desk calculator and a typewriter. During the task physiological arousal was measured using GSR.

After the task participants were asked to complete four puzzles. Two of them were insoluble. Frustration was measured in terms of the time that participants persisted at these tasks.

RESULTS:
1 Participants did adapt to the noise. Their GSR levels and number of errors were considerably reduced by the end of the first set of tasks.
2 Participants in the random noise conditions made more errors and later showed less task persistence.

INTERPRETATION: Unpredictable noise leads to lower levels of performance and patience. Why?
1 We can 'tune out' constant stimuli while still attending at a preconscious level, but unpredictable stimuli require continued attention.
2 Noise and/or attention decreases the amount of psychic energy available and therefore less is available to deal with stress.

EXPERIMENT II
METHOD: Experiment. Participants listened to random noise while performing the same tasks.
Condition 1 *Button:* Participants were given a button to press to stop the noise, though they were asked to resist if possible.
Condition 2 *No button:* Participants in this condition did not receive this option.

RESULTS: Participants in the button condition were significantly more persistent on the insoluble task than those given no control over the noise.

INTERPRETATION: Perceived control avoids a sense of helplessness and anxiety, which would increase stress and frustration.

RELATED STUDIES:
Cohen *et al.* (1991) studied the common cold. They gave half of their 420 volunteers nose drops containing the virus. The other half received a placebo. Those participants who felt their lives were unpredictable and uncontrollable were twice as likely to develop colds as those suffering low stress.

Gardner (1978) repeated Glass *et al.*'s study and found no negative effects. Then he realised that this time participants had been asked to sign a consent agreement saying that they understood their rights as a participant. This gave them a sense of control. He tested this by giving the consent forms to only half the participants. The half without consent forms did experience stress whereas the other half did not.

---

4 Work stress.   The pressures of work and the work environment are a major cause of stress, both as major life events and as hassles and uplifts. Similar stress is experienced by paid workers, volunteers, students or housewives.
  - Typical *causes*: Job uncertainty, organisational change, interpersonal conflicts, sexual harassment, punitive management, lack of control, work overload, under-utilisation of skills, responsibility for others, difficult tasks, shift work, decision-making, lack of support, and dangerous, unpleasant or uncomfortable work environment.
  - *Effects*: Absenteeism, high job turnover, alcohol and drug abuse, and poor performance in terms of quantity and quality.
  - The *costs* of work stress are high. This can be measured in terms of psychological and physical problems as well as financial value for any employer. A good employer balances costs by offering benefits to increase worker morale and production and decrease absenteeism.

Burnout

Burnout is the erosion of the human spirit which results from chronic exposure to high levels of work stress. Like all work stress, the effects on work performance and personal health are enormous. It is a problem particularly for those who work in the human services professions. For example, nurses, teachers, social workers and policemen.

Maslach and Jackson (1982) measured burnout in terms of three psychosocial components:
1 *Emotional exhaustion:* Working with people, and particularly those who are in difficulty, is a strain on psychic resources.
2 *Depersonalisation:* Both worker and client experience deindividuation. For example, a nurse regarding patients as objects. The same is true for the patient who fails to see the person behind the nurses' uniform.
3 *Perceived inadequacy:* The worker experiences low job satisfaction because they feel their efforts fail to produce the desired results.

Possible remedies include: provision of support groups and more varied work activities.

⑤ <u>Cataclysmic events</u>. Shock is the body's defence against sudden trauma, physical or psychological. All energy is concentrated on maintaining the vital systems. This happens when a person is seriously injured. A prolonged state of shock may be caused when a person is involved in a natural or man-made disaster. For example, a plane crash, a major flood, war imprisonment, a rape, or a kidnap.

Post-traumatic stress disorder (PTSD)

A disabling reaction to stress following a traumatic event. These are exceptional events which threaten survival. The response does not always appear immediately after the event but may be delayed. The reactions are long-lasting:
1 *Reliving:* The person relives the event recurrently in flashbacks and dreams.
2 Emotional *numbness* and avoidance of things which serve as a reminder.
3 General *anxiety* and arousal not previously present, including over-alertness, trouble concentrating, impairments of memory, irritability and outbursts of anger.
4 *Guilt* about surviving.

The label PTSD is relatively new but the symptoms have been long recognised. For example as shell shock or combat fatigue. It is now recognised by health workers as a serious condition which can affect someone's ability to lead a normal life. Lack of control may be one of the key factors, since such traumas disorder our orderly world. Treatment includes psychological therapy and antidepressant drugs.

Psychological reactions to stress

The effects can be classified as follows:
- *Adaptive.* Anger and aggression are ways of getting rid of the stressor. *Optimum* levels of any emotion will be associated with increased arousal, concentration and performance.
- *Pleasurable.* For example, emotional highs or loud music produce agreeable pressure. Selye uses the term **eustress** to signify pleasant stress associated with fulfilment.
- *Maladaptive.* When levels of anger, aggression, anxiety, depression or arousal generally become too high, performance will be impaired. This is especially true for cognitive tasks which require greater concentration.

The Yerkes-Dodson Law (1908) expresses this relationship between arousal and performance.

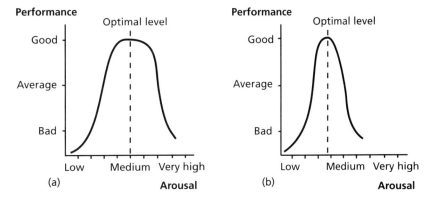

Fig. 10.1 The Yerkes-Dodson Law: (a) a simple task (b) a complicated task

There are four classic psychological responses to stress:

1 Anger and aggression are covered in Unit 7.1.

2 Anxiety:
- An *innate* response to threatening situations.
- It can also be *learned* through reinforcement. The case of Little Albert (Watson and Rayner, 1920, described in Unit 3.1) demonstrated how conditioned emotional responses (CERs) can be produced by classical conditioning. In the same way, we may learn to experience anxiety in situations where it has been present in the past. For example, walking into a room where you took an examination.

3 Depression, apathy or irritability.   Depression is an *innate* response to certain situations. It can be a realistic response and possibly even a healthy one. Evidence about coping with stress (see below) suggests that people who refuse to face reality will suffer more health problems. In some cases, avoiding depression may be avoiding reality.
   However, chronic depression is not healthy. It may be *learned*:

EXAMPLE   **Seligman (1975) Learned helplessness and depression**

- Normally, an individual experiences stress and responds in such a way as to remove the stressor. They are in control.
- However, if the response has no effect then the individual *learns* that there is no point responding. The individual learns to be helpless and apathetic.
- At another time, the individual may be in a situation where control is possible, but the individual will not respond because they have learned a pattern of non-response.

In humans the picture is not quite as simple. Learned helplessness can be a response to stress or to failure. This may lead to depression when the individual blames their failure on themselves (internal) rather than on external factors. This is particularly true if such failure is seen as unchanging (stable) and relevant to all aspects of their personality (global) rather than to specific characteristics. (See also Units 8.1 and 8.2.)

---

4 Cognitive effects.   Optimum levels of stress improve performance, but too much leads to loss of concentration and poor performance on mental tasks. A person may be less able to cope and therefore stress overwhelms them.

5 Compensatory behaviour.   For example, smoking, excess drinking or eating, and deviant sexual behaviour (see studies on overcrowding, Unit 6.3). These may act as additional factors in causing poor health.

6 Individual and cultural differences.   A person's ability to cope and the social support available will affect the degree to which any stressor disturbs their psychic resources (see DeLongis *et al.*, 1988, earlier in this unit).
- *Learned:* Different cultures teach different styles of coping. For example, the Japanese approach is to try to accept problems as opposed to the Western approach which aims to take control and change a stressful problem (Wade and Tavris, 1993).
- *Innate:* Such differences in coping styles can also be explained in terms of inherited temperamental differences (see Unit 8.4).

EXAMPLE   **Friedman and Rosenman (1974) Type A behaviour and heart disease**

RESEARCH QUESTION: Are specific styles of coping related to coronary heart disease (CHD)?

TYPE	COPING BEHAVIOURS	ASSOCIATED WITH
A	Competitive, ambitious, impatient, restless, subjective sense of time, pressurised.	heart disease, cancer, risk taking pastimes
B	Lacks the above.	
C	Nice, industrious, conventional, sociable, repressed emotional reactions. Reacts to stress or threat with helplessness and hopelessness.	cancer

PARTICIPANTS: 3154 healthy men aged between 39 and 59, living around San Francisco in 1960.

METHOD: Longitudinal, interviews. Friedman and Rosenman (1959) set up the Western Collaborative Group Study to test the long-term effects of stress on certain types of people. They devised a set of 25 questions to assess the way a person typically responds to those everyday pressures that would create feelings of impatience, competitiveness or hostility. For example, they were asked how they would cope with having to wait in a long queue or working with a slow partner.

Participants' answers were recorded as well as the *way* that they responded. The interview was conducted in a provocative manner to try to elicit type A behaviour. For example, the interviewer might speak slowly and hesitantly, so that a type A person would want to interrupt.

Participants were then classed as A1 (type A), A2 (not fully type A), X (equal amounts of type A and B), and B.

RESULTS: Eight and a half years later, 257 of the total sample had developed CHD, about 70% of these had been assessed as type A, whereas half as many were type B.

INTERPRETATION: This offers strong support to the idea that aspects of a person's temperament are associated with CHD. The key factor may be stress.

EVALUATION:Twenty-two years later, 214 men had died from CHD, 56% were type A and 44% were type B, a rather less impressive difference. It is possible that death is not as good an indicator as illness, because some people take preventive measures once they know they are ill.

RELATED STUDIES: Morris *et al.* (1981) questioned a group of women seeking treatment for a breast lump. They found that those women who turned out to have a cancerous lump, had reported that they both experienced and expressed far less anger than those women who did not have cancer. This suggests a link between cancer and the suppression of anger. Emotional suppression is linked with increased stress, lowered effectiveness of the immune system and illness.

Physiological reactions to stress

Stress is an emotion and therefore physiological reactions follow the same pattern as for any emotion (see Unit 10.1). Stress has particularly intense and longer-lasting effects.

- Stress activates the **hypothalamus** and the **pituitary** in the brain.
- These stimulate the autonomic nervous system (ANS) and the production of **ACTH** (adrenocorticotrophic hormone).
- ACTH leads to production of adrenal hormones from the **adrenal glands** located just on top of both kidneys.
- The adrenal hormones are:
  - **Adrenalin** (epinephrine), from the sympathetic ANS which arouses the organism.
  - **Noradrenalin** (norepinephrine), parasympathetic ANS which activates the return to normal functioning.
- ACTH may also block certain nervous pathways thus *reducing* anxiety.

SHORT-TERM EFFECTS
Increased heart rate, respiration, sweating and so on (see Unit 10.1). In short, arousal ready for fight or flight.

LONG-TERM EFFECTS
1. General adaptation syndrome (GAS). Selye (1956) described a model for prolonged stress in terms of the physiological reactions. Stress from any source will trigger off the following sequence of events:
   - *Alarm reaction.* Release of ACTH and adrenalin in readiness for fight or flight.
   - *Stage of resistance.* Hormone production maintained at a lower level as the body gets used to the stressor.
   - *Stage of exhaustion.* Eventual depletion of body's resources. Adrenal glands not functioning properly leading to drop in blood sugar levels. This leads to various psychosomatic disorders such as high blood pressure, heart disease, asthma and ulcers.

   Evaluation:
   - Selye thought that GAS was a nonspecific response to *any* stressor. In fact, different stimuli lead to different stress responses.
   - No two people respond in the same way (individual differences) nor does the same person always respond in the same way (situational differences).
   - Selye's contribution was to alert medicine to the importance of stress.

2. Reduced immune response. The immune system protects us from disease. The main components of the system are antibodies, T-cells and B-cells. The presence of adrenalin seems to inhibit the production of these components.

RESEARCH EXAMPLE | **Kiecolt-Glaser** *et al.* **(1984) The immune system under stress**

RESEARCH QUESTION: Can a link be demonstrated between stress and a lowered immune response?

PARTICIPANTS: Seventy-five first year medical students, volunteers.

METHOD: Natural experiment (using a naturally occurring stressor). The researchers took a blood sample one month before the students' final examinations, and again during their exams. The samples were tested for the presence of antibodies and T-cell activity.

On both occasions the students were also given questionnaires on psychiatric symptoms, loneliness and life events.

RESULTS:
1 T-cell activity was significantly lower on the second occasion, when the students were presumably most stressed.
2 It was particularly low for students who reported feeling most lonely, and those experiencing other stressful life events and psychiatric symptoms such as depression or anxiety.

INTERPRETATION: Stress is associated with a lowered immune response. This effect is stronger where social support is lacking.

---

3 Ulcers.   Noradrenalin increases the production of digestive juices in the stomach. This is a rebound effect following stress. The effects may be ulcers or more general disorders.

RESEARCH EXAMPLE | **Brady (1958) Ulcers in 'Executive' Monkeys**

RESEARCH QUESTION: Brady placed his monkey participants in 'restraining chairs' and conditioned them to press a lever. They were given shocks every 20 seconds unless the lever was pressed in the same time period. This investigation came to an abrupt halt when many of the monkeys suddenly died. Post-mortem examination showed that the monkeys had raised hormone levels and that ulcers were the cause of death. The ulcers were not due to the restraint because other monkeys had been kept in restraining chairs for up to six months with no deaths occurring. Were the ulcers due to the electric shocks or to the stress?

PARTICIPANTS: Monkeys.

METHOD: Experiment. To test their question, they used a yoked control. Another monkey also received the shocks but had no control over the lever. Only the 'executive' monkey received the psychological stress of having to press the lever but both monkeys received the shocks.

RESULTS: After 23 days of a six-hours-on, six-hours-off schedule the executive monkey died due to a perforated ulcer.

FOLLOW UP: Brady thought that stress might be related to the reinforcement schedule. He tried various routines, such as eighteen-hours-on and six-hours-off, or thirty-minutes-on, thirty-minutes-off. However, no monkeys died from ulcers. He then tested the stomachs of executive monkeys on a six-hour-on, six-hour-off schedule.

RESULTS: They found that stomach acidity was greatest during the rest period.

INTERPRETATION: Two effects were noted in relation to stress:
1 *Work-related stress*: emotional strain rather than physical distress had profound effects.
2 *Rest-related* stress: the key factor seems to be the relationship between stress and rest time. It is now understood that stress leads to sympathetic arousal, when this stops the parasympathetic system rebounds and this is when *excessive* digestive juices are released.

APPLICATIONS: Don't switch directly from work to rest. You should lower your arousal levels gradually.

EVALUATION:
1 One criticism made of the study in general is that the monkeys were *not randomly* selected, the 'executive' was chosen because it was faster at learning an avoidance response. This may of course have parallels with the human world.
2 The study shows stress in *animals* and may not apply to humans.
3 The nature of the experiment raises *ethical* questions. Are researchers justified in exposing animals to such stress, especially when they know that the result is likely to be death?

RELATED STUDIES:
Weiner *et al.* (1957) used army recruits to show how some people are more likely to develop ulcers in response to stress. Prior to basic training, the soldiers were tested and classed as over-secretors or under-secretors of digestive enzymes. After four months of stressful training, 14% of

the over-secretors had developed ulcers whereas none of the under-secretors had. This shows that individual differences moderate the effects of stress on physiological processes.

Northfield *et al.* (1993) have presented strong evidence to suggest that it is not stress at all which leads to ulcers and stomach cancer but the presence of a bacterium, *helicobacter pylori*. This challenge to a long-held view has yet to be fully accepted.

Ways of measuring stress

1. Self-report, participants asked how stressful an experience was (e.g. Holmes and Rahe).
2. Behavioural measures, giving participants a task to assess their level of frustration (e.g. Glass *et al.*).
3. Physiological measures
   - The *size of the adrenal gland*, which becomes enlarged under prolonged stress.
   - From the *amount of cortisol* in the urine, a hormone produced by the adrenal gland.
   - Testing the *galvanic skin response* (GSR), a measure of activity in the ANS.
   - Other measures of *ANS activity* such as increased heart rate, blood pressure, and respiration.
   - The *polygraph* (also known as the lie detector) is a machine which records any of these bodily functions (see Unit 10.1).

Coping with stress

Coping with stress can be achieved by reducing the problem or reducing the stress. Coping with long-term stress involves different problems than short-term stress.

PROBLEM-FOCUSED STRATEGIES

Aim: To reduce the problem or your view of it.

1. Direct action.   Deal directly with the problem. This may involve physical action or cognitive problem-solving.
2. Avoidance.   Become involved in a different activity to 'take your mind off' the problem, such as going to the cinema or painting a room.
3. Take control.   A person who feels in control suffers less harmful consequences of stress (see Glass *et al.*). Therefore, even if you can't do anything about the threatening stimulus, at least increase your sense of control. For example, the stress created by an impending GCSE exam cannot be 'solved' but you can reduce the related stress by increasing your knowledge about what the exam is likely to entail.
4. Cognitive redefinition.   Changing the way you think about the problem. Ego defence mechanisms, such as intellectualisation and rationalisation are ways of consciously reshaping the problem. For example, taking the view that things could be worse.

RESEARCH EXAMPLE   **Lazarus *et al.* (1965) Gruesome accidents in a sawmill**

RESEARCH QUESTION: Can beliefs (cognitive appraisals) about a threatening event reduce or eliminate the associated stress response?

PARTICIPANTS: Sixty-six college students, most were paid $2.00 per hour.

METHOD: Experiment. Participants were shown a stressful film called *Woodshop*. It contained scenes of gruesome accidents in a sawmill. There were three experimental conditions.
Group 1: *Denial.* Participants were told that the people were actors, the events were staged and no one was actually injured.
Group 2: *Intellectualisation.* They were asked to consider the film in terms of its value for promoting safety at work.
Group 3: *Control.* No instructions.
Stress was assessed by measuring participants' GSR and heart rate while they watched the film. They were also asked at the end to evaluate how stressful they thought the film was.

RESULTS: Groups 1 and 2 showed lower physiological stress while watching the film and reported less after the film.

INTERPRETATION: The same event may be threatening, or not, depending on how its contents are appraised. Cognitive appraisal affects both physiological and psychological stress. This can be used to explain individual differences in stress response to the same stressors.

RELATED STUDIES: Speisman *et al.* (1964) showed a film called *Subincision in Arunta* about Aboriginal puberty rites where a boy's penis is cut with a knife. The film's sound track was altered so that for some participants the trauma was emphasised, for others the traditions of the tribe were stressed (intellectualisation). There were also denial and control conditions. The highest GSR was for the 'trauma' group and the lowest for the 'intellectualisation' group.

EMOTION-FOCUSED STRATEGIES
Aim: To reduce the physiological state of arousal or tension.

1. Coping style.   There are individual differences in the way that people cope with emotions. Some people prefer to repress their emotions. The evidence suggests that this approach is more likely to lead to stress and health problems than a coping style which is the opposite (see Kiecolt-Glaser *et al.*).

2. Relaxation.   Meditation, self-hypnosis and biofeedback techniques are all forms of relaxation which decrease activity of ANS, so decreasing stress. It is advisable to avoid sudden changes from work to rest. Taper off with gentle exercise or a meal to absorb the digestive juices (see Brady). Some people use alcohol or drugs as a means of relaxing.

3. Physical exercise.   Intense activity may be a means of releasing tension and therefore decreasing anxiety. It is cathartic.

4. Emotional discharge.   Another form of catharsis. Expressing tension through crying, anger or humour.

5. Social support.   Seeking help or comfort from close friends and family. Therapy offers a kind of social support. People who lack social support are much more vulnerable to stress.

6. Drugs.   Anxiolytic drugs such as Valium reduce anxiety but may become addictive. Alcohol and non-prescription drugs may be used for relaxation.

RESEARCH EXAMPLE | **Kamarck *et al.* (1990) Social support reduces cardiovascular response**

RESEARCH QUESTION: Does social support affect cardiovascular illness?

PARTICIPANTS: Thirty-nine female psychology student volunteers. Females were used because previous research indicates that they may be more responsive. Smokers and persons suffering from ill health were excluded.

METHOD: Experiment, deception. Each participant attended the laboratory session alone or they were asked to bring a close same-sex friend.
1 Participants were given various difficult mental tasks (stressful situation).
2 The participant's cardiovascular reactions (blood pressure and heart rate) were measured before and after the tasks.
3 The participants were assessed for mood, personality and friendship patterns.
In the 'friend' condition, partners were asked to be supportive and to touch the participant on the wrist throughout the work. The partner wore a headset and did their own task to prevent the participant feeling they were being evaluated.

RESULTS:
1 In general the participants who were with a friend showed lower physiological reactions than those who were alone.
2 This was true for Type A participants, but Type B participants showed slight increases in blood pressure when with a friend.

INTERPRETATION: This shows that social support directly influences stress responses, at least for individuals (Type A) who are likely to suffer from stress.

APPLICATIONS: Revising with a friend may reduce stress.

RELATED STUDIES: Brown and Harris (1978) interviewed 400 women living in Camberwell, London. Some of them had experienced a stressful event in the preceding year, but not all developed any serious psychological problems such as depression. Those who did develop such problems shared one important factor, the absence of a close, supportive relationship.

Quick test 10.2

1 One of the factors that increases stress in commuters is the delays caused by traffic jams. Suggest **one** other factor in commuting that will cause stress. (*MEG, 1992*)

2 Name **two** life events which are known to cause stress in humans. (*MEG, 1991*)
3 Give **one** criticism of the Holmes and Rahe Life Events Scale as a means of measuring stress.
4 Describe **two** psychological effects of stress.
5 What is **one** advantage of the stress response?
6 Outline an example from everyday life when increased physiological arousal has **positive** effects on a person.
7 (a) The General Adaptation Syndrome has three phases: stage of resistance, stage of exhaustion, alarm reaction. Place them in the correct order:
   (b) What happens when a person has reached the final stage?
8 According to the Yerkes-Dodson Law, what happens to performance as arousal increases?
9 The term *locus of control* refers to how much control individuals believe that they have over the events that happen to them. What effect does locus of control have on stress? (*MEG, 1991*)
10 Describe **two** emotion-focused strategies for reducing stress.

Summary

SOURCES OF STRESS	PSYCHOLOGICAL REACTIONS TO STRESS	PSYCHOLOGICAL REACTIONS TO STRESS	MEASURING STRESS	EMOTION-FOCUSED STRATEGIES
1 Life events (Rahe *et al.*)	1 Anger and aggression	A Short-term effects	1 Self-report	1 Coping style
2 Daily events (DeLongis *et al.*)	2 Anxiety	B Long-term effects:	2 Behavioural measures	2 Relaxation
3 Environmental stimuli (Glass *et al.*, Baron & Ransberger)	3 Depression, apathy or irritability	1 GAS (Selye) 2 Reduced immune response (Kiecolt Glaser *et al.*)	3 Physiological (adrenal gland, cortisol, ANS activity, polygraph)	3 Physical exercise 4 Emotional discharge
4 Work stress (e.g. burnout)	4 Cognitive 5 Compensatory behaviour	3 Ulcers (Brady)		5 Social support
5 Cataclysmic events (e.g. PTSD)	6 Individual differences			6 Drugs

APPLICATIONS: Coping with stress

10.3 Biological bases of behaviour

THE STORY OF PHINEAS GAGE

Vermont, USA, 1848. Phineas Gage was a young railroad foreman working with explosives. An accidental discharge caused an iron bar to be fired into his head. It entered just below his left eye and out of the top of his skull, damaging a large part of his frontal cortex. Amazingly, he survived and suffered no more than momentary loss of consciousness. His higher mental abilities, such as speech, thought and memory, were unaffected. In the fullness of time, however, it became apparent that his personality was profoundly altered. Before the accident he was mild-mannered, friendly and efficient. Afterwards he became foul-mouthed, ill-tempered, impatient and unable to stick to any plan (Harlow, 1868).

This was the first confirmation that the front of the brain plays an important role in personality. Since that time researchers have been collecting more information (using less radical means) about the role specific areas of the brain play in human behaviour.

DEFINITIONS		
reductionism	A way of explaining complex behaviour using the smallest and simplest units available. Biological reductionism reduces behaviour to the action of nerves, cells and chemical reactions.
hemisphere	One half of a sphere. The brain is separated in two hemispheres, left and right.
laterality	Sidedness (lateral = side). The question of which hemisphere of the brain controls a particular task. The term *laterality* can also be used to refer to the fact that, when both hemispheres are capable of a particular function, one side is *preferred* over the other.
cerebral dominance	The side of the brain which has greater control over a particular function. Also called **hemispheric** dominance.
contralateral	One hemisphere controls the *opposite* side of the body.
bilateral	A function is equally represented by both sides of the brain.
localisation	Particular areas of the cerebral cortex are associated with specific physical or behavioural functions.
homeostasis	The balanced physiological state in terms of body temperature, fluids, blood pressure, etc. which is vital to an organism's survival. Arousal interferes with this.
endocrine system	The system of glands which produce hormones.

Brain: Structure and function

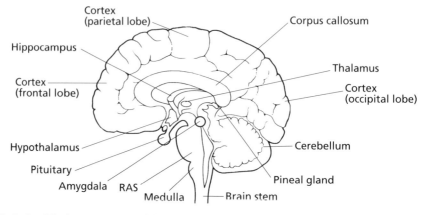

Fig. 10.2 A simplified cross-section of the brain

Name	Location and structure	Function
cortex (**or cerebral cortex**)	In the forebrain. The outermost layer of grey matter.	Higher cognitive and intellectual behaviour. It is divided into two halves (hemispheres) joined by fibres (including the **corpus callosum**).
Each half has four lobes: **frontal lobe**	At the front, the largest part.	• The motor cortex: Fine voluntary movements, inhibits inappropriate beheaviours and is associated with thinking and planning.
parietal lobe	Between the frontal and occipital lobe.	• Somatosensory cortex: Interpretation of bodily sensations of touch, pain, pressure and temperature.
temporal lobe	On the side, below the occipital lobe.	• Contains the auditory cortex for hearing and balance. Also contributes to memory, language, emotion and perception.
occipital lobe	At the back.	• Includes the visual cortex.
corpus callosum	Between the two brain hemispheres.	A large set of nerve fibres that form the main connection between the right and left hemispheres of the cerebral cortex (see 'Split-brain operations' below).
thalamus	Two footballs joined from side to side, lying under the corpus callosum.	Great relay station of the brain. It receives sensory data, performs some processing and passes the data on to the cerebral cortex.
hypothalamus	Below the thalamus, ('hypo' means under). It is about the size of a baked bean.	Integrates the activity of the ANS. Therefore it is the cognitive centre for emotions, stress, motivation and homeostasis.
pituitary gland	Attached to the base of the hypothalamus, on the anterior side.	An endocrine gland located in the brain. Controls hormonal secretions and other ANS glands.
hippocampus	Located between the thalamus and the cortex, shaped like a seahorse (hippocampus means seahorse).	Involved in learning and storing new information in memory.
limbic system	Includes parts of the cortex and hypothalamus plus the hippocampus, amygdala and other structures.	Important in emotion and motivation.
medulla	At the base of the brain stem.	The 'vital centre', controlling heartbeat, breathing, swallowing, blood pressure, digestion, etc.
cerebellum	Behind the medulla. A large structure with many folds.	Coordinates voluntary movement, muscle tone and body balance.
reticular activating system (RAS)	Found in the core of the brain stem.	Related to sleep, arousal, consciousness and attention.
brain stem	The general area which connects the spinal column to the higher brain.	The absence of any activity in the brain stem is critical in decisions regarding life and death. Includes the medulla, reticular activating system, and cerebellum.

Cerebral dominance

Some brain functions are equally represented on both sides of the brain (**bilateral**). Other functions are **lateralised** or **localised**. This means that they are dominant on one side of the brain or they are present in only one side.

1 Right and left contralateral functions. The brain is divided into two hemispheres (halves), the right and left. The main connections between muscles and sense receptors are to the opposite side of the brain. The right side of the body is connected to the left hemisphere and vice versa.

2 Handedness. Ninety per cent of people are right-handed. Analysis of drawings show that this figure is constant in all parts of the world and since prehistoric times. In right-handed people the *right* side of the body is preferred for most motor activity. This means that the *left* hemisphere is dominant.

3 Language. The left hemisphere contains areas related to language. For example,
- **Broca's area** is in the left frontal lobe. It is associated with speech production and writing.
- **Wernicke's area** is in the left temporal lobe. It is connected to the visual and auditory cortex and is related to language comprehension.

Many left-handers have bilateral dominance for language, brain damage to either side will impair language. Left-handers who have left hemisphere language dominance, have to use the other hemisphere to control their writing hand (left hand controlled by right hemisphere). This may be associated with the strange inverted writing posture used by some left-handed people.

4 Emotion. The right hemisphere controls emotional expression and the understanding of other people's expressions. It contributes emotional content to speech. The left side of the face (controlled by the right hemisphere) generally smiles more broadly and expresses more emotion than the right side.

5 Visual and spatial tasks. For example, imagery, artistic expression, pattern recognition. Such tasks are often performed better by the right hemisphere.

6 Vision. The left visual field of *both* eyes is sent to the right hemisphere, and the right visual fields go to the left hemisphere. To do this, part of the optic nerve crosses over (see Unit 2.1).

7 Hearing. Both left and right auditory cortex receive input from both ears.

8 Mixed dominance. In some people, there is no clear laterality. It is possible that this is associated with a variety of problems such as stuttering and dyslexia. Such language difficulties may be due to the presence of two competing language centres.

Ways of studying the brain

1 Techniques with no side effects:
- *EEG (electro-encephalogram).* Microelectrodes are attached to the patient's scalp. They record general electrical activity in that area of the brain. This is useful in understanding states of awareness, such as phases of sleep.
- *X-ray tomography* (CAT and PET scans). The brain is dyed using radioactive substances, such as glucose, which are injected into the bloodstream. Active areas of the brain take up more of these substances. The scan might show a tumour (tumours are areas of active growth) which can then be associated with some abnormal behaviour. More simply, the technique can be used to see what part of the brain is working while the participant is engaged on a particular task.
- *Neurospinal fluid, blood and urine.* Can be checked for traces of chemicals. For example, large amounts of cortisol in the urine indicates stress.
Problems:
- You cannot be certain that a *primary cause* has been located. For example, if you sever a person's vocal chords they cannot speak, however that does not mean that the vocal chords are central to the process.

2 Deliberate damage:
- *Ablation.* Removal of parts of the brain. In the case of H.M., the hippocampus was removed from both hemispheres in an effort to relieve his epilepsy. As a result he was no longer able to remember any new things (see Unit 4.1).

- *Lesions.* Cutting connections which gives the appearance that a section of the brain has been destroyed. Lobotomies are performed using this technique. Prefrontal lobotomies severe the connections within the frontal lobes resulting in personality changes (see Unit 7.1).
- *Implanting electrodes.* Hubel and Wiesel (see Unit 2.1) placed electrodes in cats' brains to trace activity of the visual cortex. This is different from using microelectrodes on the scalp.

Problems:

- You again cannot be certain that a *primary cause* has been located.
- You cannot be sure that the damage caused in surgery is limited to specific parts. There may be other minor injury.

3 Brain injury or illness:

- *Accidental damage.* For example, the case of Phineas Gage (see beginning of this unit) or head injuries resulting in damage to a distinct area.
- *Brain operations.* For example, *split-brain* operations demonstrate the functional asymmetry of the brain with respect to verbal and non-verbal tasks (see below).
- *Post-mortem examinations.* Looking at the brains of people with known problems. For example, schizophrenics' brains have been found to be about 6% lighter than other mental patients.

Problems:

- It is usually not possible to make before and after *comparisons* of patient. Instead comparisons are made between 'normal' individuals and those having a disorder. There is no control for individual differences.
- The process of brain injury is *traumatic.* This may lead to changes in behaviour rather than the injury itself.

RESEARCH EXAMPLE | **Split-brain operations**

This procedure is used in patients suffering from severe epileptic seizures as a means of restricting the spread of the electrical forces which occur in an attack. The fibres (the corpus callosum) connecting the two cerebral hemispheres and the optic connection are cut. This creates two independent brains.

Sperry (1968) studied the effects of such an operation. A classic test was to place such a participant behind a screen with their hands free to handle objects unseen.

If an object is to the left side of the screen, it is recorded in the right hemisphere only. If the participant is asked to pick up the object they can only do this with their left hand (controlled by their right hemisphere) and cannot say what the object is (speech is controlled by the left hemisphere).

Patients do learn ways of communicating between hemispheres. For example, an experimenter might show a letter to the left visual field and ask if it was the letter A. Language comes from the left hemisphere, which would have to guess the answer. The right hemisphere knows the answer and hears the answer given. If this is incorrect, the right hemisphere can make the face frown (both sides control the facial muscles). The left hemisphere, feeling the frown, realises it was wrong and can change the answer!

The procedure raises an interesting philosophical question. Do split-brain patients have two minds or one?

Quick test 10.3

1 What is **one** problem with using patients who have suffered brain damage as a means of studying the brain? (*MEG, sample Foundation*)
2 What is a typical behaviour of a split brain patient?
3 What is *reductionism*? Give an example.
4 What is meant by the term *localisation of function*? (*MEG, 1993*)
5 Name **two** functions of the cortex which are *bilateral*.

Summary

WAYS OF STUDYING THE BRAIN	1 Techniques with no side effects 2 Deliberate damage 3 Brain injury/illness

Chapter 11
Research techniques

Throughout this book there has been an emphasis on research. All psychological theory depends on research. To understand psychology you must understand the means of gathering data, and the practical and ethical considerations related to this.

11.1 Methods

DEFINITIONS

research	Any honest attempt to study a problem systematically.
research method	A way of doing things in a systematic manner.
research technique	The specific procedures used in a variety of research methods.
research design	The overall plan of action to maximise meaningful results and minimise ambiguity using research techniques. *Control* is an important feature of design.
research aims	The stated intentions of what question(s) are planned to be answered. For example, 'to investigate the effects of colour on mood' or 'to see if there are sex differences in colour preferences'.
hypothesis	A formal, unambiguous statement of what you predict. The research will either prove or disprove this prediction. For example, 'red will be less relaxing than blue' or 'women will prefer red more than men'.
scientific method	A series of procedures which produce an objective body of facts.
experiment	A procedure which tests an hypothesis by controlling an independent variable and observing its effect on a dependent variable. The element of *control* is crucial in order to be able to claim a *cause and effect* relationship.
ecological validity	An assessment of how true-to-life a particular method of study is, as opposed to artificially created laboratory situations.
psychometrics	The measurement of anything which is psychological.
validity	The property of being true, correct, conforming with reality.
reliability	Consistency or dependability. The degree to which a particular test or experiment gives the same result when used repeatedly under similar conditions.
standardisation	Establishing a set of norms for a test so that you can compare a person's score with an average.

cross-generational problem	A sample in a longitudinal study may be unrepresentative because of events specific to that generation, such as the Vietnam War or Aids.
cohort effect	In cross-sectional studies observed differences between generations may be due to social changes rather than age. For example, adults today are taller than their parents because of improved diet.
social desirability bias	A preference to answer questions in a socially acceptable way to make oneself 'look good'.
response bias	A tendency to give the same kind of answer. For example, preferring to answer yes rather than no.
standardised instructions or procedure	A clear outline of what the experimenter says and does to make sure that every subject is tested under exactly the same circumstances. This also makes replication possible.

Types of study

For any method there is a compromise between conflicting advantages and disadvantages.

1 Scientific experiment.   The relationship between two things is investigated by deliberately producing a change in one variable (the **independent variable** or IV) and recording what effect this has on the other variable (the **dependent variable** or DV). There is a tendency to use the term 'experiment' too loosely. This detracts from the rigorous nature of a true experiment.

Control and *replication* are key concepts. If an experimental result is 'true' it should be possible to reproduce it. Therefore an experimenter should provide sufficient detail for anyone else to attempt to replicate the work thus enhancing its validity.

The scientific method is a much broader concept. It is discussed in Chapter 1.

EXAMPLES: Tinbergen (Unit 3.3), Asch (Unit 5.1), Milgram (Unit 6.1).

Advantages:
- It is possible to claim that the IV is a *cause*.
- The extraneous variables can be well *controlled*.
- It can be *replicated*.

Disadvantages:
- It is an *artificial* situation, usually conducted in a laboratory to maximise control, and therefore the results may not generalise to real-life.
- Total *control* is in reality never possible. The results may be affected by, for example: experimenter bias, demand characteristics, volunteer bias, sample bias (see below). There may be extraneous variables beyond control or unknown to the experimenter.
- Some classes of participants, such as *children*, react poorly under experimental conditions.
- In some situations it would be *unethical* to manipulate exposure to certain conditions. For example, the effects of early deprivation on children.

2 Field experiment.   An experiment conducted in more natural surroundings, where the participants are unaware that they are participating in a psychology experiment. The independent variable is still manipulated.

EXAMPLES: Hofling *et al.* (Unit 6.1), Piliavin *et al.* (Unit 7.2).

Advantages:
- It has greater relevance for *real life*.
- The technique avoids *experimenter effects* such as participant bias and demand characteristics, because the participants are unaware of the experiment.

Disadvantages:
- Inevitably extraneous variables are harder to *control*.
- Some *design* problems remain, such as sample bias and demand characteristics.
- It is more time-consuming and *expensive* than laboratory experiments.

③ Natural experiment.   If conditions vary naturally, the effects of an independent variable can be observed without any intervention by the experimenter. It is still an experiment in the sense that a cause and effect are being identified, but not a 'true' experiment since the IV is not manipulated. For example, a researcher can compare pupil performance before and after a school introduces a new teaching programme. **Twin studies** rely on natural control of genetic factors so that the effects of environment can be observed (see item 10).

EXAMPLES: Operation Head Start (Unit 4.3), Williams (Unit 9.2), Festinger *et al.* (Unit 9.3).

Uses:
- Where conditions vary *naturally*.
- The only way to study cause and effect where there are *ethical* objections to manipulating variables.

Advantages:
- As for field experiments.

Disadvantages:
- Participants may be aware of being studied and show improvements just because of this (the **Hawthorne effect**, see Unit 11.2).
- Inevitable loss of *control* over extraneous variables.
- Such *conditions* are not always possible to find.

④ Correlation.   Strictly speaking this is not a method but a technique of data analysis (see Unit 11.3). A numerical value is calculated to represent the degree to which two sets of data are consistently related. The reason for the relationship can only be supposed. The terms IV and DV are not used, the variables are called **co-variables**.

EXAMPLES: Freedman (Unit 6.3), Patterson *et al.* (Unit 7.1), Rahe *et al.* (Unit 10.2).

Uses:
- Where experimental manipulation would be *unethical* or impossible.
- Indicates a *trend*.
- It is a good *starting point* for later experimental studies where cause might then be investigated.

Disadvantages:
- It establishes a *relationship* only, not a cause and effect.
- The relationship may be due to other *extraneous* variables. For example, height and IQ are linked because diet influences both.
- Correlations only deal with *linear* relationships. There are many other kinds of relationships, such as the curvilinear association in the Yerkes-Dodson effect (see Unit 10.2). These may be overlooked by simply calculating the correlation coefficient.

⑤ Observation.   Behaviour is observed in its natural environment or in written records. All variables are free to vary and interference is kept to a minimum. No independent variable is manipulated, but nevertheless a hypothesis may be tested.

In a sense, all research involves observation. It is both a method and a technique: either the overall design of the study or a technique for collecting data for experimental or correlational studies.

EXAMPLES: Lorenz (Unit 3.3), Hovland and Sears (Unit 5.3), Mead (Unit 9.2).

Uses:
- When behaviour is studied for the *first time*, observation is needed to establish possible relationships.
- It is good for working with young *children*, wild *animals* and uncooperative participants.
- It offers a way to study behaviour where there are *ethical* objections to manipulating variables.

Advantages:
- It gives a more *realistic* picture of spontaneous behaviour. It has high ecological validity.
- If the observer(s) remain undetected, the method avoids most *experimenter effects*, such as experimenter bias, demand characteristics, evaluation apprehension, etc.

Disadvantages:
- It is not possible to infer *cause and effect*.
- It is difficult to *replicate* and therefore you cannot be certain that the result was not a 'one off'.

- It is not possible to *control* extraneous variables.
- *Observer bias:* The observer sees what he 'wants' to see.
- *Observer reliability:* There are likely to be differences between different observers (low inter-observer reliability) or the same observer on different occasions.
- Where participants know they are being watched (disclosed observations) they may *behave unnaturally.* Even non-participant observers, by their mere presence, can alter a situation.
- Where observation is undisclosed there may be *ethical* objections. Participants have a right to informed consent.

6 Survey.   A group of self-report methods for collecting data. Oral or written, highly structured or very loose. This includes questionnaires, attitude scales, opinion polls, or interviews.

EXAMPLES: Adorno *et al.* (Unit 5.3), Hartshorne and May (Unit 7.2).

Uses:
- Where *large samples* are needed to provide sufficient data.

Advantages:
- There is a good *trade off* between the time spent and the amount of data gathered.
- It gives access to *information* not available from direct observation.

Disadvantages:
- It is possible to draw conclusions about correlations but *not cause and effect.*
- It relies on *self-report,* which is open to problems such as social desirability bias.
- People often don't actually *know what they think* and therefore are open to suggestion and response biases.
- There is evidence that people are *inconsistent,* what they say and what they do are different (see Unit 9.1). Therefore a measure of what people say they do may not be representative of behaviour.
- It is impossible to control for *personal interpretations* of a question, any attempts to explain questions could lead to experimenter bias.
- The method relies on *linguistic competence* and therefore excludes certain participants, such as children.
- The *sampling technique* is particularly critical.

7 Psychological Tests.   Written or oral tasks designed and carefully tested to measure a factor or assess some ability. Reliability, validity and standardisation are key issues (see Unit 4.3). They are generally used as a tool rather than a method of research in themselves.

There is some degree of overlap between psychological tests and survey methods. They both draw on some similar techniques but psychological tests are designed to measure rather than sample.

Kinds of tests include: personality tests, intelligence tests, tests of specific abilities, aptitude tests, achievement tests, sociograms.

EXAMPLES: Shields (Unit 4.3), Bem (Unit 9.2), Hargreaves (Unit 9.3).

Advantages:
- Provides *large amount* of information easily.
- Presents uniform situation so that participants can be *compared.*

Disadvantages:
- Constructing valid and reliable tests is very *difficult.*
- *Designer bias,* any test is biased in the direction of the author's views. An example of this is *culture bias,* especially in intelligence tests.

8 Case Study.   A detailed account of a single individual, small group, institution or event. It might contain data about personal history, background, test results, interviews.

EXAMPLES: Operation Head Start (Unit 4.3), Robertson and Robertson (Unit 8.1).

Uses:
- Where a behaviour is *rare.*
- To provide *insights* from an unusual perspective

Advantages:
- Gives in-depth picture producing *rich data.*
- Relates to *real life.*

Disadvantages:
- Usually involves recall of earlier history and therefore is *unreliable.*

- Close relationship between experimenter and participant introduces *bias*.
- *Cause and effect* are difficult to establish.
- *Not rigorous* methodology, often unstructured and unreplicable.
- Limited sample, lacks *generalisability*.
- Time consuming and *expensive*.

⑨ Cross-sectional study.   Groups of individuals of different ages are compared at the same point in time.

EXAMPLES: Samuel and Bryant (Unit 4.4), Piaget (Unit 9.1), Kohlberg (Unit 9.2).

Uses:
- Provides a picture of *development over time*.
- Can compare the effect of some treatment with a *control group*.

Advantages:
- Quick and relatively *inexpensive*, particularly in comparison to alternative of longitudinal studies.
- Easily *replicated*.
- Relatively easy to *modify* because it's quick and can be repeated easily.
- Avoids *cross-generational* problem (see longitudinal method below).

Disadvantages:
- *Participant variables* can never be matched perfectly.
- Participants used may not be comparable, differences may be due to social changes from one generation to another rather then age (= *cohort effect*).
- Can't provide data on *cause and effect*.

⑩ Longitudinal study.   One group of individuals is studied over a long period of time, taking periodic samples of behaviour.

EXAMPLES: Sameroff *et al.* (Unit 4.3), Hodges and Tizard (Unit 8.1).

Uses:
- As for cross-sectional studies, but can draw conclusions on cause and effect.

Advantages:
- Repeated measures are used, therefore participant variables are *controlled*.

Disadvantages:
- Once the study has started cannot *modify* the design.
- Impossible to *replicate* because of changes in society.
- Requires a large investment of time and *money*.
- Participants may *drop out* or be 'lost'. The remaining group therefore would become less representative.
- *Cross-generational* problem: The sample used may be unrepresentative because of events specific to that generation.

⑪ Cross-cultural study.   Different cultures compared with regard to certain practices, e.g. child-rearing, literacy, taboos, language and thought. A kind of natural experiment in the sense that practices are found to vary naturally between cultures.

EXAMPLES: Turnbull (Unit 2.3), Pettigrew (Unit 5.3), Fox (Unit 8.1), Mead (Unit 9.2).

Uses:
- Indicates *universal* and therefore innate behaviours.
- Enables us to observe how some *social practices* may be linked with certain outcomes, for example how gender stereotypes affect male and female behaviour.

Advantages:
- Suggests, but doesn't prove, *cause and effect*.
- *Rich data*, provides interesting insights into our own practices.
- Widens the *scope* of psychology to include a greater proportion of the human population.

Disadvantages:
- A non-native observer may *not understand* language or practices.
- An outsider may have *cultural biases*.
- Practices may *not* be *directly comparable*.
- Observations are only a sample of that cultures' behaviour, they may *not be typical*.
- Cannot be *certain* that an observed practice is actually the cause.
- *Costly* and time-consuming.

⑫ Twin studies.   Using naturally-occurring genetic and environmental variations. Monozygotic twins (MZ) have identical genes, they develop from a single egg.

Dizygotic twins (DZ) develop at the same time but are only as similar as siblings, they grow from two separate eggs.

EXAMPLES: Shields (Unit 4.3), Goldsmith and Gottesman (Unit 8.4).

Advantages:

- MZ twins provide a naturally-occurring *matched* sample, controlling genetic factors. Any differences between participants should be due to experience.
- Where MZ twins have been *reared apart*, we can observe the effects of a different environment on the 'same' person.

Disadvantages:

- Even MZ twins are born *different* due to influences in their mother's womb.
- Twins reared together may not have had the *same experiences*, though it is assumed that they have.
- Studies using twins rely on a *small* population, particularly when looking at those reared apart.

⑬ Animal studies.   Not all research with animals is laboratory based. Some is naturalistic observation. There are three questions in relation to research with animals:

- In what ways are animals preferable to human participants?
- Can we generalise from animal to human behaviour?
- What is ethical in terms of the use of animal participants?

The last question is governed by legislation. The Animals Act (1986) requires all research using animals in this country to be licensed by the Home Office.

EXAMPLES: Hubel and Wiesel (Unit 2.1), Lorenz (Unit 3.3), Harlow (Unit 8.1).

Uses:

- To study *animal behaviour*. For example, to provide better zoo conditions or breeding endangered species.
- When it is not possible to study humans, animal studies can indicate *possibilities*.
- To discover *innate* aspects of human behaviour.

Advantages:

- Animals are *cheaper*.
- There are *fewer* ethical problems, some procedures would be impossible with human participants.
- The *behaviourist* view is that animals produce the same behaviours as humans only in a less complex manner, therefore it is easier to study these behaviours in animals.
- They can be *conditioned* more successfully.
- They are less susceptible to *experimenter bias*.
- *Life cycles* are shorter enabling many generations to be followed.

Disadvantages:

- Animals can't report what they are *thinking*, which makes assessment difficult.
- Simply because structures are the same doesn't mean they perform the same *function*.
- Humanists argue that humans are *qualitatively different* from animals. Certain features of humans, such as consciousness and language, mean that it might never be appropriate to generalise from animals.
- The effects of *learning* cancel out inherited behaviour so that the same rules do not apply to animals and humans.

Quick test 11.1

1 In a research project, a psychologist asked fathers how much they participated in child-caring tasks. What is **one** problem with collecting data this way? (*MEG, 1994*)

2 Sometimes psychologists use animals as subjects [participants] in experiments. Explain **one** disadvantage of using animals as subjects [participants]. (*SEG, 1990*)

3 What is the main difference between an experiment and other methods of research?

4 Give one advantage and one disadvantage of using observation rather than a laboratory-based experiment.

5 Give **one** reason why psychologists carry out cross-cultural research.

Summary

METHOD OF STUDY	MAJOR ADVANTAGE	MAJOR DISADVANTAGE
1 Scientific experiment	Can suggest cause and effect.	Artificial.
2 Field experiment	Greater ecological validity than scientific experiment.	Some loss of control over extraneous variables.
3 Natural experiment	Allows study of cause and effect where ethically the factors could not be manipulated.	Such conditions not always possible to find.
4 Correlation study	Suggests possible relationships.	Cause and effect not shown.
5 Observation	High ecological validity, avoids subject bias.	Lacks control, no cause and effect.
6 Survey	Provides large amounts of data for analysis.	Unreliable data due to, for example, response bias, poor sampling, people don't know what they think.
7 Psychological tests	Provides large amounts of data about psychological abilities.	Validity and reliability, especially designer bias.
8 Case study	Provides insights about unusual behaviours.	Limited retrospective data.
9 Cross-sectional	Indicates how behaviour may change with age, relatively quickly and cheaply.	Cohort effect and lack of control for subject variables.
10 Longitudinal	Allows control of participant variables when studying changes which occur with age.	Costly, time-consuming, cross-generational problem.
11 Cross-cultural	Can investigate possible universal (innate) behaviours.	Observations of another culture may be atypical, misunderstood, not directly comparable and biased.
12 Twin studies	Can distinguish between nature and nurture.	In practice MZ twins are not exactly identical, and twins reared together do not have the same environments.
13 Animal studies	Fewer ethical objections. Necessary for studying animal behaviour.	Hard to generalise to human behaviour.

11.2 Design: Carrying out practical research

Research enters the design phase after a hypothesis has been developed. Steps in good research design:

1. Decide on the *aims* of the study, based on current theory.
2. Write an unambiguous *hypothesis*.
3. Define the *variables*.
4. Select the *sample*.
5. Use *controls*, for two reasons:
   - A *baseline*: it is necessary to have some measure of behaviour before or without the influence of the independent variable so that it is possible to see if any change has taken place.
   - Eliminating *extraneous* variables, so that only the independent variable can influence the dependent variable.
6. Analyse *results*.
7. Reach *conclusions* and adjust *theory*.

VARIABLES

The main concepts:

variable	A thing that changes.
experimental variables	The variables being studied, the IV and DV.
independent variable (IV)	The one which is specifically manipulated so that we can observe its effect on the DV. Theoretically the IV is independent of any changes in other variables. It is sometimes called the **treatment**, **experimental** or **controlled** variable.
dependent variable (DV)	The variable which is being measured or assessed. Any change should be due only to changes in the IV.
extraneous variable	Any variable other than the IV or DV. It may affect the DV and mean that it cannot properly be claimed that the IV has caused the observed change in the DV. This means that every effort must be made to *control* extraneous variables that might have an effect.
controlled variable	Any variable which is controlled. The IV or any extraneous variable.
participant (subject) variables	The characteristics of the research participants, such as age, intelligence, sex, manual dexterity. If one group of participants happens to be older or better educated, it may bias the results and explain differences between the experimental and control groups. Therefore it is important for both groups to have a balance.
demographic variables	Participant variables used to characterise populations, such as age, sex and socio-economic status. Rather than **personal variables** such as IQ and attitudes.

Selecting the sample

Deciding how and where to get your participants. The importance of an unbiased sample lies in the fact that are researcher aims to be able to *generalise* from the study, therefore the sample must be *representative* of the target population. You could not test 100 ten-year-old girls and make statements about all women or people generally.

In reality all samples are biased in some ways, most commonly:

- *Small sample size* invariably leads to bias because only a small range of participants are tested.
- *Opportunity sampling* is the most common sampling practice. This has led to much of psychological theory being based on a target population of male college students.

The main concepts:

sampling	Sampling is a research technique used in: • Observational studies as a means of selecting observations (see Unit 11.1). • Experiments, surveys and other studies as a means of selecting the participants from the target population.
population	Total number of cases about which a specific statement can be made (sometimes called the target population).
sample	Part of a population selected such that it is considered to be representative of the population as a whole. A truly representative sample is an abstract ideal.
sampling population	The population from which the sample is actually drawn. This in itself may be unrepresentative, selecting a sample from one school or from the Monday morning shoppers is biased from the start.
random sampling	Every member of the population has an equal chance of being selected, therefore it is an unbiased sample. Can be achieved with random number tables or numbers drawn from a hat.
quasi-random or **systematic sampling**	For example, every tenth case.
probability techniques	Any method where a sample is selected using a probability concept. Random sampling is an example.
bias	A prejudice, a leaning in one direction.
biased	Not equally distributed.
biased sampling	Some participants are more or less likely to be selected than they should be given their frequency in the population. This leads to systematic errors in the data.
opportunity or **accidental sampling**	Selecting participants because they are *available*. For example, asking people in the street. This is probably the most common method of sampling used. It is sometimes mistakenly regarded as random whereas it is invariably biased.
volunteer sample	Participants who become part of an experiment because they volunteer when asked. This is not random.
quota sampling	The population is divided in distinct sections or strata. A fixed number of samples or quota are taken from each section. Also called **stratified** sampling. Popular in market research, for example an interviewer might be expected to get responses from five people from different age groups.
behaviour sampling	Recording behaviour for specific time periods, chosen to

E xaminer's tip

Note that a 'sampling population' is different from a 'population', and can be used to explain an opportunity sample.

Control: Providing a baseline

The main concepts:

experimental treatment	Essentially the IV, the procedure which is applied to participants to see how it affects their behaviour.
experimental group	The group of participants who receive the experimental treatment.
control group	The participants who receive no treatment and act as a comparison with the experimental group for control purposes.
order effects	When participants are tested on two (or more) conditions (A and B) their performance may be improved or depressed by certain factors such as practice, fatigue or boredom.
repeated measures	The same participant is tested before and after the experimental treatment, therefore *all* participants are exposed to the IV and tested on the DV.
matched pairs	Participant variables are controlled by matching pairs of participants on key attributes. Only the experimental group is exposed to the IV, the control group receives no treatment. Pairs of participants, one from each group, are compared in terms of their performance on the DV.
independent measures	Comparison is made between two unrelated groups of participants. The participants are in groups not pairs. One group receives the experimental treatment, the other doesn't. Their performance on the DV is compared. It is *assumed* that individual differences are evenly distributed between both groups.
random allocation	In independent measures, participants are randomly assigned to experimental or control group to control for participant variables.
counterbalancing	An experimental procedure for controlling irrelevant factors, especially order effects.

METHODS OF PROVIDING A BASELINE

1. Repeated measures (or test–retest, own control):
   Advantages:
   - Good *control* for irrelevant participant variables.
   - Related measures *statistics* are more sensitive.
   - Needs *fewer* participants.
   Disadvantages:
   - *Order effects* can affect final performance.
   - Participants may *guess* the purpose of the experiment after the first test.

2. Matched pairs:
   Advantages:
   - Used where repeated measures are not possible.
   - *No* order effects or other problems of repeated measures design.
   - Participant variables *partly* controlled.
   - Can use related design *statistics* which are more powerful.
   Disadvantages:
   - Matching is *difficult*, time-consuming and may waste participants.
   - Some participant *variables* are inevitably present.

3. Independent measures:
   Advantages:
   - Used where repeated measures are not possible
   - *No* order effects and other problems of repeated measures.

Disadvantages:
- Lacks *control* of other participant variables.
- Needs *more participants*.
- *Statistical* measures less powerful.

SOME SOLUTIONS TO PROBLEMS RAISED

1 Counterbalancing.   Give half the participants condition A first while the other half get condition B first. Therefore some participants receive AB, and others BA. An alternative method is ABBA: each participant is given two A conditions and two B conditions, and a mean calculated for each. A **counterbalance check** can be used to see if the counterbalancing worked.

2 Equivalent measures.   Where a participant is re-tested, the test must be given in two equivalent forms to prevent advantages gained through practice. Equivalent forms can be created by taking one test and randomly placing equivalent items in form A or form B. These forms can then be counterbalanced.

3 Random allocation.   Any bias in placing participants in experimental or control groups can be overcome by randomly determining the group they are placed in.

Control: Eliminating extraneous variables

The main concepts:

experimenter effect **experimenter bias**	An experimenter has expectations about the outcome of an experiment and may indirectly and unconsciously communicate these to the participant (human or animal). This affects the participants' behaviour. This is different from the **experimental effect**, which is the effect of the experimental treatment.
interviewer bias	Ways that an interviewer or tester subtly influences a respondent's answers. For example, using leading questions or nonverbal cues.
participant bias	Ways that a participant's behaviour is prejudiced. For example, through expectations about the experiment or demand characteristics.
demand characteristics	Those features of an experimental setting that 'invite' the participant to behave in particular ways. They bias a participant's behaviour.
single blind	Participants are not informed of the aim of the experiment until after it is finished. This attempts to control participant bias.
double blind	Neither participant nor experimenter are aware of the 'crucial' aspects of the experiment. This avoids both participant and experimenter bias.
placebo	A 'treatment' which appears the same as the real thing, but does not have its critical effects. A control for the effects of expectations because participants think they are receiving the experimental treatment when they are not.

PROBLEMS WHICH MAKE CONTROL DIFFICULT

1 Environmental conditions.   These may vary randomly or systematically, such as noise or temperature.

2 Investigator biases.   Experimental results may be subtly and unconsciously affected by investigator expectations.
- **Experimenter bias:** Rosenthal and Jacobsen (1968) provided empirical evidence for the notion that things frequently turn out as one expected (**self-fulfilling prophecy**), not because the expectations were correct but because the expectations caused alterations in behaviour (see Unit 8.2).

- **Interviewer bias:** Loftus *et al.* (1970) showed that they could manipulate a participant's answers by asking a question either as 'a headlight ...' or '*the* headlight ...'. (see Unit 4.1). Greenspoon (1955) (**Greenspoon effect**) was able to alter participants' responses by using subtle reinforcement of 'right' or' wrong' answers. He said 'mm-hmm' whenever the participant said a plural word or 'huh-uh' after other responses. This led to increased production of plural words in random word generation.

3 Participant biases.   Results may also be affected by aspects of participant behaviour.
- **Demand characteristics:** One example is the participant's attempts (not necessarily conscious) to guess what the experiment is about, and do (or not do) what is expected of them. Orne (1962) tested this by telling participants they were taking part in an experiment investigating sensory deprivation. In fact participants were not deprived at all, yet they displayed the classic symptoms, in other words they did what they were expected to do.
- **Hawthorne effect:** A person's performance may improve, not because of the experimental treatment, but because they are receiving unaccustomed attention. Such attention increases self-esteem and leads to improved performance. The effect is named after the Hawthorne electrical factory where it was first observed by Mayo (1933).
- **Volunteer bias:** Volunteers are atypical participants, they are usually more highly motivated and perform better than randomly selected participants.
- **Response bias:** A preference for making any particular response rather than another, independent of the relevant response, usually in order to give socially acceptable answers.

CASE STUDY   **Why do psychologists often seem to find what they expected?**

Several reasons have already been suggested: the self-fulfilling prophecy, the Greenspoon effect, demand characteristics and the Hawthorne effect. There are many other ways to understand the willingness of participants to perform as expected:

1 The experiment as a social situation.   For social reasons people like to appear in a good light. They may adjust their behaviour in line with what they perceive as socially acceptable behaviour. This is true even when performing anonymously or when answering questions on paper. Asch's classic conformity study (see Unit 6.1) demonstrated how reluctant participants are to disagree with a group of strangers. People prefer to behave socially rather than anti-socially.

2 The participant is not a passive subject.   Orne (1962) says that the picture of the participant as an automaton is a foolish ideal. More realistically a person who takes part in an experiment should be seen as a true participant and not a subject. This naturally involves the participants' active search for clues.

3 Evaluation apprehension.   A participant is aware of being 'tested' and wants to appear normal and create a good impression. They may feel that a psychologist can 'read their mind'. In order to overcome anxiety and uncertainty, the participant tries guess what the experimenter really wants.

4 The experimenter's expectations.   There are pressures on a researcher to produce useful results. Even in double blind situations the experimenter is not 'expectation free'.

5 Of course, it may be that the results confirm expectations because the hypothesis is true. Careful planning and attention to extraneous factors enables psychologists to report valid results.

SOME SOLUTIONS TO PROBLEMS RAISED

1 Environmental conditions:
- **Systematic elimination:** Where extraneous variables vary systematically it should be possible to eliminate or balance them.
- **Random variables:** At best one can assume that the effects will be equally spread across all conditions.

2 Experimenter and subject variables, removing bias:
- **Single blind technique:** Used in almost all experiments so that participants are unaware of the experimental conditions or aim, thus preventing their expectations interfering with performance. They may still be influenced by experimenter bias.

- **Double blind technique.**
- **Placebos**.
- **Undisclosed observation:** In a field or natural experiment, the participant has no expectations because they are unaware of being part of an experiment.
- **Standardised instructions:** Helps to prevent experimenter bias.

Other techniques

pilot study	A smaller, preliminary study which makes it possible to check out standardised procedures and general design before investing time and money in the major study. Any problems can be adjusted.
debriefing	Participants should be informed of the aim of the study after they have taken part. They should be told of any deceptions that were involved.
operational definitions	Defining a variable or hypothesis in terms of **operations**. For example, hunger is operationally defined as being without food for 24 hours. This removes ambiguity.
confederate or stooge	A person who appears in an experiment as a participant, but is instructed by the researcher to act in certain ways to influence the real participants. The real participants do not know this.

Quick test 11.2

1 In some experiments, the researcher measures behaviour before and after the period of study. Why is this?
2 (a) What is meant by choosing a sample *at random*?
   (b) Suggest **one** way in which you could choose a sample at random. (*NEAB, 1993*)
3 Describe **two** practical problems that GCSE students might have when they try to use children as subjects [participants] in their investigations. (*MEG, 1992*)
4 Give **two** methods of controlling *order effects*?
5 What is a control group and what is it for? (*SEG, 1992*)

Summary

Steps in research design:

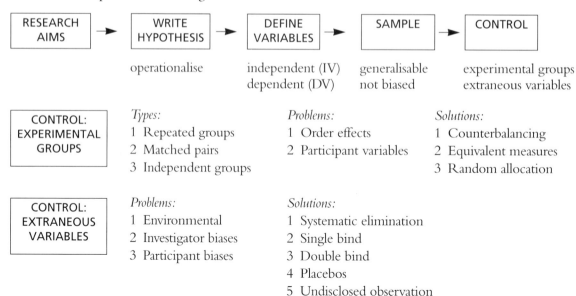

| RESEARCH AIMS | → | WRITE HYPOTHESIS | → | DEFINE VARIABLES | → | SAMPLE | → | CONTROL |

| | operationalise | independent (IV) dependent (DV) | generalisable not biased | experimental groups extraneous variables |

| CONTROL: EXPERIMENTAL GROUPS | *Types:* 1 Repeated groups 2 Matched pairs 3 Independent groups | *Problems:* 1 Order effects 2 Participant variables | *Solutions:* 1 Counterbalancing 2 Equivalent measures 3 Random allocation |

| CONTROL: EXTRANEOUS VARIABLES | *Problems:* 1 Environmental 2 Investigator biases 3 Participant biases | *Solutions:* 1 Systematic elimination 2 Single bind 3 Double bind 4 Placebos 5 Undisclosed observation |

11.3 Statistical treatments

statistic	• Number(s) used to represent data (**numerical** statistics). • The collection, classification and analysing of data (**numerical** or **graphical** statistics). • Formula based on probabilities (**inferential** statistics).
descriptive statistics	Numerical and graphical methods which are not based on probabilistic calculations.
numerical statistics	Either measures of central tendency (averages) or of dispersion (range, spread or distribution).
graphical statistics	Methods of visually displaying data.
inferential statistics	Commonly called **statistical tests**. GCSE students may want to use these in their coursework, but no understanding is necessary.
data	Facts gathered in research. Data is the raw material, it becomes **information** once it is meaningfully analysed. Data may be: • *Nominal* (named categories) e.g. Winter, Spring, Summer, Autumn. • *Ordinal* (ordered or ranked) e.g. hot, warm, cool, cold. • *Interval* (numerical scale with equal intervals) e.g. Centigrade.
significance	The extent to which research results are due to the experimental treatment rather than chance. A 5% (0.05) level of significance states that we are 95% confident that the results are due to the IV. This is the most commonly used level; 1% is stringent and used in research affecting human health; 10% is rather thin but worth reporting.
normal distribution	A bell-shaped curve with the mean, median and mode all at the same point. Many biological characteristics are distributed in this way. For example height: the majority of children age 5 will score around the mean with fewer at either extreme. See IQ in Unit 4.3.
parametric statistics	A group of statistical tests which are based on certain assumptions about the data used. They are more *powerful* tests because they are more likely to produce a significant result. The data should be interval, normally distributed and of similar variance. However, parametric tests are *robust* and therefore can be sometimes used when these conditions don't apply.

Numerical statistics: Measures of central tendency

Measures of central tendency are ways of giving the most *typical* or *central* value. The term 'average' is mistakenly used for the following measures:

❶ Mean ($\overline{X}$ or arithmetic mean).   Add up all the values and divide by N (the number of values).

❷ Median.   The middle or central value in an ordered list. Place all values in order, find the mid-point. If the mid-point lies between two numbers work out the mean of these values.

❸ Mode.   The modal group, the most common. Place values in order and find the value or values occurring most frequently. This information is automatically shown in a bar chart. Some data may contain more than one mode. **Bimodal** means two modes.

Numerical statistics: Dispersion

❶ Range.   The distance between lowest and highest values.

❷ Standard deviation(s).   The difference between each value and the mean is calculated. The mean of these differences is calculated. This is the most accurate measure because it takes the distance between all values into account. Mathematical calculators will work it out for you.

❸ Variance (s^2).   The standard deviation squared.

Graphical statistics: Displaying data in tables and graphs

When you have collected data, it can be grouped so that it has meaning.

❶ Common methods:
  - *Table:* Numerical data is arranged in columns and rows.
  - *Bar chart:* Visual display of frequency, shows the mode(s).
  - *Pie chart:* Frequency is translated into degrees of a circle.
  - *Pictogram:* Frequency is represented by suitable pictures.

❷ Methods suitable for ordinal and interval data only:
  - *Histogram:* Differs from a bar chart in that the area of the bars *must* be proportional to the frequencies represented.
  - *Frequency polygon:* Mid-point of each bar joined to show continuous change, not suitable for data which is not continuous.
  - *Line graph:* Suitable for continuous data.
  - *Curved lines:* A sketch of an approximate line may be the best way to represent the data rather than using a jagged line graph. Useful for bimodal data or a normal curve.
  - *Ogive:* A line of cumulative frequency where frequencies are progressively added to each other.
  - *Scattergram:* Used for correlations. Each pair of values is plotted against each other to show if a consistent trend is present. The *line of best fit* is a precisely calculated line and not just the line that appears to represent the data.

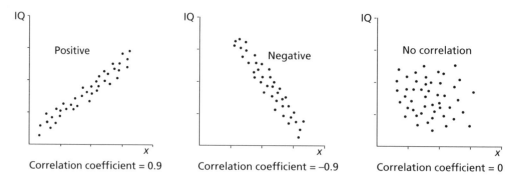

Fig. 11.1 Scattergrams (one dot = one person)

Inferential statistics

❶ Correlation.   The numerical value given for a correlation represents the extent to which two variables change together.
  - A correlation of $+1.0$ represents the highest possible *positive* correlation. The two sets of variables increase together.
  - A correlation of -1.0 represents the highest possible *negative* correlation. As one variable increases, the other decreases.
  - A correlation of 0 represents a totally random relationship: *zero* correlation.
  - The sign (whether it's + or −) tells you whether the correlation is positive or negative. The *magnitude* (size of the numbers) tells you whether the data is in fact

correlated. The closer you get to 0, the less relationship there is. A value of 0.4, for 20 subjects, is considered significant.

- The inferential tests which are used to calculate correlation are either **Spearman's rho** or **Pearson's product-moment**.
- The numerical value produced by such tests is called a **coefficient of correlation**.

② <u>Tests of difference.</u>   These determine whether one group of data is *significantly different* from another group.

- If the *mean* and the *standard deviation* from each set of data are the same, then the sets of data are essentially the same.
- For related data (related or matched samples) the most common tests are: the **related t–test** and the **Wilcoxon** test.
- For independent samples the most common tests are: the **independent t–test** and the **Mann–Whitney** test.

③ <u>The Chi-square test of association</u> (χ^2).   This test can assess both correlation and difference. The test looks at the data you collected and compares this with a theoretical distribution which would occur if there was no relationship.

Quick test 11.3

1 In what way is a graph a statistic?
2 Name three measures of central tendency (mistakenly called 'averages').
3 What kind of graph might you use for ranked data?
4 How might you choose to represent correlated data?
5 What kind of correlation is shown by a line which goes from bottom left to top right?

Summary

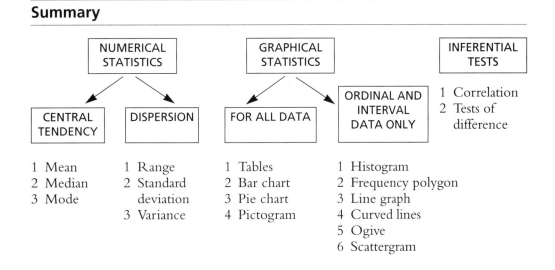

NUMERICAL STATISTICS		GRAPHICAL STATISTICS		INFERENTIAL TESTS
CENTRAL TENDENCY	DISPERSION	FOR ALL DATA	ORDINAL AND INTERVAL DATA ONLY	1 Correlation 2 Tests of difference
1 Mean 2 Median 3 Mode	1 Range 2 Standard deviation 3 Variance	1 Tables 2 Bar chart 3 Pie chart 4 Pictogram	1 Histogram 2 Frequency polygon 3 Line graph 4 Curved lines 5 Ogive 6 Scattergram	

11.4 Ethical and practical considerations

Ethics is that which is deemed acceptable in human behaviour in pursuit of certain goals or aims. It is not simply a question of 'right', but of balance between the interests of the participant and the scientific value of the research. The British Psychological Society (BPS) suggests that the aim of psychological research is to seek greater understanding of behaviour in order to 'ameliorate the human condition and enhance human dignity'.

Essential points of the ethical guidelines

When designing research, you should avoid:

1. Deception.   It is often difficult to avoid deception because otherwise participants' behaviour will be biased. Where deception is involved, participants should be thoroughly debriefed afterwards about the nature of the research and of their deception.
2. Risk to participants.   Participant's psychological or physical well-being should not be endangered.
3. Invasion of privacy.   The Data Protection Act must be followed.
4. Distress.   Participants should not be insulted, offended or angered.
5. Stress.   Participants should not feel they have harmed or upset someone else.
6. Change.   Plan to leave things as they were prior to any research.
7. Animals.   Research involving animals requires extreme caution and should be avoided unless specifically necessary. It is only permitted in this country under licence from the Home Office.

Briefing subjects:

8. Informed consent.   Wherever possible permission must be obtained from all participants. Participants should be *informed*, they should have some prior understanding about what the research will entail *before* becoming involved. If young children are involved, parents must provide informed consent.
9. Right to withdraw.   Participants should be aware that they can stop at any time.
10. Confidentiality.   Participants should be assured of the confidentiality of the data produced, as stated in the Data Protection Act.

After the research:

11. Debriefing.   Participants should be told the original research aims, informed of any deception involved and, when possible, given the results of the research. During debriefing it is helpful to ask participants if they were aware of the research aims. If they were, their data may have to be discarded.
12. Participants should be offered the chance to withhold their data.
13. All investigators should report their findings honestly.

Quick test 11.4

1 Describe **one** ethical problem that GCSE students would have to consider when carrying out a study on children. (*MEG, 1992*)
2 Field experiments have certain practical advantages but ethical drawbacks. Give **one** example of an advantage and **one** drawback in field experiments.
3 (a) Explain the term *debriefing* as it is used by psychologists.
  (b) Identify **two** points which you would make in a debriefing. (*NEAB, 1994*)

Summary

Ethics must be considered when designing research, and when briefing and debriefing participants.

Exam questions

You should spend no more than 15 minutes per question. Answers and a mark scheme are provided on page 258.

Chapter 1

Investigating children

Psychologists have produced a number of theories on children and how they develop. To do this they have to collect evidence to support their theories. Three psychologists who have carried out research on children are Albert Bandura, Sigmund Freud and Jean Piaget.

1 Briefly describe how these psychologists collected their evidence. (2 + 2 + 2)
(MEG, 1993)

2 There are numerous practical and ethical problems that arise when psychologists attempt to study children. Choose **one** of the psychologists and describe **two** ethical or practical problems with their work. (2 + 2)   *(MEG, 1993)*

3 Explain what is meant by the *nature/nurture debate* in psychology? (5)   *(SEG, 1993)*

4 There are a number of different ways to explain how children learn. Select **one** of the psychologists above and outline his theoretical approach to learning. (5)

Chapter 2

1 The following are definitions of perception.
  (i)   reception of visual information   ☐
  (ii) interpretation of visual information   ☐
  (iii) interpretation of sensory information   ☐
  (iv) recognising shapes and patterns   ☐
  (v)   reception of sensory information   ☐
Tick the box which corresponds to the best definition of perception. (1)

2 Two groups of subjects [participants] were shown the picture below, which shows faces at different distances from the viewer. Group A subjects [participants] were told that the circle was a coin and Group B subjects [participants] were told that the circle was a very large beach ball.
  (a) To which face did each group think the circle was nearer?
      Group A .... Group B............................. (1)
  (b) Explain your answer to part (a) and say what this tells you about distance perception. (3)

Face X   Face Y

    ○

3 The diagram on the right shows an illusion.
  (a) What is the illusion called? (1)
  (b) Give one explanation of the illusion. (3)

4 Describe a study which attempts to test the explanation given in 3(b). (5)

5 Some psychologists say: 'Illusions only occur under artificial conditions. They don't tell us anything about normal perception.'
  (a) What do psychologists mean by this statement? (2)
  (b) Do you agree with this statement. Give two reasons for your answer. (4)
(NEAB, 1988)

Chapter 3

1 What is meant by the term *learning*? (2)

2 During World War Two, the signal to call sailors to battle stations was a bell sounding at 100 rings per minute.
For sailors this signal became associated with the sound of guns and bombs.
15 years after the war ex–sailors and students took part in the following study.
They all listened to a bell five times. Each time it was sounded at a different number of rings per minute. On each occasion their heart rates were measured.
The results are displayed below.

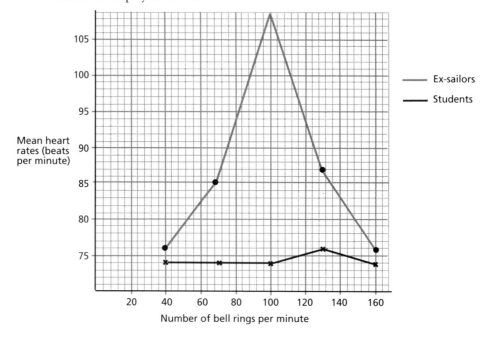

(a) Describe the results of the study. (3)
(b) How might the theory of *Classical Conditioning* explain the ex-sailors' mean heart rate when there were 100 rings per minute? (5)
(c) Explain what is meant by the term *generalisation*. Refer to the results of the study in your answer. (3)

3 An alarm has been invented to keep operators working at their desks. A ring is worn on an operator's finger and is attached to a watch which can give a small electric shock. If the finger stops moving for more than 30 seconds the operator receives an electric shock.
(a) Explain how this is an example of *punishment*. (2)
(b) Give **one** reason why this punishment might not keep people typing. (2)
(c) Suggest another way to keep keyboard operators typing. Refer to principles of conditioning in your answer. (3)   (*NEAB, 1994*)

How the alarm works

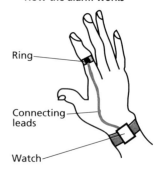

Ring

Connecting leads

Watch

Chapter 4

Two groups each of 10 subjects [participants] were given the following list of letters to learn:

F B I B B C G C S E I T V O B E

The 16 letters were projected onto a screen in 5 sets as shown below.

Order of presentation

	Set 1	Set 2	Set 3	Set 4	Set 5
Group 1	FBI	BBC	GCSE	ITV	OBE
Group 2	FB	IBBC	GC	SEIT	VOBE

The participants were asked to recall the sets of letters 24 hours later.
The results of the experiment were as follows:

Group	Total number of sets of letters recalled correctly
1	40
2	20

1 Describe the results in words. (1)

2 What can be concluded about memory from these results? (3)

3 State, from the information given, **one** variable that has not been controlled in the presentation of the sets of letters. (1)

4 Explain how you would use **either** the Method of Loci **or** the Peg Word System to remember the following list.
    Eggs, Carrots, Bread, Coffee, Butter, Cornflakes, Baked Beans. (4)

5 Marian has just seen a bank robbery. State **two** psychological factors which might affect the reliability of her memory of the event. (1 + 1)

6 Marian is interviewed by the police. How might the way in which they question her affect her memory of the event? Support your answer with psychological evidence. (4)

7 The police took Marian back to the bank where the robbery took place. Describe a study which suggests that this will improve her recall of the event. (5)   (*NEAB, 1991*)

Chapter 5

1 What is meant by a stereotype? (4)

2 Give **one** example of a stereotype and explain how it might affect someone's behaviour. (4)

3 Explain the difference between prejudice and discrimination. (8)

4 From what you have learned in psychology, describe **one** way in which discrimination might be reduced. (14)   (*SEG, 1996*)

Chapter 6

A psychologist investigated conformity by using the autokinetic effect. This is where a stationary spot of light, seen in a completely dark room, seems to move.
Participants in the dark room were shown a stationary spot of light.
The psychologist told the participants that she was going to move the light, but she did not move it.
The participants were asked to judge how far the spot of light had moved in each of two conditions.
    Condition 1: When viewing alone.
    Condition 2: When viewing in groups of three.
The results can be seen in the table below:

	Estimated distance moved (cm)	
	MEAN	RANGE
CONDITION 1	14	5–20
CONDITION 2	14	12–15

Participants' judgements

1 Describe the results of the experiment. (2)

2 (a) What is meant by the term *conformity*? (2)
  (b) Explain **one** criticism of the study of conformity described above. (2)

3 All the participants said that their estimates of distance moved had not been influenced by those of the other people present in condition 2. Tick the box which best describes this kind of conformity. (1)

COMPLIANCE   IDENTIFICATION   INTERNALISATION
    □   □   □

4 Explain the difference between compliance and internalisation. (3)

5 Sometimes people show obedience in the presence of others. Describe a study which investigates obedience. (5)

6 (a) State **two** factors that psychologists have discovered increases obedience. (2)
(b) What have we learned from studies of obedience that can be applied to everyday situations? (3)   (*NEAB, 1994*)

Chapter 7

The job interview

'A few years ago I went for a job at Stratford in East London. I took the train into St. Pancras and then took the tube out from central London to Stratford. When I got on the train I noticed that there was a battered old suitcase near the door. As the train travelled out to the East End people got off at various stops. Eventually I realised that there were only four people left in the carriage, and the other three had got on after me. This meant that the suitcase had been left. Could it be a bomb I wondered?

I looked away to pretend it wasn't there, and saw a poster from London Transport that said you should always report unattended suitcases. I thought about stopping the train by pulling the communication cord, but we were in a tunnel so that would have been daft. I noticed that nobody else on the train seemed worried so maybe it was OK after all.

I thought I might tell the guard at the next stop, but then the train would have been delayed and I would have been late for my job interview. I decided to wait until I got to Stratford, where I needed to go, and then tell the guard, and anyway there were other people on the train – they could do something if they wanted. But when I got to Stratford I just got off the train and hurried out of the station.'

1 *Diffusion of responsibility* is when a person knows that other people are present so that the responsibility for helping does not fall on him or her alone. Give an example of diffusion of responsibility in the text. (1)   (*MEG, 1993*)

2 *Pluralistic ignorance* is when the inactivity of people misleads everyone into acting as if there is nothing wrong. Give an example of pluralistic ignorance in the text. (1)   (*MEG, 1993*)

3 Some people might have called the behaviour in the text *bystander apathy*, suggesting that the writer did not help because he did not care. However, there are some very good reasons why people don't always help. Describe **three** reasons why people might not help in an emergency. (2 + 2 + 2)   (*MEG, 1993*)

4 Describe **one** other psychological study of bystander behaviour. (5)   (*MEG, 1993*)

5 Suggest **one** way by which London Transport could try to encourage its passengers to help more often. (2)   (*MEG, 1993*)

6 Most of the research on helping behaviour has been conducted in a laboratory environment. Give **one** disadvantage with this method. (2)   (*MEG, 1993*)

7 What is the difference between *altruism* and *helping behaviour*? (1)

8 Give an everyday example of altruistic behaviour. (2)

Chapter 8

Two little boys

A tragic account of two boys in central Europe was described by Koluchova. She told how the mother of the boys died when they were young, and their father remarried a woman who did not like the boys. The boys were brought up in a cellar, with straw instead of a bed, and received very little care. They were often beaten, they had no toys, and were often kept locked in a cellar. They were not discovered by the authorities until they were 7 years old. When they were examined it was found that they could not talk, they could not recognise pictures and they were retarded.

They were fostered by two sisters who offered them a warm and caring environment. Previous research suggested that these children would be unlikely to recover fully, and would remain affected by their early experience all their lives. The boys, however, made steady progress over a number of years, and by the age of fourteen they had developed an average level of intelligence, and appeared to be well adjusted.

1 Give **two** important factors of child care that the boys were deprived of. (2) (*MEG, 1991*)

2 (a) What was the short-term effect of their early upbringing on the boys? (1)
  (b) What was the long-term effect? (1)   (*MEG, 1991*)

3 These children recovered from their experience, but many other studies show how early life experiences have a damaging long-term effect on children. Describe **one** study that shows the long-term damage caused by poor early experience. (5)   (*MEG, 1991*)

4 Why do some children never recover from their early experience? (2)   (*MEG, 1991*)

5 Explain the difference between *deprivation* and *privation*. (2)

6 Most children experience some temporary loss of their attachment figure in early life. Give **one** example from everyday life of when this might occur. (2)

7 Describe **one** way that a parent might reduce any ill effects which might occur. (2)

8 The Ainsworth Strange Situation is a way of measuring *separation anxiety*. Which are the key points when a child will show separation anxiety. (3)

Chapter 9

Source A

Kohlberg investigated moral development by giving individuals a story that had a moral dilemma. An example is a story about a man called Heinz who stole an expensive drug (that he could not afford) for his wife because she would die without it. He became desperate because the chemist would not let him pay for it over a period of time. Kohlberg's participants were asked whether the man was right or wrong to steal the drug and to explain their answer. He analysed the answers and concluded that moral behaviour develops in stages. They are shown below:

Stage of moral reasoning	Moral behaviour is that which:
Pre-conventional morality Stage 1 Stage 2	Avoids punishment. Gains reward.
Conventional morality Stage 3 Stage 4	Gains approval and avoids disapproval of others. Is defined by rigid codes of 'law and order'.
Post-conventional morality Stage 5 Stage 6	Is defined by a 'social contract' generally agreed on for the public good. Is based on abstract ethical principles that determine a person's own moral code.

There is a connection between Kohlberg's stages and age, as shown on the graph below:

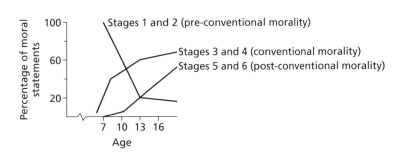

1 Use the graph above to answer the following questions:
   (a) What percentage of 13 year olds gave conventional morality answers? (1)
   (b) How does the percentage of pre-conventional morality statements change with age? (1)
   (c) Which is the most common form of moral reasoning for 13 year olds? (1)

2 Kohlberg used stories that had a moral dilemma. From your knowledge of psychology, describe **one** other way of measuring moral development. (2)

3 In his study it was Kohlberg himself who analysed the answers given by his participants. Why might this be a problem? (2)

4 Outline **one** criticism, other than the one in question 3, that has been made of Kohlberg's theory. (2)

5 Some psychologists suggest that moral behaviour may be learnt as a result of observation and imitation. Choose **one** example of moral behaviour from everyday life and explain how it can be learnt in this way. (3)   *(MEG Higher tier, 1996)*

6 Use the Source to answer this question: What was the moral dilemma for the man whose wife was ill? (2)

7 Kohlberg used the interview method with his participants. Give **one** advantage and **one** disadvantage of this method. (4)

8 Briefly describe **one** other theory of moral development (other than Kohlberg's) that you have studied. (4)   *(MEG Foundation tier, 1996)*

Chapter 10

Something in the Air

Are you among the growing number of people who are weather sensitive? Teachers have claimed for many years that school children are harder to control when it is windy and some people claim that they feel irritable and depressed just before a storm. But now there is evidence to support these claims. Recent research suggests that as many as 30–40% of the population may be sensitive to weather.

But what aspects of the weather causes these changes? One theory is that weather conditions such as lightning and wind cause air electricity to increase and this affects our social behaviour. Research has shown that suicides, accidents and some types of crime increase when the air electricity rises.

1 According to the text, what aspect of the weather affects our behaviour? (1) *(MEG, 1993)*

2 According to the text, what is **one** way that weather affects our behaviour? (1)
        (MEG, 1993)

3 Why would it be difficult to show that weather causes changes in social behaviour? (2)
        (MEG, 1993)

4 (a) Weather is one factor that can cause stress. What is meant by the term *stress*? (2)

   (b) Describe **one** way in which psychologists can measure stress. (2)   *(MEG, 1993)*

5 Describe some of the other factors in the environment which cause stress *(Hint: you might like to describe two or more factors which are known to cause stress, and include relevant studies)* (8)

6 Describe **two** physiological effects of stress. (2 + 2)   *(MEG, 1993)*

Chapter 11

A GCSE Psychology student carried out a field study into superstitious behaviour. The student's definition of superstitious behaviour was choosing to walk round a ladder instead of going straight under it.

The student wanted to find out if young people were more superstitious than older people. The student had noticed an empty ladder left behind by some building workers. The ladder was standing on a wide pavement and resting against the wall. The student observed for one hour and recorded whether or not people walking along the pavement:

(i)   carried on walking straight under the ladder, or

(ii) moved to the side to walk round the ladder to continue their journey.

The record sheet of the student is shown below.

	Walked round the ladder	Walked under the ladder
Young people	11111 11111 11111 11111 11111 11111	11111 11111 11111 11111 11111 11111
Older people	11111 11111	11111 11111 11111 11111 11111 11111

1 What was the aim of this study? (1)

2 Use the information in the record sheet to complete the following sentences with the correct numbers.

(a) ...... young people walked under the ladder out of a total of ...... young people. (1)

(b) ...... older people walked round the ladder out of a total of .... older people. (1)

3 Calculate the percentages and complete the table below. (2)

	Percentage who walked round the ladder	Percentage who walked under the ladder
Young people		
Older people		

4 (a) What conclusion can the student draw from the results of this study about the behaviour of the people the student observed? (1)

(b) Explain why the above results cannot be used to predict the superstitious behaviour of **all** young people. (2)

5 The student decided to record only the behaviour of people walking on their own. Give an explanation for this decision. (2)

6 What is a field study? (1)

7 Which **one** of the following is the most accurate statement about a well-designed field study?

All variables can be controlled. ☐

Cause and effect can be determined. ☐

The results can be generalised. ☐ (1)

8 The people in this study did not give their consent to have their behaviour recorded. Do you think this ethical issue should have prevented the student from carrying out this study? Explain your answer. (2)

9 Another student in the same psychology group decided to investigate superstitious behaviour by using a questionnaire. The student piloted the questionnaire. How should this have been done? (2)

10 Explain **one** advantage and **one** disadvantage of studying superstitious behaviour using a questionnaire method rather than a field study method. (2 + 2)   (*NEAB, 1993*)

Answers to exam questions

Most answers can be marked using the following mark scheme:

★ Questions or part questions worth 2 marks: *name* the problem/method/factor (*1 mark*) and *describe* it (*1 mark*).

★ Questions for 3 marks, either:
- Name the factor (*1 mark*), describe it (*2 marks*).
- An attempt (*1 mark*), an answer that makes sense (*2–3 marks*).

★ Questions for 4 or 5 marks: Description of a study. All exam boards place much emphasis on familiarity with empirical evidence, 'studies'. There are often questions asking you to 'describe a study'. For full marks this should include:
- the names of the researchers,
- the aim,
- some details of the method,
- the results
- the conclusion, the meaning of the results.

It is not necessary to give the date of the research, the exact results, participant details or even criticisms. The mark scheme for such questions is:
1–2 marks: anecdotal evidence; 3–4/5 marks: accurate description. (max. 4/5)

★ Questions for 6 or 9 marks: Essays
1–2 or 1–3 marks: muddled or inaccurate description of theory/research, list of factors;
3–4 or 4–6 marks: accurate but brief description, examples of results;
5–6 or 7–9 marks: detailed and accurate description, ethical or practical problems.
(Extra marks may be given for a clear and coherent answer.)

Chapter 1

1 Bandura: Experiment; Freud: Case study; Piaget: Clinical interview, observation.
2 marks each. (max. 6)

2 Bandura: Distress to participants (ethical), children particularly susceptible to demand characteristics (practical).
Freud: Invasion of privacy (ethical), limited sample (practical).
Piaget: Demand characteristics, limited sample (practical).
2 marks each. (max. 4)

3 The question as to whether behaviour is determined by inherited/innate factors or by experience/environment. Additional detail can be given with reference to a particular area of study, such as perception or intelligence. Some mention could be made about whether the question is either/or or a bit of both. (max. 5)

4 Bandura: Social learning theory, reinforcement, imitation and modelling.
Freud: Biological forces predispose children to particular kinds of learning at different stages. Identification with parents and authority figures is important.
Piaget: Learning depends on maturation and experience, the processes of assimilation, accommodation and equilibrium. (max. 5)

Chapter 2

1 (iii) interpretation of sensory information. (max. 1)

2 (a) Group A: Face X, Group B: Face Y. (max. 1)
(b) The larger face (X) is closer. If the circle is a coin it also must be closer to you and therefore to face X. This shows how distance perception draws on relative size.
1 mark for explanation, 2 marks for explanation of distance perception and relative size. (max. 3)

3 (a) Müller-Lyer. (max. 1)

(b) The line with the ingoing fins looks like the corner of a building, and therefore is in some sense further away (buildings are more distant objects). The line with the outgoing fins looks like the corner of a room, a near object. The same retinal image, created by a more distant object should represent a longer line. (max. 3)

4 For example: Segall *et al.* (max. 5)

5 (a) The fact that they 'trick' the perceptual system and are invented drawings means they are not related to normal perceptual processes. (max. 2)

(b) For example: No. Visual illusions are normal, relatively consistent phenomena, subject to the same rules as everything else we perceive (*2 marks*). They are unconscious over-extensions of the simple rules of perception (*2 marks*). (max. 4)

Chapter 3

1 A relatively permanent change in behaviour, the effects of experience.
1 mark: Change or experience mentioned; 1 mark: Relatively permanent or the equivalent. (max. 2)

2 (a) There was little difference between ex-sailors and students when the number of rings was high or low (*1 mark*), but around the 100 rings per minute, the ex-sailors had much increased heart rates (*2 marks*). (max. 3)

(b) The bell rung at a particular frequency is the CS (*1 mark*), the sound of guns and bombs is the UCS (*1 mark*), heart rate is the UCR (*1 mark*). The soldiers come to associate the particular bell ring with the sounds of guns and bombs (*1 mark*) so that the bell sound alone leads to a fear response (increased heart rate, CR) (*1 mark*). (max. 5)

(c) Once the conditioned response is learned (fear response to the bell) it occurs in response to other similar stimuli (*2 marks*), in this case the bell ringing at lower or higher frequencies (*1 mark*). (max. 3)

3 (a) The wearer receives an aversive stimulus (*1 mark*) <u>after</u> doing the wrong thing (*1 mark*). (max. 2)

(b) For example: may produce hostility and a desire to rebel, wearer may get used to the punishment. (*1 mark if muddled or inaccurate*). (max. 2)

(c) For example: use positive reinforcement (*1 mark*) such as bonus pay for extra work (*2 marks*) OR negative reinforcement (*1 mark*) such as pay deducted for poor work (*2 marks*). (max. 3)

Chapter 4

1 Group 1 recalled more than group 2. (max. 1)

2 Memory is improved (*1 mark*) by organising information (*1 mark*) relevantly or meaningfully (*1 mark*). (max.3)

3 For example: order, familiarity, length. (max.1)

4 Method of Loci: for each item form a strong visual image (*1 mark*) and then place each item (*1 mark*) along a familiar route (*1 mark*). To recall the list you walk along the route (*1 mark*). OR Peg Word System: pair each word (*1 mark*) with an already known list (*1 mark*), for example the list one-bun, two-shoe, three-tree: Associate egg with bun, carrots with shoe, bread with tree by forming an image of the pair (*1 mark*). To recall the list count 1, 2, 3 etc. (*1 mark*). (max. 4)

5 For example: her motivation to remember, emotional involvement.
Psychological factors only. (max. 2)

6 For example: the language they use, OR the cues they provide. Evidence, for example: Loftus, Loftus *et al.*, Carmichael *et al.*
2 marks for the way memory affected; 2 marks for evidence. (max. 4)

7 For example: Abernethy, Godden and Baddeley. (max. 5)

Chapter 5

1 For example, the social perception of individuals on the basis of group membership or physical characteristics, ignoring personal characteristics. Is usually inaccurate and resistant to change. *1–2 marks for an answer which shows limited knowledge, 3–4 marks for increasing accuracy and knowledge.* (max 4)

2 An example of a stereotype: old people are hard of hearing. The effects could be that you speak more loudly to old people, you talk about them behind their backs, you think they are dumber. *1 mark for an example, a further 1–2 marks for a brief or simple explanation of its affect on behaviour, plus a further 1 mark for a full explanation.* (max. 4)

3 Prejudice is the attitude, discrimination is the behaviour. *1–3 marks for limited knowledge of prejudice or discrimination, 4–6 marks for either both terms described with partial accuracy or one term described in detail, 7–8 marks for both terms described with increasing accuracy.* (max. 8)

4 For example: increasing social contact, challenging stereotypes, promoting positive images or reducing the need for ego defence. *1–3 marks for some understanding of discrimination, 4–6 marks for some effects plus a brief description of a means of reduction, 7–9 marks for some reference to psychological research, 10-14 marks for an increasingly accurate answer which is evidently based on psychology.* (max. 14)

Chapter 6

1 When a participant worked within a group (*1 mark*) their answers were very similar (*1 mark*). (max. 2)

2 (a) For example: a change in opinions and behaviour (*1 mark*) as a result of group pressure (*1 mark*). (max. 2)
  (b) For example: participants may have been conforming because the situation was ambiguous, or they may have been trying to please the experimenter. (max. 2)

3 Internalisation. (max. 1)

4 Compliance means going along with the behaviour of others (*1 mark*) but does not involve an internal change of opinion (*1 mark*) whereas internalisation means that your opinions have also changed (*1 mark*). (max. 3)

5 For example: Milgram, Hofling *et al.*, Gamson *et al.* (max. 5)

6 (a) For example: Deindividuation, gradual changes, size of group, fear of dissent, individual differences. (*1 mark each*) (max. 2)
  (b) Relevant point from study (*1 mark*), link with everyday situation (*2 marks*).

Chapter 7

1 There were other people on the train who could do something. (max. 1)

2 Nobody else was worried. (max. 1)

3 For example: Lack of personal responsibility, lack of attention, ambiguity, fear of doing the wrong thing, personal danger, time consuming. (*2 marks each reason*) (max. 6)

4 For example: Darley and Latané, Clark and Word, Piliavin *et al.* (max. 5)

5 For example: Posters (*1 mark*) showing helpful behaviour (*1 mark*), OR reward scheme (*1 mark*) for good Samaritans (*1 mark*). *One answer plus explanation.* (max. 2)

6 For example: Lack of realism. (max. 2)

7 Altruism involves some risk to the altruist, which is not the case with helping behaviour. (max. 1)

8 For example: Saving a drowning person (*1 mark*) which has the risk of drowning yourself (*1 mark*). (max. 2)

Chapter 8

1 For example: Physical care, mental stimulation, emotional stimulation. (*1 mark each*) (max. 2)

2 (a) They could not talk/recognise pictures/they were retarded. (max. 1)
  (b) They recovered reasonably, had average intelligence, appeared well adjusted. (max. 1)

3 For example: Harlow, Hodges and Tizard, Bowlby. *The study must show long-term effects.* (max. 5)

4 For example: Remedial help comes too late, not offered appropriate emotional care. (max. 2)

5 Privation is the total lack of attachment (*1 mark*) whereas deprivation is the breaking of attachment bonds (*1 mark*). (max. 2)

6 For example: A short stay in hospital, childcare arrangement while mother works, visit to grandparents while parents on holiday. (max. 2)

7 For example: when together with child give quality time, explain arrangement to child, give child something from home to take with them. (max. 2)

8 When the parent leaves (*1 mark*) and when the parent returns (*1 mark*).
3 marks for having both right. (max. 3)

Chapter 9

1 (a) About 55–57% (*1 mark*). (max. 1)
   (b It increases from zero at age 7 to 40% at age 16. *(1 mark).* (max. 1)
   (c) Conventional. *(1 mark).* (max. 1)

2 For example, Piaget's game of marbles or moral stories. *1 mark for naming plus 1 mark for describing.* (max. 2)

3 Interviewer bias influencing his interpretations. *1 mark for problem stated plus 1 mark for some detail.* (max. 2)

4 For example, gender bias, culture bias, age bias to questions, over idealistic. *1 mark for problem stated plus 1 mark for some detail.* (max. 2)

5 An example of moral behaviour: not telling a lie. *(1 mark)* (max. 1)

   Explanation: could be learned through imitation of parents. *1 mark for limited response plus 1 mark for detail.* (max. 2)

6 Whether to steal the drug. *(2 marks)* (max. 2)

7 Advantage: for example, access to information not available from observation. *(2 marks)* (max. 2)
   Disadvantage: for example, interviewer bias, dishonesty, inconsistency. *(2 marks)* (max. 2)

8 For example, Piaget or learning theory. *1–2 marks for muddled or inaccurate description, 3–4 marks for increasingly accurate and detailed description.* (max. 4)

Chapter 10

1 Increase in air electricity. (max. 1)

2 Increased suicides, accidents or some types of crime. (max. 1)

3 Can't control the weather (*1 mark*) therefore can't be certain that observed effects due to weather (*1 mark*). (max. 2)

4 (a) A state of psychological tension (*1 mark*) produced by physical or psychological pressure (*1 mark*). (max. 2)
   (b) For example: Self-report, experiment (put participant under stress and observe behaviour), size of adrenal gland, GSR. *One method only plus description.* (max. 2)

5 For example: Noise (Glass *et al.*), overcrowding (Calhoun), pollution, poor architecture. *1–4 marks: 2 or more factors described; 5–8 marks: supported with relevant studies.* (max. 8)

6 For example: Physiological exhaustion, reduced immune response, ulcers. *(2 marks each, name and describe)* (max. 4)

Chapter 11

1 To see if age affected superstitious behaviour OR to see if young people were more superstitious than older people. (max. 1)

2 (a) 30 out of 60. (max. 1)
   (b) 30 out of 40. (max. 1)

3

50%	50%
25%	75%

2 marks if all 4 right, 1 mark if 2 or 3 right. (max. 2)

4 (a) Young people are different/more superstitious than older people. (max. 1)
(b) For example: A small sample may be biased, can't generalise to all young people, there are different kinds of superstitious behaviour. (max. 2)

5 For example: Each person in a group may not actually make the decision of which way to go themselves, difficulty in recording large numbers could lead to inaccuracy. (max. 2)

6 A study conducted in a natural environment. (max. 1)

7 The results can be generalised. (max. 1)

8 For example: Yes (invasion of privacy, no informed consent) OR no (not harmful, anonymous therefore no threat to privacy). *1 answer only.* (max. 2)

9 For example: Write out the questions, give to a similar sample as intended to use later, check how well the respondents understood the questions. (*1 mark each*) (max. 2)

10 Advantage: Informed consent (ethical), or more information (practical).
Disadvantage: respondents may not tell truth (practical), artificial.
(*2 marks each*) (max. 4)

Answers to quick tests

Quick test 1.1

1 The question whether behaviour is determined by genetic/inherited factors or a product of experience/the environment.
2 The scientific study of behaviour (and experience).
3 Any physiological system: muscles, blood, hormones, nerves, brain and also genetic factors.
4 The mind or mental processes.
5 The focus is on behaviour rather than underlying causes.
6 Cognitive.
7 Humanism.
8 The study of behaviour in terms of its adaptive value and using naturalistic observation.
9 Psychodynamic and developmental.
10 The scientific method is a general approach to all research whereas an experiment is a highly controlled method of conducting research.

Quick test 2.1

1 Yes.
2 Photoreceptors.
3 The nerve fibres from the retina collect inside the eye and have to pass through the retina to reach the brain. The point where the retina is holed is the blind spot.
4 The optic chiasma.
5 The right visual field from both the right and left eyes.
6 A stationary or moving dot, direction of movement.
7 Some depth is perceived using monocular cues such as relative size, linear perspective, texture gradient.
8 The difference between the views seen by each eye.

9 The illusion created when stationary lights appear to move if the distance between the lights and the timing is right.
10 Cinema or television.

Quick test 2.2

1 Perceptions are based on sensations. Sensations are an unaltered record. Perceptions are constructed from this raw data with the help of other factors such as expectations, prior experience, etc.
2 Figure/ground., similarity, proximity, closure, continuity.
3 Visual constancy refers to the process of maintaining the same perception despite changing retinal images.
4 Shape, brightness, colour, size and depth.
5 Perceptual set.
6 You have no objects to use for comparison to estimate distance.
7 A picture which has more than one interpretation.
8 They show how expectations can alter what image you see.
9 An object which has positive emotional significance might be seen as larger, or if it has negative emotional significance it is less likely to be perceived.
10 Perception based entirely on sensory data rather than influenced by perceptual set.

Quick test 2.3

1 For example: difficult to test responses, prone to experimenter effects, immobile therefore can't easily assess responsiveness.

2 Inherited, present not just from birth.

3 They can tell what they are experiencing.

4 They do not develop the ability to see horizontal lines.

5 For example: misinterpretation of language or practices, cultural bias, limited sample.

Quick test 3.1

1 Moro, Babinski, grasping, rooting, stepping, sucking.

2 An association between a stimulus and a response which occurs after a single presentation of that stimulus. For example, a dog bite, rat learning to avoid poison.

3 Latent learning.

4 For example: speed or accuracy in problem solving, such as in a maze, obtaining food OR avoidance of an aversive stimulus.

Quick test 3.2

1 Social learning theory introduced cognitive factors, the notion that learning can be achieved through observation and imitation rather than just direct reinforcement.

2 Vicariously, by observing someone else being rewarded or punished for a particular behaviour.

3 For example: similarity (same sex, same age), status.

4 The concept of identification with a role model.

5 For example: lacks realism, artificial.

Quick test 3.3

1 A innate tendency to a particular kind of learning which takes place during a critical or sensitive period, occurs rapidly and has a lasting effect.

2 For example: bird song, most parenting behaviours. Any behaviour which is inherited, found even in individuals reared in isolation, found in all members of the species.

3 Keeps animal close to caretaker for food and protection.

4 The study of behaviour in its natural environment. Explaining behaviour in terms of its adaptive or survival value.

5 Helps chances of survival. If an animal had to learn everything it would take a long time.

6 The sign stimulus is a signal which triggers an instinctive response, a fixed action pattern is an innate or partly learned response to a sign stimulus.

7 For example: a goose's egg, the red spot on a herring gull's beak, red underbelly of male stickleback.

8 Important variables can be controlled to determine cause and effect.

9 Animals are seen in their natural setting, where their behaviour is normal rather than altered by artificial, laboratory conditions.

10 (a) A biologically-determined period of time during which an animal is exclusively receptive to certain changes.

(b) For example: a bird imprinting on the first thing it sees on hatching.

Quick test 4.1

1 (a) Primacy is the first thing you heard, recency is the most recent.

(b) Coding (acoustic versus semantic), duration (a few seconds versus a lifetime), capacity (less than seven chunks versus infinite), controlled by different areas of the brain (evidence from brain damage).

2 A technique for improving your memory.

3 For example: repetition, organisation, cues, loci system, keyword system, abbreviations, peg word system.

4 Context dependent remembering or forgetting.

5 Imagery helps connect or organise pieces of information in memory and this helps memory recall.

6 (a) Any group of letters devoid of meaning.

(b) Advantage: for example, not influenced by previous experience, easy to use.

Disadvantage: for example, not typical of the kind of thing people use their memory for, may not reflect how we use memory in everyday life.

7 Motivated forgetting, because it hurts and they'd rather not go.

8 For example: leading questions, emotional state at the time of the incident leads to forgetting, memory is a reconstruction biased by expectations, just because you were there doesn't mean you saw everything, gender or race bias.

9 For example: set, learning, expectation, motivation, language.

10 For example: free recall, recognition, paired-associate learning.

Quick test 4.2

1 1-C, 2-D, 3-A, 4-B, 5-E.

2 (a) An algorithm is a set of instructions which guarantees a solution, a recipe for success. A heuristic is a set of procedures which facilitate problem-solving, a tool box for solving problems.

(b) A schema is a structured concept. Scripts are schema about events, they are plans for action. Both are based on experience, and used to generate future expectations and behaviour.

3 For example: assimilation and accommodation, prototype formation, hypothesis testing.

4 Rigidity of thought, our tendency to view objects as serving only the function for which they are commonly used.

5 The scientific method is the process of providing an answer (or a theory) for a problem rather than generating many novel ideas.

6 A problem which requires novel solutions. For example: where to go on holiday, doing creative subjects at school/college, marketing, how to think of an answer for this question.

7 For example, knowing exactly what a person is thinking, being sure that two people are using the same problem solving method when they describe them the same.

8 For example: computers are logical, lack emotion.

9 Face validity (questions look like they test creativity), predictive validity (people who do well are more likely to be artistic).

10 A computer program written by Newell and Simon to solve heuristic problems and illustrate one kind of human problem solving.

Quick test 4.3

1 Monozygotic twins came from the same egg and are identical genetically. Dizygotic twins came from separate eggs and are as close genetically as any brother or sister.

2 For example: MZ twins are usually very small samples, MZ twins are not identical because of different intrauterine experiences even before birth, twins reared apart often still have similar environments (e.g. the same school and neighbourhood, they may not have been separated for a suitably long period).

3 For example: famial studies (Bouchard and McGue), adoption studies (Skodak and Skeels), social class (Sameroff *et al.*), birth order (Zajonc and Markus), intervention programmes (Lazar and Darlington).

4 For example: genes, diet, educational background or social class of parents, quality of home and school stimulation.

5 For example: Operation Headstart (initial gains which soon disappeared in terms of IQ and language, in adolescence differences were again apparent probably due to more positive attitudes towards education).

6 Intelligence quotient: mental age multiplied by chronological age, divided by 100.

7 The extent to which a test actually represents a person's intellectual abilities.

8 For example: personal factors on the day, temperature in the room, tester bias, culture bias.

9 For example: they can't take written tests, more open to suggestion from tester, can't be tested on verbal items.

10 For example, developing special intervention programmes, identifying children from enriched backgrounds as those who will succeed.

Quick test 4.4

1 (a) Object permanence, reflex activities (e.g. sucking), repetitive motions (e.g. kicking).
   (b) Conservation, moral relativity, non-adult approaches to problem solving
   (c) Logical, abstract thought, idealism, systematic thinking.

2 Approximately 9 months.

3 The inability to see things from another person's point of view.

4 For example: asking child if two displays of counters are the same, changing the array and asking again if they are the same. Also done with volume (water in a beaker), mass (balls of clay).

5 At the right time (when the child is 'ready') provide the opportunity to develop new modes of thinking by asking questions and supplying appropriate toys/activities.

6 It means that they only take on new information processes when they are ready. They discover knowledge for themselves, assimilating and accommodating it.

7 (a) Variant structures change as a child gets older, invariant structures are present throughout life.
   (b) Assimilation is the process of placing new information within existing schema. Accommodation is the process of modifying existing schema to fit new information which does not otherwise fit.
   (c) Concrete thinking is not abstract, systematic or logical. Formal thinking is.

8 It made the task seem more understandable. In Piaget's original experiment the child might give a different answer the second time because it made sense, otherwise why did the experimenter change the display?

9 (a) Pre-operational.
   (b) Animism, make-believe play.
   (c) For example: egocentric thought, centration, moral realism.

10 Enactive, iconic and symbolic modes.

Quick test 4.5

1 For example: child bored, doesn't pay attention, has got what they wanted anyway using incorrect language.

2 For example: using 'motherese', positive reinforcement, parental speech characteristics such as echoic responses, framing, expansion. Could mention studies which show effects, for example: Cazden.

3 Chomsky.

4 For example: vowels, syllables, nouns, verbs.

5 (a) The rules of language.
   (b) Speech using only the key words combined using grammar so that meaning is conveyed.
   (c) A biologically-determined period of time during which the organism is exclusively

receptive to certain changes. After this period learning of the particular behaviour cannot take place.

6 For grammar, but not for vocabulary or a more general communication system.

7 Pre-linguistic (cooing, turn-taking, babbling, echolalia, gestures), one word utterances (words, holophrases), two-word utterances (pivot grammar, telegraphic speech), grammar (over-generalising, overextension, underextension, pragmatics).

8 When a rule is applied incorrectly the child cannot be imitating something they have heard but must be generating their own words using grammar.

9 For example: if animals can learn language then this suggests that the nativist position is wrong, as a means of getting insight into another world, for the same reason as all scientific work: curiosity.

10 For example: what then will happen to them, what right have we got to interfere with animals in this way? Criticism can be either practical or ethical. Agreement or disagreement should be based on weighing ends (what has been learnt) against means (the criticism you have made).

Quick test 5.1

1 The tendency for the impression you form to be influenced by one outstanding trait, it is assumed that the person possesses all positive or negative traits, the tendency for the overall good or bad impression to influence perception of all character traits.

2 For example: primacy, recency, centrality, kind of signal (verbal or nonverbal), inconsistent information, the traits you possess yourself.

3 Bias.

4 Non-linguistic behaviours which can nevertheless be vocal. For example: facial expression, sighs, position of the body.

5 Psychologists propose theories of personality, these are explicit theories. Each individual also holds expectations about people (such as what other traits an intelligent person is likely to have). These are implicit theories.

6 Concepts or stereotypes held about people or things, a structured cluster of concepts.

7 Gatekeepers control the flow of information, so affecting what you know and particularly your stereotypes.

8 The hypothesis that the media over-report certain crimes, therefore giving people the impression that they are more common than they actually are.

9 For example: your behaviour such as accent, manners (Dion *et al.*), first impressions (Luchins), nonverbal behaviours indicate confidence (Leathers).

Quick test 5.2

1 For example: women are better cooks, men are more intelligent.

2 For example: through increased contact, advertising campaigns, direct teaching.

3 People hold gender stereotypes, assuming that women do inferior, feminine jobs.

4 Prejudice against sex or gender.

5 They simplify the world, reducing it to manageable proportions.

Quick test 5.3

1 He organised cooperative activities such as camping, making meals or cooking, they had t-shirts and caps with the group name on them.

2 For example: lack of informed consent of the participants themselves, distress to participants.

3 Discrimination is behaviour arising from a prejudice. Prejudice is a biased attitude towards a group.

4 For example: rigid cognitive style, favourable self-image, traditionalist, lack of interest in psychology.

5 People conform to group norms, one of which may be to hold certain prejudices.

Quick test 5.4

1 For example: Increased contact between men and women in joint activities, advertising campaigns, legislation regarding employment.

2 They encourage people to cooperate over a task which is mutually beneficial.

3 A classroom method where each member of a group has a small part of a group project to complete. At the end each member must tell the rest of the group what they have found out and then they are all tested on the project. Each member has a piece of the jigsaw which is necessary to all group members.

4 For example: prejudices are deeply rooted in human nature and individual personalities, they are an important part of group membership and increase the self-esteem of members, people are reluctant to change attitudes, increased contact may result in increased hostility, attitudes will not change if competition over scarce resources persists.

5 For example: using an attitude survey before and after to assess hostility and/or liking, assessing self-esteem or academic performance of minority groups, observing behaviour in a naturalistic setting of members from different groups.

Quick test 6.1

1 Conformity.
2 Ingrational conformity.

3 For example: a group larger than three, size of majority opinion, fear of seeming the odd one out, a conformist personality, when you are new to a group and concerned with being accepted, anonymity.

4 Advantage: for example, in some situations there is no right behaviour but group norms are a means of determining this, a means of expressing group membership and establishing social contact. Disadvantage: for example, may treat outgroup members unreasonably, may behave in a different manner from how you would on your own.

5 Because information is lacking (informational social influence).

6 For example: lack of realism, demand characteristics, influence of authority figure, problem of generalising the results, ethics.

7 For example: a soldiers life might depend on it, a small child crossing the road.

8 For example: distress to subjects, deception, informed consent.

9 Losing a sense of individuality, such as wearing a uniform or a mask.

10 It is important to distinguish between those group processes which are related to our culture and those which may be basic to human nature. Cross-cultural research is one way of discovering universal behaviours.

Quick test 6.2

1 Nondominant responses.

2 In coaction two people are performing side-by-side. This results in improved quantity rather than quality.

3 For example: performing on stage to a real audience rather than just rehearsing, cyclists performance in a cycle race rather than just practising.

4 Social inhibition and social loafing.

5 For example: making each person's work identifiable, increasing competition between workers, offering rates for piece work, making opportunities for workers to evaluate their own work.

Quick test 6.3

1 For example: increases conformity, reduces individuality and reference to personal beliefs, others treat the recruit as a policeman.

2 For example: contact with other people decreases loneliness, increased arousal in pleasant circumstances heightens mood.

3 For example: create more open space with mirrors or larger aisles, create pleasant atmosphere with music/lighting/decoration, increase shoppers sense of control.

4 For example: the degree of control we feel we have, the extent to which we are free to come and go in the crowded situation, individual

differences in experiencing arousal or coping with stress.

5 For example: the culture you live in, your age or gender, characteristics of the other person, where you are (indoors or outdoors).

Quick test 7.1

1 It is a form of ritualised aggression where opponents walk side-by-side. This enables them to assess each other's size and condition.

2 For example: mating, territory, food.

3 For example: good for the survival of the species as a whole, even the victor might be injured, could be attacked by a predator while fighting.

4 For example: less recognition of appeasement signals, more learnt/cultural influences, human behaviour less innately controlled.

5 (a) For example: give them hormones, remove their genitals, change their diet.
  (b) For example: rewards for passivity, non-violent models on TV, direct teaching about nonviolence.

Quick test 7.2

1 Behaviour which benefits another at a possible risk to the altruist.

2 For example: performing prosocial acts (acting as a good model), telling their children (direct instruction), having warm relationships with their children (learning empathy).

3 For example: social norms, imitating the behaviour of others, direct instruction.

4 For example: diffusion of responsibility, ambiguous or novel situations where other people define the norms of behaviour, fear of others thinking they're doing it wrong, or thinking that it's your fault.

5 For example: the emergency doesn't seem serious enough, doesn't notice any emergency, danger to self.

6 Yes, even though it was not conducted in the laboratory the researchers controlled an independent variable (the behaviour of the 'victim') and observed the effect on a dependent variable (the behaviour of passengers).

7 For example: lack of consent, distress to participants, no right to withdraw, participants not informed of results.

8 For example: using a stooge to create an emergency and observing what the participant does to help, questionnaire.

9 For example: can't generalise to real world, demand characteristics.

10 (i) C (ii) B

Quick test 8.1

1 A close, emotional two-way bond between two people that is lasting. It ensures safety and food

for an infant, and is a basis for later emotional relationships.

2 Where the behaviour of two people is coordinated, each partner's behaviour leads to a response.

3 For example: lack of emotional sensitivity, prolonged separation, poor quality rather than quantity of care, child-rearing style (e.g. not warm, loving, accepting).

4 For example: to avoid breaking the attachment bond, to help the healthy emotional development of the child.

5 For example: isolating causal factors because the data is often correlational, following the children over time to observe long term effects. Can be overcome, for example: using matched samples, setting up a longitudinal study with large numbers of children.

Quick test 8.2

1 A's belief about B affects A's behaviour (e.g. encouragement), such expectations alter B's beliefs about himself thus altering his behaviour, B's behaviour now confirms A's original beliefs.

2 For example: believing a bank is about to collapse, all customers withdraw their money thereby bringing about the bank's collapse; or thinking that someone else thinks you're attractive makes you behave more confidently thus becoming more attractive.

3 For example: teachers expect middle-class children to do better, peer group pressure leads to forming positive or negative attitudes towards school and achievement, teaching style, the teacher as a model.

4 Such labels convey a stereotype of that group. Stereotypes generate expectations. The self-fulfilling prophecy explains how expectations may affect someone else's behaviour by altering their self-concept.

5 For example: thinking up a new label, encouraging more integration in normal activities, raising the image through high profile activities.

Quick test 8.3

1 A trait is basically an adjective. It is a tendency to act in a particular way.

2 Introverts have higher levels of cortical arousal and are able to concentrate for longer periods of time without rests.

3 Looks at personality from the point of view of subjective experience. An idiographic approach.

4 The id.

5 During the phallic stage as a result of the child overcoming the Oedipus complex through identification with the same sex parent.

6 We all generate hypotheses or expectations, test them against reality and modify them. This is the same process as the scientific method.

7 An idiographic approach.

8 (a) Giving love and approval to another even though their behaviour may not always meet expectations.

(b) It gives the child confidence leading to high self-esteem and self-acceptance. This allows for healthy personality development.

9 The self is the impression you have of yourself now, the ideal self is the person you would like to be.

10 For example: assumes that normal behaviour is developed in the same way that abnormal, not reasonable to generalise from a biased sample.

Quick test 8.4

1 For example: activity level, emotionality, soothability, fearfulness, sociability.

2 For example: active, irregular, irritable, finds newness distressing, responds to newness by withdrawing or being slow to adapt.

3 It assumes that the children's behaviour is entirely determined by nature, whereas they have had experiences in the womb and just after birth which may already have affected their behaviour.

4 The tendency to withdraw from unfamiliar people or situations.

5 Parents either are able to manage the child's temperament, in which case possible problems are minimised, or there is a clash and problems are made worse.

Quick test 9.1

1 The process by which a child learns the social values, norms and roles of their culture.

2 As emotions develop, a child comes to understand that other people have emotions too. In other words, they learn empathy. Without this, a person has no reason to consider the feelings of another.

3 For example: could be effective way of shaping behaviour, can act as positive reinforcement through attention, may be counterproductive because increases resentment, child may learn to tolerate.

4 For example: using the concept of punishment, outlining stages of development, emphasising self-control.

5 The phallic stage.

6 Piaget's theory assumes that moral development, like cognitive development, is linked to maturation. Freud's theory was also based on appropriate ages but emphasised the emotional side and identification with parents.

7 The 5-year-old is heteronomous whereas the older child should have become autonomous. Moral absolutes, rules from a higher authority, making up for any damage done (atonement) and importance of consequence versus mutually agreed rules, reciprocity and importance of intentions.

8 For example: younger children may not understand them, they demand that the reader make certain assumptions, they may not be relevant to the sample.

9 For example: peers act as models and reinforcers, friendship is important in developing empathy and a moral understanding.

10 Theoretically moral behaviour should be based on moral principles. In reality people often act for other reasons such as convenience or they use different kinds of morals in different situations.

Quick test 9.2

1 For example: women used to sell washing powder (assumes that only women are interested), men used in ads about gardening or DIY.

2 For example: change the stereotypes used on TV, offer different models to imitate, direct instruction about equality and stereotypes.

3 The stage when a child realises that their gender is fixed.

4 For example: Margaret Mead found that men and women in different societies performed different sex roles. This suggests that such roles are not innate but culturally determined.

5 For example: parents act as models, positively and negatively reinforce sex-appropriate and inappropriate behaviours, consistency of reinforcement, their relationship with the child will determine whether the child wishes to identify and imitate their behaviour, parental expectations, the toys they provide.

6 Having both masculine and feminine characteristics.

7 The Oedipus conflict: in the phallic stage young boy loves mother, jealous of father, but father is more powerful, therefore feared. Resolution leads to identifying with rival, the father, and taking on appropriate gender behaviour.

8 For example: media use stereotypes to paint a more complex picture from a minimum of information, people also prefer information which is consistent with their stereotypes (confirmatory bias). These stereotypes act as models which readers/watchers imitate, particularly when they are rewarded.

9 For example: ability to be good parents, intelligence, school achievement, empathy. The question says 'might' therefore only innate differences should be excluded.

10 Men are born with better visual spatial ability OR people expect that men are better and these expectations encourage them to develop such an ability.

Quick test 9.3

1 People select partners whose physical attractiveness matches that of their own. Balance may be achieved by other factors such as status.

2 For example: choice of marriage partner, sociogram.

3 For example: it's rewarding and comforting to spend time with people who support your attitudes, it increases your sense of self-esteem.

4 Children change from friendship based on doing things to more emotional relationships involving empathy and confidences.

5 For example: proximity, familiarity, shared activities.

Quick test 9.4

1 Firm control, plus explaining why a behaviour is wrong, emphasises child as active agent rather than an obedient one.

2 For example: an authoritative style, warm and close family relationships, emotional responsiveness, able to meet child's emotional and intellectual needs, consistent behaviour from parents.

3 For example: acting as models, positive and negative reinforcement, behaviour shaping, identification with parents' attitudes, direct instruction.

Quick test 10.1

1 For example: they haven't learned certain expressions, they lack empathy for other people's emotions (egocentric).

2 For example: increased or decreased heart rate, blood pressure and respiration, changes in sweat production, release of adrenalin.

3 Galvanic skin response, indicating increased electrical conductivity in the skin due to sweating. Emotion causes ANS arousal. ANS arousal leads to sweating. Therefore an increased GSR indicates raised level of emotion.

4 B → A → C

5 For example: Schachter and Singer, Dutton and Aron.

6 The subjective experience of emotion is due to either specific arousal states (James-Lange) OR general arousal plus cognitive cues (Cognitive Labelling).

Quick test 10.2

1 For example: noise, lack of control, unpredictability.

2 For example: death of spouse or close family member, divorce, changing jobs, moving house.

3 For example: the scale muddles different kinds of events, it does not allow for individual differences in coping.

4 For example: loss of concentration, impairment on cognitive tasks, feelings of depression or irritability, anger and aggression, anxiety.

5 It prepares an organism for situations which threaten well-being by increasing arousal for fight or flight.

6 For example: some people perform better in exams or in a public competition, stress increases concentration and enhances performance.

7 (a) Alarm reaction, resistance, exhaustion.

(b) The body's resources are depleted, particularly the adrenal gland. This leaves the individual vulnerable to infection.

8 Performance increases up to a point, over that it decreases. There is an optimum level of arousal.

9 It reduces it.

10 For example: relaxation, physical exercise, catharsis, social support.

Quick test 10.3

1 For example: don't know what they could do before damage occurred, difficult to know the exact nature and extent of the injury, the process of damage is traumatic which itself could lead to changes in behaviour.

2 For example: they are shown an object in their left visual field but cannot say what it is though they can recognise it with either hand.

3 A kind of explanation which reduces behaviour to the simplest, smallest units. For example: biological reductionism explains behaviour in terms of nervous impulses and hormones.

4 The cerebral hemispheres are specialised for performing different types of tasks.

5 For example: sensations, some motor movements, vision, hearing.

Quick test 11.1

1 For example: social desirability bias, people don't know what they think, and/or they don't tell the truth, method relies on linguistic competence, father may overestimate his activity.

2 For example: human behaviour more complex and less innate, ethical objections such as can't give consent.

3 An experiment enables a cause and effect to be identified. Experiments can be realistic when conducted in the field or the study of naturally occurring variables.

4 Advantage: for example, reduces ethical objections, good for working with children or animals, more naturalistic/realistic, avoids experimenter effects. Disadvantage: for example, can't infer cause and effect, observer bias, not replicable, participants may behave unnaturally if they know they're being watched or if they're in a strange environment.

5 For example: to discover universal behaviours, to compare the effects of certain cultural practices, to observe the effects of learning.

Quick test 11.2

1 To be able to see if the independent variable has had any effect.

2 (a) Every member of the population being sampled has an equal chance at being selected.

(b) For example: names out of a hat, using a random number table.

3 For example: attention span, fear of experimenter, distress, influenced by peers, influenced by experimenter (demand characteristics).

4 For example: counterbalancing, equivalent measures to avoid practice effects.

5 The control group receives no extra treatment and provides a means of comparison with the experimental group, which is given the experimental treatment (the independent variable).

Quick test 11.3

1 It is a means of representing data which has been classified and organised.

2 Mean, median, mode.

3 A table, bar chart (or histogram), pie chart, pictogram, frequency polygon, line graph, ogive.

4 Using a scattergram.

5 Positive.

Quick test 11.4

1 For example: distress of child, informed consent from parents/guardians, cannot understand debriefing.

2 Practical advantage: for example: more realistic, no demand characteristics.

Ethical drawback: for example, lack of informed consent, debriefing, possible distress or invasion of privacy.

3 (a) Information passed to participants after the research is completed.

(b) For example: inform participants of any deception, tell them the results or that you will post the results later, offer the chance to withhold their data, ask for any comments, ask if they were aware of the true purpose of the research (you might have to ignore their data).

Index